MODERN

FORMAL

LOGIC

MODERN

FORMAL

LOGIC

THOMAS J. McKAY
Syracuse University

Macmillan Publishing Company
New York

Collier Macmillan Publishers
London

Macmillan Publishing Company
866 Third Avenue, New York, New York 10022

Collier Macmillan Canada. Inc.

Library of Congress Cataloging-in-Publication Data

McKay, Thomas J.
    Modern formal logic / Thomas J. McKay (date)
      p.   cm.
    Includes index.
    ISBN 0-02-379286-8
    1. Logic, Symbolic and mathematical.   2. Logic, Modern.
  I. Title.
BC135.M38 1989
160–dc19

88-234
C

Printing: 1 2 3 4 5 6 7   Year: 9 0 1 2 3 4 5 6 7 8

PREFACE

Modern logic has developed a systematic way of understanding some of the principles of correct reasoning. The focus of this book is the conveying of that understanding. This book is designed for introductory courses that focus on formal logic and for symbolic logic courses. Such courses can develop students' understanding of the principles of reasoning, and this book will aid in that development.

The book covers a full range of logical concepts and contains a number of features helpful to students. I've included numerous worked exercises illustrating concepts and rules and providing models for completing the exercises. There are extensive exercises interspersed within the chapters so that students can immediately apply the concepts and rules and test their understanding. (Answers for nearly half of the exercises appear in Appendix B). Most chapters include summaries in the form of lists of key terms and concepts, and summary lists of deductive rules that appear in the chapter. In a number of places I've included boxed material for further study; these sections are optional and geared to those who wish to pursue a specific area in depth.

An introductory chapter acquaints students with the basic concepts of justification, argument, validity, and soundness. Part A is devoted to truth-functional analysis applied to a full range of logical concepts. In addition to truth-tables, truth-trees are introduced in an optional chapter (4). The concepts of counterexample and model are introduced and explored throughout Part A. Part B introduces the method of derivation for showing validity, inconsistency, equivalence, logical truth, and contradiction (Chapters 6–8). The book develops a full system, including conditional proof and indirect proof. The concept of a model for showing invalidity, consistency, inequivalence, and contingency is developed further (Chapter 9). Part C introduces the language of predicate logic (Chapter 10) and develops the system of derivation (Chapter 11) and the concept of a model (Chapter 12). The presentation of predicate logic includes relations and multiple quantification. Instructors who wish to include the study of identity, definite descriptions, or function symbols will find this covered in a separate chapter (15).

A new approach to the teaching of quantification enhances the availability of the material in Part C. The notation of *relativized* quantification is used rather than the more traditional unrelativized notation. In 1981 I taught a basic graduate course in logic in which I used both standard (unrelativized) and relativized quantification. I introduced relativized quantification because it provides the opportunity for a significantly more general treatment of quantifiers and because it makes better connections with English syntax. The course was very successful, and I noticed two unexpected collateral effects: students with little knowledge of modern logic mastered the representation of English very easily when working with relativized quantification, and relativized quantification provided several nice insights into English syntax even for those of us who already had some logical sophistication.

My graduate students felt very strongly that relativized quantification provided a better way to present quantification logic to beginning students, and they strongly urged me to try this approach in our undergraduate introductory course. Buoyed by their encouragement, I wrote chapters on quantificational logic to replace those of the textbook I was using. The new approach was even more successful than I had expected. Students learning about the systematic study of validity for the first time have learned more quickly, have developed better ability in the symbolization of English sentences, and have acquired a deeper understanding of sentence structure and logical relationships. Relativized quantification preserves the structure of English sentences much more closely than the usual notation does, and this makes it easier for students to build on the knowledge of natural language that they already have. Relativized quantification has the full logic scope of modern logic, and in fact it allows for the possibility of analyzing additional quantifier words. By preserving the structure of natural language, relativized quantification has many of the advantages of naturalness and easy learnability that are associated with Aristotelian logic. It has the added advantage of greater scope and easy translatability into standard logic.

I have tried to make the book flexible. The minimal course on basic concepts, truth-functions, and sentential deriviation would be Chapters 1–8 (with the possibility of excluding Chapter 4 and the material on truth-trees in Chapter 5). One could then study quantificational logic using Chapter 10 and pages 214–241 of Chapter 11. By adding Chapter 9, the rest of Chapter 11, and all of Chapter 12, one can do a fuller treatment of logical concepts other than validity. Chapter 13 introduces standard (unrelativized) quantificational notation. Chapter 14 consists of further discussion of the representation of arguments, emphasizing the treatment of enthymemes and the properties of relations. Chapter 15 develops identity, definite descriptions, and function symbols, and Chapter 16 gives a systematic semantics for quantificational logic.

In the last twenty years many people have contributed to the study of relativized quantification and intermediate quantifiers. My work with this has been influenced by the work of Richard Montague, Anil Gupta, Jon Barwise, Robin Cooper, James McCawley, Mark Brown, and Philip Peterson. Several graduate students initially encouraged the writing of an introductory textbook using relativized quantification, with Terrance Swift, Merry McInerney and Eric Pearson the most insistent among them. Mark Brown gets special thanks for his ideas, his help, and his encouragement throughout the development of the introductory course and this textbook. Several sections of the book are developments of ideas he had. I thank him and Stewart Thau for using (and thus testing) the book when they taught the course. My teaching assistants have made many helpful comments and suggestions. Thousands of undergraduates have contributed to the testing of early versions of the book, and their contribution, more than any other, shows that this works. Their comments have led to many improvements in coverage and presentation.

Macmillan has provided me with a number of very fine reports with some excellent suggestions that have brought about a number of improvements. Helen McInnis has been wonderfully helpful in shaping this project and has been especially skillful at getting me to attend to the suggestions that were made.

T. J. M.

CONTENTS

PART I   FUNDAMENTAL CONCEPTS AND
TRUTH-FUNCTIONAL ANALYSIS   1

CHAPTER 1   INTRODUCTION   3
Justification and Reasons   3
Arguments   4
Maintaining Coherent Belief   7
Validity and Soundness   8
Considering the Possibilities   10
Recognition, Understanding, and Practice   12
Deductive Validity and Inductive Strength   12
A Terminological Note   15

CHAPTER 2   TRUTH-FUNCTIONAL REPRESENTATION:
CONJUNCTION, DISJUNCTION,
NEGATION   16
Compound Sentences   16
Truth-Functional Structure   18
English Connectives: And   20
Negation   25
Multiply Compound Sentences   26
Disjunction   28
Parentheses   31
Syntax and Semantics   32

CHAPTER 3   TRUTH-FUNCTIONAL ANALYSIS   44
Arguments: Validity and Invalidity   44
Inconsistency of Sets of Sentences   50
Equivalence of Pairs of Sentences   53
Tautologous, Contradictory, and Contingent
    Sentences   56
Validity: Some Special Cases   59

CHAPTER 4   TRUTH TREES   62
               Consistency and Inconsistency   62
               Validity and Invalidity   70
               Equivalence and Inequivalence   73
               Tautologous, Contradictory, Contingent   76

CHAPTER 5   CONDITIONALS: REPRESENTATION,
               ANALYSIS, TRUTH-TREES   79
               Conditionals   79
               Biconditionals   84
               Truth-Functional Connectives   84
               Symbolizing English   85
               Logical Characteristics: Truth-Functional
                   Analysis   92

PART II   DERIVATIONS AND MODELS   103

CHAPTER 6   INFERENCE RULES   105
               Showing That a Conclusion Follows   106
               Modus Ponens, Simplification, and Disjunctive
                   Syllogism   108
               Modus Tollens, Conjunction, and Hypothetical
                   Syllogism   112
               Addition and Constructive Dilemma   115
               Strategies for Constructing Derivations   117

CHAPTER 7   EQUIVALENCE RULES   122
               Double Negation, Commutativity, Associativity,
                   and DeMorgan's Theorems   122
               Redundancy, Distribution, and Conditional
                   Exchange   127
               Contraposition, Exportation, and the Biconditional
                   Rule   130

CHAPTER 8   CONDITIONAL PROOF AND INDIRECT
               PROOF   135
               Conditional Proof   135
               Indirect Proof   143
               Proof by Cases   149

Appendix 8A   Additional Rules   154
Appendix 8B   A Smaller Systems of Rules   158

CHAPTER 9   DERIVATIONS AND EXAMPLES   163
Showing Invalidity   163
Inconsistency and Consistency   168
Equivalence and Inequivalence   174
Tautologous, Contradictory, or Contingent   178

PART III: QUANTIFICATIONAL LOGIC   185

CHAPTER 10   THE LANGUAGE   187
Predicative Expressions   187
Nouns   189
Predicates and Names in Quantificational
    Logic   190
Relative Clauses   192
The Universal Quantifier   193
The Existential Quantifier   199
More on Representing English   204

CHAPTER 11   DERIVATIONS   214
Existential Quantifier Introduction   214
Universal Quantifier Exploitation   220
Existential Quantifier Exploitation   227
Quantifier Negation   233
Universal Quantifier Introduction   235
Inconsistency   244
Equivalence   247
Logical Truths   249
Contradictions   250
Appendix 11A   Additional Valid Argument
    Forms and Equivalences   251

CHAPTER 12   PREDICATE LOGIC TRUTH-TREES   254
Truth-Trees and Models   255
Negated Sentences   259
Limits of Predicate Logic Truth-Trees   263
Invalidity   265

Inequivalence   269
Contingency   271

CHAPTER 13   Unrelativized Quantification   276
Formulas   276
Derivation Rules   280

CHAPTER 14   ENGLISH ARGUMENTS   287
Enthymemes   287
Properties of Relations   291

CHAPTER 15   IDENTITY, DEFINITE DESCRIPTIONS, AND
FUNCTION SYMBOLS   297
Identity   297
Definite Descriptions   302
Function Symbols   306
Derivational Rules for Identity   310
Derivational Rules for Function Symbols   312
Derivational Rules for Definite Descriptions   314

CHAPTER 16   QUANTIFIER SEMANTICS   316
Other Quantifiers   317
Systematic Semantics   319
Systematic Semantics for Predicate Logic   323

APPENDIX A   SET THEORETIC CONCEPTS   329

APPENDIX B   ANSWERS TO SELECTED EXERCISES   331

INDEX   397

PART I

FUNDAMENTAL

CONCEPTS AND

TRUTH-FUNCTIONAL

ANALYSIS

1

INTRODUCTION

JUSTIFICATION AND REASONS

People often give reasons for their beliefs. They may wish to confirm their beliefs, to convince others, or to develop new beliefs on the basis of beliefs already held. Sometimes the reasons given will justify the beliefs and sometimes they will not. Each of the following examples might illustrate an attempt to justify a belief.

1. The Democrats do not have an adequate solution to the deficit problem, so we should not vote for their candidates.
2. I know from a class survey that none of my students last semester was studying engineering, and Carol was among my students. Thus I can be sure that Carol was not studying engineering last semester.
3. If John were to fail chemistry, he would not graduate. John will not fail chemistry. Therefore, he will graduate.

In each case, reasons are given for accepting some claim.

Logic is the systematic investigation of reasoning. In particular, when a belief is justified on the basis of other beliefs given as reasons for it, the logician would like to be able to identify the principles connecting the reasons with the conclusion they justify. The study of logic will provide analytical tools that will enable us to understand and evaluate people's attempts to give justifying reasons.

You might or might not feel pretty confident about your *ability to distinguish* good reasoning from bad, but here we will develop something deeper—an *understanding* of what makes some reasoning good and an ability to *show* that a claim follows from the reasons offered for it. We can develop a systematic formulation of the fundamental elements of a large body of reasoning. Knowledge of this system of fundamental elements can serve as a firm basis for an understanding of good reasoning, for the ability to show that

3

a conclusion follows, and for the ability to make evaluations of the reasoning of others.

ARGUMENTS

When *reasons* are given to justify a belief, an *argument* is being presented; so logic, the study of the standards of reasoning, can also be described as the study of characteristics that distinguish acceptable arguments from those that are not acceptable.

The word *argument* is often used to refer to a dispute. But in the logician's sense, an argument need not involve any dispute. For example, an argument could consist of new reasons for an old, uncontroversial belief.

> **4.** Jennifer advised me to invest in this company, I followed her advice, and now I am rich because of it. As I have always done, I should trust her financial advice.

Or an argument could consist of reasons leading to a completely new belief that no one disagrees with because previously no one had any opinion about it.

> **5.** The blue feathers and the particular kind of nest found here clearly show that blue jays lived here last summer.

The study of logic involves learning standards for the appraisal of completed pieces of reasoning, arguments. The processes and attitudes involved in the production of the reasoning are not a part of this study.

An argument has two components. The reasons presented as justifications are the *premises* of the argument, and the claim that they are intended to justify is the *conclusion*.

> **6.** Since almost everyone is disappointed with Democratic policies (premise), the Republicans will score significant gains in the next election (conclusion).
> **7.** The cost of transporting needed raw materials to our manufacturing plant has become high (premise). There are other regions nearer the source of supply, where transportation costs are low (premise). In addition, construction costs are low there (premise), and labor costs will be lower than at our present location (premise). Thus we should consider moving (conclusion).
> **8.** The new drug RXQ should not be sold to the public (conclusion), because it contains three known carcinogens and has not been sufficiently tested (premise).
> **9.** Someone is knocking at the back door (premise). The meter man must be here (conclusion).

Logic can be characterized as the discipline that systematically describes the relationship between these two components, telling us when the premises could justify the conclusion.

Of course, people are not always presenting arguments when they speak or write. We tell stories, present facts without argument, ask questions, make exclamations, express admiration, and much more. But whenever reasons are presented for accepting some claim, we have an argument, and giving and evaluating reasons are key elements of intelligent belief formation. When we are using arguments to convince others of a conclusion, the premises and conclusion will be sentences we assert to convince others. When we are confirming our own beliefs or developing new beliefs on our own, the premises and conclusion might be beliefs that are never stated out loud. (Consider examples 4 and 9 above. Most often, such conclusions could be drawn without saying or writing anything.)

Our goal in studying logic is to develop systematic standards for appraising arguments. In doing so, we focus on how language is used in formulating arguments, because sentences that could be used in expressing beliefs are more visible and more easily studied than beliefs themselves (especially unexpressed beliefs). We study the relationships among sentences that can make them suitable to be the premises and conclusions of good arguments, and we formulate systematic standards for evaluating the relationship between premises and conclusion.

Recognizing Arguments in Ordinary Language

In principle we can take any set of sentences as premises, and any single sentence as a conclusion, and apply our evaluative standards, asking whether the argument with those premises and that conclusion is valid. But most often we are interested in particular arguments because someone has *presented* the argument as a reason for accepting the conclusion. In doing so, the speaker must state the premises and conclusion and there must be something that determines which sentence is the conclusion. In order to consider a paragraph or series of paragraphs presenting an argument and to evaluate whether the argument presented is valid, we must be able to identify the premises and conclusion of the argument being presented. Several **indicator words** aid us in doing this. If we see one of these, we can suspect that a conclusion is about to follow.

So
Hence
Thus
Therefore
It must be that

"The president is very unpopular, *so* the opposition party will make significant electoral gains." The word 'so' helps to make it clear what is premise and what is conclusion.

We also have words indicating that a premise is about to follow.

For

Since

Because

Due to the fact that

"*Since* the president is very unpopular, the opposition will make significant electoral gains." These indicator words aid in identifying premises and conclusion.

But all of these aids must be used with care. Many of these words, expecially 'since', 'because', and 'so', have other uses, to indicate temporal, causal, or other types of connections.

Since Tuesday he has not studied.

It broke *because* it dropped.

He shouted 'Help!' *so* that everyone would look at him.

These statements of temporal relationship and causal sequence are not arguments. Nothing is presented as a reason (a premise) for thinking that some other thing (a conclusion) is true.

It is important to note as well that an argument can be presented without any of these indicator words.

The president is very unpopular, and his party has not used its Senate majority effectively. The opposition will make significant gains in the next election.

As long as we find some sentence or sentences asserted as reasons for believing a further claim, we know that we have an argument. Here what is said in the first sentence might be given as a reason for accepting the second. (The absence of indicator words makes it harder to know whether an argument is being given, and it is generally better style to use indicator words to let your audience see clearly when premises are offered in support of a conclusion.)

Even when it is clear that an argument is being presented and clear what the conclusion is, it is not always clear just what the entire argument is. Sometimes critical premises are left unstated because they are taken to be general knowledge or taken to be assumptions indicated in an obvious way by the rest of what is said.

Whales must have lungs, because all mammals have lungs.

It is clear that the conclusion is that whales have lungs. But that conclusion is connected with the explicitly stated premise, "all mammals have lungs," only if we assume that whales are mammals. The speaker can take that for granted because it is generally known and because context clearly indicates that the speaker is making this assumption.

EXERCISE 1a

For each passage below, determine whether it presents an argument. If it does, indicate what the conclusion is.

1. Hyenas must live in large groups, because all scavengers live in large groups, and hyenas are scavengers.

2. After a day in the Land Rover, John loves to see the huge congregation of animals at the water hole.

3. Since last summer, when he took his safari vacation, he carries his binoculars everywhere.

4. Since hyenas are not felines, they must be canines.

5. Bob will be angry unless someone brings the binoculars. But if John doesn't bring them, no one will. So if John doesn't bring the binoculars, Bob will be angry.

6. Bob was angry because he had no binoculars.

7. You have no respect for my opinions, I wouldn't discuss that with a jerk like you, and I'm sure that I'm right anyway.

8. If Bob is opposed to killing animals, he shouldn't eat meat.

9. Bob is opposed to killing animals, so he should not eat meat.

10. Bob is opposed to killing animals. Because of this, he didn't join the safari.

MAINTAINING COHERENT BELIEF

Logical connections are important in another context beside that of justifying a conclusion (giving an argument). Logical evaluation can lead us to revise or withdraw beliefs when we see that they stand in logical conflict. Thus I might believe these two things:

Al is trustworthy.
No one trustworthy would take the books from my room without asking.

But later I may find evidence leading me to believe the following:

Al took the books from my room without asking.

I now have a problem. At least one of these three beliefs is false; the three sentences are logically connected in a way that makes it impossible for all of them to be true. Perhaps Al is not worthy of continued trust; perhaps there is some special reason that could lead someone trustworthy to take the books without asking (maybe the room was flooding); or perhaps the evidence is misleading—Al didn't really take them. I may be led to look for further information to help me to decide which of the three claims is false, but even without further information, logic is sufficient to establish that they cannot all be true.

The principles at work in arguments are also at work here. Some *sets* of beliefs are logically acceptable, but others are not. All of the analytical techniques that help us to distinguish acceptable arguments from unacceptable arguments will also help in distinguishing logically unacceptable sets of beliefs from logically acceptable sets. A set of sentences or beliefs like those in our example is an *inconsistent* set because there is no possible way for all of them to be true; at least one is false. Thus it is not fully acceptable to believe all three. You are sure to be wrong about at least one of them if you do. Although our main focus will be the study of arguments, we will sometimes apply our analytical skills to showing the inconsistency of sets of sentences. In addition, it will be very useful later to discuss some of the relationships that exist between inconsistent sets of sentences and arguments.

VALIDITY AND SOUNDNESS

We need additional precise terminology to help us to focus on justification. Consider the following two arguments. (Here we will follow the useful practice in logic of writing premises separately and marking the conclusion with a special symbol, '∴'. Ordinarily, when we present arguments in English, we use such words as 'therefore', 'thus', and 'so' to indicate the conclusion. But the special symbol makes the conclusion stand out more visibly.)

1. If Socrates was human, then he was warm-blooded.
   Socrates was human.
   ∴   Socrates was warm-blooded.
2. If Socrates was a plumber, then he used a plunger.
   Socrates was a plumber.
   ∴   Socrates used a plunger.

We can all readily recognize 1 to be a good argument. But is 2 a good argument? That question should not be quite so easy to answer, because the question itself is too crude. There are two importantly distinct factors that go into making an argument good.

Argument 2 has both bad features and good features. On the bad side, it has a false premise, so it cannot be a convincing argument among those of us who recognize the premise's falsity. But on the good side, the premises have the right sort of connection with the conclusion. *If the premises were true, the conclusion would have to be true as well.* In this book we are concerned primarily with the study of this *connection* between premises and conclusion; that is, we are concerned with what it would be for premises to support or justify a conclusion if they were true. This key concept of logic is the concept of *valid* argument, and this concept can be explained in either of two ways:

1. In a valid argument, if the premises were all true, the conclusion would also be true.
2. In a valid argument, it is not possible for the conclusion to be false when all the premises are true.

The study of logic is the systematic characterization of the validating relationships that can exist between premises and conclusion. These characterizations enable us to *understand* what makes some arguments valid and provide us with resources for *showing* that arguments are valid.

When it is possible for an argument to have true premises with a false conclusion, the argument is *invalid*. No special relationship guarantees that if the premises are true, the conclusion must also be true. In other words, there is no guarantee that truth will be preserved when the step is taken from the premises to the conclusion in an invalid argument.

Both of the preceding examples, 1 and 2, are valid arguments. The premises and conclusion are connected in the right sort of way; it is not possible for the conclusion to be false when the premises are true. In any possible situation in which the premises are true, the conclusion is also true. But 1 can be seen to be a much better argument than 2 when we consider the other evaluative factor, the facts about Socrates. Every premise of 1 is true, but that does not apply to 2. So let us introduce another important term of evaluation.

A **sound** argument is an argument with both of the following features:

1. It is valid.
2. All of its premises are true.

In seeking to establish new truths on the basis of things already known, we are seeking sound arguments. Because they are valid and have true premises, they must also have true conclusions. (Valid argument preserves truth, so that if we start with all true premises in a valid argument, we are certain to have a true conclusion.) An *unsound* argument, on the other hand, is one that fails one or both of the conditions for soundness; either it is invalid or it has one or more false premises.

Logic alone cannot usually certify that an argument is sound. The principles of *valid* argument are logic's domain of study and analysis, and the question of soundness generally depends on nonlogical facts, for example, on the historical fact that Socrates was not a plumber. Logic is concerned with more general features of argument, features that can characterize an argument no matter what its subject matter. The principles of reasoning and justification studied here apply to reasoning about every subject matter.

Notice that validity is a concept that involves the full range of truth-value possibilities. In a valid argument, it is *impossible* to have the premises true with the conclusion false; that is, in *every* possible situation, if the premises are true, the conclusion is true. In trying to show that an argument is valid, do not try to determine whether the conclusion is actually true or false and do not try to determine the actual truth-values of the premises. Validity has to do with the full range of truth-value possibilities, and the *actual* truth-values represent *just one* truth-value possibility. In a valid argument, the premises and conclusion constitute a unit such that *in every possible situation*, if the premises were true, the conclusion would have to be true. In showing that an argument is valid, one must consider the full range of possibilities, checking to see whether connections exist that rule out the possibility of true premises with a false conclusion.

Some examples may make clearer how we are concerned with truth-value possibilities, not with actual truth-values.

1. If John were to fail chemistry, he would not graduate. John will not fail chemistry. Therefore, he will graduate.
2. All primates have some broad teeth. All mammals that eat vegetables have some broad teeth. So all primates are mammals that eat vegetables.
3. Some dogs won't dance unless they get birthday cake. Anything that won't dance will be painted blue. So some dogs will be painted blue unless they get birthday cake.

We can determine that only example 3 is valid, even though 2 consists of true sentences, 3 consists of false sentences, and 1 consists of sentences concerning which we have no idea what the truth-value is. (The actual truth-values are of no significance here.) In both examples 1 and 2 we can think of possible situations in which the premises would be true and the conclusion false. In example 1, John might pass chemistry but fail some other course he needed for graduation. In example 2, it might have been that many creatures that did not eat vegetables, including some primates that did not eat vegetables, had broad teeth. Nothing in the premises rules this out, so the premises do not guarantee that the conclusion is true. But for example 3 there is no possible situation in which the premises are true with the conclusion false. (Of course, none of these examples are sound arguments. Examples 1 and 2 are invalid, and example 3 has one or more false premises.)

For 1 and 2 we were able to describe possible situations in which the premises would be true with the conclusion false. Our doing this makes the case that the argument is invalid, and the possible situation described is called a "counter example" to the claim of validity or it is called a "model" that shows invalidity for that type of argument.

CONSIDERING THE POSSIBILITIES

The definition of validity in terms of possible situations gives us an especially useful way to think of validity. To establish that an argument is valid, it seems that we must somehow show that *no possible situation* exists in which the premises are true with the conclusion false. We will develop techniques for doing that throughout this book. But this definition tells us immediately how we could show someone that an argument is *invalid:* an example of just *one possible situation* in which the premises are true with the conclusion false will guarantee invalidity.

Suppose that someone were to argue in the following way:

Since some lawyers are senators (premise), and since some senators are old (premise), it must be that some lawyers are old (conclusion).

One way to see that this is *invalid* is to see clearly that there could be a possible situation in which the premises were true with the conclusion false. For example, if things became so bad with the law profession that we decided to kill off all the lawyers and start over again, allowing no one over 30 to become a lawyer, then after a short while we might have a situation in which the premises were true with the conclusion false. If a few of the new, young lawyers were elected to the senate (joining some of the old nonlawyers already there), there could be a situation in which these were true:

Some lawyers are senators.
Some senators are old.

But the following would be false:

Some lawyers are old.

Thus the argument cannot be valid because it is possible for the premises to be true with the conclusion false.

Note how we need just *one possible situation* to show invalidity. This situation can be very farfetched as long as it is clearly a possible situation. If we try to describe a situation in which some simple valid argument has true premises with a false conclusion, we will not succeed. For example, imagine a situation in which these sentences are true:

If Socrates was human, then he was warm-blooded.
Socrates was human.

Now try to add to the situation that the following sentence is *false* (while the others are still true):

Socrates was warm-blooded.

These is no such possible situation. To make the conclusion false, one must also falsify at least one of the premises. So attempts to show invalidity fail.

With more complex arguments, it is not so obvious when the attempt to describe a possible situation succeeds and when it fails. We will develop techniques of argument evaluation that can be applied to both simple and complex arguments.

RECOGNITION, UNDERSTANDING, AND PRACTICE

Many people (though not all) can *distinguish* good violinists from bad ones. A much smaller number *understand* some of the things that make someone a good violinist. A few people can even *explain* what makes one performance of a violin piece better than another. Understanding and explaining what makes good violin playing are of course very different from playing the violin well.

Often, people can do pretty well at *distinguishing* simple valid arguments from invalid arguments. Our studies, though, will take us beyond that to an *understanding* of some of the logical connections that make for valid reasoning, and we will begin to develop the ability to *explain* why some arguments are better than others. We can develop the ability to *show conclusively* that something is correctly reasoned.

Understanding what constitutes good reasoning is different from reasoning well, just as understanding what constitutes good violin playing is different from playing the violin well. But in the case of reasoning there is, I think, a closer connection between knowledge and practice. For one thing, everyone observes and practices reasoning daily. Students will see reasoning and be forced to give reasons in almost all of their work, so that the practice that connects understanding with the exercise of the ability is much more common in the case of argument than it is in the case of violin playing. In addition, there is a systematically organized body of information about valid argument, whereas good violin playing involves a greater variety of skills and has no single systematic core of the sort that exists for the practice of giving valid arguments.

DEDUCTIVE VALIDITY AND INDUCTIVE STRENGTH

When we ask whether an argument is valid, we set a very high standard of appraisal. In a valid argument a false conclusion with true premises must be *impossible*. But premises sometimes support a conclusion even when they do not meet that high standard.

> The weather report says that a low-pressure storm system is moving over us and that it will soon rain.
> This weather report is usually right.
> The sky is completely overcast.
> ∴   It will soon rain.

These three premises support this conclusion even though the argument is not valid. It is *possible* for the premises to be true and the conclusion false, but not very likely. The support is *strong* but not absolute.

When we evaluate arguments, we do not always want to look only for the cases in which it is *impossible* for the premises to be true with conclusion false. Sometimes that evaluative standard is inappropriate because it was never intended that the argument would meet that standard. Instead, we should apply a different standard, asking whether the premises support the conclusion in some other way; for example, by making the conclusion plausible or by making it more plausible than it otherwise would be.

So we need to distinguish at least two different standards for evaluating arguments. The notion of validity introduced earlier is also known as the *deductive* standard of evaluation for arguments. Arguments meeting that standard are *deductively valid:* it is impossible for the premises to be true with the conclusion false. This is now to be contrasted with *inductive* standards for appraising arguments. An argument is *inductively strong* when the premises provide strong support for the conclusion, and additional study of justification would try to formulate standards for determining when there is an inductively strong connection between premises and conclusion.

Inductive strength comes in degrees in a way that deductive validity does not. Further premises can make an argument stronger or weaker. If we add the following to the premises:

It is raining just west of here and the front is moving east.

then our argument becomes even stronger. If we had instead added:

But clearing is reported just west of here and it has not yet rained within miles of here.

the argument would have become weaker. Adding further premises cannot make a deductively valid argument more or less valid. If an argument is deductively valid, the premises already contain enough information to guarantee that the conclusion is true (if the premises are true). *Deductive validity* does not come in degrees in the way that *inductive strength* does.

In many cases we can reconstruct slightly different arguments from a single paragraph. The arguments may even differ in whether inductive or deductive standards should apply. Consider the following example (presented at the beginning of this chapter).

I know from a class survey that none of my students last semester were studying engineering, and Carol was among my students. Thus I can be sure that Carol was not studying engineering last semester.

If we take it for granted that the class survey provided accurate information about all the students, the following deductively valid argument might be the appropriate one to consider:

> None of my students last semester were studying engineering last semester.
> Carol was one of my students last semester.
> So Carol was not studying engineering last semester.

But if we wanted to be more cautious in what we concluded from our survey, we might wish to make its role explicit.

> Each of my students answering last semester's class survey said that he or she was not studying engineering.
> Carol was one of my students.
> So Carol was not studying engineering last semester.

These premises may provide support (even strong support) for the conclusion, but the argument is not deductively valid, nor is it intended to be. There are ways in which the premises might be true and the conclusion false — if Carol did not answer the survey, or if she lied, for example.

In this book we are concerned solely with deductive validity. There is a systematic and well-understood body of theory that we will master. No similar body of systematic theory exists for the understanding of inductive strength.

EXERCISE 1b

For each example, answer the applicable questions. (Note that questions b and c are not applicable if the answer to question a is 'no', and question c is not applicable if the answer to question b is 'no'.)

- **a.** Does this passage present an argument?
- **b.** Is the argument valid?
- **c.** Is the argument sound? (You might not be able to answer this question, even in the case of some of the valid arguments.)

1. All doctors have degrees, and all lawyers have degrees. So at least some doctors must be lawyers.
2. Since all doctors have degrees, and anyone who has a degree has attended school, every doctor must have attended school.
3. Every doctor is a lawyer. Every lawyer has a degree. Thus every doctor must have a degree.
4. Some surgeons are lawyers, but no lawyers have studied medicine. So some surgeons haven't studied medicine.
5. Every surgeon in New York is licensed to do surgery. Some doctors are surgeons in New York. Thus some doctors are licensed to do surgery.
6. Doctors and lawyers have clients, and they are also similar in other ways.

7. At least some doctors perform surgery, so, since no lawyers perform surgery, not all doctors are lawyers.

8. Not all doctors do surgery. Some lawyers do medical counseling. But every doctor who does surgery does medical counseling.

A TERMINOLOGICAL NOTE

Ordinary language provides several ways of talking about the connection between premises and conclusion. If an argument is deductively valid we may say that:

The premises imply the conclusion.
The premises entail the conclusion.
The premises support the conclusion.

The conclusion follows from the premises.
The conclusion can be deduced from the premises.
The conclusion is a consequence of the premises.
The conclusion can be validly inferred (from the premises).

The argument is valid.
The reasoning is conclusive.
The inference is valid.

KEY TERMS AND CONCEPTS

ARGUMENT: A belief or sentence together with some reasons for accepting it.

CONCLUSION OF AN ARGUMENT: The belief or sentence for which reasons are given in the argument.

PREMISES OF AN ARGUMENT: The beliefs or sentences that are the reasons given for accepting the conclusion.

VALID ARGUMENT: An argument in which it is impossible that the premises are true and the conclusion false; that is, in any possible situation, if the premises are true, the conclusion is also true (also called a *deductively* valid argument).

SOUND ARGUMENT: A valid argument with true premises.

INDUCTIVELY STRONG ARGUMENT: Argument in which adequate reasons for accepting the conclusion are provided.

CONSISTENT SET OF SENTENCES OR BELIEFS: A set of sentences or beliefs that could (in some possible, although perhaps nonactual situation) all be true.

INCONSISTENT SET OF SENTENCES OR BELIEFS: Not consistent. There is no possible situation in which every member of the set is true.

INDICATOR WORDS: Preceding a conclusion: *so, hence, therefore, it must be that, thus;* preceding a premise: *for, since, because.*

2

TRUTH-FUNCTIONAL REPRESENTATION: CONJUNCTION, DISJUNCTION, NEGATION

All of us already have some ability to recognize simple valid arguments and pick out inconsistencies. In studying logic we will also develop an understanding of what makes some arguments valid and an ability to show arguments to be valid. In developing this understanding, we will also refine and extend the skills of recognition that already exist. The refinement of these skills and the development of this understanding require isolation of the elements of sentences that make recognition of valid arguments possible, and we will see how those elements of sentences are related to the connections among sentences that can make an argument valid. Once we have this understanding, we can use it as a foundation for the further skill of showing arguments to be valid.

COMPOUND SENTENCES

Suppose that we overhear this conversation:

Al: John will study hard tonight or he will fail his exam tomorrow.
Bill: But John will not study hard tonight.

We know that if both of these claims are true, then this is also true:

John will fail his exam tomorrow.

We are recognizing the valid argument (A):

(A) **1.** John will study hard tonight or he will fail his exam tomorrow.
   2. John will not study hard tonight.
   Therefore, John will fail his exam tomorrow.

And we are also recognizing that a certain set of sentences (B) is inconsistent. These cannot all be true:

(B) **1.** John will study hard tonight or he will fail his exam tomorrow.
   2. John will not study hard tonight.
   3. John will not fail his exam tomorrow.

The basis for making such judgments of validity and inconsistency is a recognition of patterns in the relationships among sentences. These patterns connect the sentences' truth-values, guaranteeing that if certain sentences [such as 1 and 2] are true, certain others [such as the conclusion of argument (A)] must be true and still others [such as 3] cannot be true.

To understand why the argument (A) is valid and why the set of sentences (B) is inconsistent, we will need to see how the sentences that constitute them are constructed out of simpler sentences. Seeing this will begin to clarify the patterns that ground the logical relationships.

Consider these five sentences:

1. John will study hard tonight.
2. John will fail his exam tomorrow.
3. John will not study hard tonight.
4. John will not fail his exam tomorrow.
5. John will study hard tonight or he will fail his exam tomorrow.

Sentences 1 and 2 are the simplest, and the others are constructed from them. Sentence 3 is the **negation** of 1, and 4 is the **negation** of 2. Sentence 5 is a more complex sentence, constructed from 1 and 2 and the **connective word** 'or'. Our study of validity begins with the examination of negations and other compound sentences, so that we can see what features can account for the validity of some arguments containing them and for the inconsistency of some sets of sentences containing them.

A sentence can appear as part of a compound sentence in many ways. Many words or phrases constitute contexts for making compound sentences from simpler ones. Here are three expressions that combine with a single sentence to make a compound sentence:

1. Mary saw that _____.
   Mary saw that *John was studying*.
   Mary saw that *she was near St. Louis*.

2. Mary believes that _____.

    Mary believes that *John will pass.*

    Mary believes that *Chicago is near St. Louis.*

3. _____ not _____. [The word 'not' after the (tensed) verb of the sentence.]

    John will not *pass.*

    Chicago is not *near St. Louis.*

    Mary has not *been near Chicago.*

    Mary did not *swim.*

There are also many *connective* words that can be used to make compound sentences from simpler ones. For example,

John will fail because *he will not study.*

John will not study, but *he will not fail.*

If *John studies,* then *he will not fail.*

John will fail unless *he studies.*

John will study and *he will fail.*

John will fail even though *he studied.*

John will study or *he will fail.*

We will develop an account of the logically relevant characteristics of 'not', 'or', 'and', 'if _____, then . . .,' and some of the other words used in making compound sentences from simpler ones. This account will enable us to understand why some arguments are valid and others are not (and why some sets of sentences are consistent and others are not). This understanding will give us the ability to develop means for showing that arguments are valid (or that sets of sentences are inconsistent).

We will call any sentence that has another sentence embedded within it a **compound sentence**. A simple sentence, with no other sentence embedded within, will be called an **atomic sentence**.

TRUTH-FUNCTIONAL STRUCTURE

The first compound sentences that we will consider are artificially created compounds. Instead of any English connective word, we will introduce a special symbol, a dot, which can be used between two sentences to construct a compound sentence.

John will study hard tonight · John will fail his exam tomorrow.

Alice drove her car to school · Alice arrived on time.

We will fix the meaning of the dot symbol so that it creates a compound sentence of a special type: a **truth-functionally compound sentence**. The truth-value of the compound sentence (i.e., whether it is true or false) will depend only on the truth-values of its constituents. In particular, in any compound sentence consisting of two sentences joined by the dot,

_____ • . . . . .

the truth-value is determined by the following table (using 'T' and 'F' for *true* and *false*):

_____	. . . . .	_____ • . . . . .
T	T	T
T	F	F
F	T	F
F	F	F

There are four possible combinations of truth-values for the two constituent sentences. (These are listed on the rows of the table.) If both constituent sentences are true, the compound sentence created by joining the constituents by the dot symbol is true (first row). In the other three cases, in which at least one constituent sentence is false, the compound sentence is false.

A *truth-functional compound* is any sentence fulfilling the following condition: its truth-value depends on the truth-values of the simpler sentences occurring in it and on nothing else. (Later we use similar tables to define **truth-functional connectives** other than the dot symbol.) The dot symbol, called the **conjunction** connective, is used in creating compound sentences that we will call *conjunctions*, and the sentence constituents are called the (left and right) *conjuncts* of the conjunction.

We can immediately see that certain arguments involving compound sentences created with the dot symbol must be valid. For example:

John will study • John will pass.
So, John will pass.

must be valid argument.

John will study	John will pass	John will study • John will pass
1. T	T	T
2. T	F	F
3. F	T	F
4. F	F	F

There are four possible different situations regarding John's studying and passing—it is possible for him to study and pass, to study and not pass, to not study and yet pass, and to not study and not pass. Each of these situations is represented on a row of the table, so the full range of possible situations is considered. It is impossible for this argument to have a true premise and a false conclusion; there is no possible situation (no row of the table) in which the premise is true and the conclusion is false. In the one situation (row 1) in which the premise is true, the conclusion is also true. Thus we know, simply because of this use of the dot symbol, that the argument must be valid. We have listed every possible type of situation, and there is none in which the premise is true and the conclusion is false.

Consider another argument involving the dot symbol.

John will study.
So, John will study · John will pass.

Looking back at the table, we find two rows (1 and 2) in which the premise is true, and in one of those (row 2) the conclusion is false. Thus this is not a valid argument because there is (at least) one type of possible situation in which the premise is true and the conclusion false.

ENGLISH CONNECTIVES: AND

Although the dot symbol is not a part of ordinary English, the word 'and' usually functions in a similar way when it is used to connect sentences.

John will study	John will pass	John will study and John will pass
T	T	T
T	F	F
F	T	F
F	F	F

This accurately represents the truth-value for this compound sentence in each of the four possible situations. So the word 'and' is a device in English that can be used to make compound sentences of the type made with the dot symbol. And for the same reason

John will study and John will pass.
So, John will pass.

is valid. There is no possible situation in which the premise is true and the conclusion is false.

Our analysis of truth-functional compounds will soon help us to analyze much more complex and interesting arguments.

Contrast

To understand truth-functional compounds, it is also valuable to see that *not all compound sentences are truth-functional*.

An earthquake occurred on Thursday *because* the moon and the sun were in alignment on Thursday.

This is a compound sentence created by joining two simpler sentences with the word 'because'. But it is not a truth-functional compound, since the facts about the truth-value of the constituents are not always sufficient to determine the truth-value of the compound sentence. If both constituents are true:

It is true that: an earthquake occurred on Thursday.

It is true that: the moon and the sun were in alignment on Thursday.

the compound sentence might be either true or false.

One can see this another way. All of the following are true:

Reagan was president in 1987.

Reagan was elected president in 1984.

Reagan was governor of California in 1967.

But these sentences have different truth-values:

Reagan was president in 1987 *because* he was elected president in 1984.

Reagan was governor of California in 1967 *because* he was elected president in 1984.

The first compound sentence is true, and the second is false. Something other than the truth-value of the constituent sentences is relevant to determining the truth-value of the compound sentence.

Contrast this with some typical compound sentences made with 'and'.

An earthquake occurred on Thursday *and* the moon and the sun were in alignment on Thursday.

Reagan was president in 1987 *and* Reagan was elected president in 1984.

Reagan was governor of California in 1967 *and* Reagan was elected president in 1984.

If the basic constituent sentences are true, all of these compounds are true. You do not need any other information to know that these compound sentences are true.

English and Symbols

There are several important facts to note in considering the relationship of our truth-functional symbol to English sentences.

First we should note that when English sentences share a substantial common part, their conjunction is usually expressed without a full repetition of the common elements.

1a. John is in class and Bill is in class.
1b. John and Bill are in class.
2a. John has a brother and John has a sister.
2b. John has a brother and a sister.

The truth-value of 1b is related to truth-values of simpler sentences ("John is in class" and "Bill is in class") in the same way that the truth-value of 1a is related to those simpler sentences. Thus 1a and 1b can both be represented by

John is in class · Bill is in class.

Similarly, 2a and 2b are both represented by

John has a brother · John has a sister.

This argument is valid for the reasons given earlier:

John has a brother and a sister.
∴   John has a brother.

The premise is truth-functionally dependent on two simpler sentences. Thus the argument may be represented in this way:

John has a brother · John has a sister
∴   John has a brother.

And that argument can be shown valid by a truth-table analysis listing the four possible combinations of truth-values for the simple sentences.

Even though we have a perfectly good English word 'and' for making these truth-functional compounds, there are several reasons for using special symbols in representing truth-functional compounds.

The first is that English words will often have many uses other than their use as truth-functional connectives. The word 'and' is also used in sentences like

1 and 1 make 2.
Gin and vermouth go well together.
Carol and Alice shared expenses.

These are not compound sentences at all. There are no simpler sentences that can be joined together to make these sentences.

Notice how these sentences contrast:

Carol and Alice live in Boston.
Carol and Alice shared expenses.

The first can be represented using the dot symbol, because its truth-value depends (in the right way) on the truth-values of two simpler sentences.

Carol lives in Boston.
Alice lives in Boston.

But if we try to break the second example into *simpler* constituents, it just doesn't work out. One could try this:

Carol shared expenses with Alice.
Alice shared expenses with Carol.

But these are not any simpler than the original. The original expresses a *relationship* between Carol and Alice, it does not merely attribute the same characteristic to each.

Another reason for using the dot symbol (rather than 'and') is that there are other English connective words that are truth-functionally the same as the dot. Consider

Al is poor *but* he is happy.

If we construct a table for considering all possible cases, we find a definite truth-value whenever we know the truth-value of the constituents, and the table corresponds to the table for the dot.

Al is poor	Al is happy	Al is poor but he is happy
T	T	T
T	F	F
F	T	F
F	F	F

The word 'but' makes compound sentences that are truth-functionally the same as those made with the dot symbol or with the word 'and'. Even if there are differences in the uses of the words 'and' and 'but', there is no difference in the way in which the *truth-values* of compound sentences made with these connectives depend on the *truth-values* of their constituent sentences. We shall use the dot symbol to represent this dependency relation in a uniform way, so that we can easily recognize common patterns in truth-value relationships even where different English words occur.

Other connective words and phrases create compounds conforming to the table of truth-dependency used for the dot symbol. For example,

> although
> on the other hand
> even though
> however
> yet

Any English sentence that can be correctly represented by a compound made with the dot symbol will be called a *conjunction*.

There is still another common type of sentence that we can represent as a conjunction.

> Alice, who is very rich, drives a Ford.

The truth-value of this sentence depends on the truth-value of two simpler sentences in the right way, so we can represent it as a conjunction.

> Alice is very rich · Alice drives a Ford.

Relative clause constructions (often with 'who', 'whom', 'that', or 'which') can usually be represented as conjunctions.

> Bill is a doctor who likes to golf.
> Bill is a doctor · Bill likes to golf.

> Carol, to whom Bill wrote a letter, never writes to anyone.
> Bill wrote a letter to Carol · Carol never writes to anyone.

(In Chapter 10 this idea will be applied in a much more general way to relative clause constructions.)

The fact that the word 'and' is not always a sentence connective and the fact that other words besides 'and' conform to the truth-table for the dot symbol are both good reasons for wanting to have a single, specially defined symbol for showing this kind of truth-functional relationship in a uniform way. But the most important reason for using a special symbol is simply that it emphasizes the logically important element (in this case, the connective element of the compound sentence). This special symbol (and the others we introduce) make the deductively relevant features of arguments more visible.

EXERCISE 2a

Which of the following sentences can be represented as *conjunctions* of simpler sentences? What are the conjuncts?

1. Bob works for GM, and so does Fred.

2. Bob and Charlie work together.

3. Bob and Alice are the same height.

4. Bob and Doris are married.

5. Bob works for GM, but Ellen works for Ford.

6. Although Bob likes Fords, he works for GM.

7. Bob works for GM because the factory is near his house.

8. Bob is taller than Fred.

9. Bob and Charlie are taller than Fred.

10. Bob owns a Ford and a Chevrolet.

11. Bob compared a Toyota and a Ford.

12. Al is a dentist, but he makes very little money.

13. Al is a dentist who make very little money.

14. Al, who is a dentist, makes very little money.

NEGATION

Negation is another truth-functional relationship that can exist between sentences. We know that these sentences:

John is a fireman.
John is not a fireman.

must have opposite truth-values.

John is a fireman	John is not a fireman
T	F
F	T

For the basic sentence, "John is a fireman," there are two possible situations — it is true or it is false. Its *negation* ("John is not a fireman") has the other truth-value in each situation.

We will represent this relationship by a '$\sim$' symbol governing a sentence. Thus we could write

$\sim$(John is a fireman)

instead of "John is not a fireman." If p is any sentence, then $\sim p$ has a truth-value opposite to p's in any situation.

p	$\sim p$
T	F
F	T

Note: From now on we will use p, q, r, p_1, p_2, . . . , q_1, q_2, etc., instead of blanks (_____ , . . . , etc.). This is standard practice in logic because it is typographically easier and visually simpler. But it should be remembered that these letters are just like *blanks* into which a particular sentence can be substituted. A general table

p	q	$p \cdot q$
T	T	T
T	F	F
F	T	F
F	F	F

tells us something about all conjunctions—that is, about any sentence that can be constructed by placing sentences in place of "the blanks" (p and q) in the table. (These "blanks," p, q, r, etc., are sometimes called *sentence variables* or *schematic letters*.) We will call $p \cdot q$, $p \cdot {\sim}q$, $p \cdot (q \cdot r)$, etc., **sentence forms**, since they represent general structures for sentences.

MULTIPLY COMPOUND SENTENCES

Let's use capital letters to abbreviate particular English sentences. Abbreviations for simple sentences may be conjoined or negated to represent compound sentences. So if $A =$ Al won, $B =$ Bill is happy, and $C =$ Charlie is happy, then

$A \cdot B$	Al won and Bill is happy.
${\sim}A$	Al didn't win.
$C \cdot B$	Charlie and Bill are happy.

Compound sentences can also be conjoined or negated to represent multiply compound sentences.

$B \cdot {\sim}A$	Bill is happy and Al didn't win.
$A \cdot (B \cdot C)$	Al won and Bill and Charlie are happy.
$A \cdot (B \cdot {\sim}C)$	Al won, and Bill is happy but Charlie isn't.
$A \cdot {\sim}(B \cdot C)$	Al won, but Bill and Charlie are not both happy.
${\sim}A \cdot B$	Al didn't win, but Bill is happy.
${\sim}(A \cdot B)$	It is not the case both that Al won and that Bill is happy.

In most of these it was necessary to use parentheses to indicate what simpler sentences are being combined to make the more complex sentence.

Negation (${\sim}$) will always be taken to govern the shortest sentence that follows it. Parentheses must be used if we wish the '${\sim}$' to govern a whole conjunction. '$\sim A \cdot B$' is the conjunction of '$\sim A$' with 'B', and '$\sim(A \cdot B)$' is the negation of '$A \cdot B$'. These are very different sentences, and they may have different truth-values. (If 'B' is false, '$\sim A \cdot B$' is false and '$\sim(A \cdot B)$' is true.)

The truth-value of a multiply compound sentence can always be determined from the truth-value of its simplest parts if the compounding elements (such as '$\sim$' and '$\cdot$') are truth-functional. If 'A' and 'B' are true, then '$\sim A$' is false, so '$\sim A \cdot B$' has one false conjunct (and one true one), so it is false.

$\sim A \cdot B$

Starting with the shortest sentences, we can determine the truth-value for longer sentences until the truth-value of the complete compound is determined. At each step the tables characterizing the truth-dependency relationships determine what the truth-value is. So if A and B are true, but C is false:

$A \cdot \sim(B \cdot C)$

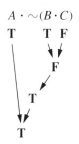

The table for conjunction (second row) is used here.

The table for negation is used here.

The table for conjunction (first row) is used here.

This can also be shown as a row of a table. Consider situations of the indicated type: A and B are true, and C is false. We determine the truth-value for '$A \cdot \sim(B \cdot C)$' by determining the truth-value for each simpler constituent.

(1)	(2)	(3)	(4)	(5)	(6)
A	B	C	$B \cdot C$	$\sim(B \cdot C)$	$A \cdot \sim(B \cdot C)$
T	T	F	F	T	T
			Determined from (2) and (3) using table for conjunction	Determined from (4) using table for negation	Determined from (1) and (5) using table for conjunction

EXERCISE 2b

If '*A*' and '*B*' stand for true sentences and '*C*' and '*D*' stand for false sentences, what is the truth value of each of the following sentences?

1. $A \cdot B$ **2.** $C \cdot B$

3. $A \cdot \sim C$ **4.** $B \cdot \sim A$

5. $A \cdot (B \cdot C)$ **6.** $(A \cdot B) \cdot \sim C$

7. $\sim(A \cdot B)$ **8.** $\sim(A \cdot C)$

9. $A \cdot \sim(B \cdot C)$ **10.** $\sim(A \cdot C) \cdot \sim D$

11. $A \cdot \sim(C \cdot \sim D)$ **12.** $A \cdot \sim(B \cdot \sim D)$

13. $\sim(\sim D \cdot A) \cdot \sim C$ **14.** $\sim(A \cdot \sim(D \cdot C))$

15. $\sim(\sim D \cdot \sim(A \cdot \sim C))$

DISJUNCTION

Another important connective is the ***disjunction*** symbol, '∨' (also called a *wedge*), the meaning of which is given by the following table.

p	*q*	*p* ∨ *q*
T	T	T
T	F	T
F	T	T
F	F	F

If *p* and *q* are sentences, then

p ∨ **q**

is a truth-functionally compound sentence which is true if one or both of the constituent sentences is true. If both are false, the compound sentence is false.

This connective corresponds to many uses of the word "or" in English. One may say

I'll see you tomorrow or sooner.

This is true if one or both of these sentences is true.

I will see you tomorrow.
I will see you sooner (than tomorrow).

It is false only if both are false. Thus 'or' seems to correspond to the table given for '∨'.

Some uses of 'or', however, may seem to fit a different pattern.

You will eat dinner or you will be punished.

A mother who says this to her child cannot fairly proceed in the following way: the child eats his dinner, then she punishes him anyway, telling him that this makes true what she originally said since both constituent sentences are true.

You eat your dinner.
You are punished.

It may seem that in this and other examples, the possibility that both of the two simple constituents of the compound are true is excluded. The mother who makes the 'or' statement may seem to affirm that one or the other is true, but not both. Such a statement would be called an *exclusive* 'or' statement, contrasting with the *inclusive* 'or' represented in our truth-table for the '∨' symbol. The truth-table for the '∨'-symbol allows for the possibility that both are true.

We will not introduce a special symbol for another type of 'or' statement, however. The exclusion of the joint truth of the simple sentences can be made explicit using the resources already available.

You'll eat your dinner or you'll be punished (but not both).
(You eat ∨ you are punished) · ∼(you eat · you are punished)
$(E \ \lor \ P) \cdot \mathord{\sim}(E \cdot P)$

Thus using '∨', ' · ', and '∼' we can explicitly represent this exclusion without any additional symbol.

E	p	$E \lor P$	$E \cdot P$	$\sim(E \cdot P)$	$(E \lor P) \cdot \sim(E \cdot P)$
T	T	T	T	F	F
T	F	T	F	T	T
F	T	T	F	T	T
F	F	F	F	T	F

Note that '$E \lor P$' is true in the first row, where both disjuncts are true, but '$(E \lor P) \cdot \sim(E \cdot P)$' is false in that case.

In some cases you may be uncertain whether to take an English 'or' sentence as *inclusive* or *exclusive*. When in doubt, treat it as an inclusive 'or', because the inclusive 'says less.'

John or Bill will be here tomorrow.

You may be unsure whether an exclusion is assumed.

$J \vee B$ At least one will be here.
$(J \vee B) \cdot \sim(J \cdot B)$ At least one will be here, *but not both.*

Notice that the second says more because it includes the first *conjoined with additional information.* It is always better to choose the minimal interpretation.

$J \vee B$

if we are unsure. We should avoid attributing to a speaker more than we are sure he or she actually said, especially when the minimal interpretation suffices in an argument analysis.

We can also use the '$\vee$' symbol in representing compound sentences made with the words 'neither' and 'nor'.

Neither John nor Bill will be here tomorrow.
$\sim(J \vee B)$

A neither-nor sentence is just the negation of a disjunction.

EXERCISE 2c

Using the following abbreviations as a guide, write an idiomatic English sentence that could be represented by the symbolized compound sentence.

A: Al speaks French.   *D:* Bill speaks Italian.

B: Bill speaks French.   *E:* Al is studying in France this year.

C: Al speaks Italian.   *F:* Bill is studying in Italy this year.

Example

$A \cdot \sim C$ Al speaks French but not Italian.

1. $A \cdot B$ 2. $C \vee D$
3. $C \cdot \sim D$ 4. $\sim(C \cdot D)$
5. $\sim C \cdot \sim D$ 6. $C \cdot E$
7. $\sim(C \vee D)$ 8. $(B \cdot \sim A) \cdot E$
9. $(C \cdot \sim A) \cdot E$ 10. $F \cdot \sim D$
11. $(B \cdot C) \cdot (E \cdot F)$ 12. $(A \cdot E) \cdot (F \cdot \sim D)$

EXERCISE 2d

Using the following abbreviations, symbolize each sentence.

A: Alice has the car.   *D:* Dan drives.

B: Boris has the car.   *E:* Emily drives.

C: Carol has the car.   *F:* Fred drives.

1. Boris and Alice don't both have the car.
2. Either Boris has the car or Carol has it.
3. Dan and Emily both drive.
4. Either Dan doesn't drive or Boris has the car.
5. Dan doesn't drive, although Boris has the car.
6. Neither Boris nor Carol has the car.
7. Boris doesn't have the car, and neither does Carol.
8. It's not true that neither Boris nor Alice has the car.
9. It's not true that Emily and Fred both drive.
10. Boris has the car and either Emily or Fred drives.
11. Alice has the car, and neither Emily nor Fred drives.
12. Neither Dan nor Fred drives, but Emily does.
13. Dan and Emily don't drive, but Fred does.
14. Either Emily drives or else Fred or Dan drives.

PARENTHESES

Parentheses are important. The numerical expression '$7-2+3$' is ambiguous because it could represent '$(7-2)+3$' (8) or it could represent '$7-(2+3)$' (2). Similarly, these symbolically represented sentences

$(A \lor B) \cdot C$

$A \lor (B \cdot C)$

have entirely different truth-conditions. For example, if A is true and C is false, then '$(A \lor B) \cdot C$' is false, but '$A \lor (B \cdot C)$' is true. Writing complex compounds without the parentheses that indicate how their constituents are composed is not permitted. The expression '$A \lor B \cdot C$' is not an acceptable way to attempt to represent any sentence.

Remember also that a negation symbol governs the shortest sentence that follows it, so

$\sim\!A \ \lor \ B$

represents a disjunction of '$\sim\!A$' with 'B'. To negate a disjunction (or a conjuction) we must enclose the compound sentence to be negated within parentheses:

$\sim\!(A \ \lor \ B)$

This negates the entire disjunction. ['$\sim\!A \ \lor \ B$' and '$\sim\!(A \ \lor \ B)$' have very different truth-conditions.]

In some cases our official notation requires parentheses even when the placement of parentheses does not affect truth-value.

$A \cdot (B \cdot C)$
$(A \cdot B) \cdot C$

Each sentence is true when all three atomic constituents is true, and each is false in every other case. However, since our dot symbol joins sentences two at a time, the expression

$A \cdot B \cdot C$

is not a sentence according to our notation. In this respect, our symbol is less flexible than most English connectives.

Alice drives and so do Betty and Carol.
Alice and Betty drive, and so does Carol.
Alice, Betty and Carol all drive.

The English word 'and' can be used to join sentences two at a time, but it can also be used to join three or more items together.

Similar remarks apply to the comparison of ' $\lor$ ' and 'or'.

Dave, Ed, or Fred will be at the party.

SYNTAX AND SEMANTICS

We can systematically present our rules of sentence formation in the following way.

Formation Rules

0. Capital letters of the alphabet stand for sentences.

1. Suppose that some expression

p

stands for a sentence. Then

$\sim$*p*

also stands for a sentence.

2. Suppose that two expressions

p

q

stand for sentences. Then the following are also sentences:

(*p* · *q*)

(*p* ∨ *q*)

Abbreviation: We can abbreviate by omitting the outer parentheses of completed expressions standing for sentences (when they are not parts of larger sentences).

For example,

(*A* ∨ *B*) · $\sim$(*A* · *B*)

is formed as follows:

I. These stand for sentences (rule 0):

A

B

II. This stands for a sentence (from I and from rule 2):

(*A* · *B*)

III. This stands for a sentence (from I and from rule 2):

(*A* ∨ *B*)

IV. This stands for a sentence (from II and from rule 1):

$\sim$(*A* · *B*)

V. This stands for a sentence (from II and IV and from rule 2):

((*A* ∨ *B*) · $\sim$(*A* · *B*))

VI. We can abbreviate the completed expression as follows:

(*A* ∨ *B*) · $\sim$(*A* · *B*)

Any expression we shall use to stand for a sentence (in this chapter) can be formulated by building it up, step by step, from basic elements according to rules 0–2 and the abbreviation principle.

Two interlocking aspects of logic have often been recognized. We have just been discussing *syntax*, the systematic study of the formation of linguistic or symbolic units. The formation principles 0–2 tell us nothing about the meanings of the symbols. (Note that nothing in 0–2 differentiates ' · ' from 'v'. They are both binary connectives.)

But we have also begun studying *semantics*, the interpretation of linguistic or symbolic units. So far, the only semantical consideration has been the question of the *truth-value* possibilities for the sentences we construct. Thus our semantics is given by the tables that characterize our truth-functional symbols.

p	$\sim p$
T	F
F	T

p	q	$p \cdot q$	$p \vee q$
T	T	T	T
T	F	F	T
F	T	F	T
F	F	F	F

This information about the truth-value dependency relations can also be given in English in a way that is parallel to the account of how sentences are formed.

0. Each capital letter has a truth-value (true or false).

1. An expression of the form

$\sim p$

is true if and only if

p

is false.

2a. An expression of the form

$p \cdot q$

is true if and only if

p

is true and

q

is also true.

b. An expression of the form

$p \vee q$

is true if and only if *at least one* of the constituent sentences

p

q

is true.

3. A sentence is false if and only if it is not true.

In this way, any sentence that can be constructed by the formation rules given earlier will have a truth-value based on the truth-values assigned to its basic constituents. (Note that the ' · ' and '∨' symbols are now differentiated by their semantical interpretations.)

EXERCISE 2e

Let 'A' and 'B' stand for true sentences and 'C' and 'D' for false sentences. Indicate the truth-value of each of the following.

1. ∼A   **2.** B ∨ C

3. ∼(B ∨ C)   **4.** ∼A · ∼(B ∨ C)

5. ∼(∼A · ∼(B ∨ C))   **6.** ∼D

7. ∼D ∨ ∼(A · ∼(B ∨ C))   **8.** ∼(∼D ∨ ∼(∼A · ∼(B ∨ C)))

EXERCISE 2f

If 'A' and 'B' stand for true sentences and 'C' and 'D' for false sentences, what is the truth-value of each of the following?

1. A ∨ C   **2.** A ∨ ∼C

3. C ∨ D   **4.** ∼A ∨ C

5. ∼A ∨ ∼B   **6.** ∼(A ∨ C)

7. A · B ∨ C)   **8.** A · ∼(C ∨ D)

9. A · ∼(B ∨ C)   **10.** C ∨ ∼(A · D)

11. B ∨ ∼(A · D)   **12.** ∼(A ∨ (B · D))

13. ∼(C ∨ (∼B · D))   **14.** ∼A ∨ ∼((B · D) · C)

A Note on Sentences and Sentence-Forms, Arguments and Argument Forms

Often there are things we would like to say about all sentences that share certain structural features. Here is an example:

Any disjunction in which the right disjunct is the negation of a conjunction and in which the left disjunct is one conjunct of the conjuction negated in the right disjunct is a true disjunction.

But there are better (shorter and clearer) ways to make the same general claim. Here is one:

Any sentence of the form . . . ∨ ~(. . . • ———) is true (no matter what sentences are placed in the blanks, as long as we replace both of the blanks . . . by the same sentence).

We can make this still clearer and even shorter by replacing the blanks by *schematic letters*—letters that do not themselves stand for particular sentences, but rather, that show where such particular sentences are to be put. Here is a way of saying the same thing using schematic letters:

Any sentence of the form p ∨ ~$(p \cdot q)$ is true.

Here the schematic letters p and q are simply substitutes for the blanks we used before. We call these schematic outlines of sentences *sentence-forms*. When a sentence fits the pattern displayed, we call it an *instance* of that form. An infinite number of sentences will be instances of any given sentence form. For example, if we abbreviate simple sentences by capital letters of the alphabet, all of these will abbreviate sentences of the form p ∨ ~$(p \cdot q)$:

A ∨ ~$(A \cdot C)$
B ∨ ~$(B \cdot A)$
$(B \cdot C)$ ∨ ~$((B \cdot C) \cdot A)$
$(B$ ∨ ~$C)$ ∨ ~$((B$ ∨ ~$C)$ ∨ $C)$

In each case, the same sentence is put in place of each occurrence of p in the sentence form and some sentence is put in place of q.

In a similar fashion we can construct **argument-forms**, exhibiting patterns that arguments may fit. Having ways like this for making general claims about sentences and about arguments is essential to the effective study of logic. Consider the difference between that following two ways of saying the same thing:

1. In an argument with two premises and a conclusion, if both premises are disjunctions and if the left disjunct of one is the negation of the right disjunct of the other, then if the conclusion is a disjunction of the left disjunct of the latter and the right disjunct of the former, the argument is valid.

2. All arguments of the following form are valid:

$p \vee q$

$\sim q \vee r$

$\therefore \quad p \vee r$

These really are two ways of saying the same thing, but the second is much shorter and much clearer. In the second you can actually see the relevant features of the pattern. For example, the two premises have a part in common. This is *described* in the first version, but it is *shown* in the second, and it is easier to recognize a pattern you can see than it is to recognize one you have only heard described. Statement 2, identifying that valid argument pattern, can be applied to the identification of valid arguments:

$A \vee B$	$(A \cdot B) \vee C$
$\sim B \vee C$	$\sim C \vee (D \vee E)$
$\therefore \quad A \vee C$	$\therefore \quad (A \cdot B) \vee (D \vee E)$
$A \vee (C \cdot D)$	$A \vee (\sim B \cdot C)$
$\sim (C \cdot D) \vee B$	$\sim (\sim B \cdot C) \vee (D \vee E)$
$\therefore \quad A \vee B$	$\therefore \quad A \vee (D \vee E)$

In each case some single sentence appears in place of each occurrence of *p*, some single sentence occurs in place of each occurrence of *q*, and some single sentence occurs in place of each occurrence of *r*. Thus each of these is an *instance* of the indicated form. Since it is a valid argument-form, each of these arguments must be valid.

How to Get an Instance of a Form

To get an instance of a form (either a sentence-form or an argument-form):

1. Replace each schematic letter in the form by a sentence (or by a letter abbreviating a sentence).
2. If the same schematic letter occurs more than once in the form, replace it by the same sentence in each of the places where it occurs in the form.
3. If a schematic letter is replaced by a compound sentence, enclose that compound sentence in parentheses.

For example, to get an instance of the argument form

1. $\sim p \vee (q \cdot p)$

   $\therefore \quad q \vee \sim p$

we can first replace *p* by some sentence, for example by the one abbreviated by '*A*', to get:

2. $\sim\!A \ \lor \ (q \cdot A)$
$\therefore \quad q \ \lor \ \sim\!A$

Then we can complete the job by replacing the schematic letter q by some sentence. If we use the sentence abbreviated '$A \cdot B$', the result is the following argument:

3. $\sim\!A \ \lor \ ((A \cdot B) \cdot A)$
$\therefore \quad (A \cdot B) \ \lor \ \sim\!A$

We can get a different instance of the same form, by choosing different replacements for the schematic letters. For example, we can replace p by '$\sim\!B$', to get

4. $\sim\!\sim\!B \ \lor \ (q \cdot \sim\!B)$
$\therefore \quad q \ \lor \ \sim\!\sim\!B$

and then replace q by '$\sim\!B$' also, to get the argument

5. $\sim\!\sim\!B \ \lor \ (\sim\!B \cdot \sim\!B)$
$\therefore \quad \sim\!B \ \lor \ \sim\!\sim\!B$

Arguments 3 and 5 are very different from one another in some respects, but both are instances of the argument-form given in argument 1. As these examples illustrate, there are various things that are *not* ruled out by rules 1–3 given above. In particular:

It is permissible to replace a schematic letter by a complex sentence.
It is permissible to replace different schematic letters by the same sentence.

How to Tell Whether a Given Sentence Is an Instance of a Form

A given sentence is an instance of a particular sentence-form if and only if it is possible, using rules 1–3 just given, to replace each of the schematic letters in the form in such a way as to produce the given sentence.

For example, the sentence

$(\sim\!A \cdot B) \ \lor \ (\sim\!A \cdot B)$

is an instance of the sentence-form

$p \ \lor \ (q \cdot r)$

because if we replace p by '$\sim\!A \cdot B$', replace q by '$\sim\!A$', and replace r by 'B', we get the sentence shown above. Saying that the sentence is of this form is really just a way of saying that the sentence is a disjunction in which the right disjunct is a conjunction.

The same sentence given above is also an instance of the form

$p \vee p$

Replacing p by '$\sim A \cdot B$' shows this. Notice, then, that the same sentence can be an instance of more than one form. (We have already seen that a form will have more than one instance.)

Notice, too, that asking whether a given sentence is of the form (i.e., is an instance of the form)

$p \cdot q$

is just a way of asking whether that sentence is a conjunction, and asking whether it is of the form

$p \vee q$

is just a way of asking whether it is a disjunction.

How to Tell Whether a Given Argument Is an Instance of a Form

There is only one new complication. In an argument-form, we do not consider the order of the premises to be significant. So both of the arguments

$A \vee B$	$\sim A$
$\sim A$	$A \vee C$
$\therefore \quad B$	$\therefore \quad C$

are considered to be instances of the argument-form

$p \vee q$
$\sim q$
$\therefore \quad p$

even though the second argument appears to have its premises in the wrong order.

Further Illustrations

A complex sentence will be properly characterized by many forms.

(s) $A \vee (B \cdot \sim A)$

It is a sentence, so it fits the form   f(1) p

It is a disjunction, so it fits the form   f(2) $p \vee q$

It is a disjunction with a right disjunct that is a conjunction, so it fits the form

f(3) $p \vee (q \cdot r)$

It is a disjunction with a right disjunct that is a conjunction the right conjunct of which is negated, so it fits the form

f(4) $p \vee (q \cdot \sim r)$

It is a disjunction with a right disjunct that is a conjunction the right conjunct of which is the negation of the left disjunct, so it fits the form

f(5) $p \vee (q \cdot \sim p)$

To get sentence (S) from the form (f1), replace p by '$A \vee (B \cdot \sim A)$'.

To get sentence (S) from the form (f2), replace p by 'A' and q by '$B \cdot \sim A$'.

To get sentence (S) from the form (f3), replace p by 'A', q by 'B', and r by '$\sim A$'.

To get sentence (S) from the form (f4), replace p by 'A', q by 'B', and r by 'A'.

To get sentence (S) from the form (f5), replace p by 'A' and q by 'B'.

Syntax and Semantics

It is a purely *syntactic* matter whether a sentence is or is not of a certain form. Only the *structure* of the sentence is important here. *Semantics*, which has to do with *meanings* and assignments of *truth values*, is irrelevant here. We can use skills of visual pattern matching to recognize that a sentence or argument has a particular form; we do not need to know anything about the meaning.

So, for example, despite the fact that the sentences 'A' and '$\sim\sim A$' will always have the same truth-value, nonetheless

'$\sim\sim A$' *is* of the form $\sim p$.

but

'A' is *not* of the form $\sim p$.

We can get '$\sim\sim A$' from $\sim p$ by replacing p by '$\sim A$', but there is no replacement for p that will yield 'A' as an instance, since there is no way we can get rid of the '$\sim$' in $\sim p$ simply by replacing p. (Logical symbols, such as '$\sim$', '$\cdot$', and '$\vee$', are fixed parts of the logical forms in which they appear. Every instance contains those elements in the corresponding place. The lower case letters p, q, etc., are blanks to be replaced in constructing an instance of a form.)

EXERCISE 2g

The column at the left contains translations of several sentences. The column at the right exhibits several numbered sentence-forms. List the numbers of each of the sentence-forms (from among those shown) of which the given sentence is an instance.

Example

$\sim B \cdot (C \vee D)$ 3,4,5

$A \vee \sim B$	**1.** $\sim p$
$\sim A \vee (B \cdot C)$	**2.** $p \vee q$
$(\sim A \vee B) \cdot C$	**3.** $p \cdot q$
$\sim (A \vee (B \cdot C))$	**4.** $\sim p \cdot q$
$(A \vee \sim B) \cdot C$	**5.** $p \cdot (q \vee r)$
$(\sim\sim A \vee B) \cdot A$	**6.** $(p \vee q) \cdot r$
$A \cdot (\sim A \vee A)$	**7.** $(p \vee \sim q) \cdot r$
$\sim (A \vee B) \cdot \sim C$	**8.** $(\sim p \vee q) \cdot r$
$(\sim A \vee B) \vee (C \cdot \sim D)$	**9.** $p \vee (q \vee r)$
$\sim A \cdot ((C \cdot D) \vee \sim E)$	**10.** $p \cdot (q \vee p)$

EXERCISE 2h

For each sentence-form, list all the sentences (from those shown) that are instances of that form.

Example

$\sim (p \cdot q)$ 4,20

$\sim p$	**1.** $A \vee B$
$p \vee q$	**2.** $\sim A \vee B$
$\sim (p \vee q)$	**3.** $A \vee \sim B$
$\sim p \vee q$	**4.** $\sim (A \cdot B)$
$p \vee \sim q$	**5.** $\sim A \vee \sim B$
$p \vee (q \cdot r)$	**6.** $\sim (A \vee \sim B)$
$p \vee (q \cdot p)$	**7.** $\sim (\sim A \vee (B \cdot C))$
$p \cdot q$	**8.** $A \vee (B \cdot C)$
$(p \vee q) \cdot r$	**9.** $\sim (A \vee (C \cdot B))$
	10. $A \cdot \sim B$
	11. $\sim A \cdot B$
	12. $A \vee (B \cdot A)$

13. $A \lor \sim A$

14. $(A \lor B) \cdot \sim C$

15. $(A \lor B) \lor \sim C$

16. $\sim(A \lor B) \lor C$

17. $\sim(A \lor (B \lor C))$

18. $(A \cdot B) \lor (C \lor (B \cdot A))$

19. $(A \cdot B) \cdot (C \lor (B \cdot A))$

20. $\sim((A \cdot B) \cdot C)$

KEY TERMS AND CONCEPTS

COMPOUND SENTENCE: Any sentence that contains one or more simpler sentences as a part.

ATOMIC SENTENCE: A sentence that is not compound.

NEGATION: The symbol '$\sim$'.

NEGATION OF A SENTENCE *p*: A sentence that is created from *p* by adding some element that has the effect of creating a sentence that always has a truth-value that is the opposite of *p*'s.

John is tall.   John is not tall.

J $\sim$J

CONNECTIVE WORD: A word that can be used to connect simpler sentences in a compound sentence.

Betty will win *or* she will be angry.

DISJUNCTION: The '$\lor$' symbol and the English word 'or' or its equivalents (when used to connect sentences). (In $p \lor q$, *p* is the left *disjunct* and *q* is the right *disjunct*.)

CONJUNCTION: The '$\cdot$' symbol and the English word 'and' and many truth-functional equivalents (when used to connect sentences). (In $p \cdot q$, *p* is the left *conjunct* and *q* is the right *conjunct*.)

TRUTH-FUNCTIONALLY COMPOUND SENTENCE: Any sentence whose truth-value depends on the truth-value of some simpler sentence or sentences but not on anything else.

TRUTH-FUNCTIONAL CONNECTIVE: Connective symbols (e.g., '$\cdot$' and '$\lor$') that can be used to construct truth-functionally compound sentences.

TRUTH-TABLE: A table that lists, row by row, all possible truth-value combinations for a set of atomic elements and uses those for computing the truth-values of compound sentences on each row.

SENTENCE-FORM: A structural pattern for sentences that are constructed with our symbols. [Example: The sentence '$A \lor (B \cdot C)$' is a disjunction. In other words, it is of the form $p \lor q$.]

ARGUMENT-FORM: A structural pattern for arguments.

$A \vee (B \cdot C)$	$(A \cdot B) \vee C$	$\sim(A \vee B)$
$\sim A$	$\sim(A \vee B)$	$(A \vee B) \vee C$
$\therefore \quad B \cdot C$	$\therefore \quad C$	$\therefore \quad C$

All three arguments are of the following form:

$p \vee q$

$\sim p$

$\therefore \quad q$

Truth-Functional Symbols Defined

p	$\sim p$
T	F
F	T

p	q	$p \cdot q$	$p \vee q$
T	T	T	T
T	F	F	T
F	T	F	T
F	F	F	F

3
TRUTH-FUNCTIONAL ANALYSIS

ARGUMENTS: VALIDITY AND INVALIDITY

We can now develop an *account* of the validity of the argument discussed at the beginning of Chapter 2.

1. John will study hard tonight or he will fail his exam tomorrow.
2. John will not study hard tonight.
3. So, John will fail his exam tomorrow.

Abbreviating our simplest sentences by '*S*' and '*E*', we can represent the argument in the following way:

$S \vee E$
$\sim S$
$\therefore\ E$

To show validity we need to show that there is no possible situation in which all of the premises are true with the conclusion false. So we consider all four possible combinations of truth-values for *S* and *E*, and the truth-values of the sentences in the argument in each possible case.

(a) *S*	(b) *E*	(c) $\sim S$	(d) $S \vee E$
T	T	F	T
T	F	F	T
F	T	T	T
F	F	T	F

One of the simple sentences, E, is the conclusion, and in every possible type of situation (on every row of the table) there is a truth-value listed for the two premises [columns (c) and (d)] and for the conclusion [column (b)]. If there is a row in which the premises are true and the conclusion is false, then arguments of this type are not valid—it is possible for the conclusion to be false when the premises are true. If there is no such row, it is valid. As we should expect, there is no such row. The only row on which both premises are true is the third, and the conclusion is also true there.

Thus we can show that whenever an argument consists of truth-functionally compound sentences related in this way, that argument must be valid. If a disjunction and the negation of the left disjunct of the disjunction are premises, and if the right disjunct is the conclusion, the argument must be valid. This will be true because of the truth-functional relationships among the sentences of the argument.

The facts developed to show that this particular argument is valid can thus be used to show a general conclusion. All arguments of the following form are valid:

$$p \lor q$$
$$\sim p$$
$$\therefore \ q$$

p	q	$\sim p$	$p \lor q$
T	T	F	T
T	F	F	T
F	T	T	T
F	F	T	F

Every argument of this form is valid because there is no way for an argument of this form to have true premises and a false conclusion. So all of these arguments must be valid:

1. The Republicans or the
   Democrats won. $R \lor D$
   It wasn't the Republicans. $\sim R$
   ∴ The Democrats won. $\therefore \ D$
2. Al won or he won't be happy. $W \lor \sim H$
   Al didn't win. $\sim W$
   ∴ Al won't be happy. $\therefore \ \sim H$
3. Al bammerizes or slammerizes. $B \lor S$
   Al doesn't bammerize. $\sim B$
   ∴ Al slammerizes. $\therefore \ S$
4. Al and Bill will both be here or
   Charlie will be angry. $(A \cdot B) \lor C$
   Al and Bill will not both be here. $\sim (A \cdot B)$
   ∴ Charlie will be angry. $\therefore \ C$

All of these are instances of the argument form, and all are valid. Note how we can make judgments of validity based on form and not content. It is easy to see that 3 is valid (if it has any content) even though we don't know what it means at all. And we do not need to know particular facts about Al, Bill, or Charlie to know that 2 and 4 are valid.

We will call an argument form *valid* when and only when every argument of that form is valid. An argument form with even one invalid instance is invalid. We will be working now to classify argument forms as valid or invalid by considering all of the combinations of truth-values that are possible for arguments of a given form. For example, consider the following argument form:

$p \lor q$

q

$\therefore\ \sim p$

This is not valid, because if p and q are both true, then the premises are true and the conclusion is false.

p	q	$\sim p$	$p \lor q$
T	T	F	T
T	F	F	T
F	T	T	T
F	F	T	F

The first row of truth-values on the table represents a possible type of situation (in which p and q are both true), and in that situation the premises ($p \lor q$ and q) will be true and the conclusion ($\sim p$) will be false. So some arguments of this type will have true premises and a false conclusion, and the argument form is not valid.

Computers will be in every
home in A.D. 2010 or sooner. $H \lor S$
They will be in every home
sooner than A.D. 2010. S
∴ They will not be in every
home in A.D. 2010. $\therefore\ \sim H$

This instance of the argument form is invalid. We can easily see that it is possible for an argument of this form to have true premises and a false conclusion.

The number of rows needed in a table listing all possible combinations of truth-values depends on the number of basic constituents. If the argument form has two basic constituents (as in the argument just considered), there are four possible combinations of truth-values, so the table has four rows. If it has three basic constituents,

$p \lor q$

$\sim q \cdot r$

$\therefore \ p \cdot r$

the table must have eight rows in order to include all possible combinations of truth-values.

(a)	(b)	(c)	(d)	(e)	(f)	(g)
p	q	r	$\sim q$	$p \lor q$	$\sim q \cdot r$	$p \cdot r$
T	T	T	F	T	F	T
T	T	F	F	T	F	F
T	F	T	T	T	T	T
T	F	F	T	T	F	F
F	T	T	F	T	F	F
F	T	F	F	T	F	F
F	F	T	T	F	T	F
F	F	F	T	F	F	F

Columns (e), (f), and (g) represent the sentences of the argument under consideration. Because there are three basic constituents (**p, q,** and **r**), there are eight rows. In every row in which both of the premises are true (this is the third row only), the conclusion is true as well. So the argument form is valid. No argument of this form can have true premises and a false conclusion.

To make sure that we always list all the possible truth-value combinations, we will find it useful to have a system. The basic constituents will be listed at the top of columns. The basic constituent farthest to the right will have rows alternating T and F. The next column (to the left) will have two rows with T and two rows with F, alternating. The next column (to the left) will have four rows with T and four rows with F, alternating. This continues, doubling each time, until all columns for basic constituents are filled. (It would not matter if we had the rows in a different order, as long as we had all of the different possibilities represented. Our system is just one way to make sure that we list all of them.)

The total number of rows needed is determined by the number of basic constituents. If the number of constituents is n, the number of rows needed to represent all combinations is 2^n.

Showing Validity and Invalidity: An Asymmetry

There is a significant asymmetry between validity and invalidity. To show validity of an argument form we must always examine every row of the truth-table to see that every possibility checks out. We must never have an instance with true premises and a false conclusion. But to show invalidity of an argument form only one example is needed. We can stop as soon as we have one possible situation in which the premises are true and the conclusion is false in an argument of that form. Thus in our previous example we really needed only one row of the truth-table.

$$p \vee q$$

$$q$$

$$\therefore \sim p$$

	Premise	Conclusion	Premise
p	*q*	$\sim p$	*p* $\vee$ *q*
T	<u>T</u>	<u>F</u>	<u>T</u>

This case suffices to show that it is possible to have true premises with a false conclusion. Consider another example.

$$(p \cdot q) \vee r$$

$$\sim p$$

$$\therefore \sim r$$

			Premise	Conclusion		Premise
p	*q*	*r*	$\sim p$	$\sim r$	*p* $\cdot$ *q*	$(p \cdot q) \vee r$
F	F	T	<u>T</u>	<u>F</u>	F	<u>T</u>

Here I have given one example, one assignment of truth-values, that makes the premises true and the conclusion false. This shows invalidity. There is also another invalidating assignment:

			Premise	Conclusion		Premise
p	*q*	*r*	$\sim p$	$\sim r$	*p* $\cdot$ *q*	$(p \cdot q) \vee r$
F	T	T	<u>T</u>	<u>F</u>	F	<u>T</u>

But only one needs to be given to show invalidity.

When we consider particular arguments rather than general argument forms, there is a different asymmetry to notice. When we establish that an *argument* is an instance of a *valid argument form*, that establishes the validity of the argument. Any instance of a valid argument form is valid, because in an argument of such a form there is no way to have true premises with a false conclusion. But showing that an argument is an instance of an invalid argument form does not show the invalidity of that argument.

$$p \vee q$$

$$p$$

$$\therefore \quad q$$

This is not a valid argument form, yet some instances of this argument form will be valid.

$(A \cdot B) \vee A$
$A \cdot B$
$\therefore \quad A$

This argument is an instance of that invalid form (substituting '$A \cdot B$' for p and 'A' for q), yet it is a valid argument. That particular argument form is not a validating argument form, but the argument has additional features that make it valid. (It is also an instance of the form

$(p \cdot q) \vee p$
$p \cdot q$
$\therefore \quad p$

That is a valid argument form, so the argument is valid.)

Summing up, we can say that we can show *validity* of an *argument form* by writing a complete truth-table. We can show validity of a *particular argument* by showing that it is an instance of a valid argument form. We can show *invalidity* of an *argument form* by giving one example (a truth-assignment or model) that shows how some argument of that form could have true premises with a false conclusion. To show *invalidity* of a *particular argument*, we would need to know that it has no validating features. Showing that it is an instance of an invalid argument form will not establish the invalidity; we also need to know that the argument form represents every feature that might be relevant to the question of whether that argument is valid. Knowing that requires a fuller knowledge of the scope of the resources involved in making arguments valid.

For example, we know that the following argument is valid:

All birds fly.
Some birds are meat-eaters.
So some meat-eaters fly.

It contains no truth-functionally compound sentences, so all we can say about it so far is that it has two premises and a conclusion; that is, it is of the form

p
q
$\therefore \quad r$

But that is not a valid form, because any argument with two premises is an instance of that form. To make a reasonable judgment about the validity of this argument, one would have to recognize that this argument has other features (like the words 'some' and 'all') that can be involved in the validation of an argument. Later, in our study of predicate logic, we will develop a fuller knowledge of the kinds of features relevant to the validation of arguments.

EXERCISE 3a

For each of these argument forms, determine whether it is *valid* or *invalid*.

1. $p \lor q$
$\sim q$
$\therefore \ p$

2. p
$\therefore \ p \lor q$

3. $p \lor q$
p
$\therefore \ \sim q$

4. $p \cdot q$
$\sim p \lor r$
$\therefore \ q \cdot r$

5. $p \lor q$
$\sim q \lor r$
$\therefore \ p \lor r$

6. $p \lor q$
$\sim p \lor r$
$\therefore \ p \cdot r$

7. $\sim(p \cdot q)$
$p \lor r$
$\therefore \ \sim q \lor r$

8. $p \lor q$
$\sim p$
$\therefore \ q \cdot \sim r$

9. $p \lor (q \cdot r)$
$\sim q$
$\therefore \ p$

10. $\sim(p \lor r)$
$\sim(q \cdot \sim r)$
$\therefore \ \sim p \cdot \sim q$

11. $\sim(p \cdot r)$
p
$\therefore \ \sim r$

12. $\sim(p \cdot q)$
$\sim p$
$\therefore \ q$

INCONSISTENCY OF SETS OF SENTENCES

We can also use our analyses of truth-functional structure to show that sets of sentences are inconsistent (i.e., that in every possible situation, at least one sentence of the set is false). Suppose, for example, that someone believes all of these things:

1. $\sim A$ Al didn't win.
2. $\sim C$ Charlie won't lose a lot of money.
3. $A \lor B$ Either Al or Bill won.
4. $\sim B \lor C$ Either Bill didn't win or Charlie will lose a lot of money.

Someone who believes everything in this set of sentences is in logical trouble. These beliefs are inconsistent, and we can use our methods of truth-functional analysis to show that there is no possible situation in which all of these are true.

There are eight possible combinations of truth-values (eight possible types of situation) involving A, B, and C.

(a) A	(b) B	(c) C	(d) ~A	(e) ~B	(f) ~C	(g) A ∨ B	(h) ~B ∨ C
T	T	T	F	F	F	T	T
T	T	F	F	F	T	T	F
T	F	T	F	T	F	T	T
T	F	F	F	T	T	T	T
F	T	T	T	F	F	T	T
F	T	F	T	F	T	T	F
F	F	T	T	T	F	F	T
F	F	F	T	T	T	F	T

The beliefs of the set under consideration are represented by the sentences with truth-values listed in columns (d), (f), (g), and (h). Check each of the eight possible situations (each of the eight rows), and you will find that on each row at least one of these four sentences is false. There is no possible situation in which all of these beliefs are true. One cannot possibly be right about all four of these things.

The general form for a set of sentences (the *set form*) of which this is an instance is

~*p*

~*q*

p ∨ *r*

~*r* ∨ *q*

Any set of sentences of this form must be inconsistent. On the other hand, a consistent set

A ∨ *B*	Al or Bill will win.
A	It will be Al.
~*B*	It won't be Bill.

will *not* be an instance of any inconsistent *set form*. The most detailed set form of which it is an instance

p ∨ *q*

p

~*q*

is consistent. If *p* is replaced by a true sentence and *q* by a false one, each sentence in such a set of this form will be true.

As with validity and invalidity, we can note an asymmetry here. To prove inconsistency of a form for a set of sentences we must examine every possible case, every row of the truth-table. To show consistency only one example, one row of the table, is needed. This form for a set of sentences

$p \cdot \sim q$

$q \vee r$

$r \vee s$

is shown consistent as soon as we give one example of a truth-assignment that makes every sentence in the set true.

p	q	r	s	S_1 $\sim q$	S_1 $p \cdot \sim q$	S_2 $q \vee r$	S_3 $r \vee s$
T	F	T	T	T	T	T	T

Every sentence in a set of this form would be true if the sentences replacing p, q, r, and s had the indicated truth-values. This one example of a truth-assignment making all of the sentences true is enough to establish consistency. (There is also one other assignment that makes them all true.)

Establishing consistency for a *form* for a set of sentences requires just one example. Showing consistency of a *particular set* of sentences requires showing that nothing about it makes it inconsistent. As with the case of showing invalidity, this requires a certain logical maturity, a general knowledge of the sorts of features that are relevant to consistency.

EXERCISE 3b

For each form for a set of sentences, determine whether it is *consistent* or *inconsistent*.

1. $p \vee q$
$p \cdot \sim q$
$\sim(p \cdot q)$

3. $p \vee q$
$\sim(p \cdot q)$
$p \cdot \sim q$

5. $(p \vee q) \cdot r$
$\sim(p \cdot r)$
$\sim q$

2. $p \vee q$
$\sim q \vee r$
$p \vee \sim r$

4. $p \vee (q \cdot r)$
$\sim q \cdot \sim p$

6. $p \vee q$
$\sim q \vee r$
$\sim(p \vee r)$

EQUIVALENCE OF PAIRS OF SENTENCES

We can also use truth-functional methods of analysis in showing that sentences are *logically equivalent;* that is, the two sentences must always have the same truth-value.

A	B	$A \cdot B$	$B \cdot A$
T	T	T	T
T	F	F	F
F	T	F	F
F	F	F	F

No matter what the situation is, '$A \cdot B$' and '$B \cdot A$' must have the same truth-value.

A more interesting example follows.

A	B	$\sim A$	$\sim B$	$A \vee B$	$\sim A \cdot \sim B$	$\sim(A \vee B)$
T	T	F	F	T	F	F
T	F	F	T	T	F	F
F	T	T	F	T	F	F
F	F	T	T	F	T	T

'$\sim A \cdot \sim B$' and '$\sim(A \vee B)$' have the same truth-value in all possible situations. They are *logically equivalent*. A number of English sentences, related to these, can also be seen to be logically equivalent.

Al is not tall, and Bill is not tall.
It is not the case that: either Al or Bill is tall.
Neither Al nor Bill is tall.
Al isn't tall, and Bill isn't tall either.

Note that when we have a pair of logically equivalent sentences there are two related valid arguments. If S_1 and S_2 are equivalent, then

S_1
$\therefore \ S_2$

S_2
$\therefore \ S_1$

are both valid. Since S_1 and S_2 cannot differ in truth-value, there is no way for one to be true with the other false. Thus, given the example of an equivalent pair of sentences just discussed, we can see that both of these arguments are valid:

$\sim(A \vee B)$
$\therefore \ \sim A \cdot \sim B$

$\sim A \cdot \sim B$
$\therefore \ \sim(A \vee B)$

To show a pair of sentences equivalent, you must consider every row of the truth-table and show that the truth-values of the sentences match in all cases. To show nonequivalence only one example is needed, to show that in at least one type of case sentences of the indicated form have different truth-values.

Thus we can show that sentences of the following form are not always equivalent.

$\sim(p \cdot q)$

$\sim p \cdot \sim q$

			S_1			S_2
p	q	$p \cdot q$	$\sim(p \cdot q)$	$\sim p$	$\sim q$	$\sim p \cdot \sim q$
T	F	F	$\underline{T}$	F	T	$\underline{F}$

In at least this one case, some sentences in a pair of sentences of this form can have different truth-values, thus they are not equivalent. (There is also another assignment that gives them different truth-values, but only one is needed to show that they are not equivalent.)

Among pairs of sentences that are *not equivalent*, we can identify several logical relationships that might hold. Most obviously, one sentence might follow from the other. For example:

John and Bill are not firemen.

John is not a fireman.

These are not equivalent, but the argument that takes the first as premise and the second as conclusion is valid.

$\sim J \cdot \sim B$
$\therefore \quad \sim J$

This will not work the other way, however. The following argument is *invalid*:

$\sim J$
$\therefore \quad \sim J \cdot \sim B$

Thus they are not equivalent, but there is a one-way relationship of logical entailment holding between them.

Some other logical relationships are also worth noting. Consider these two sentences:

Bill is a fireman, but John isn't. $B \cdot \sim J$

John is a fireman. J

These are not equivalent, but there is more to be said about their logical relationship. They cannot both be true. If one is true, the other must be false. Sentences that cannot be true together are called *contraries*. Another test of *contraries* is that each sentence entails *the negation of the other one*. Since these sentences ('$B \cdot \sim J$' and 'J') are contraries, the following arguments are both *valid*:

$B \cdot \sim J$ J
$\therefore \quad \sim J$ $\therefore \quad \sim(B \cdot \sim J)$

Each sentence entails the negation of the other. Contrary sentences cannot both be true. Note that in the case just considered, they could both be false (if 'B' is false and 'J' is false).

Sentences that are contraries are in conflict with one another. They cannot both be true. But sentences can stand in even stricter opposition: they cannot both be true *and* they cannot both be false. They must always have different truth-values. The sentences of such pairs are called *contradictories* of each other. The most obvious examples are simply a sentence and its negation.

A $B \cdot C$ $B \vee \sim C$
$\sim A$ $\sim(B \cdot C)$ $\sim(B \vee \sim C)$

Each of these is a pair of contradictories: sentences that must have opposite truth-values. More generally, we could say that two sentences are contradictories whenever each is equivalent to the negation of the other. This is a pair of *contradictories*:

$\sim A \cdot \sim B$
$A \vee B$

Accordingly, these are pairs of equivalent sentences:

$\sim A \cdot \sim B$ $\sim(\sim A \cdot \sim B)$
$\sim(A \vee B)$ $A \vee B$

When two sentences "oppose" each other, they may be contraries and not contradictories. When negation occurs in compound sentences, it is important to consider which type of opposition is occurring. For example:

John and Bill are firemen.
John and Bill are not firemen.

The most likely interpretation of these is as the *contrary* sentences

$J \cdot B$
$\sim J \cdot \sim B$

These cannot both be true. But they are not contradictories, because they can both be false (e.g., if John is a fireman but Bill isn't). The following would be true *contradictories*:

> John and Bill are firemen.
> John and Bill aren't both firemen.
> $J \cdot B$
> $\sim(J \cdot B)$

These always have opposite truth values.

EXERCISE 3c

For each pair of sentence forms, determine whether they are equivalent.

1. $p \lor q$
   $q \lor p$

2. $\sim p \lor q$
   $p \lor \sim q$

3. $\sim(p \cdot q)$
   $\sim p \lor \sim q$

4. $\sim(p \cdot q)$
   $\sim p \cdot \sim q$

5. $p \lor (q \lor r)$
   $(p \lor q) \lor r$

6. $\sim p \lor \sim q$
   $\sim(p \lor q)$

7. $\sim p \cdot q$
   $\sim(p \cdot q)$

8. $p \lor (q \cdot r)$
   $(p \lor q) \cdot r$

9. $\sim(p \cdot q) \cdot r$
   $\sim p \cdot (q \cdot r)$

10. $\sim\sim(p \lor q)$
    $\sim\sim p \cdot \sim\sim q$

TAUTOLOGOUS, CONTRADICTORY, AND CONTINGENT SENTENCES

Tautologies

Consider the truth-values possible for sentences of the form

$p \lor \sim p$

There are two possibilities (two rows) to consider.

p	$\sim p$	$p \lor \sim p$
T	F	T
F	T	T

Sentences of the form $p \vee \sim p$ are true in both of the possible types of situation. A sentence that is, like this one, true in all possible situations (on all rows of a truth-table) is called a "*logical truth*." We can tell from the logical features alone that the sentence is true. When a sentence is a logical truth in virtue of its truth-functional composition (as in the cases we are now considering), it is called a "*tautology*." The form $(p \cdot q) \vee (\sim p \vee \sim q)$ is a slightly more complex example of a *tautologous* sentence form.

p	q	$p \cdot q$	$\sim p$	$\sim q$	$\sim p \vee \sim q$	$(p \cdot q) \vee (\sim p \vee \sim q)$
T	T	T	F	F	F	T
T	F	F	F	T	T	T
F	T	F	T	F	T	T
F	F	F	T	T	T	T

Tautologies are logically special because logic can say by itself what their truth-value is. For typical sentences this is not true. Questions of factual truth-value are usually outside the scope of logic. We normally study only truth-value *relationships*. But tautologies are part of the special class of sentences (logical truths) that logic can certify as true.

Al will win or he won't.

Reagan won or he didn't.

No study of particular facts about Al's life or Reagan's life is needed to know that these are true.

Other examples of tautologous sentence forms are these:

$\sim(p \cdot \sim p)$

$((p \cdot q) \vee (p \cdot \sim q)) \vee \sim p$

$\sim(p \cdot q) \vee p$

$(p \vee \sim p) \cdot (q \vee \sim q)$

Contradictions

Now consider sentences of the form $(p \vee q) \cdot (\sim p \cdot \sim q)$.

p	q	$p \vee q$	$\sim p$	$\sim q$	$\sim p \cdot \sim q$	$(p \vee q) \cdot (\sim p \cdot \sim q)$
T	T	T	F	F	F	F
T	F	T	F	T	F	F
T	T	T	T	F	F	F
F	F	F	T	T	T	F

Sentences of this form are false in all possible situations and are called *contradictory* sentences (or *contradictions*). They are false simply because of their logical features, and contradictory sentences are the other major category of sentences concerning which logic can certify the truth-values. Here are some other instances of contradictory sentence forms:

$p \cdot {\sim}p$

${\sim}(p \lor {\sim}p)$

$(p \cdot (q \lor r)) \cdot ({\sim}(p \cdot q) \cdot {\sim}(p \cdot r))$

Note that the negation of a tautology is always contradictory, and the negation of a contradiction is always a tautology.

Contingent Sentences

If a sentence is not an instance of a tautologous form and it is not an instance of a contradictory form, it is a *contingent* sentence. It is true in some possible situations (on at least one row of its truth-table) and false in other possible situations (on at least one other row of its truth-table). A *sentence form* is *contingent* if it is neither tautologous nor contradictory. Contingent sentence forms will have both true and false instances.

Any sentence form with some true instances and some false instances will be contingent. Most of the sentence forms considered prior to this have been contingent sentence forms. For example:

$p \lor q$

$p \cdot q$

${\sim}p$

$p \cdot (q \lor {\sim}r)$

${\sim}(p \cdot q)$

Ordinary discourse consists almost completely of contingent sentences, because in ordinary discourse we are concerned to make statements that convey information about the actual world. Tautologies and contradictions are true or false in all possible worlds in virtue of the logical form; their status as true or false tells us nothing about facts particular to the actual world.

To show that a sentence form is a logical truth, we need to consider all rows of a truth-table, showing that sentences of that form are true in all possible cases. To show that a sentence form is contradictory, we also need to consider all rows, showing that sentences of that form are false in all possible cases. To show contingency we need only two examples, one true and one false. These show that it is not contradictory and is not tautologous.

Thus the form $p \cdot {\sim}(q \lor r)$ is contingent.

p	q	r	$q \lor r$	${\sim}(q \lor r)$	$p \cdot {\sim}(q \lor r)$
T	F	F	F	T	T
F	F	F	F	T	F

In at least one case it is true (thus not contradictory), and in at least one case it is false (thus not tautologous). So it is contingent.

The following table may be a useful summary of some of the information in this chapter.

	Shown by Considering Every Possible Case	Shown by Example
Argument	*Valid:* In every possible case, if premises are true, conclusion is also true.	*Invalid:* In at least one possible case, premises are true, conclusion is false.
Set of sentences	*Inconsistent:* In every possible case, at least one is false.	*Consistent:* In at least one possible case, all are true.
Pair of sentences	*Equivalent:* in every possible case, they have the same truth-value.	*Not equivalent:* In at least one possible case, they have different truth-values.
Sentence	*Logically true (tautologous):* In every possible case, true. *Contradictory:* In every possible case, false.	*Contingent:* True in at least one possible case and false in at least one possible case (two examples).

EXERCISE 3d

For each sentence form, determine whether it is *tautologous*, *contradictory*, or *contingent*.

1. $p \vee q$
2. $(p \cdot q) \vee \sim p$
3. $\sim(p \cdot q) \vee p$
4. $(p \vee q) \cdot \sim(p \cdot q)$
5. $(p \vee q) \cdot (\sim p \cdot \sim q)$
6. $(p \vee p) \cdot \sim p$
7. $(p \cdot q) \vee (p \vee r)$
8. $\sim(p \cdot q) \vee ((r \vee p) \cdot (r \vee q))$
9. $(p \cdot q) \cdot \sim(p \vee q)$
10. $p \vee (q \vee \sim p)$
11. $(p \vee \sim p) \vee q$
12. $(p \vee \sim p) \cdot q$
13. $(p \vee \sim p) \cdot (q \vee \sim q)$
14. $(p \cdot \sim p) \vee (q \cdot \sim q)$
15. $(p \vee q) \vee \sim(p \vee q)$

VALIDITY: SOME SPECIAL CASES

Exploring some special cases of valid argument can help us to see the limits of our notion of validity. Consider this argument form:

$p \cdot q$

$q \vee \sim p$

$\therefore \quad p \vee \sim p$

This argument form is valid: no argument of this form has true premises and a false conclusion.

p	q	$\sim p$	$p \cdot q$	$q \vee \sim p$	$p \vee \sim p$
T	T	F	T	T	T
T	F	F	F	F	T
F	T	T	F	T	T
F	F	T	F	T	T

The first row is the only one in which both premises are true, and there the conclusion is also true. But there is something special about this argument. Its conclusion is a tautology. Thus there is no case in which the conclusion is false. Obviously, there can be no case with true premises and a false conclusion if there are no cases with a false conclusion. No matter what premises we have, we cannot have true premises with a false conclusion if the conclusion is a tautology.

When we think about the notion of formal validity, we often think of it as consisting of "the right sort of connection" between premises and conclusion. But if the conclusion is a tautology, the conclusion must be true no matter what the premises are. Thus a "connection" is not needed in this special case. Given the premises the truth of the conclusion is guaranteed, because the truth of the conclusion is logically guaranteed even without the premises.

Thus we will accept the following general principle about validity:

Every argument with a tautologous conclusion is valid.

In such a case the premises may be pointless—the conclusion stands on its own. In such a case the argument is rather strange: it has pointless premises and a conclusion that conveys no information about the way things are (since its being true does not exclude any possible situation). But the argument is valid.

Another special case of validity occurs in arguments like the following:

$p \vee q$

$\sim p$

$\sim q$

$\therefore \quad p \cdot q$

p	q		$\sim p$	$\sim q$	$p \vee q$	$p \cdot q$
T	T		F	F	T	T
T	F		F	T	T	F
F	T		T	F	T	F
F	F		T	T	F	F

There is no situation in which the premises are true and the conclusion is false. Thus this argument is valid.

But this example may seem even stranger than the preceding one. Its premises are inconsistent. There is no possible situation in which all of the premises of this argument are true. But if the premises can never be true, we can never have true premises with a false conclusion. So the argument is valid.

This leads to a general principle that may at first seem very extraordinary:

Every argument with inconsistent premises is valid.

But arguments with inconsistent premises are always bad arguments, even if they are valid. Their deficiency is not a lack of validity; their deficiency is that *they cannot be sound arguments*. We can determine that for logical reasons alone, these arguments cannot have true premises; thus they cannot be sound. This is one case where purely logical analysis tells us something about the soundness of an argument as well as about its validity.

EXERCISE 3e

Which are valid?

1. $p \cdot q$
  $q \vee r$
  $\therefore \quad \sim(q \cdot \sim q)$

2. $p \vee q$
  $\sim q \vee r$
  $\sim(p \vee r)$
  $\therefore \quad p \cdot \sim r$

3. $p \vee \sim p$
  $q \vee p$
  $\therefore \quad q \cdot p$

4. $p \vee \sim p$
  $\sim(q \cdot \sim q)$
  $\therefore \quad (p \vee q) \cdot (\sim p \cdot \sim q)$

5. $p \vee q$
  $r \vee \sim q$
  $p \vee r$
  $\therefore \quad \sim p \vee \sim r$

4
TRUTH-TREES

Although truth-tables provide a systematic method for deciding about the validity of a wide range of argument forms, they have a serious practical limitation. They are constructed by a simple, systematic method, but that method produces tables whose size increases exponentially relative to the number of atomic constituents. An argument form with two atomic constituents has a table with 2^2 (i.e., 4) rows, but an argument form with five atomic constituents has 2^5 (i.e., 32) rows, and one with eight constituents has 2^8 (256) rows. This makes truth-tables impractical for the evaluation of some relatively simple examples.

Consider this argument form, for example:

$p \vee q$

$\sim q \vee r$

$\sim r \vee s$

$\sim s \vee t$

$\sim t \vee u$

$\therefore \ p \vee u$

This is valid, but showing validity requires a truth-table with 2^6 (64) rows and 16 columns.

In this chapter we develop another systematic procedure, truth-trees, which will often produce a much more efficient decision about the validity of an argument form or the consistency of a form for a set of sentences.

CONSISTENCY AND INCONSISTENCY

Truth-trees are most easily understood if we look first at the decision about consistency and inconsistency. To establish the consistency of a form for a set of sentences, we need one *example* of a situation (i.e., one *truth-table row* or *model*) in which every member of the set could be true. Consider this simple form for a set of sentences:

$$p \cdot \sim q$$
$$r \vee q$$

We could determine whether this is consistent by writing an eight-row truth-table and then finding at least one row on which both sentences could be true. But we can also proceed without a full table, listing the simpler sentences that must be true in order for both of these compound sentences to be true. With the first sentence, a conjunction, it is obvious what must be true:

√ 1. $p \cdot \sim q$
   2. $r \vee q$
     p Both of these must be true if $p \cdot \sim q$ is to be true.
     $\sim q$

The check mark on the first line indicates that we have listed sentences whose truth is sufficient to guarantee that the conjunction on the first line is true.

     With a disjunction, we cannot in general list things that *must* be true in order for the disjunction to be true. A disjunction presents two possibilities for situations that would make it true, and we need to branch out and consider both cases. Each of the branches on the following diagram can be thought of as one way that the disjunction could be true.

√ 1. $p \cdot \sim q$
√ 2. $r \vee q$
     p
     $\sim q$ For the second line to be true, at least one branch
  /   \   must be correct.
  r q

The check mark on the second line indicates that we have branched out to consider all of the ways that the disjunction might be true. But if both members of the original set of sentences are to be true, the branch on the right cannot be correct. It makes q true, but we already listed $\sim q$ as something that has to be true in every situation verifying the two sentences in the set. So the right branch cannot be correct, and we can eliminate that as a possible situation in which the original sentences are both true.

The possibility on the left branch remains open. If *p* and *r* are true and *q* is false, both sentences of the original set are true. We shall call the *path* beginning with sentence-form 1 (*p* · ~*q*) and ending with *r*, a *model path* for the original set. It indicates what truth-values can be given to atomic constituents to make every member of the initial set true. A situation in which sentences corresponding to *p* and *r* are true and in which the sentence corresponding to *q* is false is a *model* for the original set—a situation that makes the members of that set true. In a truth-tree diagram, each model path indicates a way to construct a model. The atomic sentences listed on the path must be true, and the negated atomic sentences listed on the path indicate which atomic sentences must be false.

In constructing a model path, we must consider the significance of each compound sentence or sentence-form. We must make sure to take note of its relationship to the truth-values of its more basic elements. We then use a check mark to indicate that it has been considered. In our example, we checked off the conjunction when we listed its conjuncts (in the third and fourth lines) and we checked off the disjunction when we branched out to consider the two cases allowed by the disjunction. An atomic constituent or the negation of an atomic constituent on a path will indicate whether a sentence is to be true or false in the model indicated by the model path.

A path is complete under two circumstances. If it contains a sentence (or sentence-form) together with the negation of the very same sentence (or sentence-form), it is closed and complete. If every sentence (or sentence-form) that is not atomic or the negation of an atomic element is checked off, the path is also complete. We show inconsistency by completing a tree in which every path is closed. We show consistency by finding at least one open, complete path (a model path).

Consider a slightly different set:

1. *p* · *q*
2. ~(*q* · *r*)
3. *r* ∨ *s*

We can begin as before, listing *p* and *q* as separate elements that must be true and checking off the first line.

√ 1. *p* · *q*
   2. ~(*q* · *r*)
   3. *r* ∨ *s*
     p
     q

Sentence-form 2 is the negation of a conjunction. Just as there is more than one way to make a disjunction true, there is more than one way to make sentence 2 true (i.e., there is more than one way to make a conjunction false). So we must branch out to consider the ways to do it.

√ 1. $p \cdot q$
   2. $\sim(q \cdot r)$
   3. $r \lor s$

p

q

$\sim q$ $\sim r$

X

We can immediately close the left path because it contains both q and $\sim q$, and we know that no model can make both of those true.

Finally, on the remaining open path, we must branch out to consider the truth-possibilities for $r \lor s$.

√ 1. $p \cdot q$
√ 2. $\sim(q \cdot r)$
   3. $r \lor s$

p

q

$\sim q$ $\sim r$

X

r s

X

Again, one path can be closed off immediately. But this leaves one open path. That path satisfies our conditions for being a *model path*.

1. The path is not closed; it does not contain any sentence and also the negation of that sentence.

2. Each sentence that is not atomic and is not the negation of an atomic sentence is checked off.

This path tells us immediately what truth-assignment would make the sentences of the original set true.

$p : T$
$q : T$
$r : F$
$s : T$

Any consistent form for a set of sentences will generate at least one model path. If a form for a set of sentences is inconsistent, every path will be closed off.

To see what happens with an inconsistent set, consider the set containing sentences 1–3:

√ **1.** $p \lor q$
   2. $\sim(q \lor r)$
   3. $r \lor \sim p$

        /   \
    p q

The first sentence requires a branching out. The second sentence is a negated disjunction. For it to be true, $q \lor r$ must be false, so $\sim q$ and $\sim r$ must both be true. This applies to each of the open paths so far developed.

√ **1.** $p \lor q$
√ **2.** $\sim(q \lor r)$
   3. $r \lor \sim p$

        /   \
    p q
   $\sim q$ $\sim q$
   $\sim r$ $\sim r$
           X

The right path now closes because it contains both q and $\sim q$. We can continue on the left path.

√ **1.** $p \lor q$
√ **2.** $\sim(q \lor r)$
√ **3.** $r \lor \sim p$

        /   \
    p q
   $\sim q$ $\sim q$
   $\sim r$ $\sim r$
  / \   **X**
r $\sim p$
X   **X**

All paths are now closed, so the original set is shown to be inconsistent. There is no consistent way to make all three of the sentences true.

With conjunction, disjunction, and negation as our logical symbols, the full set of rules for constructing model paths in truth-trees are these.

1. If a path from the first sentence contains some sentence and the negation of that very same sentence, close that path.

2. If an unchecked compound sentence on a path is a conjunction $p \cdot q$,
   add p and q to each subordinate open path. Then check off the conjunction.

3. If an unchecked compound on a path is a disjunction $p \vee q$, construct
   two branches, one with p and one with q, on each subordinate open
   path. Then check off the disjunction.

4. If an unchecked compound is a negated conjunction $\sim(p \cdot q)$, construct
   two branches, one with $\sim p$ and one with $\sim q$, on each subordinate open
   path. Then check off $\sim(p \cdot q)$.

5. If an unchecked compound is a negated disjunction $\sim(p \vee q)$, add $\sim p$
   and $\sim q$ to each subordinate open path. Then check off $\sim(p \vee q)$.

6. If an unchecked compound is double-negated, $\sim\sim p$, add p to each
   subordinate open path. Then check off $\sim\sim p$.

If all paths close, there is no model path; the inital set is inconsistent. If
some path remains open after all possible steps are done, it is a model path;
the initial set is consistent.

In working through the examples considered so far, we have always
proceeded in order through the members of our initial set of statements. It
is not necessary to do so, and it will sometimes simplify a truth-tree to do
nonbranching steps first. Thus we would get a slightly simpler tree in the
example most recently discussed if we started with the second line.

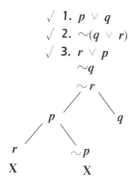

In some cases the simplification could be substantial. Consider these two
different maps for the same set.

$\sqrt{}$ **1.** $p \vee q$
$\sqrt{}$ **2.** $\sim q \vee (r \vee s)$
$\sqrt{}$ **3.** $\sim s \vee p$

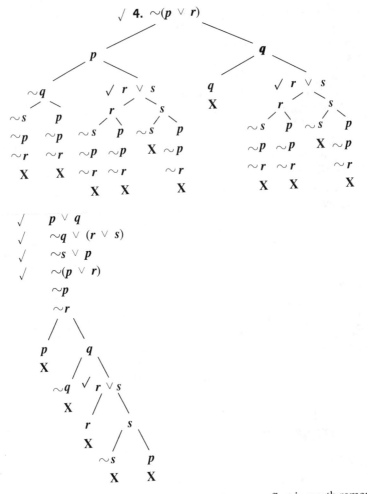

So the general guideline to do nonbranching steps first is worth remembering.

Application of the rules for constructing truth-trees can sometimes produce compound sentences farther down the path. If so, we must apply the rules to those sentences as well as to the compound sentences of the original set.

The compound sentences on the fourth line ($\sim\sim q$) and on the right branch of the sixth ($q \cdot r$) line must also be checked off to complete the tree. (In this case, the initial set is consistent, because there is an open, complete path. The model path indicates that the assignment of p:F, q:T, and r:T will make the two sentences of the initial set true.)

Examples

A.

$\checkmark$ 1. $p \lor q$
$\checkmark$ 2. $\sim(q \lor r)$
   3. $\sim(q \lor \sim s)$
    $\sim q$
    $\sim r$
    $\sim q$
    $\sim\sim s$
    s

Consistent   (p:T, q:F, r:F, s:T)

B.

$\checkmark$ 1. $p \lor \sim q$
$\checkmark$ 2. $q \lor r$
$\checkmark$ 3. $\sim(r \cdot \sim(s \cdot p))$
$\checkmark$ 4. $\sim p$

Inconsistent

C.

$\checkmark$ 1. $p \lor (q \lor r)$
$\checkmark$ 2. $\sim(r \cdot \sim q)$
$\checkmark$ 3. $\sim p \lor q$
$\checkmark$ 4. $\sim(q \lor (p \cdot r))$

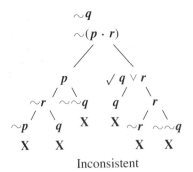

Inconsistent

EXERCISE 4a

For each set, use a truth-tree to determine whether it is consistent.

1. $p \lor q$
   $\sim p \lor q$
   $\sim q$

2. $p \lor q$
   $\sim q \cdot r$
   $\sim r \lor s$
   $\sim(p \cdot s)$

3. $p \lor (q \cdot r)$
   $\sim q$
   $\sim(p \lor r)$

4. $p \cdot (q \lor r)$
   $\sim q$
   $p \lor r$

5. $p \lor (q \lor r)$
   $\sim q$
   $\sim p \cdot \sim r$

6. $\sim p \lor \sim(q \lor r)$
   $p \lor q$

7. $p \lor (q \cdot r)$
   $\sim(r \cdot \sim s)$
   $\sim(p \lor (q \cdot s))$

8. $p \lor (q \cdot \sim r)$
   $r \lor s$
   $\sim(p \lor s)$

VALIDITY AND INVALIDITY

To use the truth-tree technique for checking for validity, we need to recognize a relationship between arguments and sets of sentences. Suppose that a certain argument with premises $P_1, \ldots, P_n$ and conclusion C is valid. Then statements 2–4 that follow must also be true.

1. The argument
   $P_1, \ldots, P_n \therefore C$
   is valid.
2. It is impossible that $P_1, \ldots, P_n$ are true and C false.
3. It is impossible that $P_1, \ldots, P_n$, and $\sim C$ are all true.
4. $\{P_1, \ldots, P_n, \sim C\}$ is inconsistent.

Every valid argument is related to a certain inconsistent set of statements. In fact, we can say in general that

An argument

$$P_1, \ldots, P_n \qquad \therefore C$$

is valid *if and only if* the set of sentences

$$\{ P_1, \ldots, P_n, \sim C \}$$

is inconsistent.

We can test an argument (or argument form) for validity by testing the related set for consistency. The related set is the set consisting of the argument's premises taken together with the negation of the conclusion. So consider the following form of argument.

$$p \vee q$$
$$r \vee \sim q$$
$$\therefore \quad p \vee r$$

To test the argument form for validity, we simply negate the conclusion and test the resulting set for consistency. (In this case, start with the third member on the list, because it does not require branching.)

$$\checkmark \quad 1. \ p \vee q$$
$$\checkmark \quad 2. \ r \vee \sim q$$
$$\checkmark \quad 3. \ \sim(p \vee r)$$
$$\sim p$$
$$\sim r$$

```
        / \
       p   q
       X  / \
         r   ~q
         X    X
```

All paths close, so the form for a set of sentences $\{ p \vee q, \ r \vee \sim q, \ \sim(p \vee r) \}$ is inconsistent. This means that the original argument,

$$p \vee q$$
$$r \vee \sim q$$
$$\therefore \quad p \vee r$$

is valid. There is no way to make the premises true with the conclusion false.

When the related set is consistent, the model path shows what assignment of truth-values in the argument form would make that premises true with the conclusion false.

Argument

$p \lor q$
$q \lor r$
$\therefore \ p \lor r$

Related Set Tested

$\checkmark \ p \lor q$
$\checkmark \ q \lor r$
$\checkmark \ \sim(p \lor r)$

$$\sim p$$
$$\sim r$$

One path is open at the end. It indicates that the truth-assignment

p:F
q:T
r:F

will make every member of a set of that form true. Thus it will make the premises true and the conclusion false in the given argument form. The form for a set is *consistent*; the argument form is *invalid*.

At the opening of this chapter we considered an argument form with six distinct atomic elements.

$p \lor q$
$\sim q \lor r$
$\sim r \lor s$
$\sim s \lor t$
$\sim t \lor u$
$\therefore \ p \lor u$

Although the truth-table would have 64 rows and numerous (640) calculations, the truth-tree is much simpler, especially if we follow our guideline to do nonbranching steps first.

$\checkmark$ **1.** $p \lor q$
$\checkmark$ **2.** $\sim q \lor r$
$\checkmark$ **3.** $\sim r \lor s$
$\checkmark$ **4.** $\sim s \lor t$

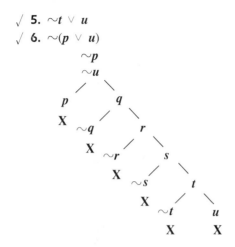

√ **5.** ~*t* ∨ *u*

√ **6.** ~(*p* ∨ *u*)

All branches close. The set 1–6 is inconsistent, so the original argument is *valid*.

EXERCISE 4b

For each argument form in Exercise 3a, use a truth-tree to determine whether or not it is valid.

EQUIVALENCE AND INEQUIVALENCE

The method of truth-trees is very helpful in testing for consistency of sets and in testing for validity of arguments (or argument forms). It can also be employed to test for equivalence of pairs of sentences, but it does not as often create a saving of time over the method of truth-tables.

Suppose that I wish to decide whether corresponding sentences of the following form are equivalent:

(p ∨ *q)* ∨ *r*   *p* ∨ *(q* ∨ *r)*

I must determine whether it is possible for them to have different truth-values. If there is some way for one to be true with the other false, they are not equivalent. I could begin by trying to find an assignment of truth-values to make the first true and the second false. In other words, I could check to see if the set {*(p* ∨ *q)* ∨ *r*, ~(*p* ∨ *(q* ∨ *r*))} is consistent.

√ **1.** *(p* ∨ *q)* ∨ *r*

√ **2.** ~(*p* ∨ *(q* ∨ *r*))

~*p*

Every path closes. That shows that we cannot make $(p \lor q) \lor r$ true and also make $p \lor (q \lor r)$ false [$(p \lor q) \lor r$ entails $p \lor (q \lor r)$]. But we might still be able to make $p \lor (q \lor r)$ true while making $(p \lor q) \lor r$ false. This would be another way of giving our original two sentences different truth-values. So we need to check the set $\{p \lor (q \lor r), \sim((p \lor q) \lor r)\}$ to see if it is consistent.

√ 1. $p \lor (q \lor r)$
√ 2. $\sim((p \lor q) \lor r)$
√ $\sim(p \lor q)$
          $\sim r$
          $\sim p$
          $\sim q$
       /   \
    p √ $q \lor r$
    X   /   \
             q r
             X   X

Each path closes. So this way of making the original sentences differ in truth-value does not work either. Thus they are equivalent, because there is no way to make them differ in truth-value.

As you can see, this method is not much better than a truth-table for this particular example. For other examples, though, it could be much better. Consider the following pair of sentence forms:

$p \lor \sim(q \lor r)$ $(p \cdot \sim q) \lor \sim r$

We can see if there is a way to make a sentence of the first form true while making a sentence of the second form false. We will test the set $\{p \lor \sim(q \lor r), \sim((p \cdot \sim q) \lor \sim r)\}$ for consistency.

√ 1. $p \lor \sim(q \lor r)$
√ 2. $\sim((p \cdot \sim q) \lor \sim r)$

$$\begin{array}{c}
\checkmark \quad \sim(p \cdot \sim q) \\
\checkmark \quad \sim\sim r \\
\cdot r \\
\diagup \quad \diagdown \\
\diagup p \qquad \checkmark \ \sim(q \lor r) \\
\diagup \quad \diagdown \\
\sim p \quad \checkmark \ \sim\sim q \quad \sim q \\
\mathrm{X} \qquad q \qquad \sim r \\
\mathrm{X}
\end{array}$$

One path remains open. Thus the assignment

p:T
q:T
r:T

will make both of the members of the set of $\{\, p \lor \sim(q \lor r),$ $\sim((p \cdot \sim q) \lor \sim r)\}$ true. So it will make sentences of the form

$p \lor \sim(q \lor r) \qquad (p \cdot \sim q) \lor \sim r$

differ in truth-value, by making the first true with the second false.

Since we quickly found an assignment that showed inequivalence, our method of truth-trees made a real savings over the truth-table method in this case.

EXERCISE 4c

Indicate whether the sentence forms are *logically equivalent*.

1. $p \cdot q$
   $q \cdot p$

2. $\sim p \lor q$
   $p \lor \sim q$

3. $\sim(p \lor q)$
   $\sim p \cdot \sim q$

4. $\sim(p \cdot q)$
   $\sim p \cdot \sim q$

5. $\sim(p \cdot q)$
   $\sim p \cdot q$

6. $p \cdot (q \cdot r)$
   $(r \cdot p) \cdot q$

7. $p \cdot \sim q$
   $\sim(q \lor \sim p)$

8. $\sim(p \lor (q \lor r))$
   $\sim p \cdot (\sim q \cdot \sim r)$

9. $p \lor (q \cdot r)$
   $(p \lor q) \cdot r$

10. $\sim(p \cdot q) \cdot r$
    $\sim p \cdot (q \cdot r)$

11. $\sim(p \lor (q \cdot r))$
    $(\sim p \cdot \sim q) \lor (\sim p \cdot \sim r)$

12. $\sim(p \cdot (q \cdot r))$
    $\sim p \lor (\sim q \cdot \sim r)$

TAUTOLOGOUS, CONTRADICTORY, CONTINGENT

In considering single sentences (or sentence forms), we find again that the method of truth-trees often does not produce a great savings over the method of truth-tables. We must see if there is a way to make the sentence true. If not, it is contradictory. But if there is a way to make it true, we must see if there is also a way to make the sentence false. If not, it is tautologous. If both work, that is, if we can make it true and we can make it false, then it is contingent.

For example, consider the form $p \vee (p \cdot q)$:

$$\sqrt{\ } \ p \vee (p \cdot q)$$

$$
\begin{array}{cc}
\diagup & \diagdown \\
p & \sqrt{\ } \ p \cdot q \\
 & p \\
 & q
\end{array}
$$

There are ways to make sentences of that form true, so it is *not contradictory*. But it might still be contingent or tautologous, so we must see if there is a way to make it false, by checking to see if we can make its negation true.

$$\sqrt{\ } \ \sim(p \vee (p \cdot q))$$
$$\sim p$$
$$\sqrt{\ } \ \sim(p \cdot q)$$

$$
\begin{array}{cc}
\diagup & \diagdown \\
\sim p & \sim q
\end{array}
$$

Open paths remain here as well, so there are ways to make sentences of the original form $(p \vee (p \cdot q))$ false. Thus this is *not tautologous*. It is a *contingent* sentence form. (In a simple example like this, it would be just as quick to write a truth-table.)

Examples

1. Consider $p \cdot \sim(p \vee q)$:

$$\sqrt{\ } \ p \cdot \sim(p \vee q)$$
$$p$$
$$\sqrt{\ } \ \sim(p \vee q)$$
$$\sim p$$
$$\sim q$$
$$\mathbf{X}$$

Contradictory

2. Consider $p \lor \sim(p \cdot q)$:

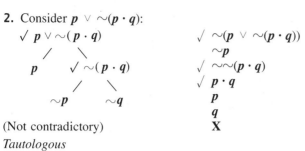

(Not contradictory)
Tautologous

3. Consider $(p \cdot q) \lor (p \cdot \sim(q \lor r))$:

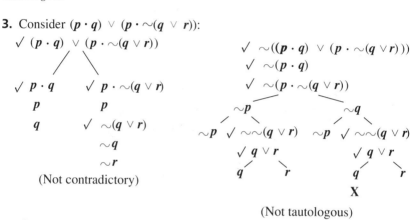

(Not contradictory)

(Not tautologous)

Contingent

EXERCISE 4d

Which of the following are tautologous, which contradictory, and which contingent?

1. $p \cdot q$
2. $p \lor (\sim p \cdot q)$
3. $p \lor \sim p$
4. $\sim p \cdot (p \cdot q)$
5. $(p \lor q) \cdot \sim(p \cdot q)$
6. $(p \cdot q) \cdot \sim(p \lor q)$
7. $(p \cdot (q \lor \sim p)) \cdot \sim q$
8. $(p \cdot r) \cdot \sim q$
9. $(p \lor \sim p) \lor q$
10. $(p \lor \sim p) \cdot q$
11. $(p \lor \sim p) \cdot (q \lor \sim q)$
12. $(p \cdot \sim p) \lor (q \cdot \sim q)$
13. $\sim((p \cdot q) \cdot \sim(p \lor q))$
14. $(p \lor q) \lor \sim(p \lor q)$
15. $\sim(p \cdot q) \lor ((p \lor r) \cdot (q \lor r))$
16. $\sim(\sim(p \cdot q) \lor r) \cdot (\sim p \lor (\sim q \lor r))$
17. $(\sim p \lor \sim p) \cdot (p \lor p)$
18. $((p \cdot q) \lor (r \cdot s)) \lor (\sim p \lor \sim q)$

Truth-Tree Rules

Double Negation

$\sim\sim p$
.
.
.
p

Conjunction

$p \cdot q$ $\sim(p \cdot q)$
.   .
.   .
.   .
p / \
q $\sim p$ $\sim q$

Disjunction

$p \lor q$ $\sim(p \lor q)$
.   .
.   .
.   .
/ \ $\sim p$
p q $\sim q$

5

CONDITIONALS: REPRESENTATION, ANALYSIS, AND TRUTH-TREES

CONDITIONALS

In representing English arguments, we will find another truth-functional connective very useful. This connective, the '$\supset$' symbol, is defined by the following table:

p	q	$p \supset q$
T	T	T
T	F	F
F	T	T
F	F	T

A sentence of the form $p \supset q$ is false in only one case, the case in which p is true and q is false.

Many arguments employ conditional statements ('if'–'then' statements). Our new symbol can often be used in representing these conditional claims.

If Alice drives, then Bill will go along.

$A \supset B$

Conditionals are employed to indicate a wide variety of types of connection and dependence. But the truth-conditions for the '$\supset$' capture the common core of all conditional statements. Someone who asserts a conditional is committed to a clearly truth-functional claim:

If Alice drives, then Bill will go along.
$A \supset B$
The following situation will not occur: Alice drives, but Bill does not go along.
$\sim(A \cdot \sim B)$

The conditional will be false if Alice drives but Bill does not go along (i.e., '$A \supset B$' is false if '$A \cdot \sim B$' is true). Any conditional statement $p \supset q$ carries with it a commitment to the corresponding claim of the form $\sim(p \cdot \sim q)$. A conditional may suggest much more than is included in this minimal truth-functional content. (It often suggests that the truth of q in $p \supset q$ is a causal result of the facts related in p, for example.) But whatever else it may suggest, every conditional assertion has at least as much informational content as this truth-functional compound.

To see that $p \supset q$ represents the truth-conditions expressed by $\sim(p \cdot \sim q)$, consider the following table:

p	q	$p \supset q$	$\sim q$	$p \cdot \sim q$	$\sim(p \cdot \sim q)$
T	T	T	F	F	T
T	F	F	T	T	F
F	T	T	F	F	T
F	F	T	T	F	T

Since the columns for $p \supset q$ and for $\sim(p \cdot \sim q)$ match each other, the two sentence-forms are equivalent; they have the same truth-value in all possible situations. Sentences of the form $p \supset q$ will capture those truth-conditions but will have syntactic features similar to those of ordinary English conditional sentences. '$A \supset B$' is like "If Alice drives, then Bill will go" in that it is a compound sentence with two simple (noncompound, nonnegated) constituents. ['$\sim(A \cdot \sim B)$' is truth-functionally equivalent, but it is a negated conjunction with another negation inside; thus it does not share the structure of the English sentence.]

Any sentence of the form $p \supset q$ will be called a *conditional*, and p is the *antecedent* of the conditional and q is the *consequent* of the conditional. Similarly, in ordinary English statements of the form 'If p, then q', the part after the word 'if' is the antecedent and the part after the word 'then' is the consequent. In English, however, the word 'then' does not always occur, and the antecedent may come after the consequent.

If Alice drives, Bill will go along.
$A \supset B$
Bill will go along if Alice drives.
$A \supset B$

Our representation of 'if'–'then' statements as truth-functional is not entirely true to the facts of ordinary conditionals. Suppose that Charlie says, "If Alice drives, then Bill will go along." Suppose now that Alice does not drive. Does this immediately show that Charlie was right? That he was wrong? The natural thing to say is that "the bet is off." The truth-values of the basic constituents (A, B) are not adequate to settle the truth-value of the conditional ("If A, then B") if Alice doesn't drive. But if English conditionals are not always truth-functional, we cannot always use truth-table methods to assess the validity of arguments employing them.

However, things are not as bad as that might suggest, because there is a common core of meaning that every conditional statement involves. Someone who says, "If p, then q" will be shown wrong (the statement will be false) if p is true and q is false. In other words, "If p, then q" involves a commitment to the falsity of $p \cdot \sim q$, that is, the truth of $\sim(p \cdot \sim q)$. Those truth-conditions are represented by $p \supset q$, and often this core of meaning is all that is relevant in the evaluation of a particular argument.

Sentences of the form $p \supset q$ have the advantage of coming out right on other equivalences as well. If we imagine a sheriff coming upon a one-car accident in the open country, there are two ways that she might express her view about the nature of the accident.

If this guy's brakes were working, then he must have been drunk.
$W \supset D$
Either this guy's brakes weren't working or else he was drunk.
$\sim W \vee D$

The English sentences are equivalent, and the formulas representing them are equivalent as well.

W	D	$\sim W$	$\sim W \vee D$	$W \supset D$
T	T	F	T	T
T	F	F	F	F
F	T	T	T	T
F	F	T	T	T

Some of the most common types of argument employ conditionals, and the '$\supset$' symbol will be used in representing them.

If the president is reelected, then
taxes will be increased. $P \supset T$
The president will be reelected. P
∴ Taxes will be increased.   ∴ T

If the president is not reelected, then
the business community will lose
confidence in the government. $\sim P \supset B$

If the business community loses confidence in the government, then there
will be little major capital invest-
ment. $B \supset L$

∴ If the president is not reelected, there will be little major capital
investment.   ∴ $\sim P \supset L$

If Dave had applied for it, he would
have been given the job. $A \supset J$

Dave was not given the job. $\sim J$

∴ He must not have applied for it.   ∴ $\sim A$

Like our other truth-functional connectives, the conditional symbol can
be used in representing multiply compound statements.

If Alice or Charlie drives, then Bill won't go along.
$(A \lor C) \supset \sim B$

If Bill doesn't go, then Ed or Fred will.
$\sim B \supset (E \lor F)$

If Gloria and Dave both stay home, then neither Ed nor Fred will go.
$(G \cdot D) \supset \sim(E \lor F)$

If Alice drives Bill will go, but if Charlie drives, then Bill will not go.
$(A \supset B) \cdot (C \supset \sim B)$

Bill will go if Ed and Fred go.
$(E \cdot F) \supset B$

If Alice drives, then Bill will go if Ed goes.
$A \supset (E \supset B)$

Since all of the symbols employed are truth-functional connectives, we
can always determine the truth-value of a compound sentence when we know
the truth-values of the parts. Suppose that A and B are true and C is false:

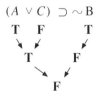

This conditional is false under those conditions, since it has a true antecedent
and a false consequent.

EXERCISE 5a

Symbolize each of the following sentences.

1. If there are ostriches in Africa, then a very large frying pan will be useful at breakfast there. (O = There are ostriches in Africa, U = A very large frying pan will be useful at breakfast in Africa)

2. If Tom can't run fast, collecting ostrich eggs will be very hazardous for him. (R = Tom can run fast, H = Collecting ostrich eggs will be very hazardous for Tom)

3. If there are ostriches in Africa, then we will make sure to take some photographs and we will tell you what an ostrich-egg omelet is like. (O, P = We will make sure to take some photographs, E = We will tell you what an ostrich egg omelet is like)

4. Ostriches live in Africa, and rheas are South American. (O, R = Rheas are South American)

5. The ostriches run fast if they see a lion. (R = The ostriches run fast, L = The ostriches see a lion)

6. If a zebra smells a lion, then the zebras and ostriches run and the lion is not successful. (S = A zebra smells a lion, Z = The zebras run, O = The ostriches run, L = The lion is successful)

7. If the flightless birds of Africa and Australia have a common ancestor, then either Africa and Australia were once much closer together or the nearest common ancestor of those birds had the ability to fly. (B = They have a common ancestor, C = Africa and Australia were once much closer together, F = The nearest common ancestor had the ability to fly)

8. If the flightless birds of Africa and Australia have no common ancestor or their nearest common ancestor had the ability to fly, then they represent an astonishing case of convergent evolution. (B, F, E = They represent an astonishing case of convergent evolution)

9. If we don't travel much in Africa, we won't see both ostriches and hippos. (T = We travel much in Africa, O = We see ostriches, H = We see hippos)

10. I want to see the lions, but today is the day for beginning our Nile excursion. (L = I want to see the lions, T = Today is the day for . . .)

11. If we see the lions, we'll miss the Nile. (L = We see the lions, M = We miss the Nile)

12. Although the herds of game animals are impressive, there is no finer sight than a pride of lions. (H = The herds are impressive, F = There is a finer sight than a pride of lions)

13. If the lions leave their kill, then if the hyenas don't move in first, the vultures clean it up. (L = The lions leave, H = The hyenas move in first, V = Vultures clean it up)

14. We won't see both lions and tigers, but if we stay next week we will see the gnus migrating. (*L*=We see lions, *T*=We see tigers, *S*=We stay next week, *G*=We see the gnus migrating)

15. Neither Africa nor Europe was in my budget last year. (*A*=Africa was in my budget, *E*=Europe was in my budget)

BICONDITIONALS

One other symbol is also of use to us.

p	*q*	*p* ≡ *q*
T	T	T
T	F	F
F	T	F
F	F	T

A statement of the form *p* ≡ *q* is true when *p* and *q* have the same truth-value. It is called a 'biconditional' symbol because *p* ≡ *q* is equivalent to (*p* ⊃ *q*) · (*q* ⊃ *p*), a conjunction of conditionals "going in both directions."

Biconditionals are very commonly employed in mathematics and philosophy, where they are most clearly expressed by the words "if and only if."

1237 is prime *if and only if* its only divisors are 1 and 1237.

An action is right *if and only if* it promotes total well-being summed over the entire population.

TRUTH-FUNCTIONAL CONNECTIVES

We can summarize the interpretation or *semantics* of our truth-functional connectives by truth-tables.

p	~*p*
T	F
F	T

p	*q*	*p* · *q*	*p* ∨ *q*	*p* ⊃ *q*	*p* ≡ *q*
T	T	T	T	T	T
T	F	F	T	F	F
F	T	F	T	T	F
F	F	F	F	T	T

We can also give this information in English.

1. If *p* is any sentence, a sentence of the form ~*p* is true if and only if *p* is false.

2. If *p* and *q* are any sentences,

    a. a sentence of the form *p* · *q* is true if and only if *p* and *q* are both true.

    b. a sentence of the form *p* ∨ *q* is true if and only if at least one of the sentences (*p* or *q*) is true.

    c. a sentence of the form *p* ⊃ *q* is true if and only if *p* is false or *q* is true.

    d. a sentence of the form *p* ≡ *q* is true if and only if *p* and *q* have the same truth-value.

3. A sentence is false if and only if it is not true.

SYMBOLIZING ENGLISH

Only If

There are a few types of sentence that many people have difficulty in symbolizing. Consider, for example, the following claim:

We will get a man to Mars by the year 2000 *only if* we continue to be technologically productive.

M only if T

This tells us that continued productivity is *necessary* to get a man to Mars. In other words, if ~*T*, then ~*M*.

$$\sim T \supset \sim M \qquad\qquad\qquad M \text{ only if } T$$

This works for 'only if' sentences in general:

p only if *q* $\sim q \supset \sim p$
If ~*q*, then ~*p*

You can reverse the order of statements and negate both to represent the 'only if' statement. We should note here that these two are equivalent:

$$\sim q \supset \sim p \qquad\qquad\qquad p \supset q$$

Thus '*p* only if *q*' would be equivalently represented by *p* ⊃ *q*.

The symbolization of 'only if' statements seems peculiar to some students because these two sentences seem very different:

1. We will get a man on Mars by the year 2000 *only if* we continue to be technologically productive.
   (*M* only if *T*)
2. If we get a man on Mars by the year 2000, we will continue to be technologically productive.
   (If *M*, then *T*?)

But this difference is due to an inadvertent change in the temporal relations of the things being discussed. The following conditional preserves the temporal relations expressed in the 'only if' statement, and it seems much better.

3. If we get a man on Mars by the year 2000, then we will have continued to be technologically productive.
   (If *M*, then *T*)

[In other words, in '*M* only if *T*', '*T*' is being used to represent the state of things before the year 2000, not after, and in sentence 2, the meaning of '*T*' is changed to represent the state of things after the year 2000.]

The words 'only if' provide one way among many to express the idea of one thing's being *necessary* for another.

In order to get a man on Mars, we must continue to be technologically productive.

Continued technological productivity *is required* (is necessary) for us to get a man on Mars.

These concepts are all related to the 'only if' idea:

p* only if *q	$\sim q \supset \sim p$
*In order for **p** to be the case, **q** must*	
be the case.	$\sim q \supset \sim p$
q*'s being the case *is required for **p	
to be the case.	$\sim q \supset \sim p$

Unless

The English 'unless' is another word for making compound sentences that sometimes produces difficulty.

We won't get a man to Mars *unless* we continue to be technologically productive.
$\sim M$ unless *T*

This is another way of saying that *T* is necessary for *M*.

$\sim T \supset \sim M$

And this is equivalent to

$M \supset T$

But here some other equivalent sentences are also worth considering.

$\sim M \vee T$
$T \vee \sim M$

These represent the same truth-conditions. In general, sentences of the form

p unless q

have truth-conditions represented equivalently by any of these types of sentences:

1. $\sim q \supset p$
2. $\sim p \supset q$
3. $p \vee q$
4. $q \vee p$

Some people find the first of these most natural, treating "unless" as "if not."

p unless q
p if not q
$\sim q \supset p$

Others find 3 and 4 very natural.

p unless q	
p or else q	$p \vee q$
q or else p	$q \vee p$

All of these have the same truth-conditions; in other words, exactly the same *truth-assignments* or *models* make each of them true.

If and Only If

Al will run for office if and only if Bill agrees to manage his campaign.

A statement like this combines an 'if' statement with an 'only if' statement.

(Al will run for office *if* Bill agrees to manage his campaign) and (Al will run for office *only if* Bill agrees to manage his campaign)

Thus we could represent it accordingly:

$(B \supset A) \cdot (\sim B \supset \sim A)$

But we can also represent it in an equivalent way by

$A \equiv B$

As we mentioned when we introduced the ' $\equiv$ ' symbol, '$A \equiv B$' is equivalent to

$(A \supset B) \cdot (B \supset A)$

Since '$\sim B \supset \sim A$' is equivalent '$A \supset B$' (and since sentences of the form '$p \cdot q$' are equivalent to the corresponding sentences of the form '$q \cdot p$'), all of these are equivalent:

$(B \supset A) \cdot (\sim B \supset \sim A)$

$(B \supset A) \cdot (A \supset B)$

$(A \supset B) \cdot (B \supset A)$

$A \equiv B$

Thus the '$\equiv$' symbol is ordinarily used to represent the connective words 'if and only if'.

Multiply Compound Sentences

In multiply compound sentences, we must determine what connectives to use, and we must also determine the correct way to group the parts of the sentence together.

1. Either the governor and the lieutenant governor will run for reelection or else the party will face a major electoral difficulty.

Isolating the connectives gives us this:

$G \cdot L \vee D$

But this is not a permissible symbolization because it needs parentheses in one way or the other:

$(G \cdot L) \vee D$
$G \cdot (L \vee D)$

In this case it is clear that the first of these two ways is correct because the English sentence incorporates several devices that indicate grouping. First, the word 'either' is employed along with the word 'or'. The word 'either' will actually indicate where the first constituent of the 'or' statement begins. Other indicators that 'G' and 'L' should be closely grouped together are parallelism of structure and elision. 'G' and 'L' are sentences that say corresponding things about the governor and the lieutenant governor, and they are grouped together in the English sentence because their common part "will run for reelection" is not repeated. Note how we can manipulate these elements to force the other grouping.

2. The governor will run for reelection, and either the lieutenant governor will run for reelection or else the party will face a major electoral difficulty.

$G \cdot (L \lor D)$

If you are having difficulty symbolizing a sentence, it is often useful to rewrite the sentence retaining the English connective words, but introducing single-letter abbreviations for the sentences. Then grouping becomes more obvious.

1. Either G and L or else D.
$(G \cdot L) \lor D$
2. G, and either L or else D.
$G \cdot (L \lor D)$

Just as 'either' can mark the beginning of a disjunction, 'both' can mark the beginning of a conjunction.

3. Both Al and either Betty or Carol will win medals.
Both A and either B or C.
$A \cdot (B \lor C)$
4. Either both Al and Betty will receive medals or Carol will.
Either both A and B or C.
$(A \cdot B) \lor C$

Similarly, 'if' indicates the antecedent of a conditional and 'then' indicates its consequent. (Note also how parallelism of sentence structure and elisions help to group sentences together.)

5. If Al runs but Bill doesn't, then Al will not win.
If A but $\sim B$, then $\sim W$.
$(A \cdot \sim B) \supset \sim W$
6. Al will run, but if Bill doesn't run, then Al will not win.
A, but if $\sim B$, then $\sim W$.
$A \cdot (\sim B \supset \sim W)$
7. If the governor runs, then neither the mayor nor the lieutenant governor will run.
If G, then neither M nor L.
$G \supset \sim (M \lor L)$

8. If the governor runs, then if he maintains his labor vote, he'll win.
If G, then if M, W.
$G \supset (M \supset W)$

9. If the governor runs, then he'll lose if he speaks too freely to the press
If G, then L if S.
$G \supset (S \supset L)$

The method of abbreviating the sentences and using English connective words becomes especially useful when 'only if' and 'unless' statements are involved. Let us agree to use these patterns for symbolization (at least for now):

p only if q $\sim q \supset \sim p$
r unless s $\sim s \supset r$

Then we can apply the method to achieve some fairly straightforward representations of multiply compound sentences.

10. If the governor runs, then he will lose unless he gets the big-city vote.
If G, then L unless B.
$G \supset (\sim B \supset L)$

11. The governor will run only if he thinks he can win and is sure that he won't need to campaign.
R only if T and S.
R only if $(T \cdot S)$.
$\sim(T \cdot S) \supset \sim R$

12. The governor will run only if he thinks he can win, and the governor is sure that he won't need to campaign.
R only if T, and S.
$(R$ only if $T)$ and S.
$(\sim T \supset \sim R) \cdot S$

The word 'without', when used as a sentence connective, can also be an indicator of sentence grouping. In simple sentences it usually indicates conjunction together with negation.

13. Bill will win without training.
W without T.
$W \cdot \sim T$

This same pattern can extend to more complex compounds if we keep in mind that 'without' is a connective that groups things together "as closely as is reasonably possible."

14. Bill will not win without training.
$\sim(W$ without $T)$.
$\sim(W \cdot \sim T)$

It would be *incorrect* to proceed in this way

$\sim W$ without T.
$\sim W \cdot \sim T$

This produces a clearly incorrect paraphrase: "Bill will not win and Bill will not train." The parentheses around the compound made with "without" surround as small a sentence as is reasonable, so the negation must be outside those parentheses.

15. The governor won't run unless he will win without campaigning.
$\sim G$ unless W without C.
$\sim G$ unless $(W \cdot \sim C)$.
$\sim(W \cdot \sim C) \supset \sim G$

16. He will run without campaigning only if he is sure that he will win.
R without C only if S.
$(R \cdot \sim C)$ only if S.
$\sim S \supset \sim(R \cdot \sim C)$

17. The governor won't run without campaigning unless both the lieutenant governor and the mayor campaign on his behalf.
$\sim G$ without C unless both L and M.
$\sim(G \cdot \sim C)$ unless $(L \cdot M)$.
$\sim(L \cdot M) \supset \sim(G \cdot \sim C)$

18. In order to win without campaigning, the governor will have to reduce taxes and increase services.
In order for W without C (to occur), R and I.
In order for $(W \cdot \sim C)$, $(R \cdot I)$.
$\sim(R \cdot I) \supset \sim(W \cdot \sim C)$

EXERCISE 5b

Symbolize each sentence. Use the symbols indicated.

I: Interest rates rise
T: Taxes rise
D: The dollar strengthens on foreign markets
B: The trade balance improves

1. The dollar will strengthen on foreign markets only if interest rates and taxes rise.

2. The dollar will not strengthen on foreign markets without both a rise in interest rates and an improvement in the trade balance.

3. If neither interest rates nor taxes rise, then the trade balance will improve unless the dollar strengthens on foreign markets.

4. Either taxes will rise without a rise in interest rates or there will be a rise in taxes with a rise in interest rates but with a dollar that is stronger on foreign markets.

5. Neither interest rates nor taxes will rise if the trade balance improves.

6. If the dollar strengthens on foreign markets, then the trade balance will not improve unless interest rates and taxes rise.

7. A rise in interest rates is necessary for an improvement in the trade balance.

8. If the dollar doesn't strengthen on foreign markets, then the trade balance won't improve if there is no rise in taxes.

9. The trade balance will improve if and only if there is a rise in taxes and a strengthening of the dollar on foreign markets.

10. If neither taxes nor interest rates rise, then the trade balance won't improve without a strengthening of the dollar on foreign markets.

LOGICAL CHARACTERISTICS: TRUTH-FUNCTIONAL ANALYSIS

Our goal in introducing truth-functional connectives is, of course, to be able to determine which logical properties apply to arguments, to sets of sentences, to pairs of sentences, or to single sentences.

Arguments: valid or invalid.
Sets of sentences: inconsistent or consistent.
Pairs of sentences: equivalent or not equivalent.
Sentences: tautologous, contradictory, or contingent.

Now that we have a way of representing English conditionals and biconditionals, we can apply truth-functional analysis to a wider range of examples.

We can use the truth-table method discussed in Chapters 3 and 4, simply employing the defining table for the '⊃' symbol. Alternatively, we can supplement our rules for constructing truth-trees (Chapter 4) and streamline some of this process.

To adapt our rules for truth-trees, we must know how to "break down" conditionals (and biconditionals) and their negations when they are encountered in working out a tree. Suppose, for example, that we have the following set of sentences:

$A \supset B$
$A \supset \sim B$
$C \supset A$
C

For a conditional $p \supset q$ to be true, either $\sim p$ must be true or q must be true. (Remember that $p \supset q$ is equivalent to $\sim p \lor q$.) So we can use this fact as a basis for our procedure.

$$\checkmark\; p \supset q$$
$$\swarrow \qquad \searrow$$
$$\sim p \qquad\quad q$$

With a conditional, the path must branch, allowing for the two ways it might be true. Thus one truth-tree for our example would be this:

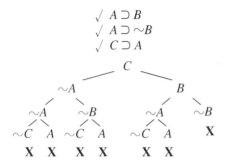

This is shown to be an inconsistent set of sentences, because all paths close. A negated conditional, $\sim(p \supset q)$, is equivalent to a conjunction, $p \cdot \sim q$, so we can devise the rule for truth-trees accordingly.

$\sqrt{}\ \sim(p \supset q)$
p
$\sim q$

For example,

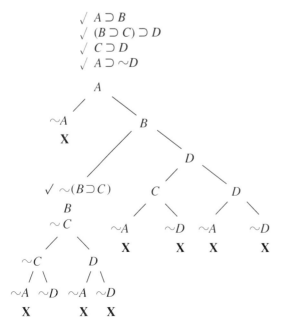

So this set of sentences is consistent, because one path remains open. (It is a *model path*.) With the *model A*:**T**, *B*:**T**, *C*:**F**, *D*:**F**, the sentences will all be true.

So we can add these to our list of truth-tree procedures from Chapter 4:

7. If an unchecked compound on a path is a conditional $p \supset q$, construct two branches, one with $\sim p$ and one with q, on each subordinate open path. Then check off the conditional.

8. If an unchecked compound is a negated conditional $\sim(p \supset q)$, add p and $\sim q$ to each subordinate open path. Then check off $\sim(p \supset q)$.

For biconditionals, the best truth-map procedure comes from recognizing that a biconditional $p \equiv q$ says that p and q have the same truth-value. There are two ways for them to have the same truth-value: they can both be true or they can both be false. Thus the procedure is this:

$$p \equiv q$$

$$\begin{array}{cc} p & \sim p \\ q & \sim q \end{array}$$

A negated biconditional $\sim(p \equiv q)$ says that p and q differ in truth-value, so the procedure is this:

$$\sim(p \equiv q)$$

$$\begin{array}{cc} p & \sim p \\ \sim q & q \end{array}$$

With both of these we make two branches and add two sentences on each branch.

The complete list of rules for model paths, then, is this:

1. If a path from the first sentence contains some sentence and the negation of that very same sentence, close that path.

2. If an unchecked compound sentence on a path is a conjunction $p \cdot q$, add p and q to each subordinate open path. Then check off the conjunction.

3. If an unchecked compound on a path is a disjunction $p \vee q$, construct two branches, one with p and one with q, on each subordinate open path. Then check off the disjunction.

4. If an unchecked compound is a negated conjunction $\sim(p \cdot q)$, construct two branches, one with $\sim p$ and one with $\sim q$, on each subordinate open path. Then check off $\sim(p \cdot q)$.

5. If an unchecked compound is a negated disjunction $\sim(p \vee q)$, add $\sim p$ and $\sim q$ to each subordinate open path. Then check off $\sim(p \vee q)$.

6. If an unchecked compound is double-negated, $\sim\sim p$, add p to each subordinate open path. Then check off $\sim\sim p$.

7. If an unchecked compound on a path is a conditional $p \supset q$, construct two branches, one with $\sim p$ and one with q, on each subordinate open path. Then check off the conditional.

8. If an unchecked compound is a negated conditional $\sim(p \supset q)$, add p and $\sim q$ to each subordinate open path. Then check off $\sim(p \supset q)$.

9. If an unchecked compound on a path is a biconditional $p \equiv q$, then on each subordinate open path, construct two branches, one with p and q and one with $\sim p$ and $\sim q$. Then check off the biconditional.

10. If an unchecked compound on a path is the negation of a biconditional, $\sim(p \equiv q)$, then on each subordinate open path construct two branches, one with p and $\sim q$ and one with $\sim p$ and q. Then check off the negated biconditional.

Truth-Tree Rules

Double Negation

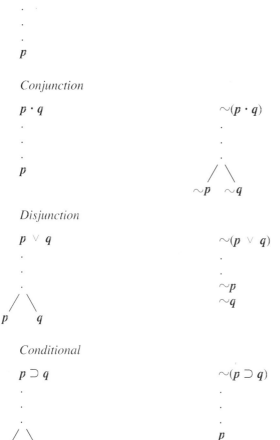

$\sim\sim p$

.

.

.

p

Conjunction

$p \cdot q$ $\sim(p \cdot q)$

.

.

.

p $\sim p$ $\sim q$

Disjunction

$p \vee q$ $\sim(p \vee q)$

.

.

.

          $\sim p$

p q $\sim q$

Conditional

$p \supset q$ $\sim(p \supset q)$

.

.

.

          p

$\sim p$ q $\sim q$

Biconditional

$p \equiv q$ $\sim(p \equiv q)$

.   .
.   .
.   .

/ \   / \
p $\sim p$ *p* $\sim p$
q $\sim q$ $\sim q$ *q*

EXERCISE 5c

For each of the argument forms shown below, indicate whether it is valid or invalid. (You will need to use truth-tables or truth-trees to work out the answer.)

Example

$p \supset q$
p
$\therefore \ \sim q$

With a Truth-Table

p	q		$p \supset q$	$\sim q$
T	T		T	F
T	F		F	T
F	T		T	F
F	F		T	T

Invalid, because on at least one row the premises are true and the conclusion is false. (p:T, q:T)

With a Truth-Tree

$\sqrt{}\ p \supset q$
p
$\sqrt{}\sim\sim q$

q
/ \
$\sim p$ q
   X

Invalid because there is at least one open path, indicating that there is some way to make the premises true with the conclusion false. (p:T, q:T)

1. $p \supset q$ **2.** $p \supset (q \lor r)$
   q q
   $\therefore \ p$ $\therefore \ p$

3. $\sim p$
∴ $\sim(p \cdot q)$

4. $p \supset (q \supset r)$
∴ $(p \supset q) \supset r$

5. $p \lor q$
$r \lor s$
∴ $q \supset q$

6. $p \lor q$
$\sim q \lor r$
$\sim p \lor \sim r$
∴ q

7. $p \supset q$
$r \supset s$
$p \lor r$
∴ $q \lor s$

8. $p \supset q$
$s \supset r$
$q \lor r$
∴ $p \lor s$

9. $p \lor q$
$\sim r \lor s$
$r \lor \sim s$
∴ $p \lor r$

10. $p \cdot (q \lor r)$
∴ $(p \cdot q) \lor r$

11. $p \supset q$
$\sim r \supset \sim q$
∴ $p \supset \sim r$

12. $p \supset (q \cdot r)$
∴ $(p \supset q) \cdot r$

13. $p \supset (q \lor \sim p)$
q
∴ $\sim p$

14. $p \lor (q \equiv \sim r)$
$\sim(q \supset p) \cdot (r \supset p)$
∴ $r \lor p$

15. $p \equiv q$
$\sim(q \equiv r)$
∴ $\sim r \supset p$

EXERCISE 5d

For each of the following forms for a set of sentences, determine whether some sets of sentences of the given form are consistent or whether all sets of sentences of the given form are inconsistent.

Example

With a Truth-Table

$p \lor q$
$p \supset q$
$\sim q$

p	q	$p \lor q$	$p \supset q$	$\sim q$
T	T	T	T	**F**
T	F	T	**F**	T
F	T	T	T	**F**
F	F	**F**	T	T

Every set of sentences of this form is *inconsistent*, because on each row (in every possible situation) at least one sentence in the set is false.

With a Truth-Tree

$\sqrt{}$ $p \vee q$
$\sqrt{}$ $p \supset q$
　　$\sim q$

Inconsistent because all paths close.

1. $p \supset q$
　　$\sim q \cdot p$

2. $p \supset q$
　　$p \supset \sim q$

3. $p \supset q$
　　$q \vee r$
　　$p \cdot \sim r$

4. $p \supset q$
　　$\sim q \cdot r$
　　$p \supset \sim r$

5. $p \supset (q \supset r)$
　　$q \cdot (p \cdot \sim r)$

6. $p \equiv q$
　　$q \equiv r$
　　$p \vee \sim r$

7. $p \equiv q$
　　$\sim q \vee r$
　　$p \cdot \sim r$

8. $p \vee q$
　　$p \supset r$
　　$q \supset r$
　　$\sim r$

EXERCISE 5e

For each pair of sentence forms, determine whether the forms are logically equivalent.

Example

$\sim p \supset q$
$\sim(p \supset q)$

With a Truth-Table

p	q	$\sim p$	$\sim p \supset q$	$p \supset q$	$\sim(p \supset q)$
T	T	F	T	T	F
T	F	F	T	F	T
F	T	T	T	T	F
F	F	T	F	T	F

Not equivalent, because on at least one row the sentences differ in truth-value.

With a Truth-Tree

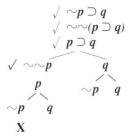

Not equivalent, because there is at least one open path, thus there is at least one way to make ∼*p* ⊃ *q* true while making ∼(*p* ⊃ *q*) false.

1. *p* ⊃ *q*
   q ⊃ *p*

2. *p* ⊃ (*q* · *r*)
   p ⊃ (*q* ⊃ *r*)

3. *p* ⊃ *q*
   ∼*q* ⊃ ∼*p*

4. *p* ⊃ ∼*q*
   q ⊃ ∼*p*

5. (*p* · *q*) ⊃ *r*
   p ⊃ (*q* ⊃ *r*)

6. (*p* ∨ *q*) ⊃ *r*
   p ∨ (*q* ⊃ *r*)

7. *p* ⊃ *q*
   ∼*p* ∨ *q*

8. *p* ⊃ *q*
   ∼(*p* ∨ *q*)

9. ∼(*p* ⊃ *q*)
   p · ∼*q*

10. ∼(*p* ⊃ *q*)
    ∼*p* ⊃ *q*

11. ∼(*p* ∨ ∼*q*)
    p ⊃ *q*

12. *p* ≡ *q*
    q ≡ *p*

13. *p* ⊃ (*q* ⊃ *r*)
    (*p* ⊃ *q*) ⊃ *r*

14. *p* ≡ (*q* ≡ *r*)
    (*p* ≡ *q*) ≡ *r*

15. ∼(*p* ≡ *q*)
    p ≡ ∼*q*

EXERCISE 5f

Which are *tautologies*, which *contradictions*, and which *contingent*?

Example

p ⊃ (*p* · *q*)

With a Truth-Table

p	*q*		*p* · *q*	*p* ⊃ (*p* · *q*)
T	T		T	T
T	F		F	F
F	T		F	T
F	F		F	T

Contingent, because on at least one row it is true and on at least one row it is false.

With a Truth-Tree

Not contradictory, because there is at least one way to make it true.

Not tautologous, because there is at least one way to make *p* ⊃ (*p* · *q*) false [i.e., to make ~(*p* ⊃ (*p* · *q*)) true]. Thus *p* ⊃ (*p* · *q*) is *contingent*.

1. *p* ⊃ *q*

2. (*p* · *q*) ⊃ *p*

3. *p* ⊃ ~~*p*

4. *p* ⊃ ~*p*

5. *p* ⊃ (*p* ∨ *q*)

6. (*p* · *q*) ⊃ (*q* · *p*)

7. (*p* ∨ *q*) ⊃ *p*

8. *p* ⊃ (*p* ⊃ *q*)

9. (*p* ∨ ~*p*) ⊃ (*p* · ~*p*)

10. (*p* · *q*) ⊃ ~(~*p* ∨ ~*q*)

EXERCISE 5g

Symbolize each argument. Determine whether it is valid.

1. Either they won't lower interest rates or they won't raise taxes. This is because if they lower interest rates, then there will be no federal

revenue problem, and they will raise taxes only if there is a federal revenue problem. (*L* = Lower interest, *R* = Raise taxes, *F* = There will be a federal revenue problem)

2. If they lower interest rates and raise taxes, then there will be no federal revenue problem. But they won't lower taxes, so there will be a federal revenue problem. (*L* = Lower interest, *R* = Raise taxes, *F* = There will be a federal revenue problem)

3. They will raise taxes only if there is a federal revenue problem. If there is inflation, then there will be a federal revenue problem. So they will raise taxes. (*R* = Raise taxes, *F* = Federal revenue problem, *I* = Inflation)

4. If they lower the taxes, then if they increase the money supply, then there will be inflation. If there is inflation, the elderly will have a rough time. Thus if they increase the money supply, the elderly will have a rough time, since they will be lowering taxes. (*L* = Lower taxes, *M* = Increase money, *I* = Inflation, *E* = Elderly have a rough time)

5. The elderly will all have a rough time unless there are lower taxes and no inflation. There will be lower taxes. Thus the elderly will not all have a rough time. (*E* = The elderly all have a rough time, *L* = There are lower taxes, *I* = There is inflation)

6. The economy is going to be in big trouble, because it cannot tolerate a drastic drop in the stock market, but there will be one. (*T* = Economy in big trouble, *D* = There is a drastic drop in the stock market)

7. The president will be reelected only if the economy improves. The economy will improve only if foreign nations cooperate. Thus the president will not be reelected, because foreign nations will not cooperate. (*R* = The president is reelected, *E* = The economy improves, *F* = Foreign nations cooperate)

8. If inflation increases, the elderly will be in financial difficulty. If taxes increase, young adults will be in financial difficulty. If young adults and the elderly are both in financial difficulty, the president will not be reelected. Thus if the president is to be reelected, inflation must not increase or taxes must not increase. (*I* = Inflation increases, *E* = Elderly in difficulty, *T* = Taxes increase, *Y* = Young adults in difficulty, *R* = The president is reelected)

EXERCISE 5h

Symbolize each sentence, then for each set of sentences determine whether it is *consistent* or *inconsistent*.

1. We will reduce energy consumption by autos only if we increase the efficiency of engines or reduce the number of miles driven. (*R* = We reduce energy consumption, *I* = We increase efficiency, *M* = We reduce miles driven)

We will not reduce the number of miles driven.
We will reduce energy consumption without increasing the efficiency of engines.

2. If emissions controls can be made to last the life of a car, then the internal combustion engine will be the cheapest to maintain and among the lowest in emissions. (L, C, E = It is among the lowest in emissions)
If it is among the lowest in emissions, it will be the dominant type of engine if it is cheapest to maintain. (D = It is dominant)
Emissions controls can be made to last the life of the car, but the internal combustion engine won't be the dominant type.

3. I have an appointment on Tuesday afternoon. (A)
I'll finish my work this week. (F)
I'll go on a picnic on Wednesday afternoon. (P)
If I have an appointment on Tuesday afternoon, then I won't be in my office. (T = I'm in office on Tuesday)
I won't be in my office on Wednesday afternoon if I go on a picnic. (W = I'm in office on Wednesday)
In order to finish my work this week I must be in my office Tuesday afternoon or Wednesday afternoon.

4. If I study on Tuesday, I'll pass my exam. (S, P)
I won't study on Tuesday.
On Wednesday I'll be in Chicago. (C)
I'll pass my exam.

5. If God exists, He is omnipotent and beneficent. (G, O, B)
If God is beneficent, He is willing to prevent evil. (B, W)
If God is omnipotent, He is able to prevent evil. (O, A)
If there is evil, either God is not willing to prevent evil or God is not able to prevent evil. (E, W, A)
There is evil. (E)
God Exists. (G)

6. Al will study only if Bill studies.
If Al doesn't study, he won't pass.
Bill will study.
Al won't pass.

7. Jack can't cram for logic and go to the party. (C, P)
Jack will be unhappy unless he goes to the party. (U)
If Jack hasn't been studying regularly, then if he doesn't cram he will fail. (S, F)
If Jack fails, he will be unhappy.
Jack has not been studying regularly, but he will not be unhappy.

8. If we are not using a good text, we will need a large number of supplementary examples. (G, S)
We are using a good text.
We will need a large number of supplementary examples.

PART II

DERIVATIONS AND

MODELS

6
INFERENCE RULES

When an argument form involves only a small number of atomic elements, truth-tables are an effective means for testing for validity. But truth-tables have several serious drawbacks.

One limitation has probably already become apparent. The number of rows in a truth-table increases exponentially relative to the number of atomic elements in the tested argument form. When there are n atomic elements, there are 2^n possible combinations of truth-values for those elements. With two or three atomic elements this is manageable. (There are four or eight combinations.) But if there are, say, six atomic elements, then there are 64 (2^6) rows in a table, which constitutes a serious clerical problem. Any more than that is not really practical with paper and pencil.

Truth-trees are an improvement over truth-tables, but truth-tables and truth-trees share a serious limitation. Neither corresponds well to our most natural ordinary methods of showing validity. If you wished to show someone that an argument was valid (that a conclusion follows from some premises), you would not usually write a truth-table and ask that it be examined to assure that no row contains true premises and a false conclusion. Similarly, you would not ordinarily provide a truth-tree asking that each path be checked step by step for correctness and closure. You had considerable experience with the justification of conclusions before you ever saw a truth-table or truth-tree. It will be possible to develop systematic methods for showing validity that conform more closely to the ordinary procedures for establishing conclusions, thereby giving us some insight into those procedures.

The most important drawback to the truth-table and truth-tree technique, however, is their limitation to truth-functional validity. Later we will explore arguments that are valid because of features other than truth-functional relationships. No procedure like truth-tables or truth-trees can be completely adequate for testing such arguments for validity. The methods for showing validity that we develop in this chapter, however, can be extended in a natural way to show validity even in cases in which the validity of an argument is not due to truth-functional relationships alone.

SHOWING THAT A CONCLUSION FOLLOWS

An example can guide us in examining our ordinary procedures for establishing that a conclusion follows from a set of premises. Suppose that we
are in a situation in which we learn that all of these things are true:

1. If Al runs for office, then Bill will be his running mate.
2. If Bill is Al's running mate, then either Charlie or Dave will be a
   campaign manager.
3. Al will run but Charlie won't be a campaign manager.

It follows that

Dave will be a campaign manager.

If someone did not immediately see that this conclusion follows, you
might show that in the following way. Working from these premises (1–3),
we can see that:

4. All will run. (3 "says so.")
5. So Bill will be his running mate. (Consider 1 and 4.)
6. So either Charlie or Dave will be a campaign manager. (2 and 5)
7. But Charlie won't be a campaign manager. (3)
8. So Dave is going to be a campaign manager. (6 and 7)

Each of these steps, 4–8, follows from some of the preceding claims in
an obviously valid way. For example, we know that if a conjunction is true,
then each of its conjuncts is true. So these are valid inference patterns:

$p \cdot q$ $p \cdot q$ If a conjunction is true, then each
                                               of its conjuncts is true.
$\therefore\ p$ $\therefore\ q$

Steps 4 and 7 are justified by the validity of these patterns and by the fact
that 3 is among the things already accepted.

3. $A \cdot {\sim}C$ 3. $A \cdot {\sim}C$
$\therefore$ 4. A $\therefore$ 7. ${\sim}C$

Step 5 is justified in a different way.

1. $A \supset B$
4. A
$\therefore$ 5. B

If 1 and 4 are both established already, step 5 can also be established, because
the following inference pattern is valid.

$p \supset q$

p

$\therefore \quad q$

If a conditional and its antecedent are both true, then the consequent must also be true.

Every argument of that form is valid. Once we make this form explicit we can see that step 6 is justified in the same way, from steps 2 and 5.

2. $B \supset (C \vee D)$

5. B

$\therefore$ **6.** $C \vee D$

This is also an instance of the valid argument pattern justifying step 5. Step 8 remains. It follows from steps 6 and 7.

6. $C \vee D$

7. $\sim C$

$\therefore$ **8.** D

The pattern of which it is an instance is another simple, obviously valid argument form.

$p \vee q$

$\sim p$

$\therefore \quad q$

If a disjunction is true and the negation of one of its disjuncts is true, then the other disjunct must be true.

Our ordinary practice in deductively justifying conclusions employs these simple inference patterns (among others). We proceed step by step, beginning with the argument's premises (our initial assumptions). Each step is justified by some previously accepted steps, and the justification involves some simple, obviously valid inference pattern. (If the pattern at some step is not valid, then the derivation will not establish the validity of the argument. If the pattern is not *obviously* valid, then the derivation might not be convincing in establishing the conclusion; people might wonder whether it is a valid step if its validity is not obvious.)

We could state the definition of a derivation in a more formal way.

A *derivation* is a sequence of sentences such that each step is either an assumption or else something that follows from previous steps by an acceptable inference pattern.

In order to make this definition applicable, we need to have a clear agreement about which inference patterns will be acceptable for the justification of steps in a derivation. These will be our *derivational rules*.

In Chapters 6–8, we develop a list of derivational rules with these features:

1. Every rule on the list preserves truth. (In other words, a conclusion is derivable only if it would have to be true whenever everything preceding it in the derivation is true. If our rules are *correct* in this way, we cannot go from true steps to false ones using the rules.)

2. Every rule on the list *obviously* preserves truth. (The derivations will be *convincing* to those who can see the correctness of the rules.)

3. The patterns embodied in the rules are commonly employed by people in justifying conclusions by derivation from premises.

4. Using just the rules on the list, the conclusion is always derivable from the premises whenever an argument is truth-functionally valid. (The system of derivational rules should be *complete* for truth-functional validity.)

5. The list is not too long to remember.

We will eventually be able to set out a method for doing derivations that has all of these desirable features.

MODUS PONENS, SIMPLIFICATION, AND DISJUNCTIVE SYLLOGISM

In the argument discussed in the preceding section, the inference pattern used to justify steps 5 and 6 is known as *modus ponens*.

Modus Ponens (MP)

$p \supset q$
p
$\therefore\ q$

From a conditional and its antecedent, the consequent may be validly inferred.

This form of argument is one of the most common patterns for simple, valid arguments.

If John is willing to give a party, then we will have a party.
John is willing to give a party. Thus we will have one.

If a conditional and its antecedent are both true, the consequent must also be true.

Inferences involving a conjunction in the premises also occured. Inferring one conjunct from a conjunction will be called *simplification*. There are two argument forms relevant here:

Simplification (Simp)

$p \cdot q$ $\qquad$ $p \cdot q$
$\therefore\ p$ $\qquad$ $\therefore\ q$

From a conjunction, each of its conjuncts may be validly inferred.

Obviously, these are valid.

Dawn and Ella are both tall.
∴ Dawn is tall.

Charlie runs for exercise but he eats too much.
∴ Charlie eats too much.

The other inference pattern we have discussed in this chapter is known as *disjunctive syllogism*. (A *syllogism* is a deductively valid argument with two premises. This particular syllogism is a fundamental use of disjunctions in inference.) As in the case of simplification, there are really two argument forms relevant here (although only one was involved in the derivation we considered earlier):

Disjunctive Syllogism (DS)

$p \lor q$	$p \lor q$	From a disjunction together with
$\sim p$	$\sim q$	the negation of one of its disjuncts,
∴ q	∴ p	the other disjunct may be validly
		inferred.

This inference pattern was frequently employed to illustrate valid argument in Chapters 1 and 2.

Reagan or Mondale won the 1984 election.
Reagan didn't win.
∴ Mondale won.

Using the indicated abbreviations for our accepted inference patterns, we can now give a fully annotated version of our derivation of the conclusion that Dave will be a campaign manager.

I. 1. $A \supset B$
    2. $B \supset (C \lor D)$
    3. $A \cdot \sim C$
    4. A 3   Simp
    5. B 1,4   MP
    6. $C \lor D$ 2,5   MP
    7. $\sim C$ 3   Simp
    8. D 6,7   DS

Each step after the premises is established on the basis of preceding steps together with some obviously valid inference pattern that we have accepted as an inference rule. This is how a derivation makes it clear that the conclusion follows.

Even just these few inference patterns (MP, Simp, DS) make a wide variety of derivations possible.

II. 1. $A \lor (B \cdot E)$
     2. $B \supset (A \lor C)$

	3. $\sim\!A$		$\therefore$	C
	4. $B \cdot E$		1,3	DS
	5. B		4	Simp
	6. $A \lor C$		2,5	MP
	7. C		3,6	DS
III.	**1.** $A \cdot [\sim\!B \cdot (C \supset D)]$			
	2. $A \supset C$			
	3. $D \supset (B \lor E)$		$\therefore$	E
	4. A		1	Simp
	5. C		2,4	MP
	6. $\sim\!B \cdot (C \supset D)$		1	Simp
	7. $C \supset D$		6	Simp
	8. D		5,7	MP
	9. $B \lor E$		3,8	MP
	10. $\sim\!B$		6	Simp
	11. E		9,10	DS

When we use derivations to show validity, we will conform to a very high standard. Every step of the derivation must be justified on the basis of some inference pattern that has been accepted into our system of derivational rules. In other words, we must have already agreed upon it as an obviously valid inference pattern.

This high standard ensures rigor of several sorts. We cannot make the mistake of drawing a conclusion that does not validly follow from the premises. Each step in a derivation that accords with our rules must validly follow from those premises because each of our rules preserves truth. We also cannot make the mistake of underestimating the resources needed in a derivation, because our method forces us at every step to be explicit about the inference pattern employed. No hidden assumptions can be the basis for a step in a derivation; the full resources of the derivational system are explicit. This kind of rigor has proved to be one of the most important factors in the development of logic, mathematics, and computer-related research over the last 100 years.

We also achieve a certain kind of security about the success of our derivations in convincing people that an argument is valid. In this chapter it is a simple matter to check the correctness of each of our rules with truth-tables. (These are valid argument forms, so truth is preserved when we move from premises to conclusion in arguments fitting these patterns.) One can also routinely and mechanically verify that the steps of the derivation are in accord with those rules; it is only a matter of verifying that the justifying steps are an instance of the premise set of the cited inference pattern and that the step justified is a corresponding instance of the conclusion of that inference pattern. For example, it is a simple, mechanical task to verify that in derivation III, step 9 ('$B \lor E$') follows from steps 3 ('$D \supset (B \lor E)$') and 8 ('D') by modus ponens. One of the justifying steps (3) is a conditional, the other (8) is the antecedent of that conditional, and the step justified (9) is the consequent. That is what it takes to be an instance of modus ponens.

In using the derivational rules of this chapter, it is important to apply them only to complete sentences justified by previous steps. They will not apply within larger sentences. Thus the following attempt to use simplification would be incorrect:

$(C \cdot S) \supset L$	If Congress passes a bill and the president signs it, then it becomes a law.
X $\therefore$ $C \supset L$ 1 Simp **X**	$\therefore$ If Congress passes a bill, then it becomes a law.

Simplification does not apply *within* the conditional. Similarly, the following would *not* be a correct application of modus ponens.

   1. $B \lor (C \supset D)$
   2. C
X $\therefore$ $B \lor D$ 1,2 MP **X**

EXERCISE 6a

MP	DS		Simp	
$p \supset q$	$p \lor q$	$p \lor q$	$p \cdot q$	$p \cdot q$
p	$\sim p$	$\sim q$	$\therefore$ p	$\therefore$ q
$\therefore$ q	$\therefore$ q	$\therefore$ p		

Using the inference patterns MP, DS, and Simp, show that each of these arguments is valid. Annotate each step, indicating what previous steps and what rule justify it.

1. $A \lor (B \cdot C)$
   $\sim(B \cdot C)$
   $\therefore$ A

2. $\sim A$
   $A \lor B$
   $B \supset C$
   $\therefore$ C

3. $\sim A \cdot (B \lor C)$
   $\sim C \lor A$
   $\therefore$ B

4. $A \supset (B \lor C)$
   $A \cdot \sim B$
   $\therefore$ C

5. $(D \lor E) \supset (E \supset F)$
   $\sim D$
   $D \lor E$
   $\therefore$ F

6. $A \lor (B \cdot C)$
   $\sim A \cdot (B \supset D)$
   $\therefore$ D

7. $A \lor (B \supset C)$
   $D \supset \sim A$
   $B \cdot D$
   $\therefore$ C

8. $A \cdot (B \supset \sim C)$
   $B \cdot (C \lor D)$
   $D \supset E$
   $\therefore$ E

9. $A \supset (B \supset C)$

$A \cdot \sim D$

$D \vee B$

$\therefore \quad C$

10. $D \vee (E \vee F)$

$(E \vee F) \supset (A \supset B)$

$\sim D \cdot \sim F$

$E \supset A$

$\therefore \quad B$

MODUS TOLLENS, CONJUNCTION, AND HYPOTHETICAL SYLLOGISM

To show validity for a wider range of arguments, we will need additional inference patterns among our rules. For example:

Modus Tollens (MT)

$p \supset q$	From a conditional together with
$\sim q$	the negation of the consequent of
$\therefore \quad \sim p$	the conditional, the negation of the
	antecedent may be validly inferred.

If the mayor is reelected, then the electorate will be ignoring his established criminal activity.	$R \supset I$
The electorate will not ignore his established criminal activity.	$\sim I$
$\therefore$ The mayor will not be reelected.	$\therefore \quad \sim R$

This valid inference pattern is another of those commonly employed in deriving a conclusion from a set of premises.

If the mayor is not reelected, then his associates will be prosecuted.	**1.** $\sim R \supset P$
If the mayor is reelected, then the electorate will be ignoring his established criminal activity.	**2.** $R \supset I$
But the electorate will not ignore his established criminal activity.	**3.** $\sim I$
So the mayor will not be reelected.	**4.** $\sim R$ 2,3 MT
Thus his associates will be prosecuted.	**5.** P 1,4 MP

Conjunctions are true if their conjuncts are true. Thus the following inference rule is valid:

Conjunction

p	From any pair of sentences,
q	their conjunction may be validly
$\therefore \quad p \cdot q$	inferred.

When we have a conjunction to establish, this rule breaks the task of establishing it into two parts.

1. $A \supset (B \vee E)$
2. $D \supset B$
3. $A \cdot \sim B$ $\therefore$ $E \cdot \sim D$
4. $\sim B$ 3   Simp
5. $\sim D$ 2,4   MT
6. A 3   Simp
7. $B \vee E$ 1,6   MP
8. E 4,7   DS
9. $E \cdot \sim D$ 5,8   Conj

Step 9 ('$E \cdot \sim D$') is a conjunction of two things that are first established separately (in steps 5 and 8).

Another useful simple inference pattern is:

Hypothetical Syllogism

$p \supset q$
$q \supset r$
$\therefore$ $p \supset r$

From a pair of conditionals such that the consequent of one is the same as the antecedent of the other, another conditional may be inferred. The inferred conditional has the same antecedent as the former conditional and the same consequent as the latter conditional.

(The English statement of this inference rule illustrates the value of using symbols to represent logical structure.)

If I miss my chemistry exam, then I'll fail chemistry. $M \supset F$

If I fail chemistry, then I won't graduate this semester. $F \supset \sim G$

$\therefore$ If I miss my chemistry exam, then I won't graduate this semester. $M \supset \sim G$

Here is a derivation employing *hypothetical syllogism*:

1. $B \supset C$
2. $A \vee \sim D$
3. $C \supset D$
4. $\sim A$ $\therefore$ $\sim B$
5. $\sim D$ 2,4   DS
6. $B \supset D$ 1,3   HS
7. $\sim B$ 5,6   MT

The conclusion could also have been derived in another way:

1. $B \supset C$
2. $A \lor \sim D$
3. $C \supset D$
4. $\sim A$
5. $\sim D$ 2,4 DS
6. $\sim C$ 3,5′ MT
7. $\sim B$ 1,6′ MT

Although it often happens that there is more than one way to derive a conclusion, there are some derivations that can be done if HS is employed but that could not have been done with only the preceding five rules.

1. $A \lor (B \supset C)$
2. $C \supset D$
3. $(B \supset D) \supset E$
4. $F \cdot \sim A$ $\therefore$ $E \cdot F$
5. $\sim A$ 4   Simp
6. $B \supset C$ 1,5   DS
7. $B \supset D$ 2,6   HS
8. E 3,7   MP
9. F 4   Simp
10. $E \cdot F$ 8,9   Conj

EXERCISE 6b

Using the six rules discussed so far—MP, MT, DS, HS, Simp, and Conj—show that each of the following is valid.

1. $A \supset (B \cdot C)$
$\sim(B \cdot C)$
$A \lor D$ $\therefore$ $D \cdot \sim A$

2. $A \lor \sim B$
$\sim A \cdot D$
$C \supset B$ $\therefore$ $D \cdot \sim C$

3. $A \supset B$
$C \supset (B \supset D)$
C $\therefore$ $A \supset D$

4. $H \supset G$
$\sim F$
$F \lor (K \cdot \sim G)$ $\therefore$ $K \cdot \sim H$

5. $A \supset \sim B$
$(C \lor D) \supset A$ $\therefore$ $(C \lor D) \supset \sim B$

6. $A \supset (B \cdot \sim C)$
$(D \supset C) \cdot A$
$\sim D \supset E$ $\therefore$ $B \cdot E$

7. $(A \cdot \sim B) \supset C$
$D \lor A$
$B \supset D$
$\sim D$ $\therefore$ C

8. $(A \cdot D) \supset (C \supset E)$
$D \supset A$
$E \supset F$
D $\therefore$ $C \supset F$

9. $B \cdot \sim A$
$D \supset A$
$C \vee A \quad \therefore \quad (B \cdot C) \cdot \sim D$

10. $A \supset (B \vee C)$
$D \vee \sim(B \vee C)$
$\sim A \supset (E \cdot F)$
$E \supset \sim H$
$\sim D \cdot G \qquad \therefore \quad (F \cdot G) \cdot \sim H$

ADDITION AND CONSTRUCTIVE DILEMMA

Two more rules will complete our first group of eight derivational rules. Consider the following argument:

Al will be in class today.
∴ Either Al or Bill will be in class today.

This argument has some strange features. But for now just focus on the central question of our study. Is that argument valid? Does the truth of the premise guarantee the truth of the conclusion? Clearly, it is valid. If a statement is true, then the disjunction of that statement with something else must also be true. To show the validity of this and related arguments, we must introduce another rule (with two argument forms):

Addition (Add)

p $\qquad\qquad\qquad$ p $\qquad\qquad$ From any sentence, any disjunction
∴ $\boldsymbol{p \vee q}$ $\qquad\quad$ ∴ $\boldsymbol{q \vee p}$ $\qquad\quad$ of which it is one disjunct may be validly inferred.

The argument above is obviously valid, but there is something strange about it, so we should see what that is. I think that the reason it seems so strange involves two factors. First, the conclusion conveys less information than the premise. Second, the conclusion is longer than the premise (less concise than the premise). Thus if you know the premise to be true, the conclusion would ordinarily be a strange thing to say, because the conclusion conveys less information, takes longer to say, and introduces irrelevant elements that merely hide a more contentful, simpler truth. But even though all of this is true, the argument is valid, so we need some such rule to show that it is valid.

This inference is not always unnatural when it occurs as a part of a derivation.

If the city or the state provides the
funds, then we'll build a new road. $\qquad$ $(C \vee S) \supset R$
The city will provide the funds. $\qquad\qquad$ C
So we will build a new road. $\qquad\qquad\quad$ ∴ R

1. $(C \lor S) \supset R$
2. C
3. $C \lor S$ 2   Add
4. R 1,3   MP

Here addition is a very natural part of the derivation.
Constructive dilemma is the last of our first eight derivational rules.

Constructive Dilemma (CD)

$p \supset q$ From two conditionals and the
$r \supset s$ disjunction of their antecedents,
$p \lor r$ the disjunction of their consequents
$\therefore \; q \lor s$ may be validly inferred.

Constructive dilemma is a fairly common form of argument.

If the Soviets are the first to land a
man on Venus, then the Hammer and
Sickle flag will be the first flag to fly
there. $R \supset H$

If the Americans are first, then the
Stars and Stripes will be the first flag
to fly there. $A \supset S$

Either the Soviets or the Americans
will be first. $R \lor A$

So either the Hammer and Sickle or
the Stars and Stripes will be the first
flag to fly on Venus. $\therefore \;\; H \lor S$

This pattern captures the essence of "argument by cases." It amounts to this:

There are two possibilities to con-
sider (P and R). $p \lor r$
In the first case, we get result Q. $p \supset q$
In the second case, we get result S. $r \supset s$
So we get either Q or S. $\therefore \; q \lor s$
There are two possibilities: we can
raise income tax rates or levy a sales
tax. $R \lor S$

If we raise income tax rates, then
wealthy Americans will be resentful. $R \supset W$

If we levy a sales tax, then the poor
will pay a larger share of taxes than
they do now. $S \supset P$

So either wealthy Americans will be
resentful or the poor will pay a larger
share of taxes then they do now. $\therefore$ $W \lor P$

In derivations, constructive dilemma can be difficult to see, because CD
involves fitting *three* separate statements into a pattern. Do a derivation to
show validity in this example:

1. $A \supset (B \supset C)$
2. $D \lor (B \lor E)$
3. $E \supset F$
4. $A \cdot {\sim}D$ $\therefore$ $C \lor F$

Even after you have done the obvious steps of simplification, modus
ponens, and disjunctive syllogism, you have to look things over carefully to
piece together the remaining steps for constructive dilemma.

5. A	4	Simp
6. $B \supset C$	1,5	MP
7. ${\sim}D$	4	Simp
8. $B \lor E$	2,7	DS
9. $C \lor F$	3,6,8	CD

It is helpful to have a guideline so that you will know when to begin
looking for things to fit into a constructive dilemma pattern. Frequently, you
can be led to productive uses of constructive dilemma if you keep it in mind
that whenever you have a disjunction in your derivation, if you cannot use it
as part of a disjunctive syllogism inference (or some other obvious inference,
such as modus ponens), you should see if you can find two conditionals that
have the disjuncts as their antecedents. Then you can make a constructive
dilemma inference.

STRATEGIES FOR CONSTRUCTING DERIVATIONS

Our eight rules formulate things that we *may* do in constructing a derivation.
But often there will be many things that we may do, and we would like
to have efficient strategies for deciding which things to do. Here are a few
simple guidelines that may help you in finding and linking relevant steps.

1. Always look for MP, MT, and DS steps. One or more of these plays
   an important role in the vast majority of the derivations you will see.
   So,
   a. if you have a conditional, $p \supset q$, find p (to do MP) or find ${\sim}q$ (to
      do MT) if you can.

    b. if you have a disjunction, look for the negation of one of the disjuncts (to do DS).

2. Simplify conjunctions.

3. Prove conjunctions by conjunction.

4. If you have a disjunction, and if neither DS nor anything else is obvious, try to find two conditionals of the right sort for CD (i.e., try to find two conditionals which have, as antecedents, the disjuncts of the disjunction).

5. If you have conditionals and you cannot do MP, MT, or CD, check for HS.

6. If a sentence letter appears only once in the premises and not at all in the conclusion, it does not link anything with anything else. It is useless.

    a. If it is a conjunct of a conjunction, then simplify, utilizing the rest of the conjunction.

      1. $B \cdot \sim A$

      2. $A \vee (D \supset E)$

      3. D $\therefore$ E

      4. $\sim A$ 1   Simp

      5. $D \supset E$ 2,4   DS

      6. E 3,5   MP

'B' can be identified here as something useless.

    b. If it is not a conjunct of a conjunction, you can often use Add to deal with it.

      1. $(A \vee B) \supset C$

      2. $D \supset A$

      3. D $\therefore$ C

      4. A 2,3   MP

      5. $A \vee B$ 4   Add

      6. C 1,5   MP

Here 'B' is again the idle element, and it is introduced in the addition step.

7. If a sentence letter appears as one element of a disjunctive conclusion but does not appear in the premises, introduce it by Add.

      1. $A \vee (C \cdot D)$

      2. $D \supset E$

      3. $C \supset F$

      4. $\sim A$ $\therefore$ $(E \cdot F) \vee G$

      5. $C \cdot D$ 1,4   DS

      6. C 5   Simp

      7. D 5   Simp

      8. E 2,7   MP

9. F	3,6	MP
10. $E \cdot F$	8,9	Conj
11. $(E \cdot F) \vee G$	10	Add

Implicational Rules for Derivations

Modus Ponens (MP)

$p \supset q$

p

$\therefore \quad q$

Modus Tollens (MT)

$p \supset q$

$\sim q$

$\therefore \quad \sim p$

Simplification (Simp)

$p \cdot q$ $p \cdot q$

$\therefore \quad p$ $\therefore \quad q$

Conjunction (Conj)

p

q

$\therefore \quad p \cdot q$

Disjunctive Syllogism (DS)

$p \vee q$ $p \vee q$

$\sim p$ $\sim q$

$\therefore \quad q$ $\therefore \quad p$

Hypothetical Syllogism (HS)

$p \supset q$

$q \supset r$

$\therefore \quad p \supset r$

Addition (Add)

p p

$\therefore \quad p \vee q$ $\therefore \quad q \vee p$

Constructive Dilemma (CD)

$p \supset q$

$r \supset s$

$p \vee r$

$\therefore \quad q \vee s$

EXERCISE 6c

Each of the following arguments is an instance of one of the valid argument forms included in the system of rules developed in this chapter. In each case, identify the rule.

1. $(A \vee B) \supset C$

$D \supset (A \vee B)$

$\therefore \quad D \supset C$

2. $A \cdot \sim(B \cdot C)$

$\therefore \quad C \vee (A \cdot \sim(B \cdot C))$

3. $\sim(A \vee B)$

$(C \cdot D) \supset (A \vee B)$

$\therefore \quad \sim(C \cdot D)$

4. $\sim(A \cdot B) \vee (C \cdot D)$

$\sim(C \cdot D)$

$\therefore \quad \sim(A \cdot B)$

5. $(A \vee B) \supset C$

$(A \vee B) \vee D$

$D \supset (E \cdot F)$

$\therefore \quad C \vee (E \cdot F)$

EXERCISE 6d

In each of the following arguments, the conclusion is derivable from the premises with just two applications of the inference rules. Complete each derivation.

1. $A \lor (B \cdot C)$
$D \supset \sim(B \cdot C)$
D $\quad \therefore \quad A$

2. $A \supset B$
$B \supset (C \lor E)$
$[A \supset (C \lor E)] \supset (D \lor F)$ $\quad \therefore \quad D \lor F$

3. $B \supset (C \lor D)$
$\sim C$
B $\quad \therefore \quad D$

4. $A \supset B$
$(C \cdot D) \lor A$
$(C \cdot D) \supset E$
$(E \lor B) \supset F$ $\quad \therefore \quad F$

5. $(A \supset B) \lor C$
$D \supset E$
$\sim C$
$A \lor D$ $\quad \therefore \quad B \lor E$

EXERCISE 6e

In each of the following arguments, the conclusion is derivable with just three applications of the inference rules. Complete each derivation.

1. $A \supset E$
$E \supset C$
A $\quad \therefore \quad A \cdot C$

2. $(B \lor A) \supset E$
$E \supset (A \cdot C)$
A $\quad \therefore \quad A \cdot C$

3. $(B \lor A) \supset (E \cdot C)$
$C \supset B$
$C \lor D$
$D \supset A$ $\quad \therefore \quad C$

4. $A \supset (C \lor D)$
$A \supset \sim C$
A $\quad \therefore \quad D$

5. $A \supset B$
$A \lor C$
$\sim B$ $\quad \therefore \quad C \cdot \sim A$

6. $B \supset \sim D$
A
$C \supset E$
$(B \lor A) \supset (B \lor C)$ $\quad \therefore \quad \sim D \lor E$

EXERCISE 6f

Use the eight inference rules of this chapter to show that these arguments are valid.

1. $A \lor \sim C$
$C \lor D$
$\sim A$ $\quad \therefore \quad D \lor B$

2. $A \supset B$
$C \supset D$
$E \supset (A \lor C)$
E $\quad \therefore \quad B \lor D$

3. $(A \supset B) \supset D$
$C \supset B$
$A \supset C$
$D \supset \sim E$ $\therefore$ $D \cdot \sim E$

4. $(A \supset B) \supset (C \lor D)$
$A \supset C$
$D \supset C$
$C \supset B$ $\therefore$ $B \lor C$

5. $(A \lor C) \supset \sim B$
$\sim D \lor B$
$A \cdot (D \lor G)$ $\therefore$ $(A \cdot G) \cdot \sim B$

6. $(A \lor B) \supset C$
$(C \lor D) \supset E$
A $\therefore$ E

7. $A \supset (B \cdot \sim C)$
$(B \lor F) \supset (D \lor C)$
$D \supset (\sim E \cdot A)$
A $\therefore$ $(D \cdot \sim E) \lor G$

8. $(B \lor \sim A) \supset (C \lor D)$
$A \supset E$
$C \supset F$
$D \supset G$
$\sim E$ $\therefore$ $F \lor G$

9. $A \supset C$
$B \supset D$
$(E \lor F) \supset (A \lor B)$
$G \cdot E$ $\therefore$ $(C \lor D) \cdot (A \lor G)$

10. $A \supset (B \cdot C)$
$C \supset E$
$(B \cdot C) \supset F$
$C \cdot \sim F$ $\therefore$ $E \cdot \sim A$

11. $A \supset [C \supset (D \cdot \sim E)]$
$\sim B \supset F$
$D \supset [A \cdot (C \lor \sim B)]$
$D \cdot G$ $\therefore$ $(D \cdot \sim E) \lor F$

12. $\sim A \supset [C \cdot \sim(D \lor F)]$
$G \supset (D \lor F)$
$B \cdot \sim A$ $\therefore$ $(B \cdot C) \cdot \sim G$

13. $(A \lor B) \supset [(C \cdot \sim D) \supset E]$
$(D \lor C) \cdot (A \supset \sim D)$
A $\therefore$ $C \cdot E$

14. $(A \cdot D) \supset E$
$(C \lor B) \supset \sim E$
$F \supset (A \cdot D)$
C $\therefore$ $\sim F$

15. $\sim A \supset (C \supset E)$
$(B \lor D) \supset [F \supset (G \cdot H)]$
$A \lor (B \lor D)$
$\sim A \cdot (C \lor F)$ $\therefore$ $E \lor (G \cdot H)$

7

EQUIVALENCE RULES

DOUBLE NEGATION, COMMUTATIVITY, ASSOCIATIVITY, AND DEMORGAN'S THEOREMS

The system of derivational rules developed in the preceding chapter is still very limited. Consider, for example, the following argument:

If Al takes the bus, then he will not be on time to meet Bill.	$A \supset \sim B$
Al will be on time to meet Bill.	B
$\therefore$ Al will not take the bus.	$\therefore \quad \sim A$

This argument is obviously valid, and it is something like *modus tollens*. But as it stands it cannot be put into the modus tollens pattern:

$$p \supset q$$
$$\sim q$$
$$\therefore \quad \sim p$$

'B' is not of the form $\sim q$ because 'B' is not a negated sentence. For an argument to fit our modus tollens pattern, the nonconditional premise must be the negation of the consequent of the conditional; but 'B' is not negated at all. A closely related argument, though, is an instance of modus tollens:

$$A \supset \sim B$$
$$\sim \sim B$$
$$\therefore \quad \sim A$$

'$\sim \sim B$' is the negation of '$\sim B$'. But '$\sim \sim B$' and 'B' are equivalent: if one argument is valid, so is the other. We now need to recognize that equivalence by adding a rule to our system of rules.

A rule based on logical equivalences allows inference in both directions. This is a difference from the rules discussed previously. (For example, 'A' is deducible from '$A \cdot B$', but not the other way around; and '$A \lor B$' is deducible from 'A', but not the other way around.) We will indicate that inference is allowed both ways by a new symbol '$::$'. So our new rules will include:

Double Negation (DN)

$$p \quad :: \quad \sim\sim p$$

With this new rule, we can derive the conclusion in our example:

1. $A \supset \sim B$
2. B $\therefore \quad \sim A$
3. $\sim\sim B$ 2   DN
4. $\sim A$ 1,3   MT

We can also use DN (in the other direction) to *eliminate* double negations:

1. $\sim C \supset D$
2. $\sim D$ $\therefore \quad C$
3. $\sim\sim C$ 1,2   MT
4. C 3   DN

Other equivalences will contribute importantly to our ability to derive conclusions from premises. For example, we know that the order of the elements in a conjunction or in a disjunction makes no difference to the truth-value. That is the basis for adding two other equivalences to our set of rules:

Commutativity (Comm)

$$p \cdot q \quad :: \quad q \cdot p$$
$$p \lor q \quad :: \quad q \lor p$$

We will want to be able to change freely the order of elements in disjunctions and in conjunctions.

1. $(A \lor B) \supset C$
2. $B \lor A$ $\therefore \quad C$
3. $A \lor B$ 2   Comm
4. C 1,3   MP

When a disjunction appears as a line of a derivation, we can write a new line in which the disjunction is commuted (as we did in line 3, above). But equivalence rules also authorize a more general interchange of formulas.

Equivalent sentences have the same truth-value in all possible circumstances, so they make the same contribution to the truth-values of larger (truth-functionally compound) sentences within which they occur. Since '$A \lor B$' is equivalent to '$B \lor A$', the formula '$(A \lor B) \supset C$' must be equivalent to '$(B \lor A) \supset C$'. '$A \lor B$' and '$B \lor A$' make the same contribution to the truth-value of the larger sentence. Thus we can use equivalence rules to justify replacement of one sentence by an equivalent sentence *within* a larger compound sentence. This gives us an alternative means for deriving the conclusion in the example most recently considered:

1. $(A \lor B) \supset C$
2. $B \lor A$
3. $(B \lor A) \supset C$ 1   Comm
4. C 2,3 MP

Here commutativity has been used to justify replacement within a larger formula.

Another important fact about conjunctions and disjunctions is captured in the *associativity* principles:

Associativity (Assoc)

$$p \cdot (q \cdot r) \quad :: \quad (p \cdot q) \cdot r$$
$$p \lor (q \lor r) \quad :: \quad (p \lor q) \lor r$$

Parentheses may be moved in a long conjunction or in a long disjunction.

Associativity and commutativity together provide the basis for reorganizing any long conjunction or long disjunction by changing the order of elements and moving the parentheses around. (Notice how these rules are used on both the entire sentence occupying a line of a derivation and on parts of sentences in the following derivation.)

1. $(A \lor B) \lor (C \lor D)$
$\quad (p \ \lor \ q) \ \lor \quad r$

$\quad p \lor (q \lor \quad r \quad)$
2. $A \lor (B \lor (C \lor D))$ 1 Assoc
$\quad p \ \lor \quad q$

$\qquad q \qquad\qquad \lor \ p$
3. $(B \lor (C \lor D)) \lor A$ 2 Comm
$\quad p \lor (q \ \lor r)$

$\quad (p \ \lor q) \ \lor \ r$
4. $((B \lor C) \lor D) \lor A$ 3 Assoc
$\quad (\ p \qquad \lor q) \lor r$

$\qquad p \qquad \lor (q \ \lor r)$
5. $(B \lor C) \lor (D \lor A)$ 4 Assoc
$\qquad p \qquad \lor \qquad q$

$\overset{q}{}\overset{\vee}{}\overset{p}{}$

6. $(C \vee B) \vee (D \vee A)$ 5   Comm

Regroupings and reorderings can always be done using Comm and Assoc. [*Do not* extend these rules beyond their legitimate sphere of applicability! There are no commutative or associative rules for conditionals; '$A \supset B$' is *not* equivalent to '$B \supset A$', and '$A \supset (B \supset C)$' is *not* equivalent to '$(A \supset B) \supset C$'. In addition, associativity does not apply to "mixtures" of disjunction and conjunction; '$A \cdot (B \vee C)$' is *not* equivalent to '$(A \cdot B) \vee C$'.]

Another pair of equivalences will be very important in derivations.

DeMorgan's Theorems (DeM)

$\sim(p \vee q)$ $::$ $\sim p \cdot \sim q$
$\sim(p \cdot q)$ $::$ $\sim p \vee \sim q$

(These equivalences are named after Augustus DeMorgan, a nineteenth-century mathematician and logician who played an important role in developing some of the techniques of modern logic.) We noticed these equivalences when we discussed symbolization of English sentences. For example, "Neither p nor q" is equivalent to $\sim(p \vee q)$ and to $\sim p \cdot \sim q$. In derivations, the DeMorgan's equivalences are very important for putting premises into "good shape" for applying simplification and disjunctive syllogism.

1. $\sim(A \cdot B)$
2. $\sim(C \vee \sim B)$ $\therefore$ $\sim(A \vee C)$
3. $\sim A \vee \sim B$ 1   DeM
4. $\sim C \cdot \sim\sim B$ 2   DeM
5. $\sim\sim B$ 4   Simp
6. $\sim A$ 3,5   DS
7. $\sim C$ 4   Simp
8. $\sim A \cdot \sim C$ 6,7   Conj
9. $\sim(A \vee C)$ 8   DeM

In the example above, notice that the derivation for the argument with lines 3 and 4 as premises and line 8 as conclusion is easily seen. (It involves only simplification, disjunctive syllogism, and conjunction.) And by DeMorgan's Theorems, 1 is equivalent to 3, 2 is equivalent to 4, and 8 is equivalent to 9.

DeMorgan's is also important in a key inference step that is often overlooked. Consider this example:

Al and Bill will both help with dinner
or else we will eat very late. $(A \cdot B) \vee C$
But Al will not help. $\sim A$
$\therefore$ We will eat very late. $\therefore$ C

If Al won't help, it is clearly not true that Al and Bill will both help. '$\sim(A \cdot B)$' follows from '$\sim A$', and we can derive it using Add and DeM.

1. $(A \cdot B) \lor C$
2. $\sim A$ $\therefore \ \ C$
3. $\sim A \lor \sim B$ 2   Add
4. $\sim(A \cdot B)$ 3   DeM
5. C 1,4   DS

Remember the sequence of steps 2–4.

$\sim p$
$\sim p \lor \sim q$ Add
$\sim(p \cdot q)$ DeM

EXERCISE 7a

Using the eight implicational inference rules together with DN, Comm, Assoc, and DeM, prove that each of the following is valid.

1. $\sim(A \cdot (B \lor C))$
    $\therefore \ \ \sim A \lor (\sim B \cdot \sim C)$

2. $(A \lor B) \lor C$
    $\therefore \ \ (C \lor A) \lor B$

3. A
    $\therefore \ \ (C \lor A) \lor B$

4. $B \supset (C \cdot \sim A)$
    $D \supset \sim C$
    D
    $\therefore \ \ \sim B$

5. $(A \lor B) \lor (C \lor D)$
    $\therefore \ \ ((B \lor D) \lor C) \lor A$

6. $\sim(A \lor B)$
    $C \supset (B \cdot D)$
    $\therefore \ \ \sim(A \lor C)$

7. $B \lor \sim(C \cdot A)$
    $\therefore \ \ \sim A \lor (\sim C \lor B)$

8. $\sim(A \cdot (B \cdot C))$
    C
    $D \supset (A \cdot B)$
    $\therefore \ \ \sim D$

9. $C \supset (\sim A \supset D)$
    $\sim B \supset \sim E$
    $(A \cdot B) \supset \sim C$
    $\therefore \ \ \sim(E \cdot \sim D)$

10. $(D \cdot E) \supset (A \lor C)$
    $B \supset \sim A$
    $(B \cdot \sim A) \supset \sim C$
    $B \cdot D$
    $\therefore \ \ \sim E$

11. $C \supset (A \cdot B)$
    $\sim B \lor \sim A$
    $D \lor (C \cdot B)$
    $\therefore \ \ \sim(C \lor \sim D)$

12. $\sim(D \lor \sim A)$
    $\sim(B \cdot \sim C)$
    $A \supset (C \supset (D \cdot E))$
    $\therefore \ \ \sim B$

13. $\sim(A \cdot C)$
$\quad \sim(C \cdot E) \supset D$
$\quad A$
$\quad \therefore \quad D \vee B$

14. $\sim(A \cdot \sim B)$
$\quad A \vee D$
$\quad \sim(C \cdot D)$
$\quad C$
$\quad \therefore \quad B$

15. $(D \vee E) \vee F$
$\quad (E \vee F) \supset (A \supset \sim B)$
$\quad \sim(D \vee F)$
$\quad E \supset B$
$\quad \therefore \quad \sim A$

REDUNDANCY, DISTRIBUTION, AND CONDITIONAL EXCHANGE

In addition to commutativity, associativity, and DeMorgan's Theorems, two other pairs of rules are based on important equivalences involving conjunction and disjunction. The first is very simple:

Redundancy (Red)

$p \qquad :: \qquad p \vee p$
$p \qquad :: \qquad p \cdot p$

One of the most common uses of this rule occurs with constructive dilemma.

If unemployment increases, then the economic outlook will be worse.	$U \supset W$
If the rate of inflation rises, then the economic outlook will be worse.	$R \supset W$
Either unemployment will increase or the rate of inflation will rise.	$U \vee R$
So the economic outlook will be worse.	$\therefore \quad W$

To show this to be valid, we need to employ only Red and CD.

1. $U \supset W$
2. $R \supset W$
3. $U \vee R$
4. $W \vee W \qquad$ 1,2,3 $\quad$ CD
5. $W \qquad\qquad$ 4 $\qquad$ Red

This type of argument is very typical of "argument by cases." The disjunctive premise, 3, tells us that these are only two cases to consider ($U \lor R$). The conditional premises tell us that in both cases we get the same result ($U \supset W$, $R \supset W$). So that result (W) is assured.

The other important pair of equivalences involving conjunction and disjunction constitutes the distribution rule.

Distribution (Dist)

$$p \lor (q \cdot r) \quad :: \quad (p \lor q) \cdot (p \lor r)$$
$$p \cdot (q \lor r) \quad :: \quad (p \cdot q) \lor (p \cdot r)$$

Although these are slightly more complex equivalences, they are easy to remember if you note that the main connective always changes. A disjunction ($p \lor (q \cdot r)$) is equivalent to a conjunction (($p \lor q) \cdot (p \lor r)$). No application of this rule will take you from a disjunction to another disjunction or from a conjunction to another conjunction.

Until we have the two key rules of the next chapter (conditional proof and indirect proof), distribution plays an important role in derivations.

The president will be reelected or else his party will be in trouble.	$R \lor T$
The president will be reelected or else the professional bureaucracy will seize control of major institutions.	$R \lor S$
So either the president will be reelected or else his party will be in trouble and the professional bureaucracy will seize control of major institutions.	$\therefore \ R \lor (T \cdot S)$

1. $R \lor T$
2. $R \lor S$
3. $(R \lor T) \cdot (R \lor S)$ 1,2   Conj
4. $R \lor (T \cdot S)$ 3   Dist

We now have a large number of equivalences involving conjunction and disjunction, but none directly involving conditionals and biconditionals. The principal equivalence that we need for conditionals is one that allows us to replace a conditional by a disjunction (or vice versa). This makes it possible to utilize our rich stock of equivalence rules involving disjunctions. The rule is *conditional exchange*:

Conditional Exchange (CE)

$$p \supset q \quad :: \quad \sim p \lor q$$

This can be illustrated by a large number of examples in which it is useful to convert conditionals to disjunctions.

I. 1. $(A \supset B) \lor C$ $\therefore$ $A \supset (B \lor C)$
  2. $(\sim A \lor B) \lor C$ 1   CE
  3. $\sim A \lor (B \lor C)$ 2   Assoc
  4. $A \supset (B \lor C)$ 3   CE

II. 1. $A \supset B$
  2. $A \supset C$ $\therefore$ $A \supset (B \cdot C)$
  3. $\sim A \lor B$ 1   CE
  4. $\sim A \lor C$ 2   CE
  5. $(\sim A \lor B) \cdot (\sim A \lor C)$ 3,4   Conj
  6. $\sim A \lor (B \cdot C)$ 5   Dist
  7. $A \supset (B \cdot C)$ 6   CE

III. 1. $\sim(A \supset B)$ $\therefore$ $A \cdot \sim B$
  2. $\sim(\sim A \lor B)$ 1   CE
  3. $\sim\sim A \cdot \sim B$ 2   DeM
  4. $A \cdot \sim B$ 3   DN

In each of these cases the key step is an equivalence rule involving disjunction (associativity in I, distribution in II, DeMorgan's Theorem in III). But to apply the rule, we needed to replace a conditional by an equivalent disjunction. This can also work the other way.

IV. 1. $\sim A \lor B$
  2. $\sim B \lor C$ $\therefore$ $\sim A \lor C$
  3. $A \supset B$ 1   CE
  4. $B \supset C$ 2   CE
  5. $A \supset C$ 3,4   HS
  6. $\sim A \lor C$ 5   CE

In IV the key step is hypothetical syllogism, even though there are no conditionals in the premises or conclusion of the argument.

EXERCISE 7b

Show that each of the following is valid (using the 15 rules discussed so far).

1. $\sim(A \lor (B \cdot C))$
  $\therefore$ $\sim(A \lor B) \lor \sim(A \lor C)$

2. $\sim A \supset A$
  $\therefore$ A

3. $A \supset (D \cdot B)$
  $C \supset (B \cdot D)$
  $A \lor C$
  $\therefore$ $B \cdot D$

4. $A \supset (B \cdot D)$
  $C \supset D$
  $A \lor C$
  $\therefore$ D

5. $A \cdot \sim B$
  $\therefore$ $\sim(A \supset B)$

6. $A \supset B$
  $\therefore$ $A \supset (B \lor C)$

7. A
$\therefore$ $B \supset (A \cdot A)$

8. $\sim A \supset B$
$\therefore$ $(A \vee C) \vee B$

9. $A \supset B$
$C \supset B$
$\therefore$ $(A \vee C) \supset B$

10. $\sim[B \vee \sim(A \supset (B \cdot C))]$
$\sim A \supset D$
$\therefore$ $D \cdot \sim A$

11. $(A \vee C) \vee (D \vee E)$
$\sim(A \cdot B)$
$C \supset \sim(B \cdot \sim A)$
$B \cdot \sim D$
$\therefore$ E

12. $\sim A \vee (B \cdot C)$
$C \supset (B \cdot D)$
$A \vee C$
$\therefore$ $B \cdot D$

13. $(\sim A \vee B) \supset D$
$C \supset B$
$\sim(A \cdot \sim C)$
$\sim(D \cdot E)$
$\therefore$ $D \cdot \sim E$

14. $\sim A \vee B$
$D \vee A$
$D \supset C$
$\therefore$ $\sim C \supset B$

15. $\sim(A \cdot C) \supset \sim B$
$D \vee B$
$\sim(D \cdot H)$
$\sim A \cdot (H \vee G)$
$\therefore$ $G \cdot \sim(A \vee H)$

CONTRAPOSITION, EXPORTATION, AND THE BICONDITIONAL RULE

Our last three equivalence rules will include some natural equivalences involving conditionals and will enable us to employ biconditionals in derivations.

So far we have only one equivalence rule directly involving conditionals (the conditional exchange rule). But there are some very natural equivalences involving conditionals that are worth separate notice. For example:

If John is a doctor, then he has a degree.
If John has no degree, then he is not a doctor.

If 3^2 is even, then 3^2 is divisible by 2.
If 3^2 is not divisible by 2, then 3^2 is not even.

Each of these is a pair of equivalent conditionals

$p \supset q$
$\sim q \supset \sim p$

Conditionals related in this way are called *contrapositives*, and we will incorporate an equivalence rule formulating this equivalence.

Contraposition (Contra)

$$p \supset q \quad :: \quad \sim q \supset \sim p$$

This rule is especially useful in connection with hypothetical syllogism and constructive dilemma.

I. 1. $A \supset \sim B$
    2. $C \supset B$ $\therefore \quad A \supset \sim C$
    3. $\sim B \supset \sim C$ 2   Contra
    4. $A \supset \sim C$ 1,3   HS

II. 1. $A \supset B$
    2. $C \supset D$
    3. $\sim B \lor \sim D$ $\therefore \quad \sim A \lor \sim C$
    4. $\sim B \supset \sim A$ 1   Contra
    5. $\sim D \supset \sim C$ 2   Contra
    6. $\sim A \lor \sim C$ 3,4,5   CD

The following rule formulates another equivalence involving conditionals:

Exportation (Exp)

$$(p \cdot q) \supset r \quad :: \quad p \supset (q \supset r)$$

This is a very natural equivalence in English.

> If the supply of oil is constant and demand increases, then the price goes up.
> If the supply of oil is constant, then if demand increases, then the price goes up.

This is often useful in derivations.

I. 1. $(S \cdot I) \supset P$ If supply is constant and demand increases, then the price goes up.

    2. $(I \supset P) \supset W$ If the price goes up if demand increases, then wholesalers make money.

    $\therefore \quad S \supset W$ $\therefore$ If supply is constant, then wholesalers make money.

    1. $(S \cdot I) \supset P$
    2. $(I \supset P) \supset W$
    3. $S \supset (I \supset P)$ 1   Exp
    4. $S \supset W$ 2,3   HS

II. 1. $(A \cdot E) \supset C$
    2. $B \supset (\sim A \supset \sim D)$
    3. $B \cdot D$ $\therefore \quad \sim C \supset \sim E$

4. $B \supset (D \supset A)$		2	Contra
5. $(B \cdot D) \supset A$		4	Exp
6. A		3,5	MP
7. $A \supset (E \supset C)$		1	Exp
8. $E \supset C$		6,7	MP
9. $\sim C \supset \sim E$		8	Contra

Our last equivalence rule will incorporate the biconditional into our deductive system. (No rule prior to this one involves it.)

Biconditional (Bic)

$$p \equiv q \quad :: \quad (p \supset q) \cdot (q \supset p)$$

A biconditional has status in our deductive system only as a conjunction of two conditionals. This makes it obvious what to do when a derivation involves a biconditional. If there is a biconditional premise, convert it to a conjunction and simplify. If there is a biconditional to derive, establish each of the two conditionals and then conjoin them.

I.	**1.** $(A \cdot B) \supset D$			
	2. $B \vee \sim(D \vee E)$			
	3. A		$\therefore$	$B \equiv D$
	4. $A \supset (B \supset D)$		1	Exp
	5. $B \supset D$		3,4	MP
	6. $B \vee (\sim D \cdot \sim E)$		2	DeM
	7. $(B \vee \sim D) \cdot (B \vee \sim E)$		6	Dist
	8. $B \vee \sim D$		7	Simp
	9. $\sim D \vee B$		8	Comm
	10. $D \supset B$		9	CE
	11. $(B \supset D) \cdot (D \supset B)$		5,10	Conj
	12. $B \equiv D$		11	Bic
II.	**1.** $B \equiv \sim D$			
	2. $\sim B \supset (C \cdot E)$			
	3. $B \supset \sim E$		$\therefore$	$D \equiv E$
	4. $(B \supset \sim D) \cdot (\sim D \supset B)$		1	Bic
	5. $B \supset \sim D$		4	Simp
	6. $\sim\sim D \supset \sim B$		5	Contra
	7. $D \supset \sim B$		6	DN
	8. $D \supset (C \cdot E)$		2,7	HS
	9. $\sim D \vee (C \cdot E)$		8	CE
	10. $(\sim D \vee C) \cdot (\sim D \vee E)$		9	Dist
	11. $\sim D \vee E$		10	Simp
	12. $D \supset E$		11	CE
	13. $\sim D \supset B$		4	Simp
	14. $\sim D \supset \sim E$		3,13	HS
	15. $E \supset D$		14	Contra
	16. $(D \supset E) \cdot (E \supset D)$		12,15	Conj
	17. $D \equiv E$		16	Bic

Equivalence Rules

1. *Double Negation (DN)*

$$p \quad :: \quad \sim\sim p$$

2. *Commutativity (Comm)*

$$p \cdot q \quad :: \quad q \cdot p$$
$$p \vee q \quad :: \quad q \vee p$$

3. *Associativity (Assoc)*

$$p \cdot (q \cdot r) \quad :: \quad (p \cdot q) \cdot r$$
$$p \vee (q \vee r) \quad :: \quad (p \vee q) \vee r$$

4. *DeMorgan's Theorems (DeM)*

$$\sim(p \vee q) \quad :: \quad \sim p \cdot \sim q$$
$$\sim(p \cdot q) \quad :: \quad \sim p \vee \sim q$$

5. *Redundancy (Red)*

$$p \quad :: \quad p \vee p$$
$$p \quad :: \quad p \cdot p$$

6. *Distribution (Dist)*

$$p \vee (q \cdot r) \quad :: \quad (p \vee q) \cdot (p \vee r)$$
$$p \cdot (q \vee r) \quad :: \quad (p \cdot q) \vee (p \cdot r)$$

7. *Conditional Exchange (CE)*

$$p \supset q \quad :: \quad \sim p \vee q$$

8. *Contraposition (Contra)*

$$p \supset q \quad :: \quad \sim q \supset \sim p$$

9. *Exportation (Exp)*

$$(p \cdot q) \supset r \quad :: \quad p \supset (q \supset r)$$

10. *Biconditional (Bic)*

$$p \equiv q \quad :: \quad (p \supset q) \cdot (q \supset p)$$

EXERCISE 7c

The following are pairs of equivalent English sentences. Indicate which of our equivalence rules is illustrated by each example.

1. Alice and Bob are both students.
Bob and Alice are both students.

2. Alice and Bob will not both take this class.
Either Alice won't take this class or Bob won't take it.

3. If John ever studied, then he passed this exam.
If John didn't pass this exam, then he never studied.

4. Alice will run for president, and either Bob or Charlie will be her running mate.
Alice will run for president with Bob as her running mate, or she will run with Charlie as her running mate.

5. If Alice runs, then if she campaigns well, she will win.
If Alice runs and campaigns well, then she will win.

6. Alice and Bob are seniors, and Charlie is too.
Alice is a senior, and Bob and Charlie are seniors too.

7. If she graduates, then she will have done a lot of work.
Either she won't graduate or else she will have done a lot of work.

8. Alice will win or else Bob and Charlie will both be unemployed.
Alice will win or else Bob will be unemployed, and, also, Alice will win
or Charlie will be unemployed.

EXERCISE 7d

Show that each of the following is valid. (Exercises 5 and 6 are difficult.)

1. $A \supset B$
$\sim C \supset D$
$\sim(B \cdot C)$
$\therefore \quad D \vee \sim A$

2. $(A \cdot B) \supset (C \vee D)$
$(E \cdot B) \supset A$
$\therefore \quad (E \cdot B) \supset (C \vee D)$

3. $B \equiv (C \cdot A)$
$C \supset \sim A$
$\therefore \quad \sim B$

4. $(A \cdot B) \supset (\sim D \supset \sim C)$
$F \supset A$
$\therefore \quad (F \cdot C) \supset (D \vee \sim B)$

5. $(B \cdot C) \equiv (A \vee D)$
$C \cdot \sim A$
$\therefore \quad B \equiv D$

6. $A \supset (B \equiv C)$
$B \cdot \sim C$
$\sim A \supset D$
$\therefore \quad D$

8

CONDITIONAL PROOF AND INDIRECT PROOF

The rules of the two preceding chapters constitute a powerful system for deriving conclusions. But two general methods of proof that are often employed were not incorporated into that inventory of techniques for deriving conclusions. These methods are not simple argument forms or equivalences, but they correspond to some natural methods of proof that require us to consider imaginatively the consequences of assumptions.

CONDITIONAL PROOF

We often establish conditional conclusions by exploring the consequences of an assumption. The conditional formulates the results of this exploration: "If that assumption were true, it would have these consequences."

The way we would establish the conclusion of the following argument can serve as an example.

> If we buy a compact disk player, we must cut down on small purchases or our financial plans will be ruined. If we buy more compact disks, we will not be cutting down on small purchases. But if we buy a compact disk player, we will buy more compact disks. So if we buy a compact disk player, our financial plans will be ruined.

The premises are these:

1. If we buy a compact disk player, we must cut down on small purchases or our financial plans will be ruined. $P \supset (C \lor R)$

2. If we buy more compact disks, we will not be cutting down on small purchases. $M \supset \sim C$

3. If we buy a compact disk player, we
will buy more compact disks. $P \supset M$

We could then proceed to consider the consequences of buying a compact
disk player.

4. Suppose that we buy a compact disk
player.   *Suppose P*
5. Then we must cut down on small pur-
chases or our financial plans will be
ruined. $C \vee R$ 1,4   MP
6. But we will also buy more compact
disks. M 3,4   MP
7. Thus we will not be cutting down. $\sim C$ 2,6   MP
8. So our financial plans will be ruined. R 5,7   DS

The assumption in step 4 (that we buy a compact disk player) leads to the
consequence in step 8 (that our financial plans will be ruined). On the basis
of this, we can conclude that a certain conditional is true.

9. If we buy a compact disk player, our
financial plans will be ruined. $P \supset R$ 4–8

Step 9 follows from the fact that our exploration of the consequences of step
4 leads us to step 8. (It follows from steps 4–8.)

   Statements 5–8 follow from the initial premises (1–3) together with an
additional supposition (4). We explore the consequences of the supposition
that we buy a compact disk player. Among those consequences is the conclusion that our financial plans will be ruined. Thus we conclude that *if* we
buy a compact disk player, *then* our financial plans will be ruined. We have
established the conditional by *assuming the antecedent* of the conditional
and showing that *the consequent is a consequence of that assumption* (taken
together with the initial premises).

   This common method for establishing conditionals is *conditional proof*.
We show that if we assume the antecedent to be true, then we can derive
the consequent.

   To formulate this procedure (exploring the consequences of an assumption)
as a rule, we need to introduce some new apparatus into our system of rules.
We need ways to indicate that

1. an *assumption* is being made (as in step 4).
2. we are exploring the consequences of that assumption (5–8).
3. steps that depend on that assumption need not follow from the initial premises alone; they follow from the premises together with the
assumption.
4. a conditional is established as the result of our explorations (9 depends
on the fact that 4 leads to 8).

Here is the notation we will use.

1. $P \supset (C \vee R)$
2. $M \supset \sim C$
3. $P \supset M$
4. P AP
5. $C \vee R$ 1,4   MP
6. M 3,4   MP
7. $\sim C$ 2,6   MP
8. R 5,7   DS
9. $P \supset R$ 4–8   CP

1. In step 4, an assumption is made. This is marked by an arrow, and we write AP (assumed premise) where we would usually write the justification for a step.
2. The line down the side from step 4 to step 8 indicates that these steps may depend upon step 4 (as well as upon the original premises). They follow from 1–3 together with the marked assumption, 4.
3. Step 9 is justified by the whole series of steps from 4 through 8. The rule of conditional proof allows us to justify a conditional on the basis of a series of steps beginning with an assumption. The conditional takes the assumption (P) as its antecedent and the last step in the series (R) as its consequent. If the assumption (P) were true, this consequence (R) would be true. ($P \supset R$)

Schematically presented, our rule of conditional proof works like this:

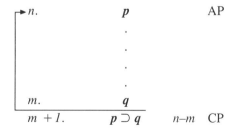

$$
\begin{array}{lll}
n. & p & \text{AP} \\
 & \cdot & \\
 & \cdot & \\
 & \cdot & \\
 & \cdot & \\
m. & q & \\
m+1. & p \supset q & n\text{–}m \quad \text{CP}
\end{array}
$$

If q is a consequence of an assumption p, then $p \supset q$ is justified by conditional proof (CP). The series of steps n–m is called a "subderivation," and the CP step *closes* the subderivation.

The conditional proof rule is an important supplement to our rules because it makes many very natural derivations possible. For example, if we had done the previous example without CP, we would have done something like this:

1. $P \supset (C \vee R)$
2. $M \supset \sim C$
3. $P \supset M$

4. $P \supset \sim C$	2,3	HS
5. $P \supset (\sim\sim C \lor R)$	1	DN
6. $P \supset (\sim C \supset R)$	5	CE
7. $(P \cdot \sim C) \supset R$	6	Exp
8. $(\sim C \cdot P) \supset R$	7	Comm
9. $\sim C \supset (P \supset R)$	8	Exp
10. $P \supset (P \supset R)$	4,9	HS
11. $(P \cdot P) \supset R$	10	Exp
12. $P \supset R$	11	Red

This derivation is nothing at all like the way one would typically try to derive the conclusion "If we buy a compact disk player, then our financial plans will be ruined." With CP we employ MP and DS as our key steps. Without CP we employ CE, Exp, HS, DN, Rep, and Comm. The CP method follows the much more natural method of exploring the consequences of an assumption.

Suppose that we buy a compact disk player. What will be among the consequences? . . . Our financial plans will be ruined. So if we buy it, our financial plans will be ruined.

There is an additional important reason to add CP to our stock of rules. We would like to be able to derive a conclusion from a set of premises whenever the argument with those premises and that conclusion is truth-functionally valid. Although the rules of the preceding chapters are not adequate to make this possible, after we add CP we have a *derivationally complete* system of rules: a system of rules that makes derivations possible for every truth-functionally valid argument.

The following simple argument cannot be shown valid using only the rules of the preceding chapters.

$A \supset B$
$\therefore \quad A \supset (A \cdot B)$

With CP, the derivation is simple.

1. $A \supset B$		
2. A		AP
3. B	1,2	MP
4. $A \cdot B$	2,3	Conj
5. $A \supset (A \cdot B)$	2–4	CP

Further examples will illustrate the utility and naturalness of this rule.

If Abilonia wins its war in Wyndom, then it will lose in Lobelia. But if it wins in Wyndom and loses in Lobelia, then Lobelia will be forced

to compromise for the sake of its alliance with Wyndom. And if Lobelia
is forced to compromise for Wyndom's sake, then there will be tension
between Lobelia and Wyndom. Thus there will be tension between Lobelia
and Wyndom if Abilonia wins its war in Wyndom.

1. $W \supset L$
2. $(W \cdot L) \supset C$
3. $C \supset T$
4. W AP   Suppose they win in Wyndom.
5. L MP   Then they'll lose in Lobelia.
6. $W \cdot L$ Conj   So both of these will happen.
7. C MP   Thus Lobelia must compromise.
8. T MP   But that will produce tension
                                    between Lobelia and Wyndom.

9. $W \supset T$ 4–8   CP   So if Abilonia wins in Wyndom,
                                    there will be tension between
                                    Lobelia and Wyndom.

If either Al or Bill goes to class, then Charlie and Dave will get the notes.
If Dave gets the notes, then Frank will get them too. So if Al goes to
class, then Frank will get the notes.

1. $(A \lor B) \supset (C \cdot D)$
2. $D \supset F$ $\therefore$ $A \supset F$
3. A AP
4. $A \lor B$ 3   Add
5. $C \cdot D$ 1,4   MP
6. D 5   Simp
7. F 2,6   MP
8. $A \supset F$ 3–8   CP

The CP strategy continues to apply when the antecedent of the conditional
conclusion is a compound sentence.

1. $A \supset (C \lor D)$
2. $B \supset F$
3. $\sim C$ $\therefore$ $(A \cdot \sim F) \supset (\sim B \cdot D)$
4. $A \cdot \sim F$ AP
5. A 4   Simp
6. $C \lor D$ 1,5   MP
7. D 3,6   DS
8. $\sim F$ 4   Simp
9. $\sim B$ 2,8   MT

10. $\sim B \cdot D$	7,9	Conj
11. $(A \cdot \sim F) \supset (\sim B \cdot D)$	4–10	CP

Sometimes in developing your strategy for deriving a conclusion you will notice that there is some useful conditional that would help you to derive the conclusion. Try proving it by CP.

$(A \supset B) \supset C$
$\sim(A \cdot D)$
$D \lor B \qquad\qquad \therefore \quad C$

In order to establish the conclusion, C, we must establish '$A \supset B$' so that we can do MP with step 1. We can establish '$A \supset B$' by CP.

1. $(A \supset B) \supset C$		
2. $\sim(A \cdot D)$		
3. $D \lor B$		
4. A		AP
5. $\sim A \lor \sim D$	2	DeM
6. $\sim\sim A$	4	DN
7. $\sim D$	5,6	DS
8. B	3,7	DS
9. $A \supset B$	4–8	CP
10. C	1,9	MP

When we proceed to do further steps after a CP step, we must take care in our justification of those steps. The CP step *closes* the subderivation. The steps within the subderivation (steps 4–8 of our example) have a special status. They are derived from the premises (1–3) together with an additional assumption (4). But after the CP step (9), the further lines of the derivation should be derived from the premises alone. This means that none of the steps appearing in the closed subderivation (4–8) may be used in the justification of steps after the CP step. In justifying step 10, only steps 1, 2, 3, and 9 may be employed. Steps 4–8 may depend upon the assumption in step 4, but step 9 ends our dependence on that additional assumption.

Our CE rule guarantees that every disjunction is equivalent to a conditional. This enables us to employ CP even in some cases in which the conclusion is a disjunction.

1. $A \supset B$		
2. $\sim B \lor (C \cdot D)$	$\therefore \quad \sim A \lor C$	
3. A		AP
4. B	1,3	MP
5. $\sim\sim B$	4	DN
6. $C \cdot D$	2,5	DS

7. *C*	6	Simp
8. *A* ⊃ *C*	3–7	CP
9. ∼*A* ∨ *C*	8	CE

In addition, we can use CP more than once when we have more than one conditional to establish.

1. *A* ⊃ *B*		
2. *C* ∨ *D*	∴ *A* ⊃ [∼*D* ⊃ (*B* · *C*)]	
3. *A*		AP
4. *B*	1,3	MP
5. ∼*D*		AP
6. *C*	2,5	DS
7. *B* · *C*	4,6	Conj
8. ∼*D* ⊃ (*B* · *C*)	5–7	CP
9. *A* ⊃ [∼*D* ⊃ (*B* · *C*)]	3–8	CP

Steps 5–7 depend on two assumptions, and the double line clearly marks this.

We can also employ subderivations that are entirely separate (neither one appearing within the other).

1. *A* ⊃ *B*		
2. *B* ⊃ (*C* · *D*)		
3. *C* ⊃ (*A* · *B*)	∴ *C* ≡ *A*	
4. *C*		AP
5. *A* · *B*	3,4	MP
6. *A*	5	Simp
7. *C* ⊃ *A*	4–6	CP
8. *A*		AP
9. *B*	1,8	MP
10. *C* · *D*	2,9	MP
11. *C*	10	Simp
12. *A* ⊃ *C*	8–11	CP
13. (*C* ⊃ *A*) · (*A* ⊃ *C*)	7,12	Conj
14. *C* ≡ *A*	13	Bic

Notice that steps 8–11 are entirely independent of steps 4–6. To establish 12 ('*A* ⊃ *C*'), we must derive 11 (*C*) from the premises (1–3) together with 8 (*A*). But 4–6 depend upon an extra assumption (4), so nothing there can be employed to justify 8–11. It would be *wrong* to try to justify step 9 (*B*) on the basis of step 5 (*A* · *B*), for example. Step 9 may depend on the premises (1–3) together with 8, but it may not depend upon the assumption in step 4.

The subderivation 4–6 is *closed*, so 5 cannot be used. Since 5 depends upon 4, that means that 9 must be justified by something other than step 5.

Justifying CP

Most people find CP to be a very natural form of inference. But it is legitimate to ask how we can justify the employment of such a technique.

For our earlier rules, justification is a simple matter. Each of the implicational inference rules is a valid argument form, thus it cannot take us from true premises to a false conclusion. If asked, we can use truth-tables to show the validity of those argument forms. Each of the equivalence rules is a correct equivalence, so the formulas related by an equivalence rule will have exactly the same truth-conditions. Thus replacement of one by the other cannot bring about any change in truth-value. We can use truth-tables to verify any equivalence used as one of our rules.

But we cannot directly employ truth-tables to verify the correctness of CP. We must use a slightly different technique, comparing two different arguments.

1. P_1
   P_2
   .
   .
   .
   P_n
   $\therefore \ A \supset C$

2. P_1
   P_2
   .
   .
   .
   P_n
   A
   $\therefore \ C$

Consider two arguments related in this way. One has n premises and its conclusion is a conditional ('$A \supset C$'). The second has $n+1$ premises, including all of the premises of the first argument ($P_1, P_2, \ldots, P_n$) and the antecedent (A) of the first argument's conclusion. The conclusion of the second argument is the consequent (C) of the conclusion of the first argument.

These are slightly different arguments. The person who gives the second argument asserts both A and C, but the person who gives the first argument does not.

But these arguments are related in an important way. One is valid if and only if the other is valid. Arguments related in this way have exactly the same invalidating conditions. (When $P_1, P_2, \ldots, P_n$, and A are true but C is false, both will have true premises and a false conclusion. In both cases, those are the only conditions under which the premises are true while the conclusion is false.) Since they have exactly the same invalidating conditions, one is valid if and only if the other is valid.

The method of CP involves an apparatus for showing arguments of the first type to be valid by doing a derivation of the conclusion for an argument of the second type. Often the derivation for the second type is easier. (It has more premises and a shorter conclusion.) That is the advantage of CP. If we show the second to be valid, we have automatically shown the first to be valid as well.

EXERCISE 8a

Derive the conclusion from the premises. (Use CP.)

1. $A \supset C$
 $\therefore$ $(A \cdot B) \supset C$

2. $(A \supset C) \cdot (B \supset C)$
 $\therefore$ $(A \lor B) \supset C$

3. $I \supset (M \supset H)$
 $\sim H$
 $\therefore$ $I \supset \sim M$

4. $A \lor (B \cdot C)$
 $C \supset \sim A$
 $\therefore$ $C \supset B$

5. $(H \cdot \sim J) \supset C$
 $C \supset E$
 $\sim J$
 $\therefore$ $H \supset E$

6. $\sim(B \cdot \sim D)$
 $\sim A \supset B$
 $C \supset (A \supset D)$
 $\therefore$ $C \supset D$

7. $A \supset (B \cdot D)$
 $B \supset (C \lor \sim D)$
 $\sim C \lor (B \cdot E)$
 $\therefore$ $A \supset (C \cdot E)$

8. $A \supset [B \lor (C \cdot D)]$
 $E \supset \sim C$
 $B \supset (E \cdot C)$
 $\therefore$ $A \supset D$

9. $A \supset (B \lor C)$
 $A \supset \sim C$
 $(A \cdot B) \supset D$
 $\therefore$ $A \supset D$

10. $A \supset B$
 $\sim(D \lor A) \supset C$
 $\therefore$ $\sim(B \lor C) \supset (D \cdot \sim A)$

11. $\sim(A \cdot (B \lor C))$
 $D \supset B$
 $E \lor C$
 $\therefore$ $A \supset (E \cdot \sim D)$

12. $B \supset (C \cdot \sim D)$
 $(C \cdot A) \supset \sim E$
 $F \supset (D \lor E)$
 $\therefore$ $A \supset (B \supset \sim F)$

INDIRECT PROOF

The system of rules we have developed is now derivationally complete. Whenever an argument is truth-functionally valid, its conclusion is derivable using the rules we have given so far. But we will introduce one more rule because it formulates a technique often employed in showing that a conclusion follows from a set of premises.

Consider the following argument.

If he used good bait and the fish weren't smarter than he was, then he didn't go hungry. But he used good bait and he did go hungry, so the fish must have been smarter than he was.

To show that the conclusion follows, we can argue in the following way:

1. $(G \cdot \sim S) \supset \sim H$

2. G

3. H

4. Suppose $\sim S$	Suppose they weren't smarter.
5. $G \cdot \sim S$	Then he would have used good bait with fish that weren't smarter.
6. $\sim H$	So he wouldn't have gone hungry.
7. $H \cdot \sim H$	But that contradicts something we already know (premise 3).
8. Thus, S	Thus, since the assumption that they weren't smarter leads to something contradictory, that assumption must be wrong. The fish were smarter than he was.

The rule of *indirect proof* formulates the idea that if an assumption leads to a contradiction, the assumption must be wrong; its contradictory is true. We will use arrows to mark the assumption and indicate dependence on that assumption just as we did for conditional proof. So the annotated, complete derivation would look like this:

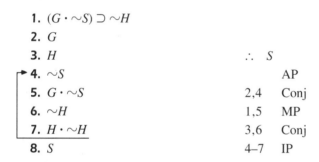

1. $(G \cdot \sim S) \supset \sim H$

2. G

3. H $\therefore$ S

4. $\sim S$ AP

5. $G \cdot \sim S$ 2,4   Conj

6. $\sim H$ 1,5   MP

7. $H \cdot \sim H$ 3,6   Conj

8. S 4–7   IP

The rule of *indirect proof* is also known as "*reductio ad absurdum*." We take an assumption and "reduce it to absurdity" by deriving an obvious contradiction. We will consider sentences of the form $q \cdot \sim q$ to be *obvious* contradictions, so our reduction to absurdity will be complete when we get such a sentence.

The rule of *indirect proof* will have two forms, presented schematically in the following ways:

We make an assumption, derive a contradiction of the form $q \cdot {\sim} q$, and then close the subderivation, concluding that the "opposite" of our original assumption must be true.

A number of examples will help to show how IP can be employed helpfully in a variety of derivations.

I.

1.	${\sim}V \supset (C \supset L)$			If the president didn't veto the bill, then if Congress passed it, it is a law.
2.	C			Congress passed it.
3.	${\sim}L$			It is not a law.
4.	${\sim}V$		AP	Suppose the president didn't veto it.
5.	$C \supset L$	1,4	MP	Then if Congress passed it, it is a law.
6.	L	2,5	MP	So it is a law (given our assumption).
7.	$L \cdot {\sim}L$	3,6	Conj	But that contradicts what we know.
8.	V	4–7	IP	So the president must have vetoed it.

II.

1.	$E \supset ({\sim}W \vee {\sim}A)$			If there is evil, then God is either unwilling or unable to prevent it.
2.	$O \supset A$			If God is omnipotent, then he is able to prevent evil.
3.	$B \supset W$			If god is beneficent, then his is willing to prevent it.
4.	$G \supset (O \cdot B)$			If God exists, he is omnipotent and beneficient.
5.	E			There is evil.
6.	G		AP	Suppose that God exists
7.	$O \cdot B$	4,6	MP	
8.	O	7	Simp	
9.	A	2,8	MP	
10.	B	7	Simp	
11.	W	3,10	MP	
12.	$W \cdot A$	9,11	Conj	
13.	$E \supset {\sim}(W \cdot A)$	1	DeM	
14.	${\sim}(W \cdot A)$	5,13	MP	
15.	$(W \cdot A) \cdot {\sim}(W \cdot A)$	12,14	Conj	That leads to contradiction.
16.	${\sim}G$	6–15	IP	So God doesn't exist.

This is a version of the famous "problem of evil." If all of the premises are true, God does not exist. (A traditional source of debate among theists is the question of which premise should be denied.)

III.	1. $\sim B \supset A$			If Beatrice is not elected, then Alice will lose her job.
	2. $C \supset (B \supset A)$			If Carol remains in power, then if Beatrice is elected, Alice will lose her job.
	3. C	$\therefore$ A		Carol will remain in power.
	4. $B \supset A$	2,3	MP	So if Beatrice is elected, then Alice will lose her job.
	5. $\sim A$		AP	Suppose Alice doesn't lose her job. What will be true?
	6. $\sim B$	4,5	MT	Beatrice wasn't elected.
	7. A	1,6	MP	So Alice will lose her job anyway.
	8. $A \cdot \sim A$	5,7	Conj	!
	9. A	5–8	IP	So Alice will lose her job.

IV.	1. $A \lor \sim B$		
	2. $B \lor \sim C$		
	3. $C \lor \sim D$	$\therefore$ $A \lor \sim D$	
	4. $\sim(A \lor \sim D)$		AP
	5. $\sim A \cdot \sim\sim D$	4	DeM
	6. $\sim A$	5	Simp
	7. $\sim B$	1,6	DS
	8. $\sim C$	2,7	DS
	9. $\sim D$	3,8	DS
	10. $\sim\sim D$	5	Simp
	11. $\sim D \cdot \sim\sim D$	9,10	Conj
	12. $A \lor \sim D$	4–11	IP

V.	1. $C \supset (\sim S \cdot \sim V)$		
	2. $\sim V \supset \sim P$	$\therefore$ $\sim(C \cdot P)$	
	3. $C \cdot P$		AP
	4. C	3	Simp
	5. $\sim S \cdot \sim V$	1,4	MP
	6. $\sim V$	5	Simp
	7. $\sim P$	2,6	MP
	8. P	3	Simp
	9. $P \cdot \sim P$	7,8	Conj
	10. $\sim(C \cdot P)$	3–9	IP

In some cases it may be useful to employ CP and IP together in a derivation:

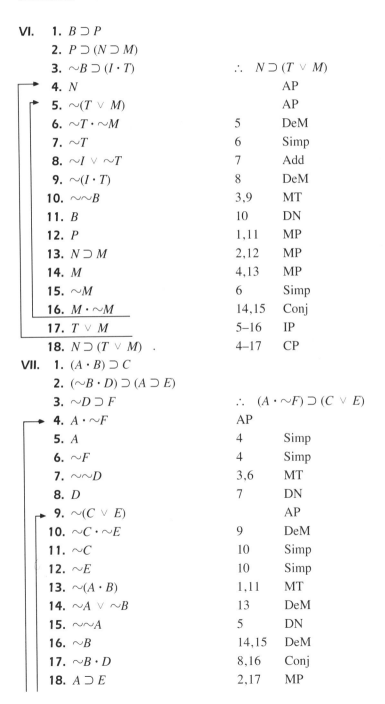

VI. **1.** $B \supset P$
  2. $P \supset (N \supset M)$
  3. $\sim B \supset (I \cdot T)$ ∴ $N \supset (T \lor M)$
  4. N AP
  5. $\sim(T \lor M)$ AP
  6. $\sim T \cdot \sim M$ 5 DeM
  7. $\sim T$ 6 Simp
  8. $\sim I \lor \sim T$ 7 Add
  9. $\sim(I \cdot T)$ 8 DeM
  10. $\sim\sim B$ 3,9 MT
  11. B 10 DN
  12. P 1,11 MP
  13. $N \supset M$ 2,12 MP
  14. M 4,13 MP
  15. $\sim M$ 6 Simp
  16. $M \cdot \sim M$ 14,15 Conj
  17. $T \lor M$ 5–16 IP
  18. $N \supset (T \lor M)$. 4–17 CP

VII. **1.** $(A \cdot B) \supset C$
  2. $(\sim B \cdot D) \supset (A \supset E)$
  3. $\sim D \supset F$ ∴ $(A \cdot \sim F) \supset (C \lor E)$
  4. $A \cdot \sim F$ AP
  5. A 4 Simp
  6. $\sim F$ 4 Simp
  7. $\sim\sim D$ 3,6 MT
  8. D 7 DN
  9. $\sim(C \lor E)$ AP
  10. $\sim C \cdot \sim E$ 9 DeM
  11. $\sim C$ 10 Simp
  12. $\sim E$ 10 Simp
  13. $\sim(A \cdot B)$ 1,11 MT
  14. $\sim A \lor \sim B$ 13 DeM
  15. $\sim\sim A$ 5 DN
  16. $\sim B$ 14,15 DeM
  17. $\sim B \cdot D$ 8,16 Conj
  18. $A \supset E$ 2,17 MP

19. E	5,18	MP
20. $E \cdot {\sim}E$	12,19	Conj
21. $C \vee E$	9–20	IP
22. $(A \cdot {\sim}F) \supset (C \vee E)$	4–21	CP

We could do without IP. Whenever we can derive a contradiction from an assumption, we can establish the negation of that assumption even without IP. Compare these:

r			r	
.			.	
.			.	
.			.	
$q \cdot {\sim}q$			$q \cdot {\sim}q$	
${\sim}r$	IP		q	Simp
			${\sim}q$	Simp
			$q \vee {\sim}r$	Add
			${\sim}r$	DS
			$r \supset {\sim}r$	CP
			${\sim}r \vee {\sim}r$	CE
			${\sim}r$	Red

Thus IP is simply a shorter way of deriving something that could be proved with the other rules.

EXERCISE 8b

Derive the conclusion from the premises. (Use IP.)

1. $A \vee C$
$C \supset D$
$D \supset A$
$\therefore \ A$

2. ${\sim}A \supset (B \vee C)$
$C \vee D$
${\sim}B \vee {\sim}D$
$\therefore \ A \vee C$

3. $A \equiv B$
$C \supset {\sim}B$
$C \supset A$
$\therefore \ {\sim}C$

4. $A \supset (D \cdot E)$
$C \vee E$
$C \supset (A \cdot {\sim}D)$
$\therefore \ E \cdot {\sim}C$

5. $A \supset (C \cdot D)$
$B \supset (E \vee {\sim}C)$
$E \supset ({\sim}A \vee {\sim}D)$
$\therefore \ {\sim}(A \cdot B)$

6. $({\sim}A \vee B) \supset C$
$A \vee {\sim}D$
$C \supset D$
$\therefore \ A$

7. $B \supset (A \cdot C)$
$(A \vee {\sim}C) \supset (B \cdot C)$
$\therefore \ A \vee C$

8. ${\sim}A \supset (B \supset C)$
$A \vee B$
$B \supset {\sim}C$
$A \supset D$
$\therefore \ A \cdot D$

PROOF BY CASES

Conditional proof and indirect proof are important proof strategies. Another important proof strategy, *argument by cases*, is not so directly embodied in our rules. Sometimes when a disjunction $p \vee q$ is available, we can prove a desired conclusion from each of the disjuncts. No matter which disjunct is true (that is, no matter which case holds), the conclusion must be true. In our system of rules, we use constructive dilemma together with the redundancy rule:

$p \vee q$
$p \supset r$
$q \supset r$
$r \vee r$ CD
r Red

The disjunction tells us that there are just two cases to consider $(p \vee q)$, and the two conditionals tell us that in each case we get the same result $(p \supset r, q \supset r)$. In a typical example in which the disjunction is available, the conditionals could be proved by conditional proof.

1. $A \supset (\sim B \cdot \sim C)$
2. $C \vee E$
3. $B \supset (E \cdot \sim D)$
4. $A \vee B$ $p \vee q$
5. A AP
6. $\sim B \cdot \sim C$ 1,5   MP
7. $\sim C$ 6   Simp
8. E 2,7   DS
9. $A \supset E$ 5–8   CP $p \supset r$
10. B AP
11. $E \cdot \sim D$ 3,10   MP
12. E 11   Simp
13. $B \supset E$ 10–12   CP $q \supset r$
14. $E \vee E$ 4,9,13   CD $r \vee r$
15. E 14   Red r

Each subderivation establishes one of the conditionals needed.

This result could be established by indirect proof also, but the derivation would be more awkward, and the derivation just given shows more clearly how the conclusion is true because it is true in each of the possible cases.

Strategy Guidelines for Constructing Derivations

1. Always look for MP, MT, DS.

2. Simplify conjunctions.

3. Prove conjunctions by Conj.

4. Use DeM on negated conjunctions or disjunctions.

5. Prove conditionals by CP (unless HS is obvious).

6. A biconditional is equivalent to a conjunction of conditionals. 2, 3, and 5 apply.

7. If you have a disjunction and you can't do DS, look for CD.

8. If you are stuck

(a) work backward from the conclusion to try to find a conditional that would be useful in deriving the conclusion, and then prove the conditional by CP.

(b) try IP. (Assume the negation of what you are trying to prove.)

(c) do a derivation "by cases." If you have some disjunction $p \vee q$ and you are trying to prove r, then establish $p \supset r$ and $q \supset r$. You can then use CD and Red to establish r.

EXERCISE 8c

Show validity by deriving the conclusion.

1. $A \supset (\sim B \vee \sim C)$
$D \supset (C \cdot E)$
$(D \vee A) \supset B$
$\therefore \quad A \supset \sim D$

2. $A \supset \sim (C \cdot D)$
$B \supset (C \vee D)$
$A \cdot B$
$\therefore \quad C \equiv \sim D$

3. $A \vee (B \cdot C)$
$C \supset \sim (A \vee D)$
$\therefore \quad (\sim B \vee D) \supset \sim C$

4. $(A \cdot B) \supset C$
$\therefore \quad (A \supset C) \vee (B \supset C)$

5. $A \supset \sim (C \cdot D)$
$\sim A \vee C$
$C \equiv D$
$\therefore \quad \sim A$

6. $A \vee (B \supset C)$
$A \supset (B \cdot D)$
$B \supset (C \vee \sim D)$
$\therefore \quad B \supset C$

7. $(\sim A \cdot B) \supset C$
$(A \cdot B) \supset D$
$(B \cdot D) \supset C$
$\therefore \quad B \supset C$

8. $(A \cdot B) \supset (C \cdot D)$
$B \supset (A \vee C)$
$(E \vee F) \supset \sim (B \cdot C)$
$C \supset (D \vee E)$
$\therefore \quad B \supset [C \cdot (D \cdot \sim E)]$

9. $B \supset C$
$B \supset D$
$(C \cdot D) \supset E$
$\therefore \quad E \vee \sim B$

10. $\sim C \supset \sim (A \vee B)$
$\sim (C \vee A) \supset B$
$\therefore \quad C$

11. $D \supset (E \cdot F)$
$D \equiv A$
$D \vee (B \cdot C)$
$\therefore \quad \sim C \supset (A \cdot F)$

12. $E \vee D$
$(D \cdot \sim A) \supset F$
$E \supset (A \vee C)$
$\therefore \quad (A \vee C) \vee F$

13. $A \supset (B \supset C)$
 $A \lor (B \cdot D)$
 $D \supset (B \supset C)$
 $\therefore \quad B \supset C$

14. $A \lor (B \cdot C)$
 $A \supset B$
 $C \supset \sim B$
 $\therefore \quad A \cdot \sim C$

15. $(C \cdot T) \supset R$
 $R \supset (S \lor L)$
 $S \supset D$
 $L \supset B$
 $\therefore \quad C \supset (\sim T \lor (D \lor B))$

16. $A \supset (B \cdot D)$
 $(G \cdot F) \supset H$
 $(B \lor D) \supset F$
 $C \supset D$
 $\therefore \quad (A \lor C) \supset (G \supset H)$

17. $B \supset (A \supset C)$
 $\sim B \supset (C \cdot D)$
 $\sim C \lor D$
 $\sim (E \cdot A)$
 $\therefore \quad A \supset ((C \cdot D) \cdot \sim E)$

18. $(A \cdot B) \supset (C \cdot E)$
 $B \supset (A \lor C)$
 $B \supset (E \lor D)$
 $E \supset \sim (C \cdot \sim D)$
 $\therefore \quad B \supset (C \cdot D)$

EXERCISE 8d

Symbolize and prove valid.

1. If the Kiwi's large egg size is an evolutionary development from a bird of similar size, then large egg size must have an adaptive value. If it is not an evolutionary development from a bird of similar size, then the Kiwi must have had some very large ancestors. So the Kiwi must have had some very large ancestors, since large egg size has no adaptive value.

2. If the flightless birds of Africa and Australia have a common ancestor, then either Africa and Australia were once much closer together or the nearest common ancestor of these birds had the ability to fly. But if they have no common ancestor or the nearest common ancestor had the ability to fly, then this is an astonishing case of convergent evolution. So either this is an astonishing case of convergent evolution, or else Africa and Australia were once much closer together.

3. Bright color in male birds must be a result of natural selection or sexual selection. If it is a result of natural selection, it must help them in adapting to their environment. If female birds are color blind, it cannot be a result of sexual selection. So if female birds are color blind, then bright color in male birds must help them in adapting to their environment.

4. If female birds are color blind, then bright color in males is not a result of sexual selection. But if it is not a result of sexual selection then if it neither camouflages them nor helps them chase away predators, then it must help in establishing territory. It can help in establishing territory only if male birds are not color blind. Bright color does not camouflage male birds, and it does not help them chase away predators. So if female birds are color blind, male birds are not color blind.

5. If female birds are color blind, then male birds are not color blind. But either both are color blind or else neither is. So female birds are not color blind.

EXERCISE 8e

Symbolize and prove valid.

1. We can reduce energy consumption by autos only if we increase the efficiency of engines or reduce the number of miles driven. We cannot reduce the number of miles driven, so we cannot reduce energy consumption by autos without increasing the efficiency of engines.

2. We will not significantly reduce energy consumption by autos unless we increase their efficiency under the most common driving conditions. To increase efficiency under the most common driving conditions, we must use an engine that is efficient at low power. Since we will have to significantly reduce energy consumption if we are to avoid economic disaster, if we are to avoid economic disaster we must use an engine that is efficient at low power.

3. If cars with high emissions are most heavily taxed, then they will become comparatively expensive. If so, people will not buy them. If people don't buy them, they will be taken off the market. Thus if cars with high emissions are most heavily taxed, they will be taken off the market.

4. If emissions controls can be made to last the life of a car, then the internal combustion engine will be the cheapest to maintain and among the lowest in emissions. If it is among the lowest in emissions, it will be the dominant engine if it is also cheap to maintain. So if emission controls can be made to last the life of the car, the internal combustion engine will be dominant.

5. If automobiles produce pollution that is costly to deal with, then if they are not to be a burden on society, they will be taxed more heavily or regulated. Regulation will be either stringent or lenient. If it is stringent, automobiles will be difficult to buy. If it is lenient, automobiles will be a burden on society anyway. Since automobiles do produce costly pollution, if they are not to be difficult to buy and they are not to be a burden on society, they must be taxed more heavily.

EXERCISE 8f

Symbolize and show valid.

1. Either they won't lower interest rates or they won't raise taxes. This is because if they lower interest rates, then there will be no federal revenue problem, and they will raise taxes only if there is a federal revenue problem. (L = Lower interest, R = Raise taxes, F = There will be a federal revenue problem)

2. If they lower taxes, then if they increase the money supply, then there will be inflation. If there is inflation, the elderly will have a rough time. Thus if they increase the money supply, the elderly will have a rough time, since they will be lowering taxes. (L = Lower taxes, M = Increase money, I = Inflation, R = Elderly have a rough time)

3. The economy is going to be in big trouble, because it cannot tolerate a drastic drop in the stock market, but there will be one. ($T=$ Economy in big trouble, $D=$ There is a drastic drop in the stock market)

4. The president will be reelected only if the economy improves. The economy will improve only if foreign nations cooperate. Thus the president will not be reelected, because foreign nations will not cooperate. ($R=$ The president is reelected, $E=$ The economy improves, $F=$ Foreign nations cooperate)

5. If inflation increases, the elderly will be in financial difficulty. If taxes increase, young adults will be in financial difficulty. If young adults and the elderly are both in financial difficulty, the president will not be reelected. Thus if the president is to be reelected, inflation must not increase or taxes must not increase. ($I=$ Inflation increases, $E=$ Elderly in difficulty, $T=$ Taxes increase, $Y=$ Young adults in difficulty, $R=$ The president is reelected)

EXERCISE 8g

Symbolize and show valid.

1. If the plasmodium parasite is found in all victims of malaria, but not in other people, then it is the source of the disease. If the plasmodium parasite is found in the anopheles mosquito and it is the source of the disease, then we should eradicate the anopheles. So we should eradicate anopheles, since plasmodium is found in all victims of malaria, in the anopheles mosquito, but not in people who do not have malaria. ($V=$ Found in all victims, $O=$ Found in others, $S=$ Is the source, $M=$ Found in anopheles, $E=$ We should eradicate anopheles)

2. Only a huge financial commitment will eradicate the mosquito if it is native to the country. Such a commitment will not be made. So we will not eradicate the mosquito if it is native. ($H=$ There is a huge financial commitment, $E=$ We eradicate the mosquito, $N=$ It is native)

3. The rivers will be full only if the monsoon rains are strong. If the rivers are not full, the mosquito will breed more readily than in recent years, and if that happens, many will die of malaria. On the other hand, if the monsoon rains are strong, there kill be extensive flood damage. So either there will be extensive flood damage or there will be many who die of malaria. ($F=$ The rivers are full, $S=$ The rains are strong, $B=$ Mosquito breeds . . ., $D=$ Many die of malaria, $E=$ There is extensive flood damage)

4. If we control the mosquito, we will use one insecticide or many. If we use just one the mosquito will become resistant, and if it becomes resistant we will lose our ability to control it. But if we use many, we don't know what effect that will have on the wildlife. So if we control the mosquito, we will have to live with uncertainty about the wildlife or with an eventual inability to control the mosquito. ($C=$ We control

the mosquito, O = We use one insecticide, M = We use many, R = The mosquito becomes resistant, L = We lose our ability to control it, K = We know what effect it has on wildlife)

APPENDIX 8A
ADDITIONAL RULES

Chapters 9–15 will employ the eight implicational rules, ten equivalences rules, CP and IP, as already developed. But there are several categories of additional valid argument forms and equivalences that one might wish to consider for inclusion in a system of inference rules. (Different instructors may select slightly different systems of inference rules.) Appendixes 8A and 8B suggest ways of doing this.

Biconditional Rules

The biconditional has a very marginal status in the system of rules developed so far. There is only one rule involving it, and that rule simply declares it to be equivalent to a conjunction of two conditionals. If we wished to give full status to the biconditional, we could introduce a number of additional rules involving it. Most obviously, we would probably want to introduce biconditional analogues of modus ponens and modus tollens.

Biconditional Inference (BI)

$p \equiv q$	$p \equiv q$	$p \equiv q$	$p \equiv q$
p	q	$\sim p$	$\sim q$
$\therefore\ q$	$\therefore\ p$	$\therefore\ \sim q$	$\therefore\ \sim p$

In addition, we might wish to add a rule analogous to hypothetical syllogism.

Biconditional Syllogism (BS)

$p \equiv q$
$q \equiv r$
$\therefore\ p \equiv r$

These five implicational inference patterns could also be supplemented by key equivalences involving biconditionals. A biconditional tells us that sentences have the same truth-value. Either both are true or both are false. This gives us an equivalence between a biconditional and a disjunction:

Biconditional Exchange (BE)

$p \equiv q \quad :: \quad (p \cdot q) \lor (\sim p \cdot \sim q)$

We also can see that a negated biconditional tells us that sentences have different truth-values.

Biconditional Negation (BN)

$$\sim(p \equiv q) \quad :: \quad p \equiv \sim q$$
$$\sim(p \equiv q) \quad :: \quad \sim p \equiv q$$

Equivalences analogous to some of those for conjunction and disjunction also obtain for the biconditional.

Biconditional Commutativity (Comm)

$$p \equiv q \quad :: \quad q \equiv p$$

Biconditional Associativity (Assoc)

$$p \equiv (q \equiv r) \quad :: \quad (p \equiv q) \equiv r$$

The existence of both of these rules implies that long strings of equivalences can be rewritten freely with elements moved around or regrouped (just as with conjunction or with disjunction). The truth-value of the long sentence will not be changed. For example, these are equivalent:

$$A \equiv ((B \equiv C) \equiv D)$$
$$(C \equiv A) \equiv (D \equiv B)$$

The equivalence can be proved using commutativity and associativity.

$A \equiv ((B \equiv C) \equiv D)$

$\qquad\qquad\qquad$ Comm

$A \equiv ((C \equiv B) \equiv D)$

$\qquad\qquad\qquad$ Assoc

$A \equiv (C \equiv (B \equiv D))$

$\qquad\qquad\qquad$ Assoc

$(A \equiv C) \equiv (B \equiv D)$

$\qquad\qquad\qquad$ Comm (twice)

$(C \equiv A) \equiv (D \equiv B)$

Avoiding Double Negation and Commutativity

To avoid double-negation steps, it is useful to recognize additional forms of key rules involving negation.

Modus Tollens +   (MT +)

$p \supset \sim q$	$\sim p \supset q$	$\sim p \supset \sim q$
q	$\sim q$	q
$\therefore \quad \sim p$	$\therefore \quad p$	$\therefore \quad p$

Disjunctive Syllogism +   (DS +)

$\sim p \lor q$
p
$\therefore\ q$

$p \lor \sim q$
q
$\therefore\ p$

DeMorgans +   (DeM +)

$\sim(\sim p \cdot \sim q)$	$::$	$p \lor q$
$\sim(p \cdot \sim q)$	$::$	$\sim p \lor q$
$\sim(\sim p \cdot q)$	$::$	$p \lor \sim q$
$\sim(\sim p \lor \sim q)$	$::$	$p \cdot q$
$\sim(p \lor \sim q)$	$::$	$\sim p \cdot q$
$\sim(\sim p \lor q)$	$::$	$p \cdot \sim q$

Conditional Exchange +   (CE +)

$\sim p \supset q$ $::$ $p \lor q$

Contraposition +   (Contra +)

$\sim p \supset q$	$::$	$\sim q \supset p$
$p \supset \sim q$	$::$	$q \supset \sim p$

These rules make it possible to avoid some double-negation steps. (Steps that many of us are inclined to avoid unofficially in any case.)

Similarly, it is attractive to add additional forms of distribution to avoid commutativity steps.

Distribution +   (Dist +)

$(p \lor q) \cdot r$	$::$	$(p \cdot r) \lor (q \cdot r)$
$(p \cdot q) \lor r$	$::$	$(p \lor r) \cdot (q \lor r)$

Other Natural Additions

There are a number of other natural candidates for our system of rules.

Pollution (Poll)

$\sim p$
$\therefore\ \sim(p \cdot q)$

$\sim p$
$\therefore\ \sim(q \cdot p)$

Destructive Dilemma (DD)

$p \supset q$
$r \supset s$
$\sim q \lor \sim s$
$\therefore\ \sim p \lor \sim r$

Convergence (Cnvrg)

$p \supset q$
$\sim p \supset q$
$\therefore\ q$

Short Dilemma (SD)

$p \supset q$
$p \vee q$
$\therefore \quad q$

Cancel and Collect (CC)

$p \vee q$
$\sim q \vee r$
$\therefore \quad p \vee r$

Contradiction (X)

$p \cdot \sim p$
$\therefore \quad q$

Excluded Middle (EM)

$\therefore \quad p \vee \sim p$

Noncontradiction (NOX)

$\therefore \quad \sim(p \cdot \sim p)$

The last three of these rules are based on the ideas that

1. $p \cdot \sim p$ is an obvious contradiction, and from a contradiction everything validly follows.
2. $p \vee \sim p$ and $\sim(p \cdot \sim p)$ are obvious tautologies, and they must always be true. (No premise is needed to justify one of those.)

A few equivalences are also attractive.

Absorption (Abs)

$p \supset q \qquad :: \qquad p \supset (p \cdot q)$

Negating a Conditional (NC)

$\sim(p \supset q) \qquad :: \qquad p \cdot \sim q$

Conditional Distribution (CDist)

$p \supset (q \vee r) \qquad :: \qquad (p \supset q) \vee (p \supset r)$
$p \supset (q \cdot r) \qquad :: \qquad (p \supset q) \cdot (p \supset r)$
$(p \vee q) \supset r \qquad :: \qquad (p \supset r) \cdot (q \supset r)$
$(p \cdot q) \supset r \qquad :: \qquad (p \supset r) \vee (q \supset r)$

EXERCISE 8h

Show that each is valid.

1. $A \equiv (B \equiv C)$
   $(A \equiv B) \equiv D$
   $\therefore \quad C \equiv D$

2. $A \equiv B$
   $C \equiv D$
   $\sim B \vee \sim D$
   $\therefore \quad \sim A \vee \sim C$

3. $A \equiv (\sim B \lor \sim C)$
$B \equiv C$
$\therefore \quad A \equiv \sim C$

4. $(A \cdot B) \supset C$
$\sim B \supset C$
$(C \cdot A) \equiv E$
$\therefore \quad A \supset E$

5. $(A \cdot B) \supset C$
$(A \cdot \sim B) \supset (D \cdot E)$
$\therefore \quad A \supset [C \lor (D \cdot E)]$

6. $[(A \cdot B) \lor C] \lor D$
$\sim D \lor E$
$\sim A$
$\therefore \quad C \lor E$

APPENDIX 8B
A SMALLER SYSTEM OF RULES

The system we have developed in Chapter 8 is derivationally complete: whenever an argument is truth-functionally valid, there is a way to derive the conclusion using our rules. So we have enough rules. In fact, there are many rules we could omit in our finished system of rules. Some of these are fairly obvious. For example, since we have the rules of modus ponens and contraposition, we do not need to have modus tollens.

Modus Tollens

$p \supset q$
$\sim q$
$\therefore \quad \sim p$

Alternative Derivation

1. $p \supset q$
2. $\sim q$
3. $\sim q \supset \sim p$ 1   Contra
4. $\sim p$ 2,3   MP

We can derive the conclusion without using modus tollens, and the derivation is reasonably short and simple. Our system would still be derivationally complete even if we omitted modus tollens from our list of derivational rules.

In fact, there are a number of reductions that could be made in the system of natural deduction rules. Here is a much smaller, but still complete, set of rules that could be used for constructing derivations.

System S

Implicational Inference Rules

MP, Add, Simp, Conj, CD

Equivalence Rules

DN, Red, Bic

Subderivation Rules

CP, IP

With System S there is some way to derive the conclusion from the premises whenever we have a truth-functionally valid argument.

A small set of rules like System S is sometimes more awkward to use. Look at the derivations for modus tollens and disjunctive syllogism, for example.

1. $p \supset q$		
2. $\sim q$		
►**3.** p		AP
4. q	1,3	MP
5. $q \cdot \sim q$	2,4	Conj
6. $\sim p$	3–5	IP

An IP would be required in order to achieve what modus tollens allows.

1. $p \vee q$		
2. $\sim p$		
►**3.** p		AP
►**4.** $\sim q$		AP
5. $p \cdot \sim p$	2,3	Conj
6. q	4–5	IP
7. $p \supset q$	3–6	CP
►**8.** q		AP
9. $q \supset q$	8–8	CP
10. $q \vee q$	1,7,9	CD
11. q	10	Red

We would require all of these steps, or something like them, in order to do what disjunctive syllogism allows. Constructive dilemma is used instead, so two conditionals leading to the conclusion must be established (by CP).

There is one advantage to such a smaller system. Since there are fewer resources, it is almost always obvious which resources *must* be used to derive a conclusion. So strategy is sometimes simpler.

If you are working *from a*

conjunction	→	then *use simplification*
disjunction	→	then *use constructive dilemma*
conditional	→	then *use modus ponens*
biconditional	→	then *use Bic*
negated statement	→	then *use IP*

If you are trying *to establish a*

conjunction	→	then *use conjunction*
disjunction	→	then *use Add or CD*
conditional	→	then *use CP*
biconditional	→	then *use BIC*
simple letter or negated statement	→	then *use IP*

If you follow these guidelines about how to use what you have and how to determine what you need, that will usually lead to a successful derivation. Use DN and Red when needed as adjuncts to your main processes.

Some derivations with System S are very long even though they are routine. Disjunctive syllogism (above) was one example. DeMorgan's equivalences are another.

1. $\sim(p \lor q)$
2. p AP
3. $p \lor q$ Add
4. $(p \lor q) \cdot \sim(p \lor q)$ Conj
5. $\sim p$ IP
6. q AP
7. $p \lor q$ Add
8. $(p \lor q) \cdot \sim(p \lor q)$ Conj
9. $\sim q$ IP
10. $\sim p \cdot \sim q$ Conj

That shows one half of the equivalence. Here is the other half:

1. $\sim p \cdot \sim q$
2. $p \lor q$ AP
3. $\sim p$ 1   Simp
4. $\sim q$ 1   Simp
5. p AP
6. $\sim q$ AP
7. $p \cdot \sim p$ 5,6   Conj
8. q 6,7   IP
9. $p \supset q$ 5–8   CP
10. q AP
11. $q \supset q$ 10–10   CP
12. $q \lor q$ 2,9,11   CD
13. q 12   Red
14. $q \cdot \sim q$ 4,13   Conj
15. $\sim(p \lor q)$ 2–14   IP

This establishes one DeMorgan's equivalence.

EXERCISE 8i

Show that the remaining rules of our full system are derivable patterns of System S. (For equivalences, do two derivations, one for each direction.)

1. Hypothetical syllogism

$p \supset q$
$q \supset r$
$\therefore \ p \supset r$

2. Commutativity

(a) $p \cdot q$ :: $q \cdot p$
(b) $p \vee q$ :: $q \vee p$

3. Associativity

(a) $p \cdot (q \cdot r)$ :: $(p \cdot q) \cdot r$
(b) $p \vee (q \vee r)$ :: $(p \vee q) \vee r$

4. Conditional exchange

$\sim p \vee q$ :: $p \supset q$

5. DeMorgan's (the other form)

$\sim(p \cdot q)$ :: $\sim p \vee \sim q$

6. Exportation

$p \supset (q \supset r)$ :: $(p \cdot q) \supset r$

7. Contraposition

$p \supset q$ :: $\sim q \supset \sim p$

8. Distribution

(a) $p \cdot (q \vee r)$ :: $(p \cdot q) \vee (p \cdot r)$
(b) $p \vee (q \cdot r)$ :: $(p \vee q) \cdot (p \vee r)$

DERIVATIONAL RULES

Implicational Rules

Modus Ponens (MP)

$p \supset q$
p
$\therefore \ q$

Modus Tollens (MT)

$p \supset q$
$\sim q$
$\therefore \ \sim p$

Simplification (Simp)

$p \cdot q$ $p \cdot q$
$\therefore \ p$ $\therefore \ q$

Conjunction (Conj)

p
q
$\therefore \ p \cdot q$

Disjunctive Syllogism (DS)

$p \vee q$ $p \vee q$
$\sim p$ $\sim q$
$\therefore \ q$ $\therefore \ p$

Hypothetical Syllogism (HS)

$p \supset q$
$q \supset r$
$\therefore \ p \supset r$

Addition (Add)

p p
∴ $p \lor q$ ∴ $q \lor p$

Constructive Dilemma (CD)

$p \supset q$
$r \supset s$
$p \lor r$
∴ $q \lor s$

Subderivation Rules

Conditional Proof (CP)

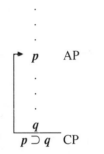

Indirect Proof (IP)

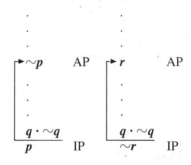

Equivalence Rules

Double Negation (DN)

p :: $\sim\sim p$

Distribution (Dist)

$p \lor (q \cdot r)$ :: $(p \lor q) \cdot (p \lor r)$
$p \cdot (q \lor r)$ :: $(p \cdot q) \lor (p \cdot r)$

Commutativity (Comm)

$p \cdot q$ :: $q \cdot p$
$p \lor q$ :: $q \lor p$

Conditional Exchange (CE)

$p \supset q$ :: $\sim p \lor q$

Associativity (Assoc)

$p \cdot (q \cdot r)$ :: $(p \cdot q) \cdot r$
$p \lor (q \lor r)$ :: $(p \lor q) \lor r$

Contrapostion (Contra)

$p \supset q$ :: $\sim q \supset \sim p$

DeMorgan's Theorems (DeM)

$\sim(p \lor q)$ :: $\sim p \cdot \sim q$
$\sim(p \cdot q)$ :: $\sim p \lor \sim q$

Exportation (Exp)

$(p \cdot q) \supset r$ :: $p \supset (q \supset r)$

Redundancy (Red)

p :: $p \lor p$
p :: $p \cdot p$

Biconditional (Bic)

$p \equiv q$ :: $(p \supset q) \cdot (q \supset p)$

9

DERIVATIONS AND EXAMPLES

In Chapters 6–8 we have concentrated on just one thing: *showing* the *validity* of arguments by deriving the conclusion from the premises. We have said nothing new about *showing invalidity* of argument forms. In addition, we have not considered the other logical concepts introduced in Chapters 1–5:

Inconsistency and consistency of *sets of sentences*.

Equivalence and nonequivalence of *pairs of sentences*.

Logical truth, contradictoriness, and contingency of *sentences*.

In this chapter we examine methods for showing invalidity. After doing so, we demonstrate how the methods employed in showing validity and invalidity of argument forms can also be employed to show that these other concepts apply to sets of sentences, to pairs of sentences, or to single sentences.

SHOWING INVALIDITY

In Chapter 3, we showed invalidity by writing truth-tables, and in Chapter 4 we showed invalidity by finding model paths in truth-trees. But neither a complete truth-table nor a complete truth-tree for an argument form needs to be presented in order to show invalidity. An argument form is invalid if there is at least one assignment of truth-values that would make some argument of that form have true premises and a false conclusion. We need just one example to show invalidity. We need only one row of the truth-table or one path in a truth-tree: one case in which the premises are true and the conclusion is false.

$p \supset q$

$r \supset q$

q

$\therefore \quad p \vee r$

	P_3		P_1	P_2	C
p	q	r	$p \supset q$	$r \supset q$	$p \vee r$
T	T	T	T	T	T
T	T	F	T	T	T
T	F	T	F	F	T
T	F	F	F	T	T
F	T	T	T	T	T
F	T	F	T	T	F
F	F	T	T	F	T
F	F	F	T	T	F

Having produced a truth-table, we can inspect it row by row to see if there is some row on which the premises are true and the conclusion false. On the *sixth row* all three premises are true and the conclusion is false. Thus we know that this is *not* a deductively valid argument form.

But we can avoid the tedious procedure of writing truth-tables in most cases. In the example, there is just one way for the conclusion to be false: p and r must both be false. And since q is one of the premises, q must be true if the premises are all to be true. This assignment

$p : \mathbf{F}$

$q : \mathbf{T}$

$r : \mathbf{F}$

can then be checked. It makes the premises true and the conclusion false. Thus we can see that the argument form is invalid without writing and checking through a complete truth-table. Only this one row of the table needs to be examined.

If we are trying to *show* invalidity, especially to convince someone else of the invalidity of an argument form, it is much simpler and more effective to present just one example that shows clearly and briefly that the argument form is not valid. Such an example is called a *counterexample* to the argument form (or a counterexample to the claim that the argument form is valid). Skill in uncovering the logically relevant features of an argument, presenting those as a general form of argument, and then constructing a counterexample to that argument form are all required to show invalidity.

English Counterexamples

The counterexample we gave was simply a truth-assignment (i.e., a model) that would make an argument of that form have true premises and a false conclusion. We can also illustrate with a more concrete example.

If Edward Kennedy is from Connecticut, then he is from New England.

If Edward Kennedy is from Maine, then he is from New England.

Edward Kennedy is from New England.

∴   Edward Kennedy is from Connecticut or from Maine.

Here it is clear that it is possible for the premises to be true and the conclusion false. It is especially clear because, for those of us who know a little bit about Edward Kennedy, it is clear that the premises *are* true and the conclusion *is* false.

An English example like the one just given is a very effective counterexample to an argument form. It makes it clear that some examples of arguments of that form are not valid, because it is an argument of that form and it is obviously invalid.

Often there is more than one truth-assignment that will make the premises true and the conclusion false. But to show invalidity it is sufficient to give just one of those assignments.

$p \supset (q \vee r)$

$\sim p$

∴ $\sim q \cdot \sim r$

When p is replaced by a false sentence and q is replaced by a true sentence, the premises are true and the conclusion is false. (It does not matter what truth-value r has.) In fact, there are three invalidating assignments:

$p:$ F	$p:$ F	$p:$ F
$q:$ T	$q:$ T	$q:$ F
$r:$ T	$r:$ F	$r:$ T

Any one of these serves as a counterexample to the argument form.

We could also construct a natural language counterexample.

If John lives off campus, he is either a junior or a senior.

John does not live off campus.

∴   John is not a junior and he is not a senior.

In this example, it should be fairly clear that it is *possible* for the premises to be true and the conclusion false (if John is a junior who lives on campus, for example). But it may be even clearer to give a more obvious example, one with evidently true premises and an evidently false conclusion.

If Cuomo is a U.S. Senator, then he is either a Republican or a Democrat.

Cuomo is not a U.S. Senator.

∴   Cuomo is not a Republican and Cuomo is not a Democrat.

It will become important (even essential) later to give English counterexamples to argument forms. But for now, truth-assignments making the premises true and the conclusion false will do just as well. Such truth-assignments schematically characterize a range of possible situations in which instances of the argument form could have true premises and a false conclusion.

EXERCISE 9a

Each of these argument forms is invalid. (a) Show that it is invalid by giving a truth-assignment that would make the premises true and the conclusion false. (b) Show invalidity by giving a natural language counterexample: an argument of that form with clearly true premises and a clearly false conclusion.

1. $p \lor q$
p
$\therefore \ \sim q$

2. $p \supset q$
q
$\therefore \ p$

3. $p \supset q$
$\sim p$
$\therefore \ \sim q$

4. $p \supset q$
$r \supset s$
$q \lor s$
$\therefore \ p \lor r$

5. $\sim(p \cdot q)$
$\sim p$
$\therefore \ q$

6. $p \supset (q \lor s)$
$s \cdot \sim p$
$\therefore \ \sim q$

EXERCISE 9b

These arguments are invalid. Show that each is invalid by indicating its logical form with as much detail as possible and showing that the logical form is not a valid form.

1. If Al has his glasses on now, he can see me. He doesn't have his glasses on. So he can't see me now.

2. Either Al or Bill bought me a copy of the chemistry text. Al bought me a copy. So Bill did not buy me a copy of the chemistry text.

3. If every sick person has eaten pickles, then pickles are bad for your health. Pickles are bad for your health. Thus every sick person must have eaten them.

4. You are permitted in only if you have a ticket. Thus, if you have a ticket, then you may go in.

5. If the earth were spherical, it would cast curved shadows on the moon. It casts curved shadows on the moon. So it must be spherical.

6. If John were a junior or a senior, he would get special parking privileges. He is not a junior and he is not a senior. Thus he does not get special parking privileges.

7. If Al were in class, then either he or Bill would bring me the notes. Bill brought me the notes. So Al was in class.

8. Flooding won't occur unless we get a heavy rainfall this spring. Thus if we get a heavy rainfall this spring, flooding will occur.

9. Flooding would occur only if we had a heavy rainfall and quick melting of the snow. Flooding did not occur. Thus we didn't have a heavy rainfall with a quick melting of the snow.

10. If Bill or Charlie enters the race, then someone from our school will win it unless the other team cheats. But neither Bill nor Charlie will enter, and the other team will cheat. Thus we won't have a winner from our school.

EXERCISE 9c

For each argument form, indicate whether it is valid or invalid. If it is valid, derive the conclusion from the premises. If it is invalid, show that it is invalid by giving a counterexample (a truth-assignment or an English argument that shows the argument form to be invalid).

1. $p \supset (q \cdot s)$
$\sim(q \lor s)$
$\therefore \quad \sim p$

2. $p \supset (q \supset r)$
$\sim q$
$\therefore \quad p \supset \sim r$

3. $(p \cdot q) \supset (r \lor s)$
$\sim r$
$\therefore \quad \sim p$

4. $(p \lor q) \supset (r \cdot s)$
$\sim r$
$\therefore \quad \sim p$

5. $(p \lor r) \lor s$
$\sim r \cdot (q \supset \sim s)$
$\therefore \quad p \lor q$

6. $(p \cdot r) \lor s$
$\sim r \cdot (q \supset \sim s)$
$\therefore \quad \sim q$

7. $p \lor (r \cdot \sim s)$
$r \supset q$
$p \supset q$
$\therefore \quad q$

8. $p \lor (r \cdot \sim s)$
$q \supset (r \cdot \sim s)$
$q \supset p$
$\therefore \quad \sim q$

EXERCISE 9d

For each of these arguments, indicate whether it is valid or invalid. If it is valid, derive its conclusion. If it is not, show invalidity by indicating its logical form in as much detail as possible and showing that its logical form is not valid.

1. Billy can't see without his glasses. Billy doesn't have his glasses. Therefore, Billy can't see.

2. Billy can see only if he has his glasses. Billy has his glasses. Therefore, Billy can see.

3. Billy can see unless he doesn't have his glasses. Billy doesn't have his glasses. Therefore, he can see.

4. Al will win only if he trains hard and sleeps well. He is not training hard. Therefore, he won't win.

5. Al and Bill did not both win the prize. But Al won, so Bill must not have won.

6. If the professor were wise, then Al and Bill wouldn't both get A's. Al is getting an A but Bill isn't. Thus the professor is wise.

INCONSISTENCY AND CONSISTENCY

If a set of sentences is inconsistent, the sentences in the set cannot all be true. We can make this evident by deriving an explicit and obvious contradiction.

1. $A \cdot {\sim}B$			
2. $A \supset (B \vee C)$			
3. ${\sim}C$			
4. A		1	Simp
5. $B \vee C$		2,4	MP
6. B		3,5	DS
7. ${\sim}B$		1	Simp
8. $B \cdot {\sim}B$		6,7	Conj

From our initial set of sentences (1–3) an obvious contradiction (of the form $q \cdot {\sim}q$) has been derived. If a contradiction follows validly from a set of sentences, those sentences cannot all be true. (A contradiction is false in every possible situation. If it validly follows from the set, there cannot be any possible situation in which all sentences in the set are true.)

By deriving an obvious contradiction we make the inconsistent character of the original set obvious. Thus our system of derivational rules enables us to show inconsistency of sets of sentences.

1. ${\sim}A \supset (C \vee D)$			
2. $C \supset D$		Initial set	
3. ${\sim}(D \vee A)$			
4. ${\sim}D \cdot {\sim}A$		3	DeM
5. ${\sim}D$		4	Simp
6. ${\sim}A$		4	Simp
7. $C \vee D$		1,6	MP
8. C		5,7	DS
9. D		2,8	MP
10. $D \cdot {\sim}D$		5,9	Conj

To say that an argument form is *valid* tells us something about all possible situations. In every possible situation, if the premises are true, the conclusion is true. Similarly, to say that a set of sentences is *inconsistent* says something about all possible situations. In every possible situation, at least one sentence in the set is false.

Derivational Rules can be adapted whenever we want to show something about every possible situation. We use them to *show validity* by deriving the conclusion of the argument from the premises. We use them to *show inconsistency* of a set by deriving a contradiction from that set.

Showing Consistency

When we wish to show the *invalidity* of an argument form or the *consistency* of a form for a set of sentences, we are in a different situation.

To say that an argument form is *invalid* says something about the existence of a certain kind of possible situation—a situation in which an argument of that form has true premises and a false conclusion. It is not an assertion about all possible situations (as a claim of validity is). To show invalidity, we construct an example rather than giving a derivation.

Similarly, a claim of *consistency* is merely the claim that in *some* possible situation every member of the set is true. It is not a claim about all possible situations. To show consistency we give an example—either a truth-assignment or a concrete example of a set of true sentences of the consistent form.

Either Al or Bill will miss class.

If Al misses, then Charlie will go.

Charlie will go if Bill misses.

$A \lor B$

$A \supset C$

$B \supset C$

We can write the logical form, representing all of the sentential connectives that appear, in the following way:

$p \lor q$

$p \supset r$

$q \supset r$

There are several combinations of truth-values that will make all members a set of this form true.

$p : \text{T}$	$p : \text{F}$	$p : \text{T}$
$q : \text{T}$	$q : \text{T}$	$q : \text{F}$
$r : \text{T}$	$r : \text{T}$	$r : \text{T}$

Any one of those is sufficient to show consistency of that form for a set of sentences. An example in natural language can also be used.

> Kennedy is from either Connecticut or Massachusetts.
> If Kennedy is from Connecticut, then he is from New England.
> Kennedy is from New England if he is from Massachusetts.

Since all of these are true, we know that it is possible for a set of sentences of the given form to be true.

Arguments and Sets of Sentences: An Important Relationship

There is an important relationship between validity and inconsistency and a correlative relationship between invalidity and consistency. The following is an inconsistent set of sentences:

A	Al is trustworthy.
$A \supset \sim B$	If Al is trustworthy, then he is not taking books from my shelf.
B	Al is taking books from my shelf.

Whenever a set of sentences is inconsistent, several valid arguments can be constructed on the basis of it.

A	A	$A \supset \sim B$
$A \supset \sim B$	B	B
$\therefore \quad \sim B$	$\therefore \quad \sim(A \supset \sim B)$	$\therefore \quad \sim A$

Each of these arguments is constructed in the following way:

1. All but one of the members of the original (inconsistent) set are taken as premises.
2. The remaining member of the original set is negated, and that negated sentence is the conclusion of the argument.

Thus for each member *p* of an inconsistent set, there is an argument which has all of the rest of the members of that set as premises and which takes $\sim p$ as conclusion. When we start with an inconsistent set, the argument constructed in this way is always valid.

It is easy to see why the argument must be valid. Let

S_1

S_2

S_3

.

.

.

S_n

stand for an inconsistent set. If there is no way for all of those sentences (S_1, $S_2, \ldots, S_n$) to be true, then

If $S_2, S_3, \ldots, S_n$ are all true, S_1 must be false; so $\sim S_1$ is true.
If $S_1, S_3, \ldots, S_n$ are all true, then S_2 must be false; so $\sim S_2$ is true.

.

.

.

If $S_1, S_2, S_3, \ldots, S_{n-1}$ are all true, then S_n must be false; so $\sim S_n$ is true.

Thus we have *n* valid arguments constructed on the basis of the set $S_1, \ldots S_n$. We can also look at this the other way around. If an argument

P_1
P_2

.

.

.

P_k
$\therefore$ C

is valid, then there is a related set of sentences that is *inconsistent*:

P_1
P_2

.

.

.

P_k
$\sim C$

These statements must all have the same truth-value.

1. *The argument ($P_1, \ldots, P_k \therefore$ C) is valid.*
2. There is no way for $P_1, \ldots, P_k$ to be true and C false.

3. There is no way for $P_1, \ldots, P_k$ to be true and $\sim C$ true.
4. There is no way for $P_1, \ldots, P_k, \sim C$ all to be true.
5. *The set* $\{P_1, \ldots, P_k, \sim C\}$ *is inconsistent.*

Thus if I have an argument that is valid

$W \vee T$	I'll walk to school or take my lunch.
$\sim W$	I won't walk to school.
$\therefore \quad T$	$\therefore$ I'll take my lunch.

There is a related inconsistent set.

$W \vee T$	I'll walk to school or take my lunch.
$\sim W$	I won't walk to school.
$\sim T$	I won't take my lunch.

In general, an argument, $P_1, P_2, \ldots, P_k \therefore \quad C$, is valid if and only if the related set of sentences $\{P_1, P_2, \ldots, P_k, \sim C\}$ is inconsistent. (This provides another way of seeing why the rule of indirect proof is sound. We can show that the argument, $P_1, P_2, \ldots, P_k \therefore \quad C$, is valid by showing that the set, $\{P_1, P_2, \ldots, P_k, \sim C\}$, is inconsistent.)

EXERCISE 9e

Show that these sets of sentences are inconsistent.

1. $A \supset C$
$A \vee C$
$\sim C$

2. $A \cdot \sim B$
$A \supset C$
$C \supset (B \vee \sim A)$

3. $A \supset (B \cdot C)$
$B \supset (D \vee \sim A)$
$C \supset (B \cdot \sim D)$
A

4. $A \vee B$
$A \supset C$
$(A \cdot C) \supset B$
$B \supset (A \cdot \sim C)$

5. $A \equiv B$
$B \equiv C$
$C \cdot \sim A$

6. $A \vee (C \cdot B)$
$\sim B$
$A \supset (B \cdot \sim D)$

7. $A \supset (\sim B \supset D)$
$A \cdot (D \supset C)$
$\sim (B \vee C)$

8. $(A \vee C) \supset (B \supset D)$
$E \supset (A \cdot B)$
$F \supset (B \cdot C)$
$(E \cdot \sim D) \vee (F \cdot \sim D)$

9. $S \supset \sim F$
$\sim (S \vee C) \supset T$
$\sim (T \cdot M)$
$\sim C$
$F \cdot M$

10. $\sim (B \equiv C) \supset A$
$D \supset \sim A$
$A \supset (D \cdot C)$
$B \equiv \sim C$

EXERCISE 9f

Prove that these are *inconsistent* sets of sentences.

1. The extinction of the dinosaurs was gradual (taking place over a period of 2 million years).

   If the extinction has been caused by an extraterrestrial impact, it would not have been gradual.

   If there are abnormally high amounts of iridium in the sediments from the period of extinction, then the extinction was caused by an extraterrestrial impact.

   There are abnormally high amounts of iridium in the sediment from the period of extinction.

2. The Ice Age extinction of shallow-water animals was caused by the lowering of sea levels.

   If the Ice Age extinction had been caused by the lowering of sea levels, then it would have been worldwide and all similar periods of lowering would have been accompanied by mass extinctions.

   But the Ice Age extinction of shallow-water animals was not worldwide.

   Not all similar periods of sea-level lowering were accompanied by mass extinctions.

3. She'll either resign her position without a fight or be removed against her will.

   If she resigns without a fight, she will be admitting guilt.

   If she is removed against her will, she will be humiliated.

   She won't admit guilt or be humiliated.

4. If our candidate can't get a huge turnout of black voters, then she won't win any southern states.

   If she supports affirmative action quotas, she will lose support among blue-collar workers.

   If she loses any blue-collar support, she'll lose the election.

   She will lose the election if she doesn't win any southern states.

   She won't get a huge turnout of black voters without Jesse Jackson's vigorous support.

   Jackson won't support her vigorously unless she supports affirmative action quotas.

   Our candidate will win.

EXERCISE 9g

Show that each form for a set of sentences is consistent (i.e., that for some set of sentences of the given form, all members of the set are true).

1. $p \cdot \sim q$
   $q \supset r$
   $(p \cdot r) \supset s$
   $\sim s$

2. $p \vee (q \vee r)$
   $\sim p \supset (\sim q \supset r)$
   $\sim (p \vee r)$

3. $p \supset (q \vee r)$
   $q \supset s$
   $r \supset s$
   $\sim s$

4. $p \supset q$
   $p \supset \sim q$
   $p \vee q$

5. $(p \vee q) \supset r$
   $q \supset \sim r$
   $\sim p$

6. $p \equiv \sim q$
   $q \vee (s \cdot r)$
   $\sim s$

7. $p \supset (q \cdot r)$
   $q \cdot \sim r$
   $p \vee q$

8. $(p \vee q) \supset r$
   $r \cdot \sim p$

9. $(p \cdot q) \vee r$
   $q \cdot (p \vee r)$

10. $(p \vee r) \supset s$
    $(s \cdot r) \supset q$
    $p \vee \sim q$

EXERCISE 9h

For each of the following forms for a set of sentences, either (A) show inconsistency by deriving a contradiction or (B) show consistency by giving an assignment of truth-values that would make all members of the set true.

1. $p \supset q$
   $q \supset (s \cdot r)$
   $\sim (p \cdot r)$

2. $p \equiv q$
   $q \vee s$
   $\sim (s \cdot p)$

3. $p \supset q$
   $r \supset q$
   $\sim p \supset r$
   $\sim q$

4. $p \equiv (q \cdot s)$
   $(s \cdot t) \supset r$
   $(p \cdot t) \cdot \sim r$

5. $p \supset (q \vee r)$
   $(q \cdot s) \supset t$
   $p \cdot \sim (r \cdot t)$

EQUIVALENCE AND INEQUIVALENCE

Equivalence

Two sentences are *equivalent* to each other if they have *the same truth-value in all possible situations*. We saw earlier that we could determine whether sentences are equivalent by writing a truth-table or a truth-tree. But we should now consider how to apply our derivational techniques so that we can avoid writing a whole truth-table to show equivalence.

If we wish to *show* that two sentences, for example

$$p \supset q \qquad p \supset (p \cdot q)$$

are equivalent, we can derive each from the other. This will show that they are equivalent: whenever the first is true, the second must also be true, and whenever the second is true, the first must also be true. Thus they must always match in truth-value.

1. $p \supset q$		
2. p		AP
3. q	1,2	MP
4. $p \cdot q$	2,3	Conj
5. $p \supset (p \cdot q)$	2–4	CP

1. $p \supset (p \cdot q)$		
2. p		AP
3. $p \cdot q$	1,2	MP
4. q	3	Simp
5. $p \supset q$	2–4	CP

The fact that we can do these two derivations, deriving each sentence from the other, shows that the sentences are equivalent. It is impossible for one to be true with the other false; they must always have the same truth-value.

Sometimes a condensation of this procedure is possible. Consider these two derivations to show equivalence:

1. $\sim(p \supset q)$		
2. $\sim(\sim p \vee q)$	1	CE
3. $\sim\sim p \cdot \sim q$	2	DeM
4. $p \cdot \sim q$	3	DN

1. $p \cdot \sim q$		
2. $\sim\sim p \cdot \sim q$	1	DN
3. $\sim(\sim p \vee q)$	2	DeM
4. $\sim(p \supset q)$	3	CE

These two derivations involve only equivalence rules, and they are just the same, except that each is an upside-down version of the other. Rather than write out both derivations, we can abbreviate by writing the equivalence rule *between* the two steps that it links. If only equivalence rules are employed, we will then know that the derivation can go in both directions.

$\sim(p \supset q)$

CE

$\sim(\sim p \vee q)$

DeM

$\sim\sim p \cdot \sim q$

DN

$p \cdot \sim q$

The abbreviation of the rule name is placed to indicate that the formulas above and below it are equivalent in virtue of the application of that rule. This summarizes the *two* derivations we gave before.

This condensation will often work, but it will not always work. Sometimes there is no way to prove an equivalence using only equivalence rules, so two separate derivations are needed. [The condensation would not have worked in the first example we considered, $(p \supset q) \quad :: \quad (p \supset (p \cdot q))$.]

EXERCISE 9i

Show that these pairs are *equivalent*.

1. $p \supset (q \cdot r)$ $(p \supset q) \cdot (p \supset r)$

2. $(p \vee q) \supset r$ $(p \supset r) \cdot (q \supset r)$

3. $(p \cdot q) \supset r$ $(p \supset r) \vee (q \supset r)$

4. $\sim(p \equiv q)$ $p \equiv \sim q$

5. $p \equiv (q \equiv r)$ $(p \equiv q) \equiv r$

6. $p \equiv q$ $q \equiv p$

7. $(p \vee q) \supset q$ $p \supset q$

8. $(p \vee q) \cdot \sim(s \vee r)$ $[(p \cdot \sim r) \vee (q \cdot \sim r)] \cdot \sim s$

9. $p \vee q$ $p \vee (q \cdot \sim p)$

10. $(p \cdot q) \supset (r \vee s)$ $(p \cdot \sim r) \supset \sim(q \cdot \sim s)$

11. $p \supset (\sim q \supset r)$ $q \supset (\sim p \supset r)$

12. $(p \vee q) \supset (r \cdot q)$ $(p \supset (r \cdot q)) \cdot (q \supset r)$

Inequivalence

To show that two sentence forms are *not equivalent*, we must show that there is some way for corresponding sentences of those forms to have different truth-values. We must *give an example* to show that this is possible. The example could be a truth-assignment that produces different truth-values for the sentences. Thus to show that

$$p \supset q \qquad p \vee q$$

are not equivalent, we can give one of these two truth-assignments:

$$p : T \qquad p : F$$
$$q : F \qquad q : F$$

The first assignment ($p : T$, $q : F$) makes $p \supset q$ false and $p \vee q$ true. The second ($p : F$, $q : F$) makes $p \supset q$ true and $p \vee q$ false. In both cases, corresponding sentences of those forms would differ in truth-value. Just giving one of those assignments is sufficient to indicate that the sentence forms are not equivalent.

We can also show inequivalence by giving English examples of sentences of the indicated form that differ in truth-value.

If Edward Kennedy is president, then he is commander-in-chief of the military.
Either Edward Kennedy is president or he is commander-in-chief of the military.

Clearly, these are not equivalent.

To show inequivalence we must find a truth-value assignment that falsifies one while making the other true. This might work in only one direction. For example:

$$p \cdot q \qquad\qquad\qquad p \vee q$$

We could not make $p \cdot q$ true while making $p \vee q$ false. If $p \cdot q$ is true, then p and q are both true, so $p \vee q$ must also be true. The form $p \vee q$ is deducible from $p \cdot q$, but not the other way around. To show that they can differ in truth-value, we must present a truth-assignment that makes $p \vee q$ true with $p \cdot q$ false. One of the following assignments would show inequivalence:

$$p : \mathbf{F} \qquad p : \mathbf{T}$$

$$q : \mathbf{T} \qquad q : \mathbf{F}$$

We can summarize our discussion so far with the following table:

	Shown by Derivation	Shown by Example
Argument	*Valid:* Conclusion is *derivable* from premises.	*Invalid:* Example with *premises true, conclusion false.*
Set of sentences	*Inconsistent:* An obvious *contradiction* $(q \cdot \sim q)$ is *derivable*.	*Consistent:* Example with *all* sentences in the set *true*.
Pair of sentences	*Equivalent: Each is derivable from the other.*	*Inequivalent:* Example in which the two sentences *differ* in *truth-value*.

EXERCISE 9j

Show that these pairs are *not equivalent*.

1. $p \supset q$		$q \supset p$
2. $p \supset (q \supset r)$		$(p \supset q) \supset r$
3. $\sim(p \supset q)$		$\sim p \supset q$
4. $\sim(p \supset q)$		$p \supset \sim q$
5. $p \vee q$		$\sim q \vee \sim p$
6. $(p \cdot q) \supset r$		$(p \supset r) \cdot (q \supset r)$
7. $(p \vee q) \supset r$		$(p \supset r) \vee (q \supset r)$
8. $p \vee q$		$[(p \cdot r) \vee (q \cdot r)] \vee \sim r$

EXERCISE 9k

For each of these pairs, show that the sentence forms are *equivalent* or show that they are *not equivalent*.

1. $p \supset (q \lor r)$ $(p \supset q) \lor (p \supset r)$

2. $\sim p \equiv q$ $\sim(p \equiv q)$

3. $(\sim p \cdot r) \equiv q$ $\sim(p \cdot r) \equiv q$

4. $(p \supset q) \lor r$ $p \supset (q \lor r)$

5. $p \cdot (q \lor \sim r)$ $(r \supset (q \cdot p)) \cdot p$

6. $p \lor \sim(q \lor r)$ $(q \supset p) \cdot (r \supset p)$

7. $p \cdot (q \lor (r \cdot p))$ $(p \cdot q) \lor (r \cdot p)$

8. $p \supset (p \lor r)$ $q \lor \sim q$

TAUTOLOGOUS, CONTRADICTORY, OR CONTINGENT

The remaining family of logical concepts are those that apply to single sentences or sentence forms. A form for a single sentence will fall under one of these classifications:

1. *logically true (tautologous): Every assignment* of truth-values makes sentences of that form *true*.

2. *contradictory: Every assignment* of truth-values makes sentences of that form *false*.

3. *contingent: At least one assignment* makes some sentences of that form *true*, and *at least one assignment* makes some sentences of that form *false*.

Since the first two concepts involve showing something about *every assignment* of truth-values, we should expect to be able to employ derivational methods in place of truth-table methods to show that the concepts apply.

Proving Tautologies

Any argument with a tautologous conclusion is valid. A tautology does not really need premises to support it. Its truth is inevitable because of its logical form.

This way of viewing the matter—a tautology stands on its own without the need of premises to support it—provides a basis for establishing tautologies using our system of derivational rules. If a sentence can be derived without there being any premises to serve as the basis of the derivation, the sentence must be a tautology.

With the rules of conditional proof and indirect proof, we have a way of beginning derivations even when there are no premises. For example, we can show that $p \supset (p \lor q)$ is tautologous by the following derivation:

1. p			AP
2. $p \lor q$		1	Add
3. $p \supset (p \lor q)$		1,2	CP

The sentence form $p \supset (p \lor q)$ has been established by our rules without there being any premises from which it is derived. Since it can be established in this way, it is a tautology. Anything derivable from an empty set of premises is tautologous.

Instead of saying that a tautology is "derived" by our rules, it seems better to say that it is *established* or *proved* using the rules alone. There is nothing it is derived *from*.

We will always start out a proof of a tautology with an AP step. Either conditional proof or indirect proof must be employed in the proof. In general, we should expect to be able to use conditional proof to establish conditionals and things equivalent to conditionals, and we should use indirect proof when no strategy employing conditional proof is evident.

Examples

I. $[p \cdot ((p \lor q) \supset r)] \supset (p \cdot r)$

1. $p \cdot ((p \lor q) \supset r)$			AP
2. p			Simp
3. $(p \lor q) \supset r$			Simp
4. $p \lor q$		2	Add
5. r		3,4	MP
6. $p \cdot r$		2,5	Conj
7. $[p \cdot ((p \lor q) \supset r)] \supset (p \cdot r)$		1–6	CP

II. $p \lor {\sim}p$

${\sim}(p \lor {\sim}p)$	AP
${\sim}p \cdot {\sim}{\sim}p$	DeM
$p \lor {\sim}p$	IP

III. $[p \cdot ({\sim}p \lor q)] \supset (p \cdot q)$

$p \cdot ({\sim}p \lor q)$	AP
p	Simp
${\sim}p \lor q$	Simp
${\sim}{\sim}p$	DN
q	DS
$p \cdot q$	Conj
$[p \cdot ({\sim}p \lor q)] \supset (p \cdot q)$	CP

IV. $(p \supset q) \supset ((p \lor q) \supset q)$

1. $p \supset q$		AP
2. $p \lor q$		AP
3. $\sim\sim p \lor q$	2	DN
4. $\sim p \supset q$	3	CE
5. $\sim q \supset \sim p$	1	Contra
6. $\sim q \supset q$	4,5	HS
7. $\sim\sim q \lor q$	6	CE
8. $q \lor q$	7	DN
9. q	8	Red
10. $(p \lor q) \supset q$	2-9	CP
11. $(p \supset q) \supset ((p \lor q) \supset q)$	1-10	CP

V. $[(p \cdot q) \lor (p \cdot \sim q)] \lor \sim p$

p	AP
$\sim(q \lor \sim q)$	AP
$\sim q \cdot \sim\sim q$	DeM
$q \lor \sim q$	IP
$p \cdot (q \lor \sim q)$	Conj
$(p \cdot q) \lor (p \cdot \sim q)$	Dist
$p \supset [(p \cdot q) \lor (p \cdot \sim q)]$	CP
$\sim p \lor [(p \cdot q) \lor (p \cdot \sim q)]$	CE
$[(p \cdot q) \lor (p \cdot \sim q)] \lor \sim p$	Comm

VI. $p \supset (q \supset p)$

1. p		AP
2. q		AP
3. $p \lor p$	1	Red
4. p	3	Red
5. $q \supset p$	2-4	CP
6. $p \supset (q \supset p)$	1-5	CP

EXERCISE 91

Show that these are tautologous.

1. $(p \cdot \sim(p \cdot q)) \supset \sim q$
2. $\sim(p \cdot \sim(p \lor q))$
3. $(p \lor q) \supset ((p \supset q) \supset q)$
4. $(p \cdot (\sim p \lor q)) \supset [(q \supset r) \supset (p \supset (q \cdot r))]$
5. $(p \supset q) \supset [(q \supset r) \supset (p \supset (p \cdot r))]$
6. $(p \equiv q) \supset ((p \lor r) \equiv (q \lor r))$
7. $(p \equiv q) \supset ((p \supset r) \equiv (q \supset r))$
8. $p \supset ((q \cdot p) \equiv q)$

9. $p \supset ((p \supset q) \equiv q)$

10. $(p \equiv q) \equiv ((p \cdot q) \vee (\sim p \cdot \sim q))$

11. $((p \equiv q) \equiv q) \equiv p$

12. $((p \supset q) \cdot (q \supset r)) \vee (r \supset p)$

13. $r \supset (p \vee \sim(q \cdot p))$

14. $(p \cdot \sim p) \supset q$

15. $(p \supset q) \vee (q \supset r)$

Establishing Contradictoriness

A contradiction is false under every truth-value assignment. To show that a sentence is contradictory, we can use the technique that we use to show that a set of sentences is inconsistent. We derive an obvious contradiction—something of the form $q \cdot \sim q$. (A contradictory sentence is, by itself, sufficient to constitute an inconsistent set of sentence.) By showing that something of the form $q \cdot \sim q$ is derivable, we make the contradictory character of the sentence obvious.

1. $[(p \vee q) \cdot (q \supset p)] \cdot \sim p$			
2. $\sim p$		1	Simp
3. $(p \vee q) \cdot (q \supset p)$		1	Simp
4. $p \vee q$		3	Simp
5. $q \supset p$		3	Simp
6. q		2,4	DS
7. p		5,6	MP
8. $p \cdot \sim p$		2,7	Conj

Since $p \cdot \sim p$ is derivable, the original sentence ($[(p \vee q) \cdot (p \supset q)] \cdot \sim q$) is contradictory.

This leaves us one question. How can we show that sentences of the form $q \cdot \sim q$ are contradictory? We cannot do it by deriving something of the form $q \cdot \sim q$, since that just leaves us where we started. Instead, we should say that this is a contradiction that is *already obvious*. The use of our full system of derivational rules, with indirect proof, depends upon our accepting this as a ground-level, obvious contradiction. We do not use our rules to show that it is contradictory by deriving some more obvious contradiction. Sentences of this form are the most obviously contradictory ones. (Similarly, we cannot use our rules to show that MP is valid. The validity of MP is a starting point in our system or rules.)

But we have another way to show that $q \cdot \sim q$ is contradictory. We can write a truth-table, something that is particularly easy in this case. And we could also exploit a more general fact to establish that it is contradictory:

> The negation of a contradiction is a tautology.
>
> Since this general fact obtains,
>
> $\sim(q \cdot \sim q)$
>
> must be a tautology. This can be established (without using IP) as follows:
>
> | | | |
> |---|---|---|
> | $\rightarrow$ 1. q | | AP |
> | 2. $q \supset q$ | 1–1 | CP |
> | 3. $\sim q \lor q$ | 2 | CE |
> | 4. $\sim q \lor \sim\sim q$ | 3 | DN |
> | 5. $\sim(q \cdot \sim q)$ | 4 | DeM |
>
> Since $\sim(q \cdot \sim q)$ is a tautology, $q \cdot \sim q$ must be contradictory.

Some Additional Examples

In each case we show that the starting sentence-form is contradictory by deriving something of the form $q \cdot \sim q$:

I.
1. $[\sim(q \cdot p) \supset p] \cdot \sim p$		
2. $\sim p$	1	Simp
3. $\sim(q \cdot p) \supset p$	1	Simp
4. $(\sim q \lor \sim p) \supset p$	3	DeM
5. $\sim q \lor \sim p$	2	Add
6. p	4,5	MP
7. $p \cdot \sim p$	2,6	Conj

II.
1. $(p \equiv \sim q) \cdot \sim(p \lor q)$		
2. $p \equiv \sim q$	1	Simp
3. $\sim(p \lor q)$	1	Simp
4. $\sim p \cdot \sim q$	3	DeM
5. $(p \supset \sim q) \cdot (\sim q \supset p)$	2	Bic
6. $\sim q \supset p$	5	Simp
7. $\sim q$	4	Simp
8. p	6,7	MP
9. $\sim p$	4	Simp
10. $p \cdot \sim p$	8,9	Conj

III.
1. $r \equiv \sim r$		
2. $(r \supset \sim r) \cdot (\sim r \supset r)$	1	Bic
3. $r \supset \sim r$	2	Simp
4. $\sim r \lor \sim r$	3	CE
5. $\sim r$	4	Red
6. $\sim r \supset r$	2	Simp
7. r	5,6	MP
8. $r \cdot \sim r$	5,7	Conj

EXERCISE 9m

Show that these are contradictory.

1. $p \cdot \sim(p \vee q)$

2. $(p \supset (q \cdot r)) \cdot \sim(r \vee \sim p)$

3. $((p \supset q) \supset p) \cdot \sim p$

4. $((p \equiv \sim q) \equiv \sim p) \equiv \sim q$

5. $((p \supset q) \cdot (\sim p \supset q)) \equiv \sim q$

6. $\sim(p \vee \sim(q \cdot p))$

7. $\sim(p \supset q) \cdot \sim(q \supset r)$

8. $(\sim(p \supset q) \vee \sim(q \supset r)) \cdot \sim(r \supset p)$

Showing Contingency

To show that a sentence-form is *contingent* we must establish that it is *not contradictory* and that it is *not tautologous*. Thus we must show that there is some way for sentences of that form to be true and that there is some way for sentences of that form to be false. So two assignments of truth-values are needed to establish contingency.

$p \cdot (q \vee r)$ is contingent.

p : **T**	
q : **T**	This assignment (among others)
r : **T**	makes it true.
p : **F**	
q : **T**	This assignment (among others)
r : **T**	makes it false.

We establish *invalidity*, *consistency*, and *inequivalence* by giving examples. To establish contingency we must give *two examples*.

The following table summarizes our logical concepts and the preferred methods for showing that they apply.

	Shown by Derivation	Shown by Example
Argument	*Valid: Derive* conclusion from premises.	*Invalid:* Example with *true premises* and a *false conclusion*.
Set of sentences	*Inconsistent: Derive* an obvious *contradiction* $(q \cdot \sim q)$.	*Consistent:* Example with *all sentences* in the set *true*.

	Shown by Derivation	Shown by Example
Pair of sentences	*Equivalent: Derive each from the other.*	*Inequivalent:* Example in which the sentences have *different truth-values.*
Sentence	*Logically true (tautologous): Derive* the sentence *without premises.*	*Contingent:* Two examples—one making it true and one making it false.
	Contradictory: Derive an *obvious contradiction* ($q \cdot \sim q$) from the sentence.	

EXERCISE 9n

Show that each of these is *contingent*.

1. $p \supset (q \lor r)$
2. $p \lor (q \cdot \sim p)$
3. $p \supset \sim p$
4. $p \equiv (p \cdot q)$
5. $(p \lor q) \supset (p \cdot q)$
6. $(p \lor (q \cdot r)) \supset ((p \lor q) \cdot r)$

EXERCISE 9o

For each of these, show that it is *tautologous*, that it is *contingent, or* that it is *contradictory*.

1. $p \supset (p \cdot q)$
2. $(p \cdot q) \supset (p \lor q)$
3. $(p \cdot \sim q) \supset \sim(p \supset q)$
4. $p \equiv (q \equiv \sim p)$
5. $p \supset \sim(q \cdot \sim p)$
6. $(\sim p \cdot \sim q) \equiv (p \lor q)$
7. $(p \supset q) \supset ((p \lor q) \supset q)$
8. $(p \supset (q \lor r)) \supset (p \supset r)$
9. $(p \supset (q \cdot r)) \supset (\sim q \supset \sim p)$
10. $p \supset [(q \lor r) \lor (p \cdot \sim(q \lor r))]$

PART III

Quantificational Logic

10

THE LANGUAGE

Many simple arguments are valid but cannot be shown valid using the methods of earlier chapters. For example,

1. All humans are mortal.
Socrates is human.
∴ Socrates is mortal.

2. Every canine eats meat.
All hyenas are canines.
∴ All hyenas eat meat.

3. Some felines are gray.
All felines sleep.
∴ Some gray things sleep.

4. Some professors are lawyers.
∴ Some lawyers are professors.

5. Al gave Betty a bracelet.
∴ Someone gave Betty something.

The earlier chapters dealt with compound sentences (sentences containing other sentences), yet these arguments (1–5) contain no compound sentences. To understand these arguments we will need to analyze the internal structure of sentences and isolate some elements that are important for validity.

PREDICATIVE EXPRESSIONS

In a sentence that is not compound, the principal verb of the sentence determines a great deal about its structure.

1. Rebecca runs.
   Some swimmers run.
   All soccer players run.
2. Al hit Bill.
   Someone hit Bill.
   Al hit someone.
   Everyone hit Bill.
   Everyone hit someone.
3. Al gave a present to Carol.
   Someone gave a present to Carol.
   Al gave something to someone.
   Everyone gave a present to Carol.

In the first group of examples, the sentence has the general structure

_____ run(s)

where some noun phrase is put in the blank. This makes a simple subject-predicate sentence, where the predicative part ['run(s)'] tells us something about the subject. ('Rebecca', 'Some swimmers', or 'All soccer players'). There is just one place for a noun phrase, in the subject position, so 'runs' is called a *monadic* context or *monadic* predicate.

In addition to simple action verbs like 'runs', a very common type of *monadic* predication involves 'is' (or some other form of the verb 'to be'). In our examples of arguments (1–5), most of the sentences were of this type. For example,

All humans *are mortal.*
Socrates *is mortal.*
All hyenas *are canines.*
Some professors *are lawyers.*

These involve monadic predicates

_____ is mortal.
_____ is a canine.
_____ is a lawyer.

and in our examples we also have the monadic predicates

_____ is a meat-eater.   _____ is gray.
_____ is a feline.   _____ sleeps.

But many verb contexts are not monadic. The transitive verb 'hit' is *dyadic*, requiring two noun phrases [as in the second group of examples, (II)]. (In the case of transitive verbs such as 'hit', we can identify these noun phrases as the *subject* and (direct) *object* of the sentence.) But many other verbs are dyadic (and do not fit the subject-object nomenclature). For example, 'Al is next to Bob' involves the context

      _____ is next to . . .

And comparative relations

      _____ is taller than . . .
      _____ is more friendly than . . .
      _____ is less than . . .

are also dyadic. Predicative contexts like these, requiring more than one noun phrase, are called *relational* contexts.

The verb 'gave' expresses a *triadic* relation, requiring three noun phrases:

      _____ gave . . . to _____.

Some predicative contexts are even tetradic, as in 'Albany is farther from Buffalo than Chicago is from Dayton.'

      _____ is farther from . . . than _____ is from *****.

(We will be able to limit our study almost entirely to monadic and dyadic simple sentences, although in principle we could incorporate relational expressions of any finite level.)

NOUNS

The noun phrases in our examples are of two types. The simplest are *proper names* ('Rebecca', 'Bill', 'Socrates', etc.), and the others are constructed from the words 'some', 'every', and 'all' together with a general term. ('All humans', 'Every canine', 'Some doctors', 'someone', 'something', etc.). The words 'all', 'some', and 'every' are among the *quantifier words* of English used to make *noun phrases*. Thus the category *noun phrase* has two important subcategories:

1. *Proper names*.
2. *Quantifier phrases* (constructed from a quantifier word and a general term).

The next important thing to notice is the recurrence of general terms in the premises and conclusion of the arguments we considered. In the first example the general term 'human' appears both within a noun phrase 'All humans' in the first premise, and within the predicative portion ('is human') of the second premise. We find many other such examples, such as 'Every canine' and 'are canines' in the second argument and 'some professors' and 'are professors' in the fourth. These common elements must be represented in the same way so that we can see the linking of elements within the arguments.

So our inventory of resources will fulfill three important conditions.

1. We must have a way of representing the verb (the *predicative context*) of a sentence, reflecting the fact that this determines how many noun phrases are needed to complete the sentence. (In other words, we must show whether it is monadic, dyadic, triadic, etc.)

2. We must have ways of representing noun phrases:
(a) Proper names.
(b) Quantifier phrases.

3. Quantifier phrases must be composed of two elements, quantifier words and general terms. The general terms can also appear as the principal content of the predicative context of a sentence.

PREDICATES AND NAMES IN QUANTIFICATIONAL LOGIC

In representing sentences in a way that makes their elements and structure clear, we will employ capital letters to represent the verb (the principal monadic or relational predicative element) of the sentence. With each capital letter standing for a verb there will be lowercase letters from the end of the alphabet ('x', 'y', 'z', 'x_1', 'x_2', etc.), one for each noun phrase position associated with that verb. Thus instead of

_____ runs

as we wrote before, we would have

Rx

('x runs' or 'x is a runner'). And for ' ____ hit . . . ' we would have

Hxy

For ' ____ gave . . . to ***' we would have

$Gxyz$

These are the skeletal structures for simple sentences. We will call these *predicates* (monadic, dyadic, triadic, etc.) (Predicates that are not monadic can be called *relations* or *relational* predicates. The letters 'x', 'y', 'z', etc. that stand for noun-phrase positions are sometimes called "individual variables.")

To build real sentences on these skeletal structures, we must associate one noun phrase with each noun phrase position. When the noun phrase is a proper noun, we represent it by a single lowercase letter of the alphabet (chosen from among 'a' through 't'), and we put it in the appropriate position in the verb. If '*Hxy*' is 'x hit y' and 'c' refers to Carl and 'd' refers to 'Dave', then 'Carl hit Dave' is

Hcd

'Carl runs' is

Rc

If '*Bxyz*' is 'x is between y and z', then 'Chicago is between Buffalo and Albany' would be

Bcba

Compound Sentences with Proper Names

Before we go on to consider more complex noun phrases, we should note that we now have one type of complete sentence, and we can make compound sentences in the way already familiar to us.

Al and Brenda both run.	$Ra \cdot Rb$
Al runs and walks.	$Ra \cdot Wa$
Al runs, but he won't beat Brenda.	$Ra \cdot {\sim}Bab$
($Bxy = x$ will beat y)	
If Al runs, he won't be late.	$Ra \supset {\sim}La$

Notice in the last two examples that each of the symbolic formulas employs two uses of the name 'a' whereas the English employs 'Al' and 'he'. This use of pronouns in English, to refer to something referred to previously by a proper name, is always treated the same way, by repeating the proper name symbol.

EXERCISE 10a

Symbolize the following simple sentences and truth-functional compounds of simple sentences.

1. John Adams was president. (a = John Adams, $Px = x$ was president)

2. Henry Clay was not president. (c = Henry Clay, $Px = x$ was president)

3. John Adams and George Washington were both presidents. (g = George Washington)

4. Neither George Washington nor Henry Clay was president.

5. George Washington was taller than John Adams. (Txy = x was taller than y)

6. Both George Washington and Benjamin Franklin were taller than John Adams. (b = Benjamin Franklin)

7. Either George Washington or John Adams signed the Emancipation Proclamation. (Sxy = x signed y, e = the Emancipation Proclamation)

8. George Washington signed the Emancipation Proclamation, but John Adams did not.

9. If George Washington signed the Emancipation Proclamation, then neither John Adams nor Abraham Lincoln did. (l = Abraham Lincoln)

10. George Washington was president, but Henry Clay was taller than he was and smarter, too. (Sxy = x is smarter than y)

RELATIVE CLAUSES

A relative clause construction in English is usually signalled by one of the relativizing words 'who', 'whom', 'that' or 'which'. Sentences containing these constructions can be represented with the conjunction symbol ' · '.

> Amelia is a doctor who smokes.
> *Da · Sa*
> Amelia, who is a doctor, smokes.
> *Da · Sa*
> Melissa, whom Carol works for, swims.
> *Wcm · Sm*
> Amelia, who is a doctor, knows Melissa, whom Carol works for.
> *Da · (Kam · Wcm)*
> Dayton is a city that Melissa has visited.
> *Cd · Vmd*
> Easton, which is nearer than Dayton, is a city that Melissa has not visited.
> *Ce · (Ned · ~Vme)*
> Fred, whom Melissa thinks about, is angry.
> *Af · Tmf*

Sometimes relative clause constructions are not signalled by any of the relativizing words.

> Dayton is a city Melissa has visited.
> *Cd · Vmd*

Fred is a fireman Melissa thinks about.
Ff · Tmf

EXERCISE 10b

Symbolize the following sentences.

1. John Adams was a senator who admired George Washington. (*a* = John Adams, *g* = George Washington, *Axy* = *x* admired *y*)

2. John Adams and Henry Clay were both senators who admired George Washington. (*c* = Henry Clay)

3. George Washington and John Adams were politicians that Henry Clay did not admire. (*Lx* = *x* is a politician)

4. Henry Clay, who was a politician, did not admire John Adams.

5. Although neither George Washington nor John Adams was a politician Henry Clay admired, Benjamin Franklin was. (*b* = Benjamin Franklin)

6. Henry Clay was a politician who admired and talked about Benjamin Franklin. (*Txy* = *x* talked about *y*)

THE UNIVERSAL QUANTIFIER

We now need resources for representing noun phrases other than proper names. As we saw, quantifier phrases have two elements, a quantifier word (such as 'All', 'Some', or 'Every') and a general term such as 'dog', 'swimmer', 'meat-eater', etc. We also noted that the general term can appear in predicative contexts, such as '*x* is a dog', '*x* swims' or '*x* is a swimmer', '*x* eats meat' or '*x* is a meat-eater'. Occurrences of general terms within noun phrases and within predicative contexts must be represented in the same way (or in related ways) if we are to examine the linking of premises and conclusion that occurs in arguments.

We have already established a way of representing predicative uses of these terms.

x is a dog	*Dx*
x swims	*Sx*
x eats meat	*Ex*

The quantifier phrase 'Every dog' is equivalent to the phrase 'Every *x* such that *x* is a dog', and this fact enables us to use '*Dx*' in the quantifier phrase. Using a colon for 'such that', we can write

Every *x* : *Dx*

to represent 'Every dog'.

The phrase 'Every dog' is used to say something about all dogs. In English we have several other quantifier words for talking about all members of a class of objects. Where we use 'every dog' we can usually employ 'any dog', 'all dogs', or 'each dog' in a similar sentence to say the same thing ("Every dog swims", "All dogs swim", "Any dog swims", "Each dog swims"). We will represent these quantifier words in the same way, using a special symbol, called the *universal quantifier*,

$\forall$

and writing 'every dog', 'all dogs', 'each dog', and 'any dog' in the same way:

$(\forall x\colon Dx)$

To write a sentence such as "All dogs swim," it would be natural to expect us simply to put the noun phrase in the correct position in the predicative expression 'x swims' or 'Sx'. This would give us '$S(\forall x\colon Dx)$'. *But this is not how we will do it!* For several reasons that will soon be clear, it is necessary to associate quantifier phrases with their position in a sentence in a different way. "All dogs swim" will be written

$(\forall x\colon Dx)Sx$
Every x such that x is a dog satisfies this condition—x swims.
Every dog swims. (All dogs swim.)

Instead of just placing the noun phrase into its position within the predicative expression, we put it in front of the predicative expression and use a common placeholder 'x' (or 'y', 'z', 'x_1', etc.) to indicate that the noun phrase is associated with that position in the predicative expression. (What placeholder we use does not matter. '$(\forall x\colon Dx)Sx$' and '$(\forall y\colon Dy)Sy$' say exactly the same thing. It is only the way positions are linked that matters.)
    Suppose that 'Lxy' stands for 'x likes y'.

All dogs like Bob.	$(\forall x\colon Dx)Lxb$
Bob likes all dogs.	$(\forall x\colon Dx)Lbx$

Both sentences say something about all dogs: the first that each of them likes Bob, the second that Bob likes each of them. The quantifier phrase is associated with a different position within the predicative expression (and, of course, so is the proper name) to indicate the difference. Note that changing every 'x' to a 'y' makes no difference because it preserves the positional relationships.

All dogs like Bob.	$(\forall x\colon Dx)Lxb$	$(\forall y\colon Dy)Lyb$
Bob likes all dogs.	$(\forall x\colon Dx)Lbx$	$(\forall y\colon Dy)Lby$

A few English words—'everyone', 'everything', 'everywhere', and 'always'—are complete quantifier phrases in themselves.

Everyone	every person	$(\forall x: Px)$
Everything	every individual object	$(\forall x: Ix)$
Everywhere	every location	$(\forall x: Lx)$
Always	every time	$(\forall x: Tx)$

Now that we have made complete sentences with quantifier phrases we can use '$\sim$', ' $\cdot$ ', ' $\vee$ ', and ' $\supset$ ' to make more complex sentences.

Not all dogs swim.	$\sim(\forall x: Dx)Sx$
All dogs swim, but not all dogs like Bob.	$(\forall x: Dx)Sx \cdot \sim(\forall x: Dx)Lxb$
Although Bob likes all dogs, not all dogs like him.	$(\forall x: Dx)Lbx \cdot \sim(\forall x: Dx)Lxb$
If Bob likes all dogs, he's crazy.	$(\forall x: Dx)Lbx \supset Cb$

These examples involve the compounding of complete quantified sentences. But we will also use our sentence connective symbols for creating *compound predicates*.

Every dog is either male or female. $(\forall x: Dx)[Mx \vee Fx]$

'$Mx \vee Fx$' respresents the *compound predicate* 'is either male or female' and the sentence predicates this of all dogs. Note that this is *not* equivalent to the (false) *compound sentence*:

Every dog is male or every dog is female. $(\forall x: Dx)Mx \vee (\forall x: Dx)Fx$

We are now in a position to see a difference between 'any' and 'every'. Although they are both universal quantifier words,

Carla likes every dog.	$(\forall x: Dx)Lcx$
Carla likes any dog.	$(\forall x: Dx)Lcx$

they behave very differently in complex sentences.

Carla does not like *every* dog.	$\sim(\forall x: Dx)Lcx$
Carla does not like *any* dog.	$(\forall x: Dx)\sim Lcx$

In fact, a good guideline seems to be that 'any' will correspond to a quantifier in a quantifier phrase governing as large a predicative expression as possible, while 'every' will correspond to a quantifier phrase governing as small a predicative expression as possible. In our example, the quantifier representing 'any' has *larger scope* than the negation; the quantifier phrase applies to a compound predicative expression ($\sim Lcx$) that includes the negation. The quantifier representing 'every' has *smaller scope* than the negation; the negation applies to a sentence [($\forall x$: Dx)Lcx] that contains the quantifier phrase.

These facts about 'any' and 'every' also provide one reason (we will see others later) for prefixing quantifier phrases to predicative expressions rather than inserting them into a position as we would with symbols for proper nouns. If both 'any' and 'every' are to be represented by a universal quantifier, as seems natural in simple sentences, then

$$\sim Lc \ (\forall x\!: \ Dx)$$

would be a problem, representing only one of the two possible meanings

$$\sim(\forall x\!: \ Dx)Lcx$$
$$(\forall x\!: \ Dx)\!\sim\! Lcx$$

The existence of compound predicates raises another possibility. Such predicates could appear within quantifier phrases.

$$(\forall x\!: \ Dx \cdot Rx)Sx$$

A quantifier phrase containing a conjunction corresponds to an English noun phrase with a restrictive relative clause (usually constructed with 'that', 'which', 'who', and 'whom'). The formula above could represent

Any dog *that runs* swims.
$(\forall x$: $Dx \cdot Rx)Sx$
Every x that is both a dog and a runner fulfills this condition—x swims.

Other examples might be

Alice loves *any dog that swims*.	$(\forall x$: $Dx \cdot Sx)Lax$
Every person Alice loves is happy.	$(\forall x$: $Px \cdot Lax)Hx$
Alice loves *everyone who loves her*.	$(\forall x$: $Px \cdot Lxa)Lax$

Disjunctive and negated predicates also often occur within quantifier phrases.

Any dog that runs or swims is healthy.	$(\forall x$: $Dx \cdot (Rx \lor Sx))\ Hx$
Any dog that doesn't run is lazy or sick.	$(\forall x$: $Dx \cdot \sim Rx)\ [Lx \lor Sx]$
Apples and bananas are nourishing.	$(\forall x$: $Ax)Nx \cdot (\forall x$: $Bx)Nx$
	or
	$(\forall x$: $Ax \lor Bx)Nx$
	(These are equivalent)

(There seems to be little use for conditionals within quantifier phrases.)

One other thing about our universal quantifier is worth noting now. If the predicative expression within a universal quantifier phrase has no application, a sentence governed by that quantifier phrase will be regarded as true automatically.

All unicorns swim.   ($\forall x$: Ux)Sx

Since there are no unicorns, it is impossible to find a counterexample, a unicorn that does not swim, so we consider this to be true. This may seem an arbitrary way to proceed (to some people it may even seem incorrect), but there are compelling reasons to do this. For example, it should follow from the fact that every even number is divisible by 2 that every even prime number is divisible by 2. Furthermore, any even prime number greater than 5 must be divisible by 2.

But consider these sentences.

(1) ($\forall x$: Ex)Dxt
(2) ($\forall x$: $Ex \cdot Px$)Dxt
(3) ($\forall x$: ($Ex \cdot Px$) $\cdot$ Gxf)Dxt

If (1) is true, then (2) and (3) must also be true. But the complex predicate of (3),

($Ex \cdot Px$) $\cdot$ Gxf

is not true of anything. There are no even prime numbers greater than 5. If universal sentences of the form

($\forall x$: Ax)Bx

are automatically considered true whenever 'Ax' is not true of anything, the inferential relationships will work out in a satisfactory way. If (1) is true, (2) will be true, and if (2) is true, (3) will also be true. All arguments of this form will be valid.

($\forall x$: Cx)Dx
$\therefore$ ($\forall x$: $Cx \cdot Ex$)Dx

Other ways of resolving the problem of universal quantifier phrases with predicates lacking application will have difficulty with this inference pattern (and others). For example, suppose we said that every universally quantified sentence governed by a quantifier phrase in which the predicative expression had no application would be classified as *untrue*; then some instances of this argument form would be said to have a true premise and an untrue conclusion [the step from (2) to (3), for example]. Yet in other cases, this type of argument seems valid [as in the step from (1) to (2)]. We can say that all arguments of this form are valid if we agree (perhaps unnaturally) that something of the form ($\forall x$: Ax)Bx is true whenever Ax has no application to anything.

EXERCISE 10c

Using the universal quantifier '$\forall$' together with the other symbols discussed so far, give the symbolization for each of the following sentences.

1. Every canine eats meat. ($Cx = x$ is a canine, $Ex = x$ eats meat)
2. Not every canine eats meat.
3. All canines eat meat, but Harry is not a canine. (h = Harry)
4. Harry is a hyena, and hyenas are not canines. ($Hx = x$ is a hyena)
5. Hyenas eat meat, and they also bark. (Bx = barks)
6. Although all hyenas eat meat, not all hyenas are good cooks. ($Gx = x$ is a good cook)
7. Every hyena that eats meat is a good cook.
8. Every hyena either eats meat or is a good cook.
9. Everyone knows Bob. ($Px = x$ is a person, $Kxy = x$ knows y, b = Bob)
10. Either everyone loves Bob or not everyone knows him. ($Lxy = x$ loves y)
11. Bob knows everyone, but he doesn't love everyone.
12. Bob doesn't love anyone.
13. Bob loves any person who is a good cook.
14. Everyone who knows Bob loves him.
15. Every hyena that cooks well either loves Bob or doesn't know him.

EXERCISE 10d

Using the quantifier '$\forall$' (together with the other symbols discussed so far), write the symbolization for each sentence. Use the abbreviations indicated.

Dx: x is a dog
Mx: x eats meat
Hx: x howls
Bx: x barks
e: Ernie
d: Donald
Lxy: x barks louder than y does
Cx: x is a cat

1. All dogs howl.
2. All dogs howl and bark.
3. Ernie barks and Donald doesn't.
4. Anything that barks is a dog.

5. Every dog barks or howls.

6. Not all dogs bark, but Ernie barks and he howls too.

7. Ernie barks louder than Donald does.

8. Any dog barks louder than Donald does.

9. Ernie barks louder than any cat does.

10. Ernie barks louder than any dog that howls.

11. Any dog that barks louder than Ernie does is a meat-eater.

12. Any dog that barks louder than Ernie does barks louder than Donald does.

13. Ernie doesn't bark louder than every cat.

14. Ernie doesn't bark louder than any cat.

THE EXISTENTIAL QUANTIFIER

Another quantifier word occurring in the arguments presented at the opening of this chapter is 'some' as in 'some dogs', 'some doctors', 'someone', and 'something'. To represent English quantifier phrases involving 'some', we will follow the same pattern as before.

Some dogs   (Some x: Dx)

And as with universal quantification, we will introduce a special symbol

$\exists$

that corresponds to the quantifier word. This symbol represents the idea of *at least one* object of the indicated sort.

($\exists x$: Dx)
At least one x such that x is a dog
Some dog (or dogs)

'Some dogs swim' would be '($\exists x$: Dx)Sx'.

With the new symbol we are not able to make the distinction that we make in English between singular and plural: 'some dog' and 'some dogs'. Although this is sometimes important to the sense of the English,

Some dog bit Bill.
Some dogs bit Bill.

conveying a significant difference in meaning, it turns out to be less important for inference. For the category of basic arguments that we will study, the difference can be set aside. Both of these sentences would be represented by the same formula,

$(\exists x\colon Dx)Bxb$

The symbol '$\exists$' is called an *existential quantifier*. [Sentences with existential quantifier phrases assert the *existence* of things of the type they are about.

$(\exists x\colon Dx)Sx$

'Some dogs swim' asserts that there exists at least one dog, and it swims. If it is true, both dogs and swimmers must exist.]

In addition to its use in representing English quantifier phrases employing 'some' as their quantifier word, the existential quantifier also has the role of representing most uses of the English indefinite article 'a' (or 'an').

A dog bit Carl.	$(\exists x\colon Dx)Bxc$
Carl bit a dog.	$(\exists x\colon Dx)Bcx$

Except for occasional universal uses of 'a' (as in 'A whale is a sea mammal'), occurrences of 'a' can be represented by '$\exists$'.

There are many other quantifier concepts besides the universal quantifier ($\forall$) and the existential quantifier ($\exists$). Other noun phrases constructed in a similar way are, for example,

many dogs

most dogs

few dogs

at least three dogs

at most seven dogs

infinitely many dogs

the dog

But the core of logical studies employs only these two most important quantifiers, *all* and *some*. (In Chapters 15 and 16 we discuss the other quantifier concepts mentioned.)

The existential quantifier is the last of the symbols we need, so let us now categorize and name what we have.

Predicates

Rx, Hx, etc.	(monadic)
Bxy, Cxy, etc.	(dyadic)
$Dxyz$, etc.	(triadic)
$Fxyz_1z_2$, etc.	(tetradic)
etc.	(etc.)

Individual Variables

$x, y, z, x_1, x_2, \ldots, y_1, y_2, \ldots$, etc.

Individual Constants (Proper Names)

$a, b, c, \ldots, t, a_1, a_2, \ldots, b_1, b_2, \ldots$, etc.

Truth-Functional Symbols

$\cdot, \vee, \supset, \equiv, \sim$

Quantifiers

$\exists, \forall$

Occasionally, we may also wish to return to the employment of

Sentence Letters

$A, B, C, \ldots$

to represent unanalyzed sentences. ('It is raining', perhaps.)

These are all of the resources of *predicate logic*, the core of modern logic (also called *quantifier* or *quantificational* logic).

We can give a systematic description of formulas using these elements.

   0. 'Atomic' formulas

   (a) Any sentence letter is a formula.

   (b) A predicate letter followed by an appropriate number (monadic, 1; dyadic, 2; triadic, 3; etc.) of individual terms (variables or constants) is a formula.

   1. If X is a formula, then $\sim X$ is a formula.

   2. If X and Y are formulas, then

   $(X \cdot Y)$

   $(X \vee Y)$

   $(X \supset Y)$

   $(X \equiv Y)$

   are all formulas.

   3. If X and Y are formulas and $\textcircled{v}$ is some variable, then

   $(\exists \textcircled{v}: X)Y$

   $(\forall \textcircled{v}: X)Y$

   are formulas

Abbreviation (a): We can abbreviate by omitting the outer parentheses of completed expressions (when they are not parts of larger formulas).

Abbreviation (b): If X is a compound sentence with outer parentheses, then we can abbreviate $(\forall \textcircled{v}: X)Y$ and $(\exists \textcircled{v}: X)Y$ by omitting the outer parentheses of X.

The construction of some formulas may help to illustrate this.

Example A: $(\exists x: Ax)(Bx \cdot \sim Rxa)$.

1. These are formulas [rule 0(b)]:
   Ax
   Bx
   Rxa

2. This is a formula (from 1 and rule 1):
   $\sim Rxa$

3. This is a formula (from 1 and 2 and rule 2):
   $(Bx \cdot \sim Rxa)$

4. This is a formula (from 1 and 3 and rule 3):
   $(\exists x: Ax)(Bx \cdot \sim Rxa)$

Example B: $(\exists x: Ax)\sim Bx \supset (\exists y: Ay)(\exists z: \sim(Bz \cdot Cz))Ryz$

1. These are formulas [rule 0(b)]:
   Ax
   Bx
   Ay
   Bz
   Cz
   Ryz

2. This is a formula (1 and rule 1):
   $\sim Bx$

3. This is a formula (1 and rule 2):
   $(Bz \cdot Cz)$

4. This is a formula (3 and rule 1):
   $\sim(Bz \cdot Cz)$

5. These are formulas (1, 2, 4 and rule 3):
   $(\exists x: Ax)\sim Bx$
   $(\exists z: \sim(Bz \cdot Cz))Ryz$

6. This is a formula (5 and rule 3):
   $(\exists y: Ay)(\exists z: \sim(Bz \cdot Cz))Ryz$

7. This is a formula (5, 6 and rule 2):
   $((\exists x: Ax)\sim Bx \supset (\exists y: Ay)(\exists z: \sim(Bz \cdot Cz)) Ryz)$

8. This is an abbreviation (a) of 7:
   $(\exists x: Ax)\sim Bx \supset (\exists y: Ay)(\exists z: \sim(Bz \cdot Cz)) Ryz$

Example C: $(\exists x: Ax \cdot (\exists y: By)Rxy)(\forall z: \sim Bz)Rxz$

1. These are formulas [rule 0(b)]:
   Ax
   By
   Rxy
   Bz
   Rxz

2. This is a formula (1 and rule 1):
$\sim Bz$

3. These are formulas (1, 2 and rule 3):
$(\exists y\colon By)Rxy$
$(\forall z\colon \sim Bz)Rxz$

4. This is a formula (1, 3 and rule 2):
$(Ax \cdot (\exists y\colon By)Rxy)$

5. This is a formula (3, 4 and rule 3):
$(\exists x\colon (Ax \cdot (\exists y\colon By)Rxy))(\forall z\colon \sim Bz)Rxz$

6. This is an abbreviation (b) of 5:
$(\exists x\colon Ax \cdot (\exists y\colon By)Rxy)(\forall z\colon \sim Bz)Rxz$

EXERCISE 10e

Use the symbols of predicate logic to represent the structure of the following sentences.

Tx:	x is a truck driver	Cx:	x drives carelessly
Sx:	x speeds	Kxy:	x knows y
		a:	Alice

1. Some truck drivers speed.

2. Some truck drivers don't speed.

3. Some truck drivers speed and drive carelessly.

4. Some truck drivers who speed drive carelessly.

5. Some truck drivers who don't speed drive carelessly.

6. Some truck drivers who speed drive carelessly, but not all truck drivers who speed drive carelessly.

7. Alice is a truck driver who speeds, but she doesn't drive carelessly.

8. Some truck drivers who know Alice don't speed.

9. Alice knows a truck driver who drives carelessly.

10. Not all of the truck drivers Alice knows speed, but some of them do.

EXERCISE 10f

Symbolize each sentence. Use the abbreviations indicated.

Cx:	x is a cat	c:	Carlo
Mx:	x meows	d:	Donald
Hx:	x hisses	Bxy:	x is bigger than y

1. Some cats meow and some cats hiss.

2. Some cats meow and hiss.

3. Some cats don't meow.

4. Not all cats meow.

5. Some cats that don't hiss meow.

6. Some things that hiss are cats.

7. Some cats hiss and all cats meow.

8. Carlo is a cat who hisses, but Donald is bigger than Carlo.

9. Some cats bigger than Carlo meow but don't hiss.

10. Carlo is bigger than any cat that hisses.

11. Carlo isn't bigger than any cat that hisses.

12. Some cats that hiss but don't meow are bigger than Carlo and bigger than Donald too.

MORE ON REPRESENTING ENGLISH

We now have the resources for representing a wide range of English sentences. To do so, we must examine English more closely to see how logical relations are shown there.

Simple Logical Relationships

In our discussion of truth-functional logic (Chapter 2) we considered two ways in which claims can be opposed: either as contraries or contradictories.

> **1.** A pair of sentences are *contraries* if and only if they cannot both be true. (It amounts to the same thing to say that S and T are contraries if and only if $\sim T$ *follows from* S.)
>
> **2.** A pair of sentences are *contradictories* if and only if they must always have opposite truth-value. (It amounts to the same thing to say that S and T are contradictories if and only if $\sim T$ *is equivalent to* S.)

The statements

| Al and Bill both swim. | $A \cdot B$ |
| Al and Bill are both nonswimmers. | $\sim A \cdot \sim B$ |

are *contraries* because they cannot both be true. But they can both be false (if one swims but the other does not). The sentences

| Al and Bill both swim. | $A \cdot B$ |
| Al and Bill do not both swim. | $\sim(A \cdot B)$ |

are contradictories, though. In studying predicate logic we must again attend to the different ways of opposing a claim. Consider

1. All dogs swim.
2. No dogs swim.
3. Not all dogs swim.

2 and 3 both 'oppose' 1, but only 3 is a contradictory of 1. 1 and 3 must always have opposite truth-value, and they are properly represented as a sentence and its negation.

1. $(\forall x: Dx)Sx$
3. $\sim(\forall x: Dx)Sx$

Sentences 1 and 2, however, can both be false (if some dogs swim and some dogs do not swim). Thus they are not contradictories. There are two equivalent ways of representing 'No dogs swim'.

2. No dogs swim.	$(\forall x: Dx)\sim Sx$
	$\sim(\exists x: Dx)Sx$

The second of these makes apparent what 2 really contradicts.

4. Some dogs swim.	$(\exists x: Dx)Sx$

2 and 4 are contradictories.

Traditionally, the basic logical relationships among the simplest quantified sentences have been represented by beginning with four fundamental sentence types.

(A) All dogs swim.	$(\forall x: Dx)Sx$	Universal, affirmative
(E) No dogs swim.	$(\forall x: Dx)\sim Sx$	Universal, negative
(I) Some dogs swim.	$(\exists x: Dx)Sx$	Particular, affirmative
(O) Some dogs do not swim.	$(\exists x: Dx)\sim Sx$	Particular, negative

These are four of the most common patterns for quantified sentences of English. When these are diagrammed in a square, several important relationships can be seen.

	Affirmitive predicate	Negative predicate
Universal	**A**: All D are S.	**E**: No D are S.
	$(\forall x: Dx)Sx$	$(\forall x: Dx)\sim Sx$
Particular	**I**: Some D are S.	**O**: Some D are not S.
	$(\exists x: Dx)Sx$	$(\exists x: Dx)\sim Sx$

1. Diagonally opposed corners contradict each other.

   (a) **A** contradicts **O**. In other words:

   (i) **A** is equivalent to $\sim$**O**.
   '$(\forall x\colon Dx)Sx$' is equivalent to '$\sim(\exists x\colon Dx)\sim Sx$'.

   (ii) **O** is equivalent to $\sim$**A**.
   '$(\exists x\colon Dx)\sim Sx$' is equivalent to '$\sim(\forall x\colon Dx)Sx$'.
   (The $\sim$**A** form 'Not all D are S' is a fifth type of common basic quantified sentence form in English, equivalent to **O**, 'Some D are not S'.)

   (b) **I** contradicts **E**. In other words:

   (i) **I** is equivalent to $\sim$**E**.
   '$(\exists x\colon Dx)Sx$' is equivalent to '$\sim(\forall x\colon Dx)\sim Sx$'.

   (ii) **E** is equivalent to $\sim$**I**.
   '$(\forall x\colon Dx)\sim Sx$' is equivalent to '$\sim(\exists x\colon Dx)Sx$'. [Some people find '$\sim(\exists x\colon Dx)Sx$' to be a more natural way to represent the English **E** sentence 'No D are S'.]

2. The universal sentences **A** and **E** 'oppose' each other but are not contradictories. They oppose each other because if there are any dogs (any things of which 'Dx' is true), then **A** and **E** cannot both be true. (They are not contradictories because they can both be false.)

3. The particular sentences **I** and **O** can both be true. (And if there are no dogs, both are false.)

4. From a universal sentence (either an **A** or an **E**), together with an existence premise, the corresponding particular sentence (**I** or **O**) below it can be inferred. The needed existence premise must guarantee that the general term of the quantifier phrase applies to something. It can be represented naturally in either of two ways (using 'Ix' for 'x is a thing').

Some things are dogs.	$(\exists x\colon Ix)Dx$
Some dogs are dogs.	$(\exists x\colon Dx)Dx$

Each employs the *existential* quantifier, each states that there are dogs, and either can be used to fill out the inference from general to particular.

A	$(\forall x\colon Dx)Sx$	$(\forall x\colon Dx)Sx$
There are dogs.	$(\exists x\colon Dx)Dx$	$(\exists x\colon Ix)Dx$
$\therefore$ **I**	$(\exists x\colon Dx)Sx$	$(\exists x\colon Dx)Sx$

E	$(\forall x\colon Dx)\sim Sx$	$(\forall x\colon Dx)\sim Sx$
There are dogs.	$(\exists x\colon Dx)Dx$	$(\exists x\colon Ix)Dx$
$\therefore$ **O**	$(\exists x\colon Dx)\sim Sx$	$(\exists x\colon Dx)\sim Sx$

All of these are valid.

Only

The word 'only' causes difficulty for some students of logic, so watch out for it. The sentence 'Only dogs swim' tells us something about the class of *things that are not dogs*: none of them are swimmers.

Only dogs swim. $(\forall x: \sim Dx)\sim Sx$

It is equivalent to say

All swimmers are dogs. $(\forall x: Sx)Dx$

The same principles apply in more complicated sentences.

Only union members without jobs were admitted.
$(\forall x: \sim(Ux \cdot \sim Jx))\sim Ax$
$(\forall x: Ax)(Ux \cdot \sim Jx)$

Only those designated by some official will receive awards.
$(\forall x: \sim(\exists y: Oy)Dyx)\sim(\exists z: Az)Rxz$
$(\forall x: (\exists z: Az)Rxz)(\exists y: Oy)Dyx$

A special problem exists when 'only' is used in a noun phrase with a relative clause.

Only students with beards were admitted.

This English sentence is ambiguous, with three possible interpretations, corresponding to three places in which the negation can be placed within the noun phrase.

(a) $(\forall x: \sim(Sx \cdot Bx))\sim Ax$
(b) $(\forall x: Sx \cdot \sim Bx)\sim Ax$
(c) $(\forall x: \sim Sx \cdot Bx)\sim Ax$

The interpretations (b) and (c) can be made more compelling by special emphasis that indicates the clause to be negated.

(b) Only students *with beards* were admitted.
(c) Only *students* with beards were admitted.

Symbolization cannot be done with confidence until an interpretation is pinned down.

EXERCISE 10g

Give a predicate logic representation of each of the following sentences. Use the indicated abbreviations.

Ax: *x* can add   *j*: John
Ex: *x* is an elephant   *Kxy*: *x* knows *y*
Mx: *x* is a mathematician   *Lxy*: *x* is larger than *y*
Px: *x* is a person   *Sxy*: *x* is smarter than *y*

1. John can add.
2. Every mathematician can add.
3. Anyone who can add is smarter than John.
4. Some people can't add.
5. No one can add.
6. Only mathematicians can add.
7. Everyone knows John.
8. John doesn't know everyone.
9. John knows a mathematician who can't add.
10. Everyone John knows is a mathematician.
11. Every elephant is larger than John.
12. John is smarter than any elephant.
13. John is not larger than every elephant.
14. John is not larger than any elephant.
15. Elephants can't add.
16. John knows elephants that can add.
17. An elephant John knows is smarter than him.
18. No one John knows is smarter than him.
19. Only mathematicians are smarter than John.
20. Only mathematicians who are larger than John are smarter than him.

Multiple Quantification

To represent the sentence

Someone gave a bracelet to Alice.

we need to associate quantifier phrases with two of the noun phrase positions in the predicative context

x gave y to z *Gxyz*

There is no special problem about this; we simply prefix both quantifier phrases, using the variables to link each quantifier phrase with the appropriate noun phrase position.

($\exists x$: Px)($\exists y$: By)$Gxya$

Similarly, the sentence

Any elephant is larger than every person.

is represented by the formula

($\forall x$: Ex)($\forall y$: Py)Lxy

But when universal and existential quantifiers appear together within a sentence, caution is needed.

Every number is less than some number.

Let 'Lxy' stand for 'x is less than y'. It is clear that 'Every number' is associated with the first position ('x') in 'Lxy', and that 'some number' is associated with the second position ('y' in 'Lxy'). But that is not the only question we need to answer, for there are still two possible ways to fulfill that condition.

($\forall x$: Nx)($\exists y$: Ny)Lxy
($\exists y$: Ny)($\forall x$: Nx)Lxy

These formulas are not equivalent. The first says

Every number x satisfies the following condition—there is some number that x is less than.

The second says

Some number y satisfies the following condition—every number is less than y.

The first is true and the second is false. (The original English sentence is ambiguous because either of our formulas might represent a correct interpretation of it, although the true one is considerably more likely to be what someone intends to say.) Similarly, if 'Cxy' is 'x is a child of y', then

($\forall x$: Px)($\exists y$: Py)Cxy
(Each person is a child of someone.)

is true, but

($\exists y$: Py)($\forall x$: Px)Cxy
(Some person has this feature : everyone is his or her child.)

is false.

When the quantifier phrases governing a sentence are all existential or all universal, quantifier order is not a problem because changing the order produces an equivalent formula.

Someone x satisfies this condition—x gave a bracelet to Alice.
($\exists x$: Px)($\exists y$: By)$Gxya$
Some bracelet y satisfies this condition—someone gave y to Alice.
($\exists y$: By)($\exists x$: Px)$Gxyz$

Those are equivalent, as are these.

Any elephant is larger than every person.
($\forall x$: Ex)($\forall y$: Py)Lxy
Any person satisfies this condition—every elephant is larger.
($\forall y$: Py)($\forall x$: Ex)Lxy

After our inferential rules are introduced we will be able to show that quantifier order does not matter if all of the quantifiers in a sequence are universal, and that it does not matter when all of the quantifiers in a sequence are existential. But as we have seen, quantifier order can make a difference when we have mixed quantifiers.

When symbolizing sentences with both existential and universal quantifiers, we must sort out the sense and attempt to determine from the context of the sentence which quantifier order is meant.

EXERCISE 10h

Symbolize each sentence. Use the abbreviations indicated.

Sx: x is a scientist
Bx: x is a biologist
Cx: x is a chemist
Ex: x is eligible
Tx: x studies

Jx: x will join
Oxy: x is older than y
Wxy: x is wiser than y
b: Bill

1. All scientists study.

2. All biologists and chemists study.

3. Some biologists are older than some chemists.

4. Some biologists are wiser than all chemists.

5. Only biologists study.

6. Only biologists older than Bill are eligible.

7. No scientists older than Bill study.

8. Bill is older than some scientists who don't study.

9. Any biologist older than Bill is wiser than him too.

10. Any biologist older than Bill is wiser than every chemist.

11. No chemist older than Bill is wiser than every biologist.

12. No one who isn't older than Bill will join.

13. Only chemists older than Bill will join, but some of them are not eligible.

14. All eligible chemists are older and wiser than Bill.

Reflexives

Reflexive sentences occur when multiple noun phrase positions within a predicate are taken to refer to that same individual. In English these are signaled by pronouns with 'self' as suffix. We repeat a proper name or a variable in representing this.

John hates himself.	Hjj
John gave himself a record.	$(\exists x\!: Rx)Gjxj$
No number is less than itself.	$\sim(\exists x\!: Nx)Lxx$ or $(\forall x\!: Nx)\sim Lxx$
Someone gave himself a record.	$(\exists y\!: Py)(\exists x\!: Rx)\ Gyxy$

EXERCISE 10i

Symbolize the following, using the abbreviations indicated. (The last four are rather difficult.)

Lxy: x loves y	j: John
Wx: x is wise	b: Bill
Sxy: x is smarter than y	Rxy: x has read y
Fx: x is a philosopher	Bx: x is a book
Px: x is a person	Ix: x is a thing

1. John doesn't love everyone.

2. There is a person who loves everyone.

3. No one loves everyone.

4. No one loves anyone.

5. Anyone who loves himself is wise.

6. Only the wise love everyone.

7. Only the wise love themselves.

8. John doesn't love himself, but some people love him.

9. John doesn't love himself, but there are people who love themselves.

10. No one loves himself.

11. Anyone who loves himself is smarter than John.

12. Anyone who loves himself is smarter than any philosopher.

13. Anyone who loves himself is smarter than anyone who doesn't.

14. All philosophers have read books.

15. There is a person who has read every book.

16. Only philosophers are wise, and only they have read everything.

17. Every philosopher loves at least one person.

18. Every philosopher has read something, but some haven't read any books.

19. There is someone who has read every book that either John or Bill has read, but they are smarter than him.

20. There is a person who has read every book that any philosopher has read.

EXERCISE 10j

Symbolize these sentences. Use the abbreviations indicated.

Lx: x is a lawyer
Sx: x studies
Bx: x is a book
Oxy: x owns y
Cxy: x is y's client

Fx: x is foolish
Dx: x is a doctor
Px: x is a person
b: Bill

1. Some lawyers study.

2. Some lawyers own books.

3. Some lawyers don't own books.

4. Some lawyers who study don't own books.

5. Some lawyers who don't own books study.

6. Some lawyers have clients.

7. Not all lawyers have clients.

8. All lawyers who have clients own books.

9. Any lawyer who is his own client is foolish.

10. Lawyers either study or have clients.

11. Lawyers never study.

12. All lawyers and doctors have clients.

13. Bill doesn't have a client.

14. No one owns every book.

15. Any doctor with clients is a client of some lawyer.

16. Only lawyers and doctors have clients.

17. Anyone who is a client of some lawyer is also a client of some doctor.

18. No doctor is his own client.

EXERCISE 10k

Use the suggested abbreviations in representing the following sentences.

a: Al Px: x is a person Hxy: x heard y
b: Betty Mx: x is a musician Sxy: x saw y
c: Carla Kxy: x murdered y

1. Betty and Carla saw Al, but neither one of them heard him.

2. Not everyone heard Al.

3. Al heard everyone he saw.

4. Carla didn't hear everyone.

5. Al saw someone that Carla heard.

6. No one saw everyone that Carla heard.

7. Al didn't see anyone that Carla didn't hear.

8. Only the musicians saw Carla.

9. Every musician saw Carla, but Carla didn't hear anyone.

10. Carla saw someone who hadn't heard any musicians.

11. Either everyone who was murdered saw Carla or not everyone who was murdered was a musician.

12. Neither Carla nor anyone who was murdered was a musician.

11

DERIVATIONS

We must now supplement our system of derivational rules in a way that will enable us to show the validity of predicate logic arguments. Only a few new rules are needed to make this possible.

EXISTENTIAL QUANTIFIER INTRODUCTION

One obviously valid type of argument involving quantifiers consists in the introduction of an existential sentence on the basis of a particular example.

(I.) John is a person. Pj
John eats meat. Mj
∴ At least one person eats $(\exists x: Px)Mx$
meat.

Truths about some particular individual can serve as a basis for an existential conclusion. This is *Existential Quantifier Introduction* (EQI).

$$\ldots j \ldots$$
$$-j-$$
$$\therefore \ (\exists x: \ldots x \ldots)-x-$$

Of course, this same inference pattern is available no matter what individual we are talking about, and no matter what variable we use in the conclusion of the inference, and no matter how complex the sentences are.

Al is a person who jogs. $Pa \cdot Qa$
Al ripped and sewed a T-shirt. $(\exists z: Tz)[Raz \cdot Saz]$
∴ Someone who jogs ripped and
sewed a T-shirt. $(\exists y: Py \cdot Qy)(\exists z: Tz)[Ryz \cdot Syz]$

Bill is a doctor who hired a lawyer. $Db \cdot (\exists x: Lx)Hbx$
Bill is on trial. Tb
∴   Some doctor who hired a lawyer
is on trial. $(\exists y: Dy \cdot (\exists x: Lx)Hyx)Ty$

This must also be warranted by our rule. So to state it more generally, let us say that for any constant ⓒ and any variable ⓥ, the following is an acceptable inference pattern:

(EQI)   . . .ⓒ. . .

            —ⓒ—

     ∴   (∃ⓥ: . . .ⓥ. . .)—ⓥ—

This implicational inference rule enables us to do some simple derivations.

(II) Bill is a French dentist.	**1.** $Fb \cdot Db$		
∴ Some dentists are French.	**2.** Fb	1	Simp
	3. Db	1	Simp
	4. $(\exists x: Dx)Fx$	2,3	EQI

(III) Al is a student over 65.	**1.** $Sa \cdot Oa$		
If Al is over 65, then he is eligible for Medicare.	**2.** $Oa \supset Ma$		
∴ Some students are eligible for Medicare	**3.** Sa	1	Simp
	4. Oa	1	Simp
	5. Ma	2,4	MP
	6. $(\exists x: Sx)Mx$	3,5	EQI

(IV) Charlie loves Betty.	**1.** Lcb		
Charlie is a person who will succeed.	**2.** $Pc \cdot Sc$		
∴ Someone who will succeed loves Betty.	**3.** $(\exists x: Px \cdot Sx)Lxb$	1,2	EQI

(V) Charlie loves Betty.	**1.** Lcb		
Charlie is a person who will succeed.	**2.** $Pc \cdot Sc$		
∴ Someone who loves Betty will succeed.	**3.** Pc	2	Simp
	4. Sc	2	Simp
	5. $Pc \cdot Lcb$	1,3	Conj
	6. $(\exists x: Px \cdot Lxb)Sx$	4,5	EQI

(VI) Amelia is a doctor.	**1.** Da		
Amelia owns a horse.	**2.** $(\exists x: Hx)Oax$		
∴ Some doctor owns a horse.	**3.** $(\exists y: Dy)(\exists x: Hx)\,Oyx$	1,2	EQI

(VII) Anna is tall.   **1.** Ta

    (Anna is a person.)   **2.** Pa

    ∴   Someone is tall.   **3.** $(\exists x\colon Px)Tx$ 1,2   EQI

(VIII) Al gave a bracelet to Betty.   **1.** $(\exists x\colon Bx)Gaxb$

    (Al is a person.)   **2.** Pa

    ∴   Someone gave a bracelet

    to Betty.   **3.** $(\exists y\colon Py)(\exists x\colon Bx)\,Gyxb$

                                                                        1,2   EQI

In (VII) and (VIII) the second premise is in parentheses because it would usually remain unstated in a presentation of the argument in English. (In the context of a conversation, that sort of thing is usually obvious, so we do not need to state it.) But to make the derivation of the conclusion possible, we must sometimes explicitly state such trivial additional premises. As long as we add only trivial background premises, such as

Pa Al is a person.

$(\forall x\colon Bx)Ix$ Every bracelet is a thing.

there will be no problem. (We will explore the need for this and its limitations in a later chapter.)

Free, Bound, Open, Closed

It is useful to introduce some new terminology before we proceed further in presenting our inference rules. We must have a convenient way of talking about predicative contexts and related sentences. First we will distinguish the use of variables in complete sentences from their appearance in "bare" predicative contexts.

A *bound* occurrence of a variable is an occurrence of a variable that is associated with a quantifier.

We could put this more formally:

An occurrence of a variable ⓥ is bound within a formula if either

1. that occurrence of ⓥ is immediately preceded by a quantifier:

$\exists$ⓥ

$\forall$ⓥ

or

2. that occurrence of ⓥ is within X or within Y within a formula of one of these forms:

$(\forall$ⓥ$\colon X)Y$

$(\exists$ⓥ$\colon X)Y$

Generally, a quantifier will have at least three occurrences of a bound variable associated with it.

$(\forall x: Fx)Gx$

Each occurrence of 'x' is *bound* by the quantifier.

$(\forall x: Fx \cdot Gx)Rxy$

In this formula, each occurrence of 'x' is bound, but 'y' is not bound. Unbound occurrences of variables are also called *free* occurrences.

		free	*bound*
1.	Fx	x	
2.	$Gx \cdot Hx$	x	
3.	$(\exists y: Hy)Rxy$	x	y
4.	$(\exists y: Rxy)Sxy$	x	y
5.	$Fx \cdot (\exists x: Gx)Hx$	'x' in left conjunct	'x' in right conjunct
6.	$(\exists x: Fx)Gx \supset (\forall y: Fy)Gy$		x,y
7.	$(\exists x: Rxy)(Sxy \vee Txz)$	y,z	x
8.	$(\exists x: Fx)(\exists y: Gy)\,Rxy$		x,y

An *open formula* is a formula with at least one free occurrence of a variable.

A *closed formula* is a formula that is not open.

Only **6.** and **8.** on this list are closed. The others are open formulas. An *open formula* is what we have been calling a *simple or complex predicative context*. These are fairly technical terms, but their availability will make the statement of our rules simpler and more precise.

For a further simplification, instead of writing

$\ldots a \ldots$ $-b-$
$\ldots y \ldots$ $-x-$

to represent formulas, we will employ A, B, C, and D, adding individual variables and constants when we wish to indicate which variables appear free within the formula and which individual constants appear in corresponding positions. We will write

Ax
Aa

to stand for pairs of formulas related in the following way—the formula with the constant results from substituting that constant for *every* free occurrence of the variable.

Fx	Ax
Fb	Ab
$Fy \cdot Gy$	By
$Fb \cdot Gb$	Bb
$(\exists x: Hx)Rxy$	Cy
$(\exists x: Hx)Rxa$	Ca
$(\exists x: Rxy)Kyb$	Dy
$(\exists x: Rxa)Kab$	Da

If ⓒ is an individual constant, and ⓥ is a variable, we will say that Bⓒ is a ⓒ|ⓥ *instance* (pronounced "a c-for-v instance") of Bⓥ if and only if Bⓒ is the formula that results from replacing all unbound occurrences of ⓥ in Bⓥ by ⓒ.

We then get this improved statement of EQI:

(EQI) Aⓒ
$\quad\quad$ Bⓒ
$\quad$ ∴ $(\exists$ⓥ$: A$ⓥ$)B$ ⓥ

ⓒ is an individual constant such that

(i) Aⓒ is a ⓒ|ⓥ instance of Aⓥ.
(ii) Bⓒ is a ⓒ|ⓥ instance of Bⓥ.

This permits (I)–(VIII), as we wish. Note that it also permits this:

(IX) Al loves himself.	**1.** Laa
$\quad$ Al is a person.	**2.** Pa
$\quad$ ∴ Someone loves Al.	**3.** $(\exists x: Px)Lxa$ 1,2 EQI

'Laa' is an $a|x$ instance of 'Lxa'. 'Laa' is also an $a|x$ instance of 'Lxx' and of 'Lax', so other inferences from 1 and 2 are also possible.

(X) Al loves someone.	$(\exists x: Px)Lax$	1,2 EQI
(XI) Someone loves himself.	$(\exists x: Px)Lxx$	1,2 EQI

No Accidental Binding

Our statement of EQI also prohibits something that should not be allowed but which was not prohibited by the more informally stated version of EQI on page 215. We used this inference to illustrate EQI

1. Amelia is a doctor.	Da	
2. Amelia owns a horse.	$(\exists x: Hx)Oax$	
3. So some doctor owns a horse.	$(\exists y: Dy)(\exists x: Hx) Oyx$	1,2 EQI

But as first stated, our rule EQI would seem to allow the following inference from 1 and 2 as well.

4. $(\exists x: Dx)(\exists x: Hx)\ Oxx$ 1,2 EQI

This is a very peculiar formula, since it has two quantifiers with 'x' as the variable, creating an initially puzzling situation. It is not immediately clear which 'x' in 'Oxx' goes with the first quantifier and which with the second. We shall always read such formulas as having an 'x' variable bound by the most immediately dominant quantifier with 'x'. This makes the '$(\exists x: Dx)$' quantifier phrase irrelevant in the interpretation of 4 (since it binds no later variable in the formula), and the formula says:

4'. Some horse owns itself. $(\exists x: Hx)Oxx$
                                    $(\exists x: Dx)(\exists x: Hx)Oxx$

Clearly, this does not follow from 1 and 2. Our new statement of EQI does not allow it, because '$(\exists x: Hx)Oax$' is not an $a|x$ instance of '$(\exists x: Hx)\ Oxx$'. Since there are *no unbound* occurrences of 'x' in '$(\exists x: Hx)Oxx$', there is no $a|x$ instance of '$(\exists x: Hx)Oxx$' [except perhaps '$(\exists x: Hx)Oxx$' itself]. There is no place to substitute 'a' for 'x' since 'x' is always bound.

The easiest way to remember all of this is simply to keep in mind that *accidental binding* is prohibited. In making the inference

1. Da
2. $(\exists x: Hx)Oax$
3. $(\exists x: Dx)(\exists x: Hx)\ Oxx$ 1,2   **X**

we *accidentally* bind the second to last 'x' in 4 by the '*wrong*' quantifier [by '$(\exists x: Hx)$' instead of '$(\exists x: Dx)$']. The constant 'a' appears in 'Da' and in '$(\exists x: Hx)Oax$ ', and our inference should have preserved the cross-referencing of the term positions occupied by 'a' in those sentences. But by employing 'x' instead of some other variable, we accidentally bind one position (formerly occupied by 'a') by the wrong quantifier.

1. Da
2. $(\exists x: Hx)Oax$
3. $(\exists y: Dy)(\exists x: Hx)\ Oyx$ 1,2   EQI   *Correct*
X. $(\exists x: Dx)(\exists x: Hx)Oxx$ *Incorrect*

Even more simply, we can remember that when "putting on" a quantifier phrase, we should normally use a variable that does not already occur in the formula being quantified (so 3 is correct but **X** is not).

EXERCISE 11a

In each formula

(a) number the quantifiers in order from left to right,
(b) number each occurrence of a variable with the number of the quantifier (if any) by which it is bound, and,
(c) put a zero beneath any free occurrence of a variable.

Example:

$$\overset{1}{(\forall x:\ Ax)}\overset{2}{((\exists y:\ By)}Ryx \cdot \overset{3}{(\exists z:\ Bz)}Rzy)$$
$$1\ \ \ 1\ \ \ \ \ \ 2\ \ \ \ \ 2\ \ 21\ \ \ \ \ 3\ \ \ 3\ \ 30$$

[Note that the final occurrence of 'y' is free because there is no quantifier with 'y' governing it. The quantifier phrase '(∃y: By)' governs only 'Ryx' immediately following it.]

1. *Ray*
2. (∀y: Ay)Rxy
3. (∀x: Ax)(Ba ⊃ Rxa)
4. (∀z: Bz · Rxa)(Rzy · (∃y: Ay)Ryx)
5. (∀x: Ax)(∃y: By · Ryx)Rxy
6. (∃y: Ay)Ray · (∀z: Bz)Rzy
7. (∀x: Ax · (∃y: Ay) Rxy)Bx
8. (∀x: Ax)Bx ⊃ (∀y: Cy)Rxy
9. (∀x: Ax)Rxy · (∃y: By)[Rxy · Ryz]
10. (∀x: Ax)[Rxy · (∃y: By)(Rxy · Ryz)]

UNIVERSAL QUANTIFIER EXPLOITATION

Besides EQI there is another obviously valid inference pattern involving quantified sentences.

Every philosopher is wise.	(∀x: Fx)Wx
Socrates is a philosopher.	Fs
∴ Socrates is wise.	Ws

If some property applies to every philosopher, the premise that a particular individual is a philosopher justifies drawing the conclusion that the property that applies to every philosopher applies to that individual. This inference pattern, when stated generally, constitutes the rule of *Universal Quantifier Exploitation* (UQE).

(*UQE*) (∀ⓥ: *A*ⓥ)*B*ⓥ
            Aⓒ
       ∴ *B*ⓒ

ⓒ is some individual constant such that

(i) *A*ⓒ is a ⓒ|ⓥ instance of *A*ⓥ.
(ii) *B*ⓒ is a ⓒ|ⓥ instance of *B*ⓥ.

We can now construct derivations corresponding to quite a wide range of inferences (using UQE and EQI).

(I) All collies are canines.	**1.** (∀x: Cx)Kx		
Canines don't roar.	**2.** (∀x: Kx)~Rx		
Lassie is a collie.	**3.** Cl		
∴ Lassie doesn't roar.	**4.** Kl	1,3	UQE
	5. ~Rl	2,4	UQE

(II) All cats are mammals.	**1.** (∀x: Cx)Mx		
All mammals are warm-blooded.	**2.** (∀x: Mx)Wx		
∴ If Garfield is a cat, then	**3.** Cg		AP
Garfield is warm-blooded.	**4.** Mg	1,3	UQE
	5. Wg	2,4	UQE
	6. Cg ⊃ Wg	3–5	CP

(III) All humans are mortal.	**1.** (∀x: Hx)Mx		
Betty is not mortal.	**2.** ~Mb		
∴ Betty is not human.	**3.** Hb		AP
	4. Mb	1,3	UQE
	5. Mb · ~Mb	2,4	Conj
	6. ~Hb	3–5	IP

(IV) All doctors are smart.	**1.** (∀x: Dx)Sx		
Doris is a doctor who golfs.	**2.** Dd · Gd		
∴ Some golfers are smart.	**3.** Dd	2	Simp
	4. Sd	1,3	UQE
	5. Gd	2	Simp
	6. (∃x: Gx)Sx	4,5	EQI

(V) If Al can golf, anyone can.	**1.** Ga ⊃ (∀x: Px)Gx		
Any doctor can golf.	**2.** (∀x: Dx)Gx		
Al is a doctor.	**3.** Da		
Bill is a lab technician.	**4.** Lb		
(Lab technicians are people.)	**5.** (∀x: Lx)Px		
∴ Some lab technicians can	**6.** Ga	2,3	UQE
golf.	**7.** (∀x: Px)Gx	1,6	MP
	8. Pb	4,5	UQE
	9. Gb	7,8	UQE
	10. (∃x: Lx)Gx	4,9	EQI

(VI) All men are vain or greedy.
Greedy men are doomed.
Socrates is a man.
Socrates is not doomed.
∴   Socrates is vain.

1. $(\forall x: Mx)[Vx \lor Gx]$			
2. $(\forall x: Mx \cdot Gx)Dx$			
3. Ms			
4. $\sim Ds$			
5. $Vs \lor Gs$		1,3	UQE
6. $\sim Vs$			AP
7. Gs		5,6	DS
8. $Ms \cdot Gs$		3,7	Conj
9. Ds		2,8	UQE
10. $Ds \cdot \sim Ds$		4,9	Conj
11. Vs		6–10	IP

(VII) Al and Bill are dentists.
Every dentist golfs or plays
tennis.
Al doesn't golf.
Bill doesn't play tennis.
∴   Some dentists golf and
some don't.

1. $Da \cdot Db$			
2. $(\forall x: Dx)[Gx \lor Tx]$			
3. $\sim Ga$			
4. $\sim Tb$			
5. Da		1	Simp
6. Db		1	Simp
7. $Gb \lor Tb$		2,6	UQE
8. Gb		4,7	DS
9. $(\exists x: Dx)Gx$		6,8	EQI
10. $(\exists x: Dx)\sim Gx$		3,5	EQI
11. $(\exists x: Dx)Gx \cdot (\exists x: Dx)\sim Gx$			
		9,10	Conj

(VIII) Everything Alfonso is related
to is shaggy.
Every English shepherd is
related to Basil.
∴   If Alfonso is an English
shepherd, then Basil is shaggy
and Alfonso is related to him.

1. $(\forall x: Rax)Sx$			
2. $(\forall x: Ex)Rxb$			
3. Ea			AP
4. Rab		2,3	UQE
5. Sb		1,4	UQE
6. $Sb \cdot Rab$		4,5	Conj
7. $Ea \supset (Sb \cdot Rab)$		3–6	CP

(IX) Any doctor is able to treat
everyone.
Alice is a doctor.
Bill is not able to treat Charlie.
(Charlie is a person.)
(Bill is a person.)
∴   Some doctor is able to treat
some nondoctor.

1. $(\forall x: Dx)(\forall y: Py)\, Txy$			
2. Da			
3. $\sim Tbc$			
4. Pc			
5. Pb			
6. $(\forall y: Py)Tay$		1,2	UQE
7. Db			AP
8. $(\forall y: Py)Tby$		1,7	UQE
9. Tbc		4,8	UQE
10. $Tbc \cdot \sim Tbc$		3,9	Conj
11. $\sim Db$		7–10	IP
12. Tab		5,6	UQE
13. $(\exists y: \sim Dy)Tay$		11,12	EQI
14. $(\exists x: Dx)(\exists y: \sim Dy)Txy$			
		2,13	EQI

(X) Anyone who is married (to
someone) is happy.
Bill is married to Carol.
(Bill is a person.)
(Carol is a person.)
∴ Bill is happy.

1. $(\forall x: Px \cdot (\exists y: Py)Mxy)Hx$
2. Mbc
3. Pb
4. Pc
5. $(\exists y: Py)Mby$ 2,4   EQI
6. $Pb \cdot (\exists y: Py)Mby$ 3,5   Conj
7. Hb 1,6   UQE

Derivation Strategies

A few tips may help you to produce correct and efficient derivations using
the quantifier rules.

1. Remember that EQI and UQE are *implicational inference rules*. They
do not apply within formulas. They apply only to complete formulas.

A. If Governor Riley resigns his job,
Bono will become governor.
(Riley is a person.)

1. $Rr \supset Gb$
2. Pr

X. If someone resigns his job, Bono
will become governor.

X. $(\exists x: Px)Rx \supset Gb$
Incorrect

Someone has this characteristic:
if he resigns his job, then Bono
becomes governor.

3. $(\exists x: Px)[Rx \supset Gb]$ 1,2   EQI
Correct

B. If every day last week was sunny,
then Monday was sunny.
Friday was a day last week.

1. $(\forall x: Dx)Sx \supset Sm$
2. Df

X. So if Friday was sunny, then
Monday was sunny.

X. $Sf \supset Sm$
Incorrect

2. Although the following argument form is fairly simple, derivation of
the conclusion involves indirect proof (IP).

A. All actors are balloonists.
Charlie is not a balloonist.
∴ Charlie is not an actor.

1. $(\forall x: Ax)Bx$
2. $\sim Bc$
3. Ac AP
4. Bc 1,3   UQE
5. $Bc \cdot \sim Bc$ 2,4   Conj
6. $\sim Ac$ 3–5   IP

3. If you have an existentially quantified conclusion, that tells you a
great deal about the structure of your derivation. Your last step will almost
certainly be an EQI step. EQI requires two previous steps.

$\cdot$
$\cdot$
$\cdot$

A _____

$\cdot$
$\cdot$
$\cdot$

B_____
$(\exists x: Ax)Bx$

That divides your derivation into two parts and determines your strategy. You know that you must find some particular individual about which you can prove each of those two things (A and B).

Consider the following derivation.

1. $Fa \cdot Ga$
2. $(\forall x: Gx)(Hx \cdot Rxb)$
3. $(\forall x: Rxb)Rbx$
4. $\sim Hb$
$\therefore$ $(\exists x: \sim Gx)Rxa$

$\cdot$
$\cdot$
$\cdot$

j. $\sim G-$

$\cdot$
$\cdot$
$\cdot$

k. $R-a$
$(\exists x: \sim Gx)Rxa$

To complete this derivation, we must find some name that can fill the blank in step j and in step k, while enabling us to derive both j and k. Since 'Ga' is true according to premise 1, it is unlikely that j could be '$\sim Ga$'. (That could be derived only if the premises are inconsistent.) Since 'b' is the only other name available, it seems very likely that j must be '$\sim Gb$', so k must be 'Rba'. So we can concentrate on proving each of those. The derivation would be this.

5. Gb			AP
6. $Hb \cdot Rbb$		2,5	UQE
7. Hb		6	Simp
8. $Hb \cdot \sim Hb$		4,7	Conj
9. $\sim Gb$		5–8	IP
10. Ga		1	Simp
11. $Ha \cdot Rab$		2,10	UQE
12. Rab		11	Simp
13. Rba		3,12	UQE
14. $(\exists x: \sim Gx)Rxa$		9,13	EQI

The derivation is divided into two parts, steps 5–9 and steps 10–13, leading to the conclusion. Existentially quantified conclusions will almost always have derivations that can be segmented in this way.

4. The same principles apply for multiple quantification. Suppose that from the same four premises we had to prove a multiply quantified conclusion.

$(\exists x: {\sim}Gx)(\exists y: Hy)Rxy$

We must derive that from two preceding steps

${\sim}G-$
$(\exists y: Hy)R-y$

So our derivation has this structure.

1. $Fa \cdot Ga$
2. $(\forall x: Gx)[Hx \cdot Rxb]$
3. $(\forall x: Rxb)Rbx$
4. ${\sim}Hb$
    $\therefore$ $(\exists x: {\sim}Gx)(\exists y: Hy)Rxy$

    .

    .

    .
j. ${\sim}G$＿＿＿

    .

    .

    .
k. H- - -

    .

    .

    .
l. R＿＿＿ - - -
m. $(\exists y: Hy)R$＿＿＿ y k, l EQI
n. $(\exists x: {\sim}Gx)(\exists y: Hy)Rxy$ j, m EQI

Once we note that j is more likely '${\sim}Gb$' than '${\sim}Ga$' and also note that k is more likely 'Ha' than 'Hb', we know that l must be Rba and m must be '$(\exists y: Hy)Rby$ '. The rest (deriving j, k, and l) is easy.

5. To exploit a premise governed by a universal quantifier, we need to establish some ⓒ|ⓥ instance of the open sentence that occurs within the quantifier phrase.

$(\forall ⓥ: Aⓥ)Bⓥ$

    .

    .

    .
$Aⓒ$
$Bⓒ$

So if Aⓒ is not in the premises, try to prove it.

1. $(\forall x: \sim Gx \cdot (\exists y: Hy)Rxy)Fx$
2. $(\forall x: Gx)Hx$
3. $\sim Ha \cdot Rab$
4. Gb
   ∴ Fa

   .

   .

   .

m. $\sim Ga \cdot (\exists y: Hy) Ray$
   Fa 1, m   UQE

It is obvious what the last step must be (from 1 and m to the conclusion). So now we can concentrate on deriving m.

1. $(\forall x: \sim Gx \cdot (\exists y: Hy)Rxy)Fx$
2. $(\forall x: Gx)Hx$
3. $\sim Ha \cdot Rab$
4. Gb
5. $\sim Ha$ 3   Simp
6. Ga AP
7. Ha 2,6   UQE
8. $Ha \cdot \sim Ha$ 5,7   Conj
9. $\sim Ga$ 6–8   IP
10. Hb 2,4   UQE
11. Rab 3   Simp
12. $(\exists y: Hy)Ray$ 10,11   EQI
13. $\sim Ga \cdot (\exists y: Hy) Ray$ 9,12   Conj
14. Fa 1,13   UQE

The derivation of step 13 divides into two parts, proving each conjunct (5–9, 10–12). The derivation of step 12 divides into two parts, proving 'Hb' (step 10) and proving 'Rab' (step 11).

EXERCISE 11b

Using the rules EQI and UQE (together with the rules of sentence logic), prove that each is valid.

1. $Ha \cdot Cb$
   $(\forall x: Hx)Jx$
   $(\forall x: Cx)Jx$
   ∴ $Ja \cdot Jb$

2. $Ha \cdot Gb$
   $Ha \supset Ja$
   $Gb \supset Jb$
   ∴ $(\exists x: Hx)Jx \cdot (\exists x: Gx)Jx$

3. $Hj \cdot Fj$
   $(\forall x: Hx)Mx$
   ∴ $(\exists x: Mx)Fx$

4. $(\forall x: Ax)Bx$
   $\sim Ba$
   ∴ $\sim Aa$

5. $Da \cdot Ea$
$Ea \supset (Ga \lor Fa)$
$\sim Fa \lor Ha$
$Da \supset \sim Ha$
$\therefore \quad (\exists x: Gx)Ex$

6. $Tb \cdot Fb$
$(\forall x: Tx)Rx$
$(\forall x: Rx \cdot Fx)Mx$
$\therefore \quad (\exists x: Tx)Mx$

7. $Fa \cdot Hb$
$(\forall x: Hx)Jx$
$(\forall x: Fx)(Jx \cdot \sim Hx)$
$\therefore \quad (\exists x: Jx)\sim Hx \cdot (\exists x: Jx)Hx$

8. $(\forall x: Ax \cdot Bx)Cx$
$(\forall x: Cx)(Dx \lor Ex)$
$\sim Ea$
$\therefore \quad (Aa \cdot \sim Da) \supset \sim Ba$

9. $Ba \cdot Bb$
$(\forall x: Bx)Dx$
$(Da \cdot Ea) \supset Gb$
$\therefore \quad Ea \supset (\exists x: Bx \cdot Dx) \, Gx$

10. Rab
$Pa \cdot Pb$
$(\exists x: Px)Rxb \supset (\forall x: Px)Rxb$
$\therefore \quad Rbb$

11. $(\forall x: Fx)Gx$
$(\forall x: \sim Fx)(\forall y: Gy)Rxy$
$(\forall x: Hx)\sim Gx$
$Ha \cdot Fb$
$\therefore \quad (\exists x: \sim Hx)Rax$

12. Rab
$(\forall x: Rxb)Fx$
$\sim Fb$
$\therefore \quad (\exists x: Fx)(\exists y: \sim Fy)Rxy$

13. $(\forall x: Ax)Bx$
$Ad \cdot Cd$
$\therefore \quad (\forall x: Cx)Dx \supset (\exists x: Bx)Dx$

14. $(\forall x: Fx)(\forall y: Gy)Rxy$
$Fa \cdot (Gb \cdot Gc)$
$\sim Rbc$
$\therefore \quad (\exists x: \sim Fx)(\exists y: Fy) \, Ryx$

15. $(Aa \cdot Ca) \supset (\forall x: Bx \cdot \sim Fx)Gx$
$(\forall x: Bx)Ax$
$Ba \cdot (Bb \cdot \sim Fb)$
$\therefore \quad Ca \supset (\exists x: Gx \cdot \sim Fx)Ax$

16. Hb
$(\forall x: Fx)Gx$
$(Ga \cdot Hb) \supset Rab$
$(\forall x: Hx)Jx$
$\therefore \quad Fa \supset (\exists x: Fx)(\exists y: Jy)Rxy$

17. $(Fa \cdot Gb) \cdot Rab$
$(\forall x: Fx)Hx$
$(\forall x: Gx)Kx$
$\therefore \quad (\exists x: Hx)(\exists y: Ky) \, Rxy$

18. $Fa \cdot Ga$
$(\forall x: Gx)(Hx \lor \sim Fx)$
$(\forall x: Fx \cdot Hx)(\exists y: Gy) \, Rxy$
$\therefore \quad (\exists x: Gx)(\exists y: Gy) \, Rxy$

EXISTENTIAL QUANTIFIER EXPLOITATION

We can easily show the following argument to be valid.

All collies are canines.	**1.** $(\forall x: Cx)Kx$		
Lassie is a collie that barks.	**2.** $Cl \cdot Bl$		
$\therefore$ Some canines bark.	**3.** Cl	2	Simp
	4. Bl	2	Simp
	5. Kl	1,3	UQE
	6. $(\exists x: Kx)Bx$	4,5	EQI

But clearly we do not need information about Lassie in particular to get this conclusion. Just the premise that some collies bark should be sufficient.

All collies are canines.   **1.** $(\forall x\colon Cx)Kx$
Some collies bark.   **2.** $(\exists x\colon Cx)Bx$
∴   Some canines bark.   ∴ $(\exists x\colon Kx)Bx$

But we now have no proper name to use in connection with '$(\forall x\colon Cx)Kx$' in a UQE inference, and we have no rule at all for exploiting the existential premise.

The rule of *Existential Quantifier Exploitation* (EQE) solves these two problems together. It allows us to *introduce* an individual term on the basis of an existential premise. The premise

$(\exists x\colon Cx)Bx$

guarantees that there are collies that bark. Even though we might not already have a name for one of those collies, we can introduce an individual term as though it named one of them. (The premise says that there are some.) This will make further inference possible.

The rule EQE, then, will be the following. (Note that it allows the immediate inference of two steps on the basis of a single existential sentence.)

(EQE) $(\exists ⓥ\colon Aⓥ)Bⓥ$
            ∴ $Aⓒ$
            ∴ $Bⓒ$

(i) $Aⓒ$ is a ⓒ|ⓥ instance of $Aⓥ$.
(ii) $Bⓒ$ is a ⓒ|ⓥ instance of $Bⓥ$.
(iii) ⓒ does not appear before the first of these EQE steps. (ⓒ must be new.)
(iv)   ⓒ does not appear in the last step of the derivation.

We now can derive the desired conclusion in the following way.

1. $(\forall x\colon Cx)Kx$
2. $(\exists x\colon Cx)Bx$
3. Ca 2   EQE
4. Ba 2   EQE
5. Ka 1,3   UQE
6. $(\exists x\colon Kx)Bx$ 4,5   EQI

Qualification (iii) on EQE is important. We do not wish to allow the following:

Some men are bald.   **1.** $(\exists x\colon Mx)Bx$
Some men are not bald.   **2.** $(\exists x\colon Mx){\sim}Bx$
                                3. Ma 1   EQE

Some men are both bald and not
bald

4. *Ba*		1	EQE
5. ∼*Ba*		2	EQE
6. *Ba* · ∼*Ba*		4,5	Conj
7. (∃*x*: *Mx*)[*Bx* · ∼*Bx*]		3,6	EQI

We certainly cannot validly go from premises 1 and 2 to the contradictory conclusion that some men are both bald and not bald. Step 5 is ruled out by the qualification (iii) that says *we must introduce a new individual constant* for each existentially quantified sentence we wish to exploit.

EQE allows the introduction of two steps using a new name. That name may then be used in further inferences. But any additional EQE steps, based on other existentially quantified steps of the derivation, must introduce still another name.

1. (∃*x*: *Ax*)(∃*y*: ∼*By*)*Rxy*		
2. (∃*x*: *Bx*)*Cx*		
3. (∀*x*: *Ax* · (∃*y*: *Dy*)*Rxy*)(∀*z*: *Bz*)*Rxz*		
4. (∀*x*: ∼*Bx*)*Dx*		
∴ (∃*x*: *Ax*)(∃*y*: *Cy*) *Rxy*		
5. *Ba*	2	EQE
6. *Ca*	2	EQE
7. *Ab*	1	EQE
8. (∃*y*: ∼*By*)*Rby*	1	EQE
9. ∼*Bc*	8	EQE
10. *Rbc*	8	EQE
11. *Dc*	4,9	UQE
12. (∃*y*: *Dy*)*Rby*	10,11	EQI
13. *Ab* · (∃*y*: *Dy*)*Rby*	7,12	Conj
14. (∀*z*: *Bz*)*Rbz*	3,13	UQE
15. *Rba*	5,14	UQE
16. (∃*y*: *Cy*)*Rby*	6,15	EQI
17. (∃*x*: *Ax*)(∃*y*: *Cy*) *Rxy*	7,16	EQI

Note how the existentials in steps 1, 2, and 8 were each exploited with two inference steps in which a *new* name was introduced.

Qualification (iv) is important, because the name introduced in an EQE step is really just a derivational convenience. It should not be a part of any ultimate conclusion that is derived.

Some men are bald.   **1.** (∃*x*: *Mx*)*Bx*
∴ Al is bald.   **2.** *Ba*

We do not want such evidently invalid conclusions to be allowed. The problem here is that we have introduced an individual constant, corresponding to a real name, 'Al', rather than introducing it as a mere "quasi-name" of the sort used in an EQE inference. We know that someone is bald, but we do not have information about Al or anyone else in particular. A "quasi-name" introduced in an EQE inference can be used to proceed through a derivation, but it should not appear in the derivational goal, the last step of the derivation.

EQE enlarges our derivational capacity considerably when employed in connection with the other rules of derivation.

(I) Some professors are lawyers.	**1.** $(\exists x: Rx)Lx$		
$\therefore$ Some lawyers are professors.	**2.** Ra	1	EQE
	3. La	1	EQE
	4. $(\exists x: Lx)Rx$	2,3	EQI

(II) All surgeons are doctors.	**1.** $(\forall x: Sx)Dx$		
Some surgeons perform heart	**2.** $(\exists x: Sx)Tx$		
transplants.	**3.** Sa	2	EQE
$\therefore$ Some doctors perform heart	**4.** Ta	2	EQE
transplants.	**5.** Da	1,3	UQE
	6. $(\exists x: Dx)Tx$	4,5	EQI

(III) Some lawyers are not friendly.	**1.** $(\exists x: Lx)\sim Fx$		
All optimists are friendly.	**2.** $(\forall x: Ox)Fx$		
$\therefore$ Some lawyers are not	**3.** La	1	EQE
optimists.	**4.** $\sim Fa$	1	EQE
	5. Oa		AP
	6. Fa	2,5	UQE
	7. $Fa \cdot \sim Fa$	4,6	Conj
	8. $\sim Oa$	5–7	IP
	9. $(\exists x: Lx)\sim Ox$	3,8	EQI

(IV) Some doctors are professors.	**1.** $(\exists x: Dx)Fx$		
All professors do research.	**2.** $(\forall x: Fx)Hx$		
Any doctor who does research	**3.** $(\forall x: Dx \cdot Hx)Kx$		
merits respect.	**4.** Da	1	EQE
$\therefore$ Some doctors merit respect.	**5.** Fa	1	EQE
	6. Ha	2,5	UQE
	7. $Da \cdot Ha$	4,6	Conj
	8. Ka	3,7	UQE
	9. $(\exists x: Dx)Kx$	4,8	EQI

(V) Dave loves everyone.	**1.** $(\forall x: Px)Ldx$		
$\therefore$ It is not the case that	**2.** $(\exists x: Px)\sim Ldx$		AP
there are people Dave doesn't	**3.** Pa	2	EQE
love.	**4.** $\sim Lda$	2	EQE
	5. Lda	1,3	UQE
	6. $Lda \cdot \sim Lda$	4,5	Conj
	7. $\sim(\exists x: Px)\sim Ldx$	2–6	IP

(In the next section a simpler way to do example (V) will be introduced.)

(VI) Someone loves Betty.
Anyone who loves someone is
happy.
(Betty is a person.)
∴   Someone is happy.

1.	(∃x: Px)Lxb		
2.	(∀x: Px · (∃y: Py)Lxy)Hx		
3.	Pb		
4.	Pa	1	EQE
5.	Lab	1	EQE
6.	(∃y: Py)Lay	3,5	EQI
7.	Pa · (∃y: Py)Lay	4,6	Conj
8.	Ha	2,7	UQE
9.	(∃x: Px)Hx	4,8	EQI

(VII) Some people have relatives
they hate.
Anyone who is hated is
unlucky.
∴   Some people are unlucky.

1.	(∃x: Px)(∃y: Py · Rxy)Hxy		
2.	(∀x: Px · (∃y: Py)Hyx)Ux		
3.	Pa		
4.	(∃y: Py · Ray)Hay	1	EQE
5.	Pt · Rat	4	EQE
6.	Hat	4	EQE
7.	Pt	5	Simp
8.	(∃y: Py)Hyt	3,6	EQI
9.	Pt · (∃y: Py)Hyt	7,8	Conj
10.	Ut	2,9	UQE
11.	(∃x: Px)Ux	7,10	EQI

(VIII) Some people are not happy.
Anyone who is loved is happy.
(Dave is a person.)
∴   There are people that
Dave doesn't love.

1.	(∃x: Px)~Hx		
2.	(∀x: Px · (∃y: Py)Lyx)Hx		
3.	Pd		
4.	Pa	1	EQE
5.	~Ha	1	EQE
6.	Lda		AP
7.	(∃y: Py)Lya	3,6	EQI
8.	Pa · (∃y: Py)Lya	4,7	Conj
9.	Ha	2,8	UQE
10.	Ha · ~Ha	5,9	Conj
11.	~Lda	6–10	IP
12.	(∃x: Px)~Ldx	4,11	EQI

EXERCISE 11c

Using EQI, UQE, and EQE, prove that each of the following is valid.

1. (∃x: Fx)Gx
(∀x: Gx)Hx
∴   (∃x: Fx)Hx

2. (∃x: Fx)Gx
∴   (∃x: Gx)Fx

3. (∃x: Fx)Gx
(∃x: Fx)Hx
(∀x: Hx)Kx
(∀x: Gx)~Kx
∴   (∃x: Fx)Kx · (∃x: Fx)~Kx

4. (∃x: Fx)Gx ⊃ (Fa · Ja)
(∃x: Fx)Ex
(∀x: Ex)(Gx · Hx)
(∀x: Jx)Kx
∴   (∃x: Fx)Kx

5. $Ba \cdot (\exists x: Bx)\sim Fx$
$(\forall x: Bx)Ax$
$(Aa \cdot Ca) \supset (\forall x: Bx \cdot \sim Fx)Gx$
$\therefore\ Ca \supset (\exists x: Gx \cdot \sim Fx)Ax$

6. $Fa \cdot Ga$
$(\forall x: Gx)(Hx \lor \sim Fx)$
$(\forall x: Fx \cdot Hx)(\exists y: Ky)Rxy$
$(\forall x: Kx)Jx$
$\therefore\ (\exists x: Gx)(\exists y: Ky)Rxy$

7. $(\exists x: Fx)Gx$
$(\forall x: Fx)Hx$
$\therefore\ (\exists x: Hx)Gx$

8. $(\exists x: Fx)(\exists y: Gy)Rxy$
$(\forall x: Fx)Hx$
$(\forall x: Gx)Kx$
$\therefore\ (\exists x: Hx)(\exists y: Ky)Rxy$

9. $(\exists x: Fx)(\exists y: Fy)Rxy$
$(\forall x: Fx) \cdot (\exists y: Gy)Ryx)Hx$
$(\forall x: Fx \cdot (\exists y: Gy)Rxy)\sim Hx$
$(\forall x: Fx)Gx$
$\therefore\ (\exists x: Hx)(\exists y: \sim Hy)Ryx$

10. $(\exists x: Fx \cdot (\exists y: Gy)Rxy)Rxa$
Ha
$(\forall x: (\exists y: Hy)Rxy)Hx$
$(\forall x: Hx)(\forall y: Rxy)Ryx$
$\therefore\ (\exists x: Gx)(\exists y: Fy)Rxy$

11. $(\exists x: Fx)Gx \cdot (\exists y: Gy)\sim Ky$
$(\forall x: Gx)Hx$
$(\forall x: Fx)[Hx \equiv Kx]$
$\therefore\ (\exists x: Fx)Kx \cdot (\exists y: Gy)\sim Fy$

12. $(\exists x: Fx)\sim Kx$
$(\forall x: Gx)(\forall y: Fy)Rxy$
$(\exists x: Gx)Kx$
$(\forall x: Gx \lor Fx)Hx$
$(\forall x: Hx)(\forall y: Hy \cdot Rxy)Ryx$
$\therefore\ (\exists x: Kx)(\exists y: \sim Ky) (Rxy \cdot Ryx)$

13. $(\forall x: Fx) (\forall y: Fy \cdot Ryx)Rxy$
$(\exists x: Fx)(\forall y: Fy)\sim Rxy$
Rab
$Fa \cdot Fb$
$\therefore\ Rba \cdot (\exists x: Fx)\sim Rax$

14. $(\forall x: Hx)(\forall y: Hy \cdot Rxy) [Fx \equiv \sim Fy]$
$(\forall x: Hx \cdot \sim Fx)(\exists y: Hy)Rxy$
$(\exists x: Fx \cdot (Gx \cdot Hx))(\exists y: Hy)Rxy$
$(\forall x: Hx \cdot \sim Fx)Gx$
$\therefore\ (\exists x: Gx)(\exists y: Gy)Rxy \cdot (\exists x: \sim Fx)(\exists y: Fy)Rxy$

15. $Ac \supset (\exists y: Cy)Rcy$
$\sim Ac \supset (\exists x: Ax)(\exists y: By)Rxy$
$(\forall x: Bx)(Cx)$
$\therefore\ (\exists x: Ax)(\exists y: Cy)Rxy$

16. $(\forall x: Ax)(\exists y: By)Rxy$
$(\forall x: Bx)\sim Cx$
$(\exists x: Ax)(\exists y: Cy)Rxy$
$\therefore\ (\exists x: Ax)[(\exists y: Cy)Rxy \cdot (\exists z: \sim Cz)Rxz]$

17. $(\forall x: Fx)(\forall y: Gy \cdot Rxy)\sim Ryx$
$(\exists x: Fx)Rxx$
$\therefore\ (\exists x: Fx)\sim Gx$

18. $(\forall x{:}\ Ax \cdot (\exists y{:}\ By)Rxy)Cx$
$(\exists x{:}\ Ax)(\exists y{:}\ Cy)Rxy$
$(\forall y{:}\ Cy)(\forall x{:}\ Ax \cdot Rxy)\ (\forall z{:}\ Bz)Rxz$
$\therefore\ \ (\exists x{:}\ Bx)Cx \supset (\exists y{:}\ Cy)(\exists z{:}\ Cz)Ryz$

QUANTIFIER NEGATION

In discussing the simple logical relationships among quantified sentences (in Chapter 10), we noticed some important equivalences.

1. Not all D are S.   Some D are not S.
   $\sim(\forall x{:}\ Dx)Sx$ is equivalent to $(\exists x{:}\ Dx)\sim Sx$
2. No D are S.   It is not the case that some D are S.
   $(\forall x{:}\ Dx)\sim Sx$ is equivalent to $\sim(\exists x{:}\ Dx)Sx$

These equivalences will be incorporated as equivalence rules, Quantifier Negation (QN) rules, in our system of derivational rules.

QN

(a) $\sim(\forall ⓥ{:}\ Aⓥ)Bⓥ$ $::$ $(\exists ⓥ{:}\ Aⓥ)\sim Bⓥ$
(b) $\sim(\exists ⓥ{:}\ Aⓥ(Bⓥ$ $::$ $(\forall ⓥ{:}\ Aⓥ)\sim Bⓥ$

It is useful to have available the two other equivalences as well.

(c) $\sim(\forall ⓥ{:}\ Aⓥ)\sim Bⓥ$ $::$ $(\exists ⓥ{:}\ Aⓥ)Bⓥ$
(d) $\sim(\exists ⓥ{:}\ Aⓥ)\sim Bⓥ$ $::$ $(\forall ⓥ{:}\ Aⓥ)Bⓥ$

When we add the QN rules to the three already introduced (EQI, UQE, EQE) *we have a system of rules that make possible the derivation of a conclusion in a predicate logic argument whenever the semantic features of predicate logic guarantee that it validly follows.* No additional rules are necessary, although it will be convenient to add one more (UQI, as one might expect) in the section that follows. It is worth keeping in mind, though, that we already have a *derivationally complete* system of rules.

The strategy for employing QN rules is very much like the strategy for employing the DeMorgan's equivalences. To apply our other rules, we usually need quantified sentences rather than negated sentences. QN enables us to "drive in" the negations, making application of the other rules possible.

(I) Not everyone is wise.   **1.** $\sim(\forall x{:}\ Px)Wx$
   Anyone who is not wise will   **2.** $(\forall x{:}\ Px \cdot \sim Wx)Rx$
   perish.   **3.** $(\exists x{:}\ Px)\sim Wx$ 1   QN
   $\therefore$ Some people will perish.   **4.** Pa 3   EQE

5. ~Wa	3	EQE
6. $Pa \cdot {\sim}Wa$	4,5	Conj
7. Ra	2,6	UQE
8. $(\exists x\colon Px)Rx$	4,7	EQI

Step 1 here is immediately transformed into the more useful existential 3. Similarly, a negated conclusion is derived from an equivalent formula by QN.

(II) Some people are beggars.   **1.** $(\exists x\colon Px)Bx$
No beggars are rich.   **2.** $(\forall x\colon Bx){\sim}Rx$

∴ Not everyone is rich. **3.** Pa	1	EQE
4. Ba	1	EQE
5. ~Ra	2,4	UQE
6. $(\exists x\colon Px){\sim}Rx$	3,5	EQI
7. ${\sim}(\forall x\colon Px)Rx$	6	QN

(III) Not all people are beggars.   **1.** ${\sim}(\forall x\colon Px)Bx$
Every salesman is a beggar.   **2.** $(\forall x\colon Sx)Bx$

∴ Not all people are salesmen. **3.** $(\exists x\colon Px){\sim}Bx$	1	QN
4. Pa	3	EQE
5. ~Ba	3	EQE
▸**6.** Sa		AP
7. Ba	2,6	UQE
8. $Ba \cdot {\sim}Ba$	5,7	Conj
9. ~Sa	6–8	IP
10. $(\exists x\colon Px){\sim}Sx$	4,9	EQI
11. ${\sim}(\forall x\colon Px)Sx$	10	QN

Keep in mind that QN is an equivalence rule. It applies within formulas (to parts of formulas) as well as to complete lines of derivation.

(IV) If some people are not mortal,   **1.** $(\exists x\colon Px){\sim}Mx \supset Wa$
then Aristotle was wrong.
Not all people are mortal.

2. ${\sim}(\forall x\colon Px)Mx		
3. ${\sim}(\forall x\colon Px)Mx \supset Wa$	1	QN
∴ Aristotle was wrong. **4.** Wa	2,3	MP

(V) Anyone who doesn't own a dog   **1.** $(\forall x\colon Px \cdot {\sim}(\exists y\colon Dy)Oxy)Lx$
is lucky.   **2.** $(\forall y\colon Dy){\sim}Oay$
No dog is owned by Al.   **3.** Pa

(Al is a person.) **4.** $Pa \cdot (\forall y\colon Dy){\sim}Oay$	2,3	Conj
∴ Al is lucky. **5.** $(\forall x\colon Px \cdot (\forall y\colon Dy){\sim}Oxy)Lx$		
	1	QN
6. La	4,5	UQE

EXERCISE 11d

Using UQE, EQI, EQE, and QN, derive the conclusion.

1. $\sim(\exists x: Fx)Gx$
$(\exists x: Hx)Fx$
$\therefore\quad \sim(\forall x: Hx)Gx$

2. $\sim(\exists x: Fx)(\exists y: Gy)Rxy$
$(\exists x: Hx)Rxa$
Ga
$\therefore\quad \sim(\forall x: Hx)Fx$

3. $\sim(\forall x: Dx)Ax \supset (\forall y: Dy)By$
$(\forall x: Ax)Cx$
$\therefore\quad \sim(\exists x: Dx \cdot \sim Bx) \sim Cx$

4. $\sim(\exists x: Ax)\sim Bx$
$(\forall x: \sim Ax)(\forall y: By)Lxy$
$(\forall x: Bx)\sim Cx$
$Cd \cdot Ae$
$\therefore\quad (\exists x: \sim Cx)Ldx$

5. $\sim(\forall x: Ax)Bx$
$(\forall x: (\exists y: Ay)Rxy)(\exists z: Bz)Rxz$
$(\forall x: Ax \cdot \sim Bx)(\exists y: Cy)Ryx$
$\therefore\quad (\exists y: Cy)(\exists z: Bz)\, Ryz$

6. $(\forall x: Fx)(Ax \lor Gx)$
$(\forall x: Mx)(\forall y: Gy)Cyx$
$\sim(\exists x: Mx)Cax$
$Mb \cdot Ha$
$(\forall x: Ax)Gx$
$\therefore\quad \sim(\forall x: Hx)Fx$

7. $(\forall x: Fx)(\forall y: Gy)Rxy$
$Fa \cdot (Gc \cdot Gb)$
$\sim Rbc$
$\therefore\quad (\exists x: \sim Fx)(\exists y: Fy)Ryx$

8. $(\forall x: Hx \cdot (\forall y: Hy)\sim Rxy)Ax$
$(\exists x: Hx)Ax \supset (\forall y: Ay)By$
$\sim Bc \cdot Hc$
$\therefore\quad (\exists y: Hy)Rcy$

9. $\sim(\forall x: Fx)(\exists y: Fy)Rxy$
$(\exists x: Fx)(\forall y: Fy)Rxy$
$\therefore\quad Fa \supset (\exists x: Fx)[Rxa \;\cdot (\exists y: Fy)(\sim Ryx \cdot \sim Rya)]$

10. $\sim(\forall x: Ax)(\exists y: By)Rxy$
$(\forall x: Ax \cdot (\exists y: Cy)\sim Rxy)(\exists z: Dz)Rxz$
$(\forall x: Bx \lor Dx)Cx$
$(\exists x: Bx)Ax$
$\therefore\quad (\exists x: Ax)[(\exists y: Cy)\sim Rxy \cdot (\exists z: Cz)Rxz]$

11. $\sim(\forall x: Ax)Bx$
$(\forall x: (\exists y: Ay)Rxy)(\exists z: Bz)Rxz$
$(\forall x: Ax \cdot \sim Bx)(\exists y: Cy)Ryx$
$\therefore\quad (\exists x: Bx)(\exists y: Cy)\, Ryx$

12. $\sim(\exists x: Ax \cdot (\exists y: Cy)Rxy)Bx$
$(\forall x: Cx)(\forall y: \sim By)\sim Rxy$
$(Aa \cdot Cc) \cdot Rac$
$\therefore\quad \sim(\forall x: Ax)(\forall y: Rxy)Ryx$

UNIVERSAL QUANTIFIER INTRODUCTION

Although it is not absolutely necessary to introduce another inference rule, it is very convenient to do so. Up to now we have no direct way of deriving a universally quantified conclusion, so it is natural to expect there to be a rule of *Universal Quantifier Introduction* (UQI).

On the other hand, we cannot expect UQI to be very much like EQI.

Al is a friendly person.	$Fa \cdot Pa$
Al is a Greek.	Ga
∴ Some friendly people are Greek.	$(\exists x: Fx \cdot Px)Gx$
X All friendly people are Greek. **X**	**X**$(\forall x: Fx \cdot Px)Gx$ **X**

Clearly, the universal conclusion could not follow from premises like these.

There is a strategy commonly used in establishing universal conclusions. If we wish to prove 'All A's are B's', we say

Suppose c stands for some arbitrarily selected A.

We go on to prove

c would have to be a B.

From that fact that we can prove of any arbitrarily selected A that it must be a B, we conclude that any A must be a B. This rule will, like CP and IP, require a subderivation. In this case we use the subderivation to explore the consequences of the assumption that something is A.

┌─►Ac	AP
│ .	
│ .	
│ .	
│ Bc	
└───	
$(\forall x: Ax)Bx$	UQI

If our assumption that c is A enables us to conclude that c is B, then we can conclude '$(\forall x: Ax)Bx$', as long as no other assumptions are associated with c (i.e., as long as c is "arbitrarily selected"). The easiest way to guarantee that there is no special information associated with c prior to the AP step is to require the c not appear in any step prior to the AP step.

Consider a simple example.

All hyenas are canines.	**1.** $(\forall x: Hx)Kx$		
All canines have teeth.	**2.** $(\forall x: Kx)Tx$		
∴ All hyenas have teeth.	┌─►**3.** Hc		AP
	│ **4.** Kc	1,3	UQE
	└ **5.** Tc	2,4	UQE
	6. $(\forall x: Hx)Tx$	3–5	UQI

If we assume that 'c' refers to a hyena (3), we can show that 'c' refers to something with teeth (5). But there is nothing special about 'c'. Whenever we assume that something is a hyena, we can prove (given the two premises) that it has teeth. Thus we can conclude (6) that all hyenas have teeth.

(As an illustration of how to get by without employing UQI, here is a derivation of the same conclusion that does not employ UQI.

1. $(\forall x: Hx)Kx$		
2. $(\forall x: Kx)Tx$		
3. $(\exists x: Hx){\sim}Tx$		AP
4. Hc	3	EQE
5. ${\sim}Tc$	3	EQE
6. Kc	1,4	UQE
7. Tc	2,6	UQE
8. $Tc \cdot {\sim}Tc$	5,7	Conj
9. ${\sim}(\exists x: Hx){\sim}Tx$	3–8	IP
10. $(\forall x: Hx)Tx$	9	QN

We employ IP, QN, and EQE to get our general conclusion, and the derivation is significantly longer. But by doing this sort of thing we could do without UQI.)

The complete statement of our rule UQI is this.

(UQI) .

.

.

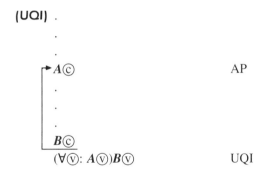

$A\copyright$	AP
$B\copyright$	
$(\forall \text{\textcircled{v}}: A\text{\textcircled{v}})B\text{\textcircled{v}}$	UQI

1. $A\copyright$ is a $\copyright\,|\,\text{\textcircled{v}}$ instance of $A\text{\textcircled{v}}$, *and vice versa*.
2. $B\copyright$ is a $\copyright\,|\,\text{\textcircled{v}}$ instance of $B\text{\textcircled{v}}$, *and vice versa*.
3. $\copyright$ does not appear in any step prior to this AP step.
4. If there is an individual constant in $B\copyright$ that was introduced in an *EQE* step, then the *EQE* step must occur before this AP step (i.e., prior to the beginning of the subderivation).

Restriction (3) guarantees that no additional assumptions are associated with $\copyright$. The UQI step depends upon what we can prove from the assumption $A\copyright$ without other special assumptions about $\copyright$.

The need for restriction (4) has not been explained previously, but without this restriction there would be a difficulty (although it is a difficulty that rarely comes up in derivations). The following argument is *invalid*:

For any number there is some number it is less than.

Anything such that every number is less than it is huge.

∴   Some huge thing is such that every number is less than it.

Premises 1 and 2 are true, yet the conclusion is false (since there is nothing such that every number is less than it). Yet without restriction (4) on UQI we could derive that conclusion.

1. $(\forall x\colon Nx)(\exists y\colon Ny)\, Lxy$

2. $(\forall z\colon (\forall x\colon Nx)Lxz)\, Hz$

   3. Nc AP

   4. $(\exists y\colon Ny)Lcy$ 1,3   UQE

   5. Lca 4   EQE

X 6. $(\forall x\colon Nx)Lxa$ 3–5   **X**

   7. Ha 2,6   UQE

   8. $(\exists y\colon Hy)(\forall x\colon Nx)\, Lxy$ 6,7   EQI

Step 6 is prohibited by restriction (4), since 'a' is introduced in step 5, an EQE step, and does not appear before step 3. Thus (4) enables us to rule out this kind of incorrect derivation.

Now that we have all of the rules that we will be employing, it is worth stating them together.

QN

$\sim(\forall \text{\textcircled{v}}\colon A\text{\textcircled{v}})B\text{\textcircled{v}}$ :: $(\exists \text{\textcircled{v}}\colon A\text{\textcircled{v}})\!\sim\!B\text{\textcircled{v}}$

$\sim(\exists \text{\textcircled{v}}\colon A\text{\textcircled{v}})B\text{\textcircled{v}}$ :: $(\forall \text{\textcircled{v}}\colon A\text{\textcircled{v}})\!\sim\!B\text{\textcircled{v}}$

$\sim(\forall \text{\textcircled{v}}\colon A\text{\textcircled{v}})\!\sim\!B\text{\textcircled{v}}$ :: $(\exists \text{\textcircled{v}}\colon A\text{\textcircled{v}})B\text{\textcircled{v}}$

$\sim(\exists \text{\textcircled{v}}\colon A\text{\textcircled{v}})\!\sim\!B\text{\textcircled{v}}$ :: $(\forall \text{\textcircled{v}}\colon A\text{\textcircled{v}})B\text{\textcircled{v}}$

UQE

$(\forall \text{\textcircled{v}}\colon A\text{\textcircled{v}})B\text{\textcircled{v}}$ ⓒ is an individual constant, where

$A\text{\textcircled{c}}$ **(i)** $A\text{\textcircled{c}}$ is a ⓒ|ⓥ instance of $A\text{\textcircled{v}}$.

∴ $B\text{\textcircled{c}}$ UQE   **(ii)** $B\text{\textcircled{c}}$ is a ⓒ|ⓥ instance of $B\text{\textcircled{v}}$.

EQE

$(\exists \text{\textcircled{v}}\colon A\text{\textcircled{v}})B\text{\textcircled{v}}$ ⓒ is some individual constant such

∴ $A\text{\textcircled{c}}$ EQE   that

∴ $B\text{\textcircled{c}}$ EQE   **(i)** $A\text{\textcircled{c}}$ is a ⓒ|ⓥ instance of $A\text{\textcircled{v}}$.

                                       (ii) $B\text{\textcircled{c}}$ is a ⓒ|ⓥ instance of $B\text{\textcircled{v}}$.

                                       (iii) ⓒ does not appear before the first of these (EQE) steps.

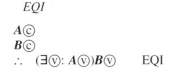

EQI

Aⓒ
Bⓒ
∴ (∃ⓥ: Aⓥ)Bⓥ   EQI

ⓒ is an individual constant such that
(i) Aⓒ is a ⓒ⎮ⓥ instance of Aⓥ.
(ii) Bⓒ is a ⓒ⎮ⓥ instance of Bⓥ.

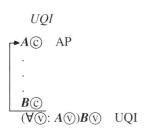

UQI

Aⓒ AP

·
·
·

Bⓒ
(∀ⓥ: Aⓥ)Bⓥ   UQI

(i) Aⓒ is a ⓒ⎮ⓥ instance of Aⓥ, *and vice versa.*
(ii) Bⓒ is a ⓒ⎮ⓥ instance of Bⓥ, *and vice versa.*
(iii) ⓒ does not appear free in any step prior to this AP step.
(iv) Any constant in Bⓒ that was introduced in an *EQE* step must occur prior to this *AP* step.

Strategy Guidelines for Constructing Derivations

In addition to the strategy principles for sentence logic, the following apply.

1. Use QN to "drive in" negations in negated premises (and negated parts of premises).
2. Exploit existentials (use EQE) as soon as possible (introducing a new name in doing so).
3. Always look for UQE steps. If you already have (∀ⓥ: Aⓥ)Bⓥ, try to establish A—if you don't already have it.
4. Always look for these steps:
   (∀ⓥ: Aⓥ)Bⓥ
   ∼Bⓒ
   ∴ ∼Aⓒ
   Prove ∼Aⓒ by indirect proof (assume Aⓒ).
5. Prove an existential '(∃x: Ax)Bx' by proving Aⓒ and Bⓒ.
6. Prove universals by UQI. To prove '(∀x: Ax)Bx', assume Aⓒ and derive Bⓒ (where ⓒ is some term not occurring outside the sub-derivation).
7. Remember that EQE, EQI, UQE, and UQI are all *implicational infer-ence rules.*

Examples

(I) All of John's brothers went to medical school.

1. (∀x: Bxj)Mx
2. (∀x: Mx)Dx

Anyone who went to medical school has had substantial debts. Anyone who has had substantial debts worries about money. ∴ All of John's brothers worry about money.

3. $(\forall x: Dx)Wx$		
▶**4.** Bcj		AP
5. Mc	1,4	UQE
6. Dc	2,5	UQE
7. Wc	3,6	UQE
8. $(\forall x: Bxj)Wx$	4–7	UQI

(II) No politican takes risks.
Every statesman takes risks.
∴ No politician is a statesman.

1. $(\forall x: Tx){\sim}Rx$		
2. $(\forall x: Sx)Rx$		
▶**3.** Ta		AP
4. ${\sim}Ra$	1,3	UQI
▶**5.** Sa		AP
6. Ra	2,5	UQI
7. $Ra \cdot {\sim}Ra$	4,6	Conj
8. ${\sim}Sa$	5–7	IP
9. $(\forall x: Tx){\sim}Sx$	3–8	UQI

(III) Every dog either barks or yelps.
Dogs that bark make terrible pets.
Dogs that yelp make terrible pets.
∴ Dogs are always terrible pets.

1. $(\forall x: Dx)(Bx \lor Yx)$		
2. $(\forall x: Dx \cdot Bx)Tx$		
3. $(\forall x: Dx \cdot Yx)Tx$		
▶**4.** Db		AP
5. $Bb \lor Yb$	1,4	UQE
▶**6.** Bb		AP
7. $Db \cdot Bb$	4,6	Conj
8. Tb	2,7	UQE
9. $Bb \supset Tb$	6–8	CP
▶**10.** Yb		AP
11. $Db \cdot Yb$	4,6	Conj
12. Tb	3,11	UQE
13. $Yb \supset Tb$	10–12	CP
14. $Tb \lor Tb$	5,9,13	CD
15. Tb	14	Rep
16. $(\forall x: Dx)Tx$	4–15	UQI

(IV) Any dog with a bone guards it.
No dog guarding a bone barks.
Every dog in the neighborhood has a bone.
∴ No dogs in the neighborhood are barking

1. $(\forall y: By)(\forall x: Dx \cdot Hxy)Gxy$		
2. $(\forall x: Dx \cdot (\exists y: By)Gxy){\sim}Rx$		
3. $(\forall x: Dx \cdot Nx)(\exists y: By)Hxy$		
▶**4.** $Dc \cdot Nc$		AP
5. $(\exists y: By)Hcy$	3,4	UQE
6. Ba	5	EQE
7. Hca	5	EQE
8. Dc	4	Simp
9. $(\forall x: Dx \cdot Hxa)Gxa$	1,6	UQE
10. $Dc \cdot Hca$	7,8	Conj
11. Gca	9,10	UQE
12. $(\exists y: By)Gcy$	6,11	EQI
13. $Dc \cdot (\exists y: By)Gcy$	8,12	Conj
14. ${\sim}Rc$	2,13	UQE
15. $(\forall x: Dx \cdot Nx){\sim}Rx$	4–14	UQI

(V) Either everyone will behave well or else no one will get privileges.
Only those with privileges will go to town.
∴   No one who does not behave well will go to town.

1. $(\forall x: Px)Bx \ \lor \ (\forall x: Px)\sim Gx$		
2. $(\forall x: Tx)Gx$		
3. $Pa \cdot \sim Ba$		AP
4. Pa	3	Simp
5. $\sim Ba$	3	Simp
6. $(\exists x: Px)\sim Bx$	4,5	EQI
7. $\sim(\forall x: Px)Bx$	6	QN
8. $(\forall x: Px)\sim Gx$	1,7	DS
9. $\sim Ga$	4,8	UQE
10. Ta		AP
11. Ga	2,10	UQE
12. $Ga \cdot \sim Ga$	9,11	Conj
13. $\sim Ta$	10–12	IP
14. $(\forall x: Px \cdot \sim Bx) \ \sim Tx$		
	3–13	UQE

(VI) Anyone who is loved loves everyone.
No one loves Chuck.
(Chuck is a person.)
∴   No one loves anyone.

1. $(\forall x: Px \cdot (\exists y: Py)Lyx)(\forall z: Pz)Lxz$		
2. $\sim(\exists x: Px)Lxc$		
3. Pc		
4. $(\forall x: Px)\sim Lxc$	2	QN
5. Pa		AP
6. Pb		AP
7. Lab		AP
8. $(\exists y: Py)Lyb$	5,7	EQI
9. $Pb \cdot (\exists y: Py)Lyb$	6,8	Conj
10. $(\forall z: Pz)Lbz$	1,9	UQE
11. Lbc	3,10	UQE
12. $\sim Lbc$	4,3	UQE
13. $Lbc \cdot \sim Lbc$	11,12	Conj
14. $\sim Lab$	7–13	UQI
15. $(\forall y: Py)\sim Lay$	6–14	UQI
16. $(\forall x: Px)(\forall y: Py) \ \sim Lxy$		
	5–15	UQI

EXERCISE 11e

Prove that each is valid.

1. $(\forall x: Fx)Gx$
$(\forall x: Hx)\sim Gx$
∴ $(\forall x: Hx)\sim Fx$

2. $(\exists x: Hx)Fx \supset (\forall x: Hx)Gx$
∴ $(\forall x: Hx \cdot \sim Gx)\sim Fx$

3. $(\forall x: Rxx)Gx$
$(\forall x: Hx)\sim Gx$
∴ $(\forall x: Fx)Hx \supset (\forall x: Fx)\sim Rxx$

4. (∀x: (∃y: Hy) Rxy)Rxa
   (∀x: Gx)Rxb · Gb
   ∴   (∀x: Gx)Hx ⊃ (∀x: Gx)Rxa

5. (∀x: Fx)(∀y: Gy)Rxy
   (∃x: Fx)(∃y: ~Fy)~Rxy
   ∴   (∃x: ~Fx)~Gx

6. ~(∀x: Ax)(Bx · Rxa)
   (∀x: Rax)Rxa
   ~(∃x: Ax)~Bx
   ∴   (∃x: Ax)~Rax

7. ~(∃x: Fx · (∃y: Gy)Rxy)Hx
   (∀x: Kx)Rxb
   ∴   Gb ⊃ ~(∃x: Fx · Hx)Kx

8. (∃x: Ax · Dxb)(∀z: Dxz)Oz
   ∴   Ob

9. (∀x: Bx · (∃y: Gy)Lxy)(∀y: Gy)Lyx
   (∃x: Gx)Lax
   Ba
   ∴   (∀y: Gy)(∃x: Bx) Lyx

10. (∀x: Fx)(∀y: Gy)~Rxy
   (∀x: Hx)(∀y: Hy)Rxy
   (∀x: Fx ∨ Gx)Hx
   ∴   ~(∃x: Fx)Gx

11. (∀x: Fx)(∀y: Gy)~Rxy
   (∀x: Fx)(∃y: Gy)Rxy
   (∃x: Hx)Rxa ⊃ ~(∃y: Gy)Ray
   Ha
   ∴   ~(∃x: Hx)Fx · ~(∃x: Hx)Rxa

12. (∀x: Fx)(∃y: Gy)Rxy
   ~(∃x: Gx)Rxx
   (∃x: Fx)Rxx
   ∴   (∃x: Fx)(∃y: Fy) Rxy · (∃x: Rxx)(∃y: ~Ryy)Rxy

13. (∀x: (∃y: Fy) Lyx)Hx
   Fa
   (∃x: Fx)Hx ⊃ (∀x: Hx)Gx
   (∃x: Hx)~Gx
   ∴   ~(∀x: Fx)(∃y: Fy)Lyx

14. (∀x: Fx)(∀y: Fy · Rxy)Ryx
   Rab · (Fa · Fb)
   (∀x: (∃y: Fy)Rxy)Rxx
   (∃x: Fx)~(∃y: Fy)Rxy
   ∴   [Rbb · (∃x: Fx)~Rxb] · (∀x: Fx · Rbx)Rxx

15. (∀x: Gx)(∀y: Fy)Lyx
   (∀x: Fx)~(∀z: Gz)Lxz
   ∴   (∃x: Gx)Gx ⊃ (∀x: Fx)[(∃y: Gy)Lxy · (∃z: Gz)~Lxz]

16. $(\forall x: Fx)Hxa$
$(\exists x: Gx)Hax$
$(\forall x: Fx \lor Gx)(\forall y: Hxy) (\forall z: Hyz)Hxz$
$Fb \cdot (\forall y: Fy)(\exists z: Gz) Hzy$
$\therefore \quad [Hba \cdot (\exists x: Gx)Hbx] \cdot (\exists y: Gy)(\exists z: Gz)Hyz$

17. $(\forall x: (\exists y: Ay) Rxy)Rxa$
$(\exists x: Ax)Rax$
$\sim(\forall x: Cx)Bx$
$(\forall x: Rxa)Bx$
$\therefore \quad [(\forall x: Ax \cdot Rxx)Bx \cdot (\exists x: Rxx)(\exists y: Ay)Rxy] \cdot (\exists x: Cx)(\forall y: Ay)\sim Rxy$

18. $(\exists x: Fx)Rxx$
$(\forall x: (\exists y: Fy)Ryx)Gx$
$\sim(\exists x: Hx)Rxx$
$\therefore \quad [\sim(\forall x: Fx)Hx \cdot (\exists y: Fy)Gy] \cdot (\forall z: \sim Gz) \sim(\exists y: Fy)Ryz$

19. $\sim(\exists x: Ax \cdot (\exists y: By)Rxy)Rxb$
$(\forall x: Rxx)Rxb$
$\therefore \quad (\forall x: Ax \cdot Rxx)\sim Bx$

20. $(\forall x: (\exists y: Fy) Rxy)Hx$
Fa
$(\exists x: Fx)Hx \supset (\forall x: Hx)Gx$
$(\exists x: Hx)\sim Gx$
$\therefore \quad \sim(\forall x: Fx)(\exists y: Fy) Rxy$

21. $(\forall x: Fx)(\forall y: Fy \cdot Rxy)Ryx$
$Rab \cdot (Fa \cdot Fb)$
$(\forall x: (\exists y: Fy)Rxy)Rxx$
$(\exists x: Fx)\sim(\exists y: Fy)Rxy$
$\therefore \quad [Rbb \cdot (\exists x: Fx)\sim Rxb] \cdot (\forall x: Fx \cdot Rbx)Rxx$

22. $(\forall x: Ax)(\exists y: By)Rxy$
$(\forall x: Bx)Ax$
$\sim(\exists x: Ax)(\sim Bx \lor \sim Cx)$
$\therefore \quad (\forall x: Ax)(\exists y: Ay) Rxy \cdot (\forall x: Ax)(\exists y: Cy) Rxy$

23. $(\forall x: Fx)(\forall y: Fy \cdot Gy)Rxy$
$(\exists y: Gy)(\forall x: Fx)\sim Rxy$
$\therefore \quad (\exists x: Gx)\sim Fx \cdot \{(\exists x: Gx)Fx \supset (\forall x: Fx) [(\exists y: Gy)Rxy \cdot (\exists z: Gz)\sim Rxz]\}$

24. $(\forall x: Fx)Rxa$
$(\exists x: Gx)Rax$
$(\forall x: Fx \lor Gx)(\forall y: Rxy) (\forall z: Ryz)Rxz$
$Fb \cdot (\forall y: Fy)(\exists z: Gz) Rzy$
$\therefore \quad Rba \cdot [(\exists x: Gx)Rbx \cdot (\exists y: Gy)(\exists z: Gz)Ryz]$

25. $(\forall x: (\exists y: Ay) Rxy)Rxa$
$(\exists x: Ax)Rax$
$\sim(\forall x: Cx)Bx$
$(\forall x: Rxa)Bx$
$\therefore \quad [(\forall x: Ax \cdot Rxx)Bx \cdot (\exists x: Rxx)(\exists y: Ay)Ryy] \cdot (\exists x: Cx)(\forall y: Ay)\sim Rxy$

26. $(\forall x: Ax)(\forall y: By \cdot Rxy)Ryx$
$\sim(\exists x: Bx)(\exists y: Cy) Rxy$
$(\forall x: Ax)(\forall y: By \cdot Rxy) (\forall z: Az \cdot Ryz)Rxz$
$\therefore \quad (\forall x: Ax \cdot (\exists y: By)Rxy)\sim Cx \cdot (\forall z: Az)[(\exists y: By)Rzy \supset Rzz]$

27. $(\forall x: Fx)(\forall y: Fy)Rxy$
$(\forall x: (\forall z: Fz)Rzx)Gx$
$\sim(\exists x: Hx)Rxx$
$\therefore \quad (\forall x: Fx)[Gx \cdot \sim Hx] \cdot (\forall x: \sim Gx)(\exists y: Fy) \sim Ryx$

INCONSISTENCY

Just as we used the derivational rules of sentence logic to show both validity of arguments and inconsistency of sets of sentences, we shall use the system of predicate logic rules for showing both. To establish that a set of sentences is inconsistent, show that a contradiction of the form $q \cdot \sim q$ is derivable. $q \cdot \sim q$ cannot be true, so if it is derivable from a set of sentences, then the members of that set cannot all be true.

All birds are feathered.	**1.** $(\forall x: Bx)Rx$		
Anything feathered flies.	**2.** $(\forall x: Rx)Lx$		
Not all birds fly.	**3.** $\sim(\forall x: Bx)Lx$		
	4. $(\exists x: Bx)\sim Lx$	3	QN
	5. Ba	4	EQE
	6. $\sim La$	4	EQE
	7. Ra	1,5	UQE
	8. La	2,7	UQE
	9. $La \cdot \sim La$	6,8	Conj

Since 9 cannot be true (no matter what individual 'a' stands for), the original set (1–3) is not consistent.

No one who knows John likes him.	**1.** $(\forall x: Px \cdot Kxj)\sim Lxj$		
Anyone who is liked likes everyone.	**2.** $(\forall x: (\exists y: Py)Lyx) (\forall z: Pz)Lxz$		
Al knows John.	**3.** Kaj		
Al likes Bill.	**4.** Lab		
(Al, Bill, and John are people.)	**5.** $(Pa \cdot Pb) \cdot Pj$		
	6. $Pa \cdot Pb$	5	Simp
	7. Pa	6	Simp
	8. $Pa \cdot Kaj$	3,7	Conj
	9. $\sim Laj$	1,8	UQE
	10. $(\exists y: Py)Lyb$	4,7	EQI
	11. $(\forall z: Pz)Lbz$	2,10	UQE

12. Lba	7,11	UQE
13. Pb	6	Simp
14. $(\exists y\!: Py)Lya$	12,13	EQI
15. $(\forall z\!: Pz)Laz$	2,14	UQE
16. Pj	5	Simp
17. Laj	15,16	UQE
18. $Laj \cdot \sim Laj$	9,17	Conj

As in sentence logic, the contradiction must be derived from the initial set of sentences alone. Any additional assumptions employed must be discharged (by CP, IP, or UQI). In other words, every subderivation must be closed.

1. $(\forall x\!: Ax \cdot Bx)Cx$		
2. $(\forall x\!: Ax \cdot Bx)\sim Cx$		
3. Aa		AP
4. Ba		AP
5. $Aa \cdot Ba$	3,4	Conj
6. Ca	1,5	UQE
7. $\sim Ca$	2,5	UQE
8. $Ca \cdot \sim Ca$	6,7	Conj
9. $\sim Ba$	4–8	IP
10. $(\forall x\!: Ax)\sim Bx$	3–9	UQI

The contradiction in step 7 does not show any inconsistency in the set consisting of the two sentences. It shows only that 1–4 constitute an inconsistent set, but 3 and 4 are additional assumptions, not part of the initial set of sentences (1 and 2). Now consider a new set, 1–3, below.

1. $(\forall x\!: Ax \cdot Bx)Cx$		
2. $(\forall x\!: Ax \cdot Bx)\sim Cx$		
3. $Ac \cdot Bc$		
4. Cc	1,3	UQE
5. $\sim Cc$	2,3	UQE
6. $Cc \cdot \sim Cc$	4,5	Conj

1–3 constitute an inconsistent set, since 6 is derivable without additional assumptions.

Subderivations may occur within proofs of inconsistency as long as they are closed.

1. $(\forall x\!: Ax \cdot (\forall y\!: By)Rxy)Cx$	
2. $(\forall x\!: Bx)Ax$	

3. $(\forall x: Ax)(\forall y: Ay) Rxy$

4. $(\exists x: Ax)\sim Cx$

5. Ae	4	EQE
6. $\sim Ce$	4	EQE
7. $(\forall y: Ay)Rey$	3,5	UQE
8. Ree	5,7	UQE
9. Bb		AP
10. Ab	2,9	UQE
11. Reb	7,10	UQE
12. $(\forall y: By)Rey$	9–11	UQI
13. $Ae \cdot (\forall y: By)Rey$	5,12	Conj
14. Ce	1,13	UQE
15. $Ce \cdot \sim Ce$	6,14	Conj

EXERCISE 11f

For each set, show that it is inconsistent.

1. $\sim(\forall x: Hx)Gx \supset (\forall x: Hx)\sim Fx$
$(\exists x: Hx \cdot \sim Gx)Fx$

2. $(\forall x: Fx)(\forall y: Gy)Rxy$
$(\forall x: Hx)\sim Rxx$
$(\forall x: Fx)Hx$
$(\exists x: Fx)Gx$

3. $(\forall x: (\exists y: Hy)Rxy)Rxa$
$Hb \cdot (\forall x: Gx)Rxb$
$(\forall x: Gx)Hx$
$\sim(\forall x: Gx)Rxa$

4. $(\forall x: Fx)(\forall y: Gy)Rxy$
$(\exists x: Fx)(\exists y: \sim Fy)\sim Rxy$
$(\forall x: \sim Gx)Fx$

5. $(\exists x: Fx \cdot Rxa)(\forall z: Rxz)Gz$
$Ga \supset (\forall x: Rxa)Hx$
$\sim(\exists x: Fx)Hx$

6. $(\forall x: Fx \cdot (\forall y: Hy)Rxy)\sim Rxx$
$(\forall x: Gx)(\forall y: Gy)Rxy$
$(\exists x: Fx)Gx$
$(\forall x: Hx)Gx$

7. $\sim(\forall x: Ax)(Bx \cdot Dx)$
$(\forall x: Bx)Dx$
$(\forall x: Cx)Bx$
$(\forall x: Ax)Cx$

8. $(\forall x: Bx)(Cx \lor Dx)$
$(\forall x: Cx)(Ax \cdot Ex)$
$(\forall x: Bx \cdot Dx)(Cx \cdot Ex)$
$(\exists x: Bx)\sim Ex$

9. $(Ca \lor Da) \supset (\exists x: Fx)Gx$
$\sim(\exists x: Fx \cdot Hx)(Gx \lor \sim Dx)$
$(\forall x: Fx)Hx$
$Fa \lor Ca$

10. $(\forall x: Kbx)Dxa$
$(\exists x: Rxc)Kbx$
$(\forall x: Rxc)(\forall y: Dxy)Dcy$
$\sim Dca$

11. $(\forall x: Ax)(\forall y: By)Rxy$
$(\forall x: Cx)Bx$
$(\forall x: Ax)Cx$
$(\exists x: Ax)\sim(\exists y: Cy) [Rxy \cdot Ryx]$

12. $(\forall x: Fx)Rax$
$(\forall y: Fy)(\forall z: Gz)Ryz$
$(\forall x: (\forall y: Gy)Rxy)(\forall z: Fz)Rxz$
$\sim(\forall x: Fx)[Rax \cdot Rxx]$

EQUIVALENCE

As we saw in Chapter 9, derivational techniques are used for showing equivalence as well as for showing validity and inconsistency. To show that two sentences are equivalent, we derive each from the other. Our predicate logic rules can also be used in this way to show equivalence.

I. '$(\forall x: Ax)[Bx \cdot Cx]$' is equivalent to '$(\forall x: Ax)Bx \cdot (\forall x: Ax)Cx$'.

1.	$(\forall x: Ax)(Bx \cdot Cx)$	
►**2.**	Ac	AP
3.	$Bc \cdot Cc$	UQE
4.	Bc	Simp
5.	$(\forall x: Ax)Bx$	UQI
►**6.**	Ad	AP
7.	$Bd \cdot Cd$	UQE
8.	Cd	Simp
9.	$(\forall x: Ax)Cx$	UQI
10.	$(\forall x: Ax)Bx \cdot (\forall x: Ax)Cx$	Conj

1.	$(\forall x: Ax)Bx \cdot (\forall x: Ax)Cx$	
►**2.**	Ac	AP
3.	$(\forall x: Ax)Bx$	Simp
4.	Bc	UQE
5.	$(\forall x: Ax)Cx$	Simp
6.	Cc	UQE
7.	$Bc \cdot Cc$	Conj
8.	$(\forall x: Ax)(Bx \cdot Cx)$	UQI

II. '$(\forall x: Ax \cdot (\exists y: By)Rxy)Cx$' is equivalent to '$(\forall y: By)(\forall x: Ax \cdot Rxy)Cx$'.

1.	$(\forall x: Ax \cdot (\exists y: By)Rxy)Cx$	
►**2.**	Bc	AP
►**3.**	$Ad \cdot Rdc$	AP
4.	Ad	Simp
5.	Rdc	Simp
6.	$(\exists y: By)Rdy$	EQI
7.	$Ad \cdot (\exists y: By)Rdy$	Conj
8.	Cd	UQE
9.	$(\forall x: Ax \cdot Rxc)Cx$	UQI
10.	$(\forall y: By)(\forall x: Ax \cdot Rxy)Cx$	UQI

1.	$(\forall y: By)(\forall x: Ax \cdot Rxy)Cx$	
►**2.**	$Ad \cdot (\exists y: By)Rdy$	AP
3.	Ad	Simp
4.	$(\exists y: By)Rdy$	Simp
5.	Bc	EQE
6.	Rdc	EQE
7.	$(\forall x: Ax \cdot Rxc)Cx$	UQE
8.	$Ad \cdot Rdc$	Conj
9.	Cd	UQE
10.	$(\forall x: Ax \cdot (\exists y: By)Rxy)Cx$	UQI

As before, if an equivalence can be demonstrated using only equivalence rules, we can write a single "two-directional" proof of equivalence (instead of two separate one-directional derivations). These work both from the top down and from the bottom up.

III. '~($\forall x$: Ax)[Bx · Cx]' is equivalent to '($\exists x$: Ax)[~Bx ∨ ~Cx]'.
   1. ~($\forall x$: Ax)[Bx · Cx]

                             QN

   2. ($\exists x$: Ax)~[Bx · Cx]

                             DeM

   3. ($\exists x$: Ax)[~Bx ∨ ~Cx]
IV. '~($\exists x$: Ax)[Bx · Cx]' is equivalent to '($\forall x$: Ax)[Bx ⊃ ~Cx]'.
   1. ~($\exists x$: Ax)[Bx · Cx]

                             QN

   2. ($\forall x$: Ax)~[Bx · Cx]

                             DeM

   3. ($\forall x$: Ax)[~Bx ∨ ~Cx]

                             CE

   4. ($\forall x$: Ax)[Bx ⊃ ~Cx]

EXERCISE 11g

Use the system of derivational rules to show that the following are *equivalent*:

1. ($\exists x$: Ax · Bx)Cx
    ($\exists x$: Bx · Cx)Ax

2. ($\forall x$: Ax)Bx
    ($\forall x$: Ax)[Ax · Bx]

3. ($\forall x$: Ax · Bx)Cx
    ($\forall x$: Ax)[Bx ⊃ Cx]

4. ($\forall x$: Ax ∨ Bx)Cx
    ($\forall x$: Ax)Cx · ($\forall y$: By) Cy

5. ~($\exists x$: Ax)[Bx · ~Cx]
    ($\forall x$: Ax · Bx)Cx

6. ($\exists x$: Ax · ($\forall y$: By)Rxy)($\forall z$: Cz)Rxz
    ($\exists x$: Ax)($\forall y$: By)($\forall z$: Cz)[Rxy · Rxz]

7. ($\forall x$: Ax)[Bx ⊃ Ba]
    ($\exists x$: Ax)Bx ⊃ Ba

8. ($\forall x$: Ax · ($\exists y$: By)Rxy)Cx
    ($\forall y$: By)($\forall x$: Ax · Rxy) Cx

9. ($\forall x$: Ax · ($\forall y$: By)Rxy)Rxx
    ($\forall x$: Ax)[~Rxx ⊃ ($\exists y$: By)~Rxy]

10. ~($\forall x$: Ax · ($\exists y$: By)Rxy)($\forall z$: Cz)Rzx
    ($\exists x$: Ax)[($\exists y$: By)Rxy · ($\exists z$: Cz)~Rzx]

11. ($\forall x$: Ax)Bx ⊃ ($\forall y$: Ay)Cy
    ($\exists x$: Ax)~Bx ∨ ($\forall y$: Ay)Cy

12. $\sim(\exists y\colon By)(\forall x\colon Ax \cdot Rxy)Cx$
$(\forall y\colon By)(\exists x\colon Ax \cdot \sim Cx)Rxy$

13. $(\exists x\colon Ax)\sim Bx \supset (\exists y\colon Cy \cdot Ay)\sim By$
$(\forall x\colon Ax)[Bx \lor (\exists y\colon Cy)(Ay \cdot \sim By)]$

14. $(\forall x\colon Ax \cdot (\forall y\colon By)Rxy)(\forall z\colon Cz)Rxz$
$(\forall x\colon Ax \cdot (\exists y\colon Cy)\sim Rxy)(\exists z\colon Bz)\sim Rxz$

LOGICAL TRUTHS

To establish something as a logical truth, we do as in Chapter 9. We derive the sentence without employing any premises. This means that we must begin with an assumption (to be discharged at the close of a subderivation). So we must employ CP, IP or UQI as a principal step.

I. '$(\forall x\colon Ax \cdot Bx)Ax$' is a logical truth.

$Ac \cdot Bc$	AP
Ac	Simp
$(\forall x\colon Ax \cdot Bx)Ax$	UQI

II. '$(\forall x\colon Ax \cdot (\forall y\colon Ay)Rxy)Rxx$' is a logical truth.

$Ac \cdot (\forall y\colon Ay)Rcy$	AP
Ac	Simp
$(\forall y\colon Ay)Rcy$	Simp
Rcc	UQE
$(\forall x\colon Ax \cdot (\forall y\colon Ay)Rxy) Rxx$	UQI

III. '$(\forall x\colon Ax \cdot Bx)Cx \supset (\forall x\colon Ax)(Bx \supset Cx)$' is a logical truth.

$(\forall x\colon Ax \cdot Bx)Cx$	AP
Ac	AP
Bc	AP
$Ac \cdot Bc$	Conj
Cc	UQE
$Bc \supset Cc$	CP
$(\forall x\colon Ax)(Bx \supset Cx)$	UQI
$(\forall x\colon Ax \cdot Bx)Cx \supset (\forall x\colon Ax)(Bx \supset Cx)$	CP

IV. '$\sim(\exists x\colon Ax)[(\forall y\colon Ay)Rxy \cdot \sim(\exists z\colon Az)Rzx]$' is a logical truth.

$(\exists x\colon Ax)[(\forall y\colon Ay) Rxy \cdot \sim(\exists z\colon Az)Rzx]$	AP
Ac	EQE
$(\forall y\colon Ay)Rcy \cdot \sim(\exists z\colon Az)Rzc$	EQE
$(\forall y\colon Ay)Rcy$	Simp
$\sim(\exists z\colon Az)Rzc$	Simp
$(\forall z\colon Az)\sim Rzc$	QN
Rcc	UQE
$\sim Rcc$	UQE
$Rcc \cdot \sim Rcc$	Conj
$\sim(\exists x\colon Ax)[(\forall y\colon Ay)Rxy \cdot \sim(\exists z\colon Az)Rzx]$	IP

EXERCISE 11h

Use the system of derivational rules to show that these are *logical truths*.

1. $(\forall x: Ax)[Ax \lor Bx]$
2. $(\forall x: Ax)[Bx \lor {\sim}Bx]$
3. ${\sim}(\exists x: Ax)[Bx \cdot {\sim}Bx]$
4. $(\forall x: Ax \cdot Rxx)(\exists y: Ay)Rxy$
5. $(\forall x: Ax)(\forall y: By) [(\forall z: Bz)Rxz \supset Rxy]$
6. $(\forall x: Ax)Bx \supset {\sim}(\exists x: {\sim}Bx)Ax$
7. $(\exists x: Ax){\sim}Bx \lor (\forall y: Ay)By$
8. ${\sim}(\exists y: By)(\exists x: Ax \cdot Rxy){\sim}Ax$
9. $(\forall x: Ax \cdot Cx)[Bx \lor (\exists y: Cy)(Ay \cdot {\sim}By)]$
10. $(\forall x: Ax \cdot (\forall y: By)Rxy)[(Bx \cdot Cx) \supset (\exists z: Cz)Rxz]$
11. $(\exists x: Ax){\sim}Rxx \supset {\sim}(\forall y: Ay)(\forall x: Ax)Rxy$
12. $(\forall x: Ax)[Bx \cdot Cx] \supset (\forall x: Ax)[Cx \lor Dx]$
13. $(\forall x: Ax \cdot Cx)Bx \supset (\forall y: Cy)[By \lor {\sim}Ay]$
14. $(\forall x: Bx \cdot (\forall y: Ay)Rxy)[Ax \supset Rxx]$
15. $(\exists x: Ax \cdot Cx){\sim}Bx \lor (\forall y: Cy)[Ay \supset By]$
16. ${\sim}(\exists y: By \cdot (\forall x: Ax)Rxy)(Ay \cdot {\sim}Ryy)$
17. $(\forall x: Ax){\sim}(\forall y: Ay)[Ryx \equiv {\sim}Ryy]$
18. $(\forall x: Ax \lor Bx)Cx \supset (\forall x: Ax \cdot (\forall y: Cy) Rxy)Rxx$

CONTRADICTIONS

Just as we show that a set of sentences is inconsistent by deriving something of the form $q \cdot {\sim}q$, we can show that a single sentence is contradictory by deriving something of the form $q \cdot {\sim}q$ from it.

I. '$(\exists x: Ax) [Bx \cdot {\sim}Ax]$' is contradictory.

1.	$(\exists x: Ax) [Bx \cdot {\sim}Ax]$	
2.	Ac	EQE
3.	$Bc \cdot {\sim}Ac$	EQE
4.	${\sim}Ac$	Simp
5.	$Ac \cdot {\sim}Ac$	Conj

II. '$(\exists x: Ax) [Rxx \cdot (\forall y: Ay){\sim}Rxy]$' is contradictory.

1.	$(\exists x: Ax)[Rxx \cdot (\forall y: Ay){\sim}Rxy]$	
2.	Ab	EQE
3.	$Rbb \cdot (\forall y: Ay){\sim}Rby$	EQE
4.	$(\forall y: Ay){\sim}Rby$	Simp
5.	${\sim}Rbb$	UQE

6. Rbb		Simp
7. $Rbb \cdot \sim Rbb$		Conj

III. '$(\forall x: Ax)Bx \equiv (\exists x: Ax)\sim Bx$' is contradictory.

1. $(\forall x: Ax)Bx \equiv (\exists x: Ax)\sim Bx$		
2. $[(\forall x: Ax)Bx \supset (\exists x: Ax)\sim Bx] \cdot$		
$[(\exists x: Ax)\sim Bx \supset (\forall x: Ax)Bx]$		Bic
3. $(\forall x: Ax)Bx \supset (\exists x: Ax)\sim Bx$		Simp
►**4.** $(\forall x: Ax)Bx$		AP
5. $\sim(\exists x: Ax)\sim Bx$	4	QN
6. $(\exists x: Ax)\sim Bx$	3,4	MP
7. $(\exists x: Ax)\sim Bx \cdot \sim(\exists x: Ax)\sim Bx$		Conj
8. $\sim(\forall x: Ax)Bx$		IP
9. $(\exists x: Ax)\sim Bx$		QN
10. $(\exists x: Ax)\sim Bx \supset (\forall x: Ax)Bx$	2	Simp
11. $(\forall x: Ax)Bx$		MP
12. $(\forall x: Ax)Bx \cdot \sim(\forall x: Ax)Bx$		Conj

EXERCISE 11i

Show that each is contradictory.

1. $(\exists x: Ax \cdot Bx)\sim Bx$

2. $(\exists x: Ax \cdot Bx)[\sim Bx \vee \sim Ax]$

3. $\sim(\forall x: Ax)[Ax \vee Cx]$

4. $(\exists x: Ax \cdot Bx)(\forall y: By)Rxy \cdot (\forall z: Bz)\sim Rzz$

5. $(\exists x: (Ax \cdot Bx) \cdot (\forall y: By)Rxy)\sim(\exists z: Az)Rxz$

6. $(\exists x: Ax)(\forall y: Ay) \, [Rxy \equiv \sim Rxx]$

7. $(\exists x: Ax)Bx \cdot ((\forall x: Ax)\sim Ax \vee (\forall y: By)\sim Ay)$

8. $(\exists y: By \cdot (\forall x: Ax) \, Rxy)(Ay \cdot \sim Ryy)$

9. $(\exists x: Ax \cdot (\forall y: By) \, Rxy)(\exists z: Cz \cdot Bz)\sim Rxz$

10. $\sim(\forall x: Ax)(\exists y: By)Rxy \cdot (\exists y: By)(\forall x: Ax)Rxy$

APPENDIX 11A
ADDITIONAL VALID ARGUMENT FORMS
AND EQUIVALENCES

Some additional inference patterns and equivalences are worth considering. Some might make valuable additional rules.

Quantificational Modus Tollens (QMT)

$(\forall \text{\textcircled{v}}: A\text{\textcircled{v}})B\text{\textcircled{v}}$
$\sim B\text{\textcircled{c}}$
$\therefore \quad \sim A\text{\textcircled{c}}$

Quantificational Contraposition (QCont)

(∀ⓥ: Aⓥ)Bⓥ   ::   (∀ⓥ: ~Bⓥ)~Aⓥ

Conversion (Conv)

(∃ⓥ: Aⓥ)Bⓥ   ::   (∃ⓥ: Bⓥ)Aⓥ

Absorption (Abs)

(∀ⓥ: Aⓥ)Bⓥ   ::   (∀ⓥ: Aⓥ)[Aⓥ · Bⓥ]

(∃ⓥ: Aⓥ)Bⓥ   ::   (∃ⓥ: Aⓥ)[Aⓥ · Bⓥ]

Derelativization (DR)

(∀ⓥ: Aⓥ)Bⓥ   ::   (∀ⓥ: Cⓥ ∨ ~Cⓥ)[Aⓥ ⊃ Bⓥ]

(∃ⓥ: Aⓥ)Bⓥ   ::   (∃ⓥ: Cⓥ ∨ ~Cⓥ)[Aⓥ · Bⓥ]

Quantificational Distribution (QDist)

(∀ⓥ: Aⓥ)[Bⓥ · Cⓥ]   ::   (∀ⓥ: Aⓥ)Bⓥ · (∀ⓥ: Aⓥ)Cⓥ

(∀ⓥ: Aⓥ ∨ Bⓥ)Cⓥ   ::   (∀ⓥ: Aⓥ)Cⓥ · (∀ⓥ: Bⓥ)Cⓥ

(∃ⓥ: Aⓥ)[Bⓥ ∨ Cⓥ]   ::   (∃ⓥ: Aⓥ)Bⓥ ∨ (∃ⓥ: Aⓥ)Cⓥ

(∃ⓥ: Aⓥ ∨ Bⓥ)Cⓥ   ::   (∃ⓥ: Aⓥ)Cⓥ ∨ (∃ⓥ: Bⓥ)Cⓥ

Quantifier Reordering (Reord)

(∀ⓥ₁: Aⓥ₁)(∀ⓥ₂: Bⓥ₂)C   ::   (∀ⓥ₂: Bⓥ₂)(∀ⓥ₁: Aⓥ₁)C

(∃ⓥ₁: Aⓥ₁)(∃ⓥ₂: Bⓥ₂)C   ::   (∃ⓥ₂: Bⓥ₂)(∃ⓥ₁: Aⓥ₁)C

Provided that

(i) ⓥ₁ does not occur free within Bⓥ₂.
(ii) ⓥ₂ does not occur free within Aⓥ₁.

Relettering (Relet)

(∃ⓥ₁: Aⓥ₁)Bⓥ₁   (∀ⓥ₁: Aⓥ₁)Bⓥ₁
∴ (∃ⓥ₂: Aⓥ₂)Bⓥ₂   ∴ (∀ⓥ₂: Aⓥ₂)Bⓥ₂

Provided that

(i)   ⓥ₂ does not occur in Aⓥ₁ or Bⓥ₁.
(ii) Aⓥ₂ is a ⓥ₂|ⓥ₁ instance of Aⓥ₁.
(iii) Bⓥ₂ is a ⓥ₂|ⓥ₁ instance of Bⓥ₁.

Universal Syllogism (US)

$(\forall ⓥ: Aⓥ)Bⓥ$
$(\forall ⓥ: Bⓥ)Cⓥ$
$\therefore \quad (\forall ⓥ: Aⓥ)Cⓥ$

Quantifier Exportation (QEXP)

$(\forall ⓥ: Aⓥ \cdot Cⓥ)Dⓥ \quad :: \quad (\forall ⓥ: Aⓥ)[Cⓥ \supset Dⓥ]$
$(\exists ⓥ: Aⓥ \cdot Cⓥ)Dⓥ \quad :: \quad (\exists ⓥ: Aⓥ)[Cⓥ \cdot Dⓥ]$

Prenexation (Prenex)

Provided that ⓥ does not occur free in *A*:

$(\exists ⓥ: Cⓥ)Bⓥ \supset A \qquad :: \quad (\forall ⓥ: Cⓥ)[Bⓥ \supset A]$
$A \supset (\forall ⓥ: Cⓥ)Bⓥ \qquad :: \quad (\forall ⓥ: Cⓥ)[A \supset Bⓥ]$
$[(\forall ⓥ: Cⓥ)Bⓥ \supset A] \cdot (\exists ⓥ: Cⓥ)Cⓥ \qquad :: \quad (\exists ⓥ: Cⓥ)[Bⓥ \supset A]$
$[A \supset (\exists ⓥ: Cⓥ)Bⓥ] \cdot (\exists ⓥ: Cⓥ)Cⓥ \qquad :: \quad (\exists ⓥ: Cⓥ)[A \supset Bⓥ]$

EXERCISE 11j

Show that each of the additional rules listed above is already derivable using the basic system of rules (UQE, UQI, EQE, EQI, QN) of this chapter. (For QMT, US, and Relet, show that the conclusion is derivable from the premises. The others are equivalence rules: show that each side is derivable from the other.)

12

PREDICATE LOGIC
TRUTH-TREES

Using the derivational rules we can show each of the following:

That an argument is *valid*.

That a set of sentences is *inconsistent*.

That a pair of sentences are *equivalent*.

That a sentence is a *logical truth*.

That a sentence is *contradictory*.

But the derivational rules are of no use when showing that the concepts above do not apply. We need a different method to show any of the following:

That an argument form is *not valid*.

That a form for a set of sentences is *consistent*.

That a pair of sentence forms are *equivalent*.

That a sentence form is *contingent*.

To show that an argument form is not valid, we generally supply an example (a "counterexample") in which invalidity is apparent.

$(\forall ⓥ: Aⓥ)Bⓥ$

$(\exists ⓥ: Bⓥ)Cⓥ$

∴ $(\exists ⓥ: Aⓥ)Cⓥ$

This argument form is not valid. We can show this by giving an example of an argument of that form that is obviously invalid.

All whales are mammals.	$(\forall x: Wx)Mx$
Some mammals swing from trees.	$(\exists x: Mx)Sx$
∴ Some whales swing from trees.	∴ $(\exists x: Wx)Sx$

Since this invalid argument is an instance of that form, the form cannot be valid.

This particular argument is so clearly invalid because its premises are simple, evidently true sentences and its conclusion is simple and obviously false. Because of this, we know immediately that it cannot be valid, and as soon as we know that it is an instance of the given form, we know that the form given cannot be a valid argument form. In general, to show that an argument form is not valid we need to show that it is *possible* for an argument of that form to have true premises and a false conclusion. This is usually shown most clearly by presenting an argument of that form that *actually* has true premises and a false conclusion, and in which this is obvious. If such a situation is actual, then of course it must be possible.

The same ideas apply to showing consistency (or nonequivalence or contingency). We can show the consistency of the following form:

$(\exists ⓥ: Aⓥ)Bⓥ$
$(\forall ⓥ: Cⓥ)Bⓥ$
$(\forall ⓥ: Aⓥ)\sim Cⓥ$

To show consistency, we can present a set of true sentences of that form. As long as it is easy to see that the sentences are true, it will be apparent that the set is consistent.

Some mammals swim.	$(\exists x: Mx)Sx$
All fish swim.	$(\forall x: Fx)Sx$
No mammals are fish.	$(\forall x: Mx)\sim Fx$

These are all true, and the set is of the form in question, so this form for a set of sentences is consistent.

TRUTH-TREES AND MODELS

It would be nice to have a *systematic* procedure for showing invalidity, consistency, nonequivalence and contingency. In Chapter 4 we developed the method of truth-trees for deciding about consistency (and about validity, equivalence, and contingency). For truth-functional logic, truth-trees constitute a *decision procedure* for consistency: a truth-tree for truth-functional logic is always finite in length, and for any form for a set of sentences, it always shows whether that set is consistent or inconsistent. Nothing as general and decisive can be devised for predicate logic. (This fact, that there can be no systematic decision procedure for all of predicate logic, was established by Alonzo Church in 1936.) But truth-trees can still be a very useful basis for constructing models to show consistency or invalidity, and in many cases they can also be used in determining that a set is inconsistent or that an argument is valid.

The truth-tree rules consist of a procedure to apply to each possible kind of sentence other than atomic sentences and their negations. So for truth-functional logic, we had these rules:

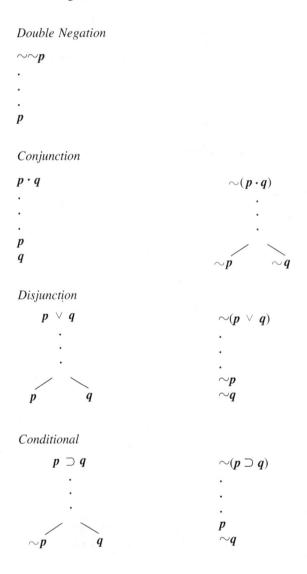

Double Negation

$\sim\sim p$
.
.
.
p

Conjunction

$p \cdot q$ $\sim(p \cdot q)$
.   .
.   .
.   .
p
q $\sim p$ $\sim q$

Disjunction

$p \vee q$ $\sim(p \vee q)$
.   .
.   .
.   .
                                                      $\sim p$
p q $\sim q$

Conditional

$p \supset q$ $\sim(p \supset q)$
.   .
.   .
.   .
                                                      p
$\sim p$ q $\sim q$

Biconditional

We will now need to augment this with four new rules, for existential sentences, for universal sentences, and for the negations of each of those. For existential sentences, the rule for constructing a truth-tree is like the rule EQE in the deductive system (Chapter 11). Whenever an existential sentence, $(\exists \text{\textcircled{v}}: A\text{\textcircled{v}})B\text{\textcircled{v}}$, is true, there is at least one individual of which $A\text{\textcircled{v}}$ and $B\text{\textcircled{v}}$ are both true. The existential sentence does not say what individual these are true of, so to write simpler sentences based on the existential we must introduce an arbitrary name, that is, a name that has not been used previously on that path of the truth-tree. Such a name will not have any prior "information" associated with it, so whatever inferences we make using that name will apply solely because it represents the sort of individual guaranteed by the existential sentence. Thus our truth-tree rule is this:

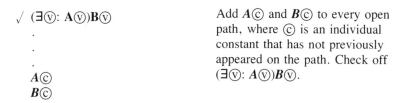

We introduce some new individual constant ⓒ that will stand in for an individual of the type guaranteed to exist by the sentence $(\exists \text{\textcircled{v}}: A\text{\textcircled{v}})B\text{\textcircled{v}}$. It is important to introduce a new constant, because an existential does not give information about any individual that has already been named.

The rule for universal sentences will introduce a new element into the construction of truth-trees. The truth-tree rule for a sentence will apply to any name:

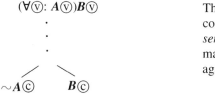

This applies for any individual constant ⓒ. *Do not check off the sentence* $(\forall \text{\textcircled{v}}: A\text{\textcircled{v}})B\text{\textcircled{v}}$ (because it may be necessary to apply the rule again, using a different constant).

Because the universal sentence is never checked off, truth-trees containing universals can sometimes continue to grow without limit. Paths for truth-functional logic were always finite because the rules for constructing the paths always produced simpler sentences and enabled us to take the compound sentences out of consideration (by checking them off). Eventually, we reached the simplest sentences: atomic sentences and the negations of atomic sentences. But no such finite procedure can apply to all of predicate logic.

In many simple examples the predicate logic truth-tree rules will work very well to give us a decision about a form for a set of sentences. In some cases, all paths will close, showing inconsistency.

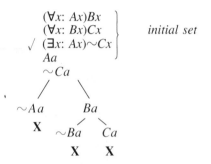

Since all paths close, we know that the initial set is inconsistent.

In some cases in which the paths do not close, we can get enough information to construct a *model* that will show consistency. A model consists of a set of individuals and an interpretation of the predicates that makes every sentence in the set true.

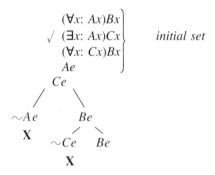

The universal sentences are never checked off, so we cannot tell immediately whether we are done. We could always use some other name (*a,b,c*, etc.) to make new branches based on one of the universal sentences. But there is no point in doing so, because the open path already describes a model that will make all of the sentences of the set true. In a universe with just one individual, denoted by '*e*', all sentences of the original set will be true if these sentences are all true:

Ae   Be   Ce

To say that a form for a set of sentences is consistent is to say that it is possible for the members of some set of sentences of that form all to be true. We need just one example of a set of that form that is true in some possible situation. A possible situation in which only a small number of individuals exist will give us an easily characterized model for the set of sentences. Additional individuals might be used in characterizing other models for the set of sentences, but we need only one model to show consistency. There is no reason to introduce additional individuals into consideration.

EXERCISE 12a

Use the method of truth-trees to determine whether the following are consistent.

1. $(\forall x: Ax \cdot Bx)Cx$
   $(\exists x: Ax)Bx$
   $(\forall x: Bx){\sim}Cx$

2. $(\exists x: Ax)Cx$
   $(\forall x: Bx){\sim}Cx$
   $(\exists x: Ax)Bx$

3. $(\exists x: Ax){\sim}Bx$
   $(\forall x: Ax)(Bx \vee Cx)$
   $(\forall x: Ax){\sim}Cx$

4. $(\exists x: Ax)(Bx \cdot Cx)$
   $(\forall x: Bx)Dx$
   $(\forall x: Cx){\sim}Dx$

5. $(\exists x: Ax)(Bx \cdot Cx)$
   $(\exists x: Bx)Dx$
   $(\forall x: Cx){\sim}(Bx \cdot Dx)$

NEGATED SENTENCES

A negated existential sentence is equivalent to a universal sentence. ${\sim}(\exists ⓥ: Aⓥ)Bⓥ$ is equivalent to $(\forall ⓥ: Aⓥ){\sim}Bⓥ$. For example, "It is not the case that some cows fly" is equivalent to "No cows fly" or "Every cow is a nonflier." We can use this as the basis for a rule for negated existential sentences simply by incorporating the quantifier negation equivalence into our truth-tree rules. So we can simply take each negated existential sentence and convert it to a universal sentence.

$\sqrt{}$ ${\sim}(\exists ⓥ: Aⓥ)Bⓥ$
   $(\forall ⓥ: Aⓥ){\sim}Bⓥ$

Similarly, the rule for the negated universal is based on another quantifier negation rule. ${\sim}(\forall ⓥ: Aⓥ)Bⓥ$ is equivalent to $(\exists ⓥ: Aⓥ){\sim}Bⓥ$. "Not all birds fly" is equivalent to "Some birds don't fly."

$\checkmark$ $\sim(\forall ⓥ: Aⓥ)Bⓥ$
$(\exists ⓥ: Aⓥ)\sim Bⓥ$

Using the new methods we might get a tree like the following:

$(\forall x: Ax)Bx$
$\checkmark$ $\sim(\exists x: Bx)Cx$
$\checkmark$ $(\exists x: Ax)\sim Cx$
Ab
$\sim Cb$

$\diagup$ $\diagdown$

$\sim Ab$ Bb
$\mathbf{X}$ $(\forall x: Bx)\sim Cx$

$\diagup$ $\diagdown$

$\sim Bb$ $\sim Cb$
$\mathbf{X}$

Such a tree helps us to find a model even though the universals are never eliminated from consideration. In the following model

one individual, b Ab Bb $\sim Cb$

each of the sentences of the original set is true. (There is no point in introducing additional individuals.)

Although there is no systematic decision procedure for full predicate logic, we are in a position to state a general result about showing consistency for sets containing only monadic predicates. Suppose that a set contains only monadic predicates and we construct a truth-tree that has, on each path, some individual constant introduced for each existentially quantified sentence on that path (i.e., each existential is checked off). Suppose also that each universal on the tree has been used with each of the individual constants to create a pair of branches. Suppose further that all of the truth-functionally compound sentences are checked off in accord with the rules for truth-trees for sentence logic. If some paths remain open after all of that, the initial set is consistent. The open path can be used as a guide for constructing a model for showing consistency when only monadic predicates are involved.

So at least in the case of examples involving monadic predicates, we can always use truth-trees to *determine* whether or not a set is consistent. We can *show* consistency in either of two ways: by giving an example in natural language or by presenting an artificial model. We can *show* inconsistency in two ways: by deriving a contradiction or by constructing a truth-tree in which all paths close.

Examples

1. $\checkmark$ $(\exists ⓥ: Aⓥ)\sim Bⓥ$
$(\forall ⓥ: Aⓥ)Cⓥ$

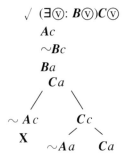

$\checkmark$ $(\exists \text{\textcircled{v}}: B \text{\textcircled{v}}) C \text{\textcircled{v}}$

Ac

$\sim Bc$

Ba

Ca

$\sim Ac \qquad Cc$

$X \qquad \sim Aa \qquad Ca$

Two paths remain open. Taking the path farthest to the right, we get the following characterization of a model:

two individuals, a and c

$$Ba \quad Ca$$
$$Ac \quad \sim Bc \quad Cc$$

With atomic sentences assigned in that way, this set of sentences of the original form will all be true.

$(\exists x: Ax)\sim Bx$	(True, since Ac and $\sim Bc$)
$(\forall x: Ax)Cx$	(True, since Cx is true of everything)
$(\exists x: Bx)Cx$	(True, since Ba and Ca)

(Note that we did not say whether or not 'Aa' is true. It does not matter; either way will work. So we do not need to say anything about that.)

We could also give a counterexample in natural language.

Some mammals are not white.	$(\exists x: Mx)\sim Wx$
All mammals have lungs.	$(\forall x: Mx)Lx$
Some white things have lungs.	$(\exists x: Wx)Lx$

2. $\checkmark$ $\sim(\exists \text{\textcircled{v}}: A \text{\textcircled{v}}) B \text{\textcircled{v}}$

$\checkmark$ $(\exists \text{\textcircled{v}}: C \text{\textcircled{v}})[A \text{\textcircled{v}} \cdot B \text{\textcircled{v}}]$

Ca

$\checkmark$ $Aa \cdot Ba$

Aa

Ba

$(\forall \text{\textcircled{v}}: A \text{\textcircled{v}})\sim B \text{\textcircled{v}}$

$\sim Aa \qquad \sim Ba$

$X \qquad X$

This form for a set of sentences is inconsistent. All paths close.

3. √ (∃ⓥ: Aⓥ · Bⓥ)Cⓥ
   (∀ⓥ: Cⓥ)Dⓥ
√ ~(∀ⓥ: Aⓥ)Dⓥ
√ (∃ⓥ: Bⓥ)~Dⓥ
√ (∃ⓥ: Aⓥ)~Dⓥ
√ *Aa · Ba*
   Ca
   Aa
   Ba
   Ab
   ~*Db*
   Bc
   ~*Dc*

Model

three individuals, *a*, *b*, and *c*

Aa	*Ba*	*Ca*	*Da*
Ab		~*Cb*	~*Db*
Bc		~*Cc*	~*Dc*

Such a model makes true all members of the following set, which is of the given form:

(∃*x*: *Ax* · *Bx*)*Cx*
(∀*x*: *Cx*)*Dx*
~(∀*x*: *Ax*)*Dx*
(∃*x*: *Bx*)~*Dx*

Example in Natural Language

Some gray mammals have tusks.
Whatever has tusks is dangerous.
Not all gray things are dangerous.
Some mammals are not dangerous.

EXERCISE 12b

For each of these, determine whether it is consistent or inconsistent.

1. ~(∀ⓥ: Aⓥ)Bⓥ
(∀ⓥ: Aⓥ)Cⓥ
~(∃ⓥ: ~Bⓥ)Cⓥ

2. (∀ⓥ: Aⓥ)(Bⓥ ∨ Cⓥ)
~(∀ⓥ: Aⓥ)Bⓥ
~(∃ⓥ: Aⓥ)Cⓥ

3. ~(∃ⓥ: Aⓥ)(Bⓥ · Cⓥ)
(∃ⓥ: Aⓥ)Bⓥ
(∃ⓥ: Aⓥ)Cⓥ

4. (∀ⓥ: Aⓥ · Bⓥ)(Cⓥ · Dⓥ)
(∀ⓥ: Aⓥ)Bⓥ
~(∀ⓥ: Aⓥ)Cⓥ
~(∀ⓥ: Aⓥ)Bⓥ

5. ~(∀ⓥ: Aⓥ · Bⓥ)(Cⓥ · Dⓥ)
~(∃ⓥ: Aⓥ)Cⓥ
~(∃ⓥ: Bⓥ)Dⓥ

LIMITS OF PREDICATE LOGIC TRUTH-TREES

The examples of truth-trees that we have considered so far have involved only monadic predicates. Once an individual is introduced on each path for each existential sentence and for each negation of a universal sentence, and once each univesal sentence is exploited with each individual constant on a path, then paths that remain open will indicate models for showing consistency. In relational examples, however, there can be a need to keep introducing new individuals without limit. Consider how we might represent these sentences:

"For any number x, there is some number y such that $x < y$"
"0 is a number"

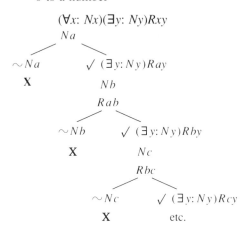

We keep coming up with new existential sentences, and we introduce appropriate individual constants (an individual b that a is related to, an individual c that b is related to, etc.). When we have such an example (in which some sentence contains two quantifier phrases together, the first universal and the second existential), a set can be inconsistent even though not all of the paths of the truth-tree are closed. This is because we might continue adding individual constants and new paths, always leaving some path open.

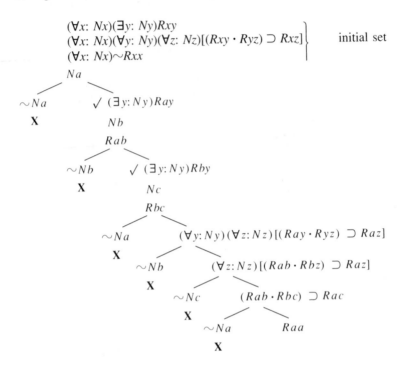

$$(\forall x\colon Nx)(\exists y\colon Ny)Rxy$$
$$(\forall x\colon Nx)(\forall y\colon Ny)(\forall z\colon Nz)[(Rxy \cdot Ryz) \supset Rxz]\Big\}\quad \text{initial set}$$
$$(\forall x\colon Nx){\sim}Rxx$$

There are many universal sentences that never get checked off, new existential sentences can always be introduced on the basis of the first sentence of the initial set, and new individual constants must be introduced every time there is a new existential. If we try to use the information we have in constructing a model, though, the model will not work.

$$Na \quad Nb \quad Nc \qquad Rab \quad Rbc \quad Rac$$

So far this may seem all right, but there must be some individual that c is related to. [Just as '$(\exists y\colon Ny)Ray$' gave birth to 'b', and that led to '$(\exists y\colon Ny)Rby$', we also get 'c' and then '$(\exists y\colon Ny)Rcy$'.] To keep the model small, we could try to make c related to a or to b. But if Rca, then the second sentence of the set can then be used to show that if Rac and Rca, then Raa [$(Rac \cdot Rca) \supset Raa$]. But since Na, ${\sim}Raa$ (from the third sentence). So 'Rca' cannot be true. Similarly, 'Rcb' cannot be true, and 'Rcc' cannot be true. So we need a new individual constant. But this reasoning continues, and new individuals must continually be added. We can never construct a model based on just a finite number of individuals.

No finite model will work to show consistency here. But the set is consistent, as we can see by interpreting Nx as 'x is a number' and 'Rxy' as 'x is less than y' and 'a' as 0. Each sentence is true.

($\forall x$: Nx)($\exists y$: Ny)Rxy
For each number x, there is a number that x is less than.

($\forall x$: Nx)($\forall y$: Ny)($\forall z$: Nz)[($Rxy \cdot Ryz$) $\supset Rxz$]
Consider any numbers x, y, and z, if $x < y$ and $y < z$, then $x < z$.

($\forall x$: Nx) $\sim Rxx$
No number is less than itself.

Na
0 is a number.

All of these are true, so the form given here must be consistent. But the fact that we used an infinite set as the basis for the model is no coincidence. No finite model suffices to show consistency. So the truth-tree method cannot be a complete decision procedure, because in at least some cases there is no finite termination and no finite path yields a successful model. Not all paths close, but the process never ends.

These limitations on the use of truth-trees are related to the fact that there can be no general decision procedure for consistency (or for related concepts like validity) for predicate logic. When we apply a routinely specifiable procedure like truth-trees and there are open paths, we do not always know whether that is because the set is consistent (but with no finite model), or whether we have just not carried the steps far enough to get all of the paths to close.

INVALIDITY

We can adapt the procedure for showing consistency and use it for showing invalidity, nonequivalence, and contingency. To show that an argument form is invalid, we consider the set consisting of the premises together with the negation of the conclusion. The argument form is invalid if and only if that set is consistent (see Chapter 4).

Examples

1. ($\forall \circledv$: $A\circledv$)$B\circledv$
   ($\exists \circledv$: $A\circledv$)$C\circledv$ $\therefore$ ($\forall \circledv$: $B\circledv$)$C\circledv$
       1. ($\forall x$: Ax)Bx
   $\checkmark$ 2. ($\exists x$: Ax)Cx
   $\checkmark$ 3. $\sim$($\forall x$: Bx)Cx
   $\checkmark$ ($\exists x$: Bx)$\sim Cx$

Ab

Cb

Bc

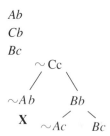
~ *Cc*

~*Ab*   *Bb*

X   ~*Ac*   *Bc*

Two open paths remain, so the initial set 1–3 is consistent. The model indicated by the path ending with '*Bc*' is this:

Two individuals, *b* and *c*   *Ab*   *Bb*   *Cb*

Bc   ~ *Cc*

With a possible situation of that sort, each of 1–3 is true. So in the original argument, the premises are true and the conclusion is false.

2. (∀ⓥ: *A*ⓥ)*B*ⓥ

(∀ⓥ: *C*ⓥ)*B*ⓥ   ∴   (∃ⓥ: *A*ⓥ)*C*ⓥ

(∀*x*: *Ax*)*Bx*

(∀*x*: *Cx*)*Bx*

√ ~(∃*x*: *Ax*)*Cx*

(∀*x*: *Ax*)~*Cx*

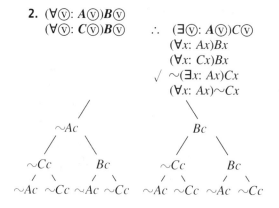

~*Ac*   *Bc*

~*Cc*   *Bc*   ~*Cc*   *Bc*

~*Ac* ~*Cc* ~*Ac* ~*Cc*   ~*Ac* ~*Cc* ~*Ac* ~*Cc*

There are eight open paths, and by following one, we can find a model. Let's consider the path farthest to the right.

One individual, *c*   *Bc* ~*Cc*

In such a one-member model, the premises will be true with the conclusion false in an argument of the form first given.

3. (∃ⓥ: *A*ⓥ)[*B*ⓥ ∨ *C*ⓥ]

(∀ⓥ: *B*ⓥ)*D*ⓥ   ∴   (∃ⓥ: *A*ⓥ)*D*ⓥ

√ (∃*x*: *Ax*)[*Bx* ∨ *Cx*]

(∀*x*: *Bx*)*Dx*

√ ~(∃*x*: *Ax*)*Dx*

(∀*x*: *Ax*)~*Dx*

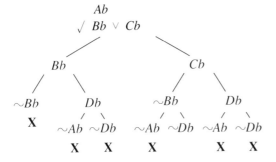

Model

One individual, *b*   *Ab*   ∼*Bb*   *Cb*   ∼*Db*

This makes the premises true and the conclusion false in an argument of the given form.

4. (∀ⓥ: *A*ⓥ)[*C*ⓥ ∨ *D*ⓥ]
    ∼(∃ⓥ: *A*ⓥ)*C*ⓥ
    (∃ⓥ: *A*ⓥ)*B*ⓥ   ∴ (∀ⓥ: *B*ⓥ)*D*ⓥ

(∀*x*: *Ax* · *Bx*)[*Cx* ∨ *Dx*]
√ ∼(∃*x*: *Ax*)*Cx*
√ (∃*x*: *Ax*)*Bx*
√ ∼(∀*x*: *Bx*)*Dx*
    (∀*x*: *Ax*)∼*Cx*
√ (∃*x*: *Bx*)∼*Dx*
    Ac
    Bc
    Ba
    ∼*Da*

∼*Ac*   ∼*Cc*
   X

        ∼*Aa*   ∼*Ca*

√∼(*Ac* · *Bc*) √ *Cc* ∨ *Dc*   √ ∼(*Ac* · *Bc*)   √ *Cc* ∨ *Dc*
 ∼*Ac* ∼*Bc*   ∼*Cc*   *Dc*   ∼*Ac* ∼*Bc*   ∼*Cc*   ∼*Dc*
  X   **X**   **X**   **X**   **X**   **X**

        √∼(*Aa* · *Ba*) √ *Ca* ∨ *Da*   √ ∼(*Aa* · *Ba*) √ *Ca* ∨ *Da*
         ∼*Aa* ∼*Ba*   *Ca*   *Da*   ∼*Aa* ∼*Ba*   *Ca*   *Da*
                 X   **X**   **X**   **X** **X**

Model (based on the open path farthest to the right)

Two individuals, *a* and *c*   ~*Aa*   *Ba*   ~*Ca*   ~*Da*

                                                           Ac   *Bc*   ~*Cc*   *Dc*

5. (∀ⓥ: *A*ⓥ)[*B*ⓥ ∨ *D*ⓥ]

(∃ⓥ: *B*ⓥ)*D*ⓥ   ∴   (∀ⓥ: *A*ⓥ)[*C*ⓥ ∨ *D*ⓥ]

(∀*x*: *Ax*)[*Bx* ∨ *Dx*]

√ (∃*x*: *Bx*)*Dx*

√ ~(∀*x*: *Ax*)[*Cx* ∨ *Dx*]

√ (∃*x*: *Ax*)~[*Cx* ∨ *Dx*]

Ba

Da

Ac

~[*Cc* ∨ *Dc*]

~*Cc*

~*Dc*

```
        /    \
  ~Ac    √ Bc ∨ Dc
   X       /   \
         Bc     Dc
        /  \     X
    ~Aa   √ Ba ∨ Da
          /   \
        Ba      Da
```

Model

Two individuals, *a* and *c*   *Ba*   *Da*

                                                   Ac   *Bc*   ~*Cc*   ~*Dc*

EXERCISE 12c

Show that these are invalid.

1. (∃ⓥ: *A*ⓥ)*B*ⓥ

(∀ⓥ: *C*ⓥ)*A*ⓥ

∴   (∃ⓥ: *C*ⓥ)*B*ⓥ

2. (∃ⓥ: *A*ⓥ)~*B*ⓥ

(∃ⓥ: *A*ⓥ)*B*ⓥ

∴   (∃ⓥ: *C*ⓥ)*D*ⓥ

3. (∃ⓥ: *A*ⓥ · *B*ⓥ)*D*ⓥ

(∀ⓥ: *C*ⓥ)*B*ⓥ

(∃ⓥ: *C*ⓥ)*A*ⓥ

∴   (∃ⓥ: *C*ⓥ)*D*ⓥ

4. ~(∀ⓥ: *A*ⓥ)[*B*ⓥ ∨ *C*ⓥ]

(∀ⓥ: *B*ⓥ)*D*ⓥ

(∃ⓥ: *C*ⓥ)*D*ⓥ

∴   (∃ⓥ: *A*ⓥ)*D*ⓥ

5. (∀ⓥ: *A*ⓥ)~*B*ⓥ
  ~(∀ⓥ: *B*ⓥ)*C*ⓥ
  (∃ⓥ: *B*ⓥ)*C*ⓥ
  ∴ (∀ⓥ: *A*ⓥ)~*C*ⓥ

6. (∀ⓥ: *A*ⓥ)~*B*ⓥ
  ~(∀ⓥ: *B*ⓥ)*C*ⓥ
  (∃ⓥ: *B*ⓥ)*C*ⓥ
  ∴ (∀ⓥ: *A*ⓥ)*C*ⓥ

INEQUIVALENCE

If it is possible for two sentences to differ in truth-value, the sentences are not equivalent. We can show that forms for a pair of sentences are not equivalent by showing that there are sentences that correspond to the forms but that can differ in truth-value. We may provide concrete English examples that differ in truth-value or we may abstractly describe models that would give opposite truth-values to a pair of sentences corresponding to the given forms. These models can be discovered by a use of truth-trees.

Form

(∀ⓥ: *A*ⓥ · *B*ⓥ)*C*ⓥ   (∀ⓥ: *A*ⓥ)(*C*ⓥ · *B*ⓥ)

Natural Language Example

Ax = *x* is a movie actor.
Bx = *x* has been a U.S. president.
Cx = *x* is well known.

Every movie actor who has been a U.S. president is well known.
(∀x: Ax · Bx)Cx

Every movie actor has been a well-known U.S. president.
(∀x: Ax)(Cx · Bx)

Truth-Tree

Model (based on the open path farthest to the left)

One individual, c Ac ~Bc

When trying to show inequivalence, we have a choice about which sentence to negate. We must consider one sentence together with the negation of the other, and at least one of those two possible combinations should yield an open path that can serve as the basis for a model showing inequivalence. In some cases, this will work in only one of the two ways. If so, then trying the one that does not work can lead to closure of all the paths. For example, if we had tried the other way in the example just considered, all paths would have closed.

√ ~(∀ⓥ: Aⓥ · Bⓥ)Cⓥ
√ (Aⓥ: Aⓥ)(Cⓥ · Bⓥ)
√ (∃ⓥ: Aⓥ · Bⓥ)~Cⓥ
√ $Ac \cdot Bc$
√ ~Cc
√ Ac
√ Bc

~Ac √ $Cc \cdot Bc$
X Cc
        Bc
        X

For the original sentences to be equivalent, *both* of the following argument forms would have to be valid:

(∀ⓥ: Aⓥ · Bⓥ)Cⓥ   (∀ⓥ: Aⓥ)(Cⓥ · Bⓥ)
∴ (∀ⓥ: Aⓥ)(Cⓥ · Bⓥ)   ∴ (∀ⓥ: Aⓥ · Bⓥ)Cⓥ

We just showed that the second of those is valid. But the sentences are not equivalent, because the first is invalid (shown by the earlier truth-tree).

Form

(∃ⓥ: Aⓥ)(Cⓥ · Bⓥ)   (∃ⓥ: Aⓥ)(Cⓥ ⊃ Bⓥ)

Natural Language Example

Ax = x is a cow
Cx = x flies
Bx = x will surprise Susan

Some cow flies and will surprise Susan. *False*

Some cow will surprise Susan if it flies. *True*

Truth-Tree

√ ~(∃Ⓥ: AⓋ)(CⓋ · BⓋ)
√ (∃Ⓥ: AⓋ)(CⓋ ⊃ BⓋ)
   (∀Ⓥ: AⓋ)~(CⓋ · BⓋ)

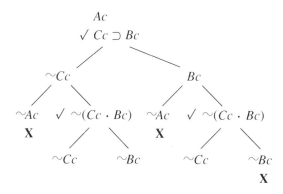

Model (based on the open path farthest to the right)

One individual, *c*   *Ac   Bc   ~Cc*

EXERCISE 12d

For each pair, show that the sentence forms are not equivalent.

1. (∀Ⓥ: AⓋ)BⓋ
(∀Ⓥ: BⓋ)AⓋ

2. (∀Ⓥ: AⓋ · BⓋ)~CⓋ
(∃Ⓥ: AⓋ)(BⓋ · ~CⓋ)

3. (∀Ⓥ: AⓋ ∨ BⓋ)CⓋ
(∀Ⓥ: AⓋ)CⓋ ∨ (AⓋ: BⓋ)CⓋ

4. (∀Ⓥ: AⓋ)[BⓋ ∨ CⓋ]
(∃Ⓥ: AⓋ)(BⓋ ∨ (∃Ⓥ: AⓋ)CⓋ

5. (∀Ⓥ: AⓋ)~BⓋ
~(∀Ⓥ: AⓋ)BⓋ

6. (∀Ⓥ: AⓋ)~[BⓋ ∨ CⓋ]
(∀Ⓥ: BⓋ)~[AⓋ ∨ CⓋ]

CONTINGENCY

To show that a sentence form is contingent, we must show that there can be sentences of that form that are true and sentences of that form that are false. We can do that by presenting two examples of sentences of that form, one true and the other false. We could also schematically describe two models, one that makes the sentence true and one that makes it false.

Truth-trees can often help in the discovery of such models. We must construct two truth-trees, one for the sentence form and one for its negation. In each case we should have an open path. One path will be a model path showing how a sentence of the given form can be true, and the other will be a model path showing how a sentence of that form can be false (i.e., how its negation can be true).

I. Form

(∀ⓥ: Aⓥ)Bⓥ

Natural Language Examples

1. $Ax = x$ is a dog
$Bx = x$ is a mammal
Every dog is a mammal.   *True*

2. $Ax = x$ is a dog
$Bx = x$ is brown
Every dog is brown.   *False*

Truth-Trees

(∀ⓥ: Aⓥ) *B*ⓥ

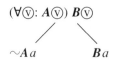

~*A a*   *B a*

√ ~(∀ⓥ: Aⓥ)*B*ⓥ
√ (∃ⓥ: Aⓥ)~*B*ⓥ
Ac
~*Bc*

No paths close. We give two models:

1. One individual, *a*   ~*Aa*   (Makes a true sentence.)
2. One individual, *c*   *Ac*   ~*Bc* (Makes a false sentence.)

II. Form

(∃ⓥ: Aⓥ · *B*ⓥ)*C*ⓥ

Natural Language Examples

1. $Ax = x$ is a dog
$Bx = x$ is brown
$Cx = x$ barks
Some dogs that are brown bark.   *True*

2. Ax = x is a dog
   Bx = x is brown
   Cx = x writes novels
   Some dogs that are brown write novels.   *False*

Truth-Trees

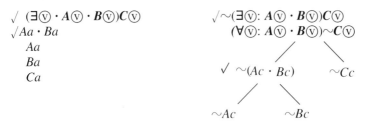

Take the one model path in the left tree to show it true, and one of the three model paths in the right tree to show it false.

Models

1. One individual, a Aa Ba Ca *True*
2. One individual, c $\sim Ac$ *False*

Two types of example require special attention when we are showing contingency.

III. Form

$$(\forall ⓥ: Aⓥ)[\sim Aⓥ \cdot Bⓥ]$$

This might at first appear to be contradictory, so you might think that there is no way for it to be true. But there is a way. If there is no individual of which '$Aⓥ$' is true, the sentence as a whole will be true. So we can make it true as well as making it false.

Natural Language Examples

1. Ax = x is an odd number divisible by 4
   Bx = x is divisible by 2
   Any odd number divisible by 4 satisfies this condition—it is not an odd number divisible by 4 and it is divisible by 2.   *True*
2. Ax = x is a dog
   Bx = x brown
   Every dog satisfies this condition—it is not a dog but it is brown.   *False*

Truth-Trees

Models

1. One individual, *a*   ~Aa   (Makes it true.)
2. One individual, *c*   Ac   (Makes it false.)

The other type of special case is illustrated by the following example:

IV. Form

(∃Ⓥ: AⓋ)[AⓋ ∨ BⓋ]

This may at first look tautologous, but it will be false if there are no individuals satisfying AⓋ.

Natural Language Examples

1. Ax = x is a dog
   Bx = x is a cat
   At least one dog is either a dog or a cat.   *True*
2. Ax = x is a unicorn
   Bx = x is a cat
   At least one unicorn is either a unicorn or a cat.   *False*

EXERCISE 12e

Show that these are contingent.

1. (∃Ⓥ: AⓋ)BⓋ
2. (∀Ⓥ: AⓋ · BⓋ)[BⓋ · CⓋ]
3. (∀Ⓥ: AⓋ)~AⓋ
4. (∃Ⓥ: AⓋ · BⓋ)BⓋ
5. ~(∀Ⓥ: AⓋ · CⓋ)BⓋ
6. ~(∃Ⓥ: AⓋ · CⓋ)CⓋ
7. (∀Ⓥ: AⓋ)BⓋ ⊃ (∀Ⓥ: BⓋ)CⓋ
8. (∀Ⓥ: AⓋ · BⓋ)CⓋ ⊃ (∀Ⓥ: AⓋ · ~BⓋ)~CⓋ

Tree Rules for Quantificational Logic

Existential

√ (∃ⓥ: Aⓥ)Bⓥ

        .
        .
        .
        Aⓒ
        Bⓒ

Add *A*ⓒ and *B*ⓒ to every open path, where ⓒ is an individual constant that has not previously appeared on the path. Check off (∃ⓥ: Aⓥ)Bⓥ.

Negation of an Existential

∼(∃ⓥ: Aⓥ)Bⓥ

        .
        .
        .

(∀ⓥ: Aⓥ)∼Bⓥ

Universal

(∀ⓥ: Aⓥ)Bⓥ

        .
        .

∼*A*ⓒ   *B*ⓒ

Add branches for ∼*A*ⓒ and *B*ⓒ to every open path. This applies to every individual constant ⓒ. *Do not check off the sentence* (∀ⓥ: Aⓥ)Bⓥ (because it may be necessary to apply the rule again, using a different constant).

Negation of a Universal

∼(∀ⓥ: Aⓥ)Bⓥ

        .
        .
        .

(∃ⓥ: Aⓥ)∼Bⓥ

13

UNRELATIVIZED QUANTIFICATION

FORMULAS

During this century work in formal logic has employed *unrelativized quantifiers*. No general term qualifies the quantifier, so that the fundamental form for formulas is this:

$(\forall ⓥ)B ⓥ$ Every individual ⓥ satisfies this condition - - - $B ⓥ$.
$(\exists ⓥ)B ⓥ$ At least one individual ⓥ satisfies this condition - - - $B ⓥ$.

It is most natural to view this as a "limiting case," equivalent to

$(\forall ⓥ: A ⓥ \vee \sim A ⓥ)B ⓥ$
$(\exists ⓥ: A ⓥ \vee \sim A ⓥ)B ⓥ$

Since '$A ⓥ \vee \sim A ⓥ$' is true of everything (no matter what '$A ⓥ$' is), the qualification in the quantifier phrase has no content, and we can abbreviate by erasing it.

$(\forall ⓥ)B ⓥ$
$(\exists ⓥ)B ⓥ$

This yields standard, unrelativized quantification.

There is no reason why we could not have such unrelativized quantifiers along with relativized quantifiers. We would simply treat '$(\forall ⓥ)$' and '$(\exists ⓥ)$' as abbreviations for the vacuously relativized quantifiers '$(\forall ⓥ: A ⓥ \vee \sim A ⓥ)$' and '$(\exists ⓥ: A ⓥ \vee \sim A ⓥ)$'.

But the usual approach to predicate logic relies on *unrelativized quantification* only, and we need to see how to do this. In the section of Chapter 11 on extra rules, we noted a pair of important equivalences:

Derelativization

$(\forall ⓥ: Aⓥ)Bⓥ$ :: $(\forall ⓥ: Cⓥ ∨ {\sim}Cⓥ)[Aⓥ ⊃ Bⓥ]$
$(\exists ⓥ: Aⓥ)Bⓥ$ :: $(\exists ⓥ: Cⓥ ∨ {\sim}Cⓥ)[Aⓥ · Bⓥ]$

Using the unrelativized quantifiers '$(\forall ⓥ)$' and '$(\exists ⓥ)$' to replace the vacuously relativized '$(\forall ⓥ: Cⓥ ∨ {\sim}Cⓥ)$' and '$(\exists ⓥ: Cⓥ ∨ {\sim}Cⓥ)$', we see these equivalences.

Relativized   *Unrelativized*

$(\forall ⓥ: Aⓥ)Bⓥ$ $(\forall ⓥ) (Aⓥ ⊃ Bⓥ)$
$(\exists ⓥ: Aⓥ)Bⓥ$ $(\exists ⓥ) (Aⓥ · Bⓥ)$

If unrelativized quantifiers are employed, a typical universally quantified sentence corresponds to a universally quantified conditional. A typical existentially quantified sentence corresponds to an existentially quantified conjunction.

Translation: Relativized to Unrelativized

Translating from relativized to unrelativized quantification is a simple matter of replacing each relativized quantification by the corresponding unrelativized quantification—a universally quantified conditional or an existentially quantified conjunction.

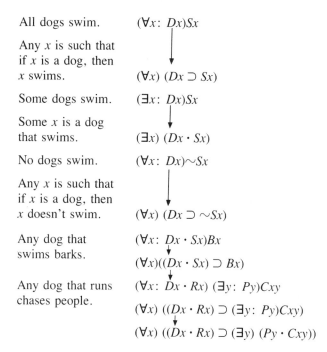

All dogs swim. $(\forall x: Dx)Sx$

Any x is such that
if x is a dog, then
x swims. $(\forall x) (Dx ⊃ Sx)$

Some dogs swim. $(\exists x: Dx)Sx$

Some x is a dog
that swims. $(\exists x) (Dx · Sx)$

No dogs swim. $(\forall x: Dx){\sim}Sx$

Any x is such that
if x is a dog, then
x doesn't swim. $(\forall x) (Dx ⊃ {\sim}Sx)$

Any dog that $(\forall x: Dx · Sx)Bx$
swims barks.
                        $(\forall x)((Dx · Sx) ⊃ Bx)$

Any dog that runs $(\forall x: Dx · Rx) (\exists y: Py)Cxy$
chases people.
                        $(\forall x) ((Dx · Rx) ⊃ (\exists y: Py)Cxy)$

                        $(\forall x) ((Dx · Rx) ⊃ (\exists y) (Py · Cxy))$

Any dog that chases people barks.

$$(\forall x: Dx \cdot (\exists y: Py)Cxy)Bx$$
$$\downarrow$$
$$(\forall x) ((Dx \cdot (\exists y: Py)Cxy) \supset Bx)$$
$$(\forall x) ((Dx \cdot (\exists y)(Py \cdot Cxy)) \supset Bx)$$

Some dogs swim and run, but some do neither.

$$(\exists x: Dx)(Sx \cdot Rx) \cdot (\exists y: Dy) \sim(Sy \vee Ry)$$
$$\downarrow$$
$$(\exists x)(Dx \cdot (Sx \cdot Rx)) \cdot (\exists y) (Dy \cdot \sim(Sy \vee Ry))$$

Anyone designated by a judge will receive an award.

$$(\forall x: Px \cdot (\exists y: Jy)Dyx) (\exists z: Az)Rxz$$
$$\downarrow$$
$$(\forall x)((Px \cdot (\exists y: Jy)Dyx) \supset (\exists z)(Az \cdot Rxz))$$
$$\downarrow$$
$$(\forall x)((Px \cdot (\exists y)(Jy \cdot Dyx)) \supset (\exists z) (Az \cdot Rxz))$$

EXERCISE 13a

Rewrite your answers to the exercises of Chapter 10, but use unrelativized quantification.

Translation: Unrelativized to Relativized

Translation from unrelativized quantification is not quite so smooth. Of course, we could always do it this way:

Translation Scheme I

| $(\forall\textcircled{v})C\textcircled{v}$ | translates to | $(\forall\textcircled{v}: D\textcircled{v} \vee \sim D\textcircled{v})C\textcircled{v}$ |
| $(\exists\textcircled{v})C\textcircled{v}$ | translates to | $(\exists\textcircled{v}: D\textcircled{v} \vee \sim D\textcircled{v})C\textcircled{v}$ |

But then typical sentences are

| $(\forall x)(Ax \supset Bx)$ | to | $(\forall x: Dx \vee \sim Dx)(Ax \supset Bx)$ |
| $(\exists x)(Ax \cdot Bx)$ | to | $(\exists x: Dx \vee \sim Dx)(Ax \cdot Bx)$ |

This is not what we usually want. Instead, we would like these translations.

Translation Scheme II

| $(\forall\textcircled{v})(A\textcircled{v} \supset B\textcircled{v})$ | to | $(\forall\textcircled{v}: A\textcircled{v})B\textcircled{v}$ |
| $(\exists\textcircled{v})(A\textcircled{v} \cdot B\textcircled{v})$ | to | $(\exists\textcircled{v}: A\textcircled{v})B\textcircled{v}$ |

When we have universally quantified conditionals and existentially quantified conjunctions, we can follow this last pattern.

But unrelativized quantifiers may also appear on other types of sentences: disjunctions, biconditionals, and so on. When this happens, we must either look for equivalent sentences in the more usual form or else shift back to translation scheme I. We can combine the two translation schemes to produce a translation from unrelativized to relativized quantification.

1. $(\forall x)((Ax \cdot Bx) \supset Cx)$
$\downarrow$
$(\forall x:Ax \cdot Bx)Cx$

2. $(\exists x)((Ax \cdot Bx) \cdot Cx)$
$\downarrow$
$(\exists x:Ax \cdot Bx)Cx$

3. $(\forall x)[(Ax \cdot (\exists y)(By \cdot Rxy)) \supset (\forall z)(Cz \supset Rxz)]$
$\downarrow$
$(\forall x:Ax \cdot (\exists y:By)Rxy)(\forall z:\ Cz)Rxz$

4. $(\exists x)\sim(Ax \lor Bx)$
$\downarrow$
$(\exists x)(\sim Ax \cdot \sim Bx)$
$\downarrow$
$(\exists x:\ \sim Ax)\sim Bx$
$\downarrow$

5. $(\forall x)(Ax \equiv Bx)$

$(\forall x)[(Ax \supset Bx) \cdot (Bx \supset Ax)]$
$\downarrow$
$(\forall x)(Ax \supset Bx) \cdot (\forall x)(Bx \supset Ax)$
$\downarrow$
$(\forall x:\ Ax)Bx \cdot (\forall x:\ Bx)Ax$

Translations 4 and 5 are produced by transforming unrelativized formulas to an equivalent form before translating.

$(\exists x)\sim(Ax \lor Bx)$ *is equivalent to* $(\exists x) (\sim Ax \cdot \sim Bx)$

$(\forall x)(Ax \equiv Bx)$ *is equivalent to* $(\forall x)(Ax \supset Bx) \cdot (\forall x)(Bx \supset Ax)$

6.(a) $(\exists x)Bx$
$\downarrow$
$(\exists x:\ Cx \lor \sim Cx)Bx$

(b) $(\exists x)Bx$
$\downarrow$
$(\exists x)(Bx \cdot Bx)$
$\downarrow$
$(\exists x:\ Bx)Bx$

EXERCISE 13b

Translate these into relativized form.

1. $(\forall x)(Ax \supset (Bx \cdot Cx))$ **2.** $(\forall x)(Ax \supset (\exists y)(By \cdot Rxy))$

3. $(\forall x)(Ax \supset Bx) \supset (\exists y)(Cy \cdot Dy)$ **4.** $(\forall x)Ax \supset (\exists y)By$

5. $\sim(\forall x)(Ax \supset Bx)$ **6.** $(\forall x)\sim(Ax \cdot Bx)$

7. $(\exists x)(Ax \cdot \sim Cx) \cdot (\exists y)(By \cdot Dy)$ **8.** $(\forall x)((\exists y)Rxy \supset (\exists y)Ryx)$

DERIVATION RULES

The rules of derivation can be slightly altered and streamlined if we employ unrelativized quantification. Keep two things in mind:

1. '$(\forall x)$' works like '$(\forall x{:}\ Cx \lor \sim Cx)$'.
   '$(\exists x)$' works like '$(\exists x{:}\ Cx \lor \sim Cx)$'.

2. We can always prove
   $p \lor \sim p$

The proof of '$p \lor \sim p$' is this:

$\sim(p \lor \sim p)$	AP
$\sim p \cdot \sim\sim p$	DeM
$p \lor \sim p$	IP

Let's use **T** to stand for sentences of the form '$p \lor \sim p$'. Since **T** can be proved independently, it is unnecessary as an argument premise and pointless as an argument conclusion. Since it applies to everything, it is empty of content as a qualifier in a quantifier phrase. Thus if we write out our quantifier rules using **T** to correspond to the tautologous formula within the quantifier phrases, we can then simply eliminate the **T**'s. This will give us our quantifier rules for unrelativized quantification.

	Vacuously Relativized	Unrelativized
EQE	$(\exists \text{\textcircled{v}}{:}\ \mathbf{T})C\text{\textcircled{v}}$ $\therefore \mathbf{T}$ $\therefore C\text{\textcircled{c}}$	$(\exists \text{\textcircled{v}})C\text{\textcircled{v}}$ $\therefore C\text{\textcircled{c}}$
EQI	$\mathbf{T}$ $C\text{\textcircled{c}}$ $\therefore (\exists \text{\textcircled{v}}{:}\ \mathbf{T})C\text{\textcircled{v}}$	$C\text{\textcircled{c}}$ $\therefore (\exists \text{\textcircled{v}})C\text{\textcircled{v}}$
UQE	$(\forall \text{\textcircled{v}}{:}\ \mathbf{T})C\text{\textcircled{v}}$ $\mathbf{T}$ $\therefore C\text{\textcircled{c}}$	$(\forall \text{\textcircled{v}})C\text{\textcircled{v}}$ $\therefore C\text{\textcircled{c}}$
UQI	$\mathbf{T}$ . . . $C\text{\textcircled{c}}$ $(\forall \text{\textcircled{v}}{:}\ \mathbf{T})C\text{\textcircled{v}}$	. . . $C\text{\textcircled{c}}$ $(\forall \text{\textcircled{v}})C\text{\textcircled{v}}$

EQE, EQI, and UQE are not very different from before. The restrictions have not been spelled out because they are exactly analogous to those for the corresponding rules with relativized quantification. (In EQI and UQE, $C\text{\textcircled{c}}$ must be a $\text{\textcircled{c}} \mid \text{\textcircled{v}}$ instance of $C\text{\textcircled{v}}$. In EQE, $\text{\textcircled{c}}$ must be a new name and $C\text{\textcircled{c}}$ must be a $\text{\textcircled{c}} \mid \text{\textcircled{v}}$ instance of $C\text{\textcircled{v}}$.)

But UQI introduces a new apparatus—a subderivation that does not begin with an assumption in the way that previous subderivation rules (CP, IP, and relativized UQI) did. Let us call this a "universal subderivation." This subderivation begins with a barrier, marking the first use of Ⓒ representing "any arbitrarily selected individual." We prove that CⒸ is true for any arbitrarily selected individual Ⓒ and close the subderivation writing the corresponding universally quantified formula '(∀Ⓥ)CⓋ'.

The restrictions on UQI are these:

1. CⒸ must be a Ⓒ|Ⓥ instance of CⓋ, and vice versa.

2. Ⓒ must not appear in any formula prior to the beginning of the universal subderivation.

3. Any name (individual constant) introduced by EQE appearing in CⒸ must appear before the beginning of the universal subderivation.

The following examples show how the rules work for typical quantified sentences. On the left is the inference rule for relativized quantification and on the right is the rule for unrelativized quantification. The middle column shows the application of the unrelativized rules to the usual sorts of sentences, universally quantified conditionals, and existentially quantified conjunctions. Additional steps are included to help make the parallel with the relativized quantifier rules more apparent.

Relativized	Parallel Unrelativized	Unrelativized: Rules
EQE		
(∃Ⓥ: AⓋ)BⓋ	(∃Ⓥ) (AⓋ · BⓋ)	(∃Ⓥ)CⓋ
∴ AⒸ EQE	∴ AⒸ · BⒸ EQE	∴ CⒸ EQE
∴ BⒸ EQE	AⒸ Simp	
	BⒸ Simp	
EQI		
AⒸ	AⒸ	CⒸ
BⒸ	BⒸ	∴ (∃Ⓥ) CⓋ EQI
∴ (∃Ⓥ: AⓋ)BⓋ EQI	AⒸ · BⒸ Conj	
	∴ (∃Ⓥ) (AⓋ · BⓋ) EQI	
UQE		
AⒸ	1. AⒸ	(∀Ⓥ) CⓋ
(∀Ⓥ: AⓋ)BⓋ	2. (∀Ⓥ) (AⓋ ⊃ BⓋ)	∴ CⒸ UQE
∴ BⒸ UQE	3. AⒸ ⊃ BⒸ 2 UQE	
	4. BⒸ 1,3 MP	

UQI
AⒸ
·
·
·
BⒸ
(∀Ⓥ: AⓋ)BⓋ UQI

AⒸ
·
·
·
BⒸ
AⒸ ⊃ BⒸ CP
(∀Ⓥ) (AⓋ ⊃ BⓋ) UQI

CⒸ
(∀Ⓥ)CⓋ UQI

Because conditionals are usually proved by CP, a conditional subderivation appears within the universal subderivation here. [This makes the parallel with relativized UQI apparent. You make the same assumption (*A*ⓒ) and derive the same consequence (*B*ⓒ) to get the desired universally quantified conclusion.]

Quantifier Negation

The fundamental idea of quantifier negation remains the same when unrelativized quantifiers are employed.

There are no *A*'s.	Everything is non-*A*.
$\sim(\exists x)Ax$	$(\forall x)\sim Ax$
Not everything is *A*.	Something is non-*A*.
$\sim(\forall x)Ax$	$(\exists x)\sim Ax$

Thus our four equivalences look much the same as before.

(a) $\sim(\exists ⓥ)A ⓥ$ :: $(\forall ⓥ)\sim A ⓥ$

(b) $\sim(\forall ⓥ)A ⓥ$ :: $(\exists ⓥ)\sim A ⓥ$

(c) $\sim(\exists ⓥ)\sim A ⓥ$ :: $(\forall ⓥ)A ⓥ$

(d) $\sim(\forall ⓥ)\sim A ⓥ$ :: $(\exists ⓥ)A ⓥ$

In typical arguments the QN rule for unrelativized quantification is used in conjunction with several equivalence rules: DeMorgan's laws, implication, and double negation.

Anything that is not a herbivore is a carnivore. Not all cows are herbivores. So some cows are carnivores.

1. $(\forall x: \sim Hx)Mx$			**1.** $(\forall x)(\sim Hx \supset Mx)$		
2. $\sim(\forall x: Cx)Hx$			**2.** $\sim(\forall x)(Cx \supset Hx)$		
3. $(\exists x: Cx)\sim Hx$	2	QN	**3.** $(\exists x)\sim(Cx \supset Hx)$	2	QN
4. Ca	3	EQE	**4.** $(\exists x)\sim(\sim Cx \lor Hx)$	3	CE
5. $\sim Ha$	3	EQE	**5.** $(\exists x)(\sim\sim Cx \cdot \sim Hx)$	4	DeM
6. Ma	1,5	UQE	**6.** $(\exists x)(Cx \cdot \sim Hx)$	5	DN
7. $(\exists x: Cx)Mx$	4,6	EQI	**7.** $Ca \cdot \sim Ha$	6	EQE
			8. Ca	7	Simp
			9. $\sim Ha$	7	Simp
			10. $\sim Ha \supset Ma$	1	UQE
			11. Ma	9,10	MP
			12. $Ca \cdot Ma$	8,11	Conj
			13. $(\exists x)(Cx \cdot Mx)$	12	EQI

Steps 2-6 of the unrelatized derivation move from '$\sim(\forall x)(Cx \supset Hx)$' (Not all cows are herbivores) to the equivalent '$(\exists x)(Cx \cdot \sim Hx)$' (Some cows are not herbivores). By generally similar steps, we could establish any of these four equivalences:

$$\sim(\exists x)(Ax \cdot Bx) \quad :: \quad (\forall x)(Ax \supset \sim Bx)$$
$$\sim(\forall x)(Ax \supset Bx) \quad :: \quad (\exists x)(Ax \cdot \sim Bx)$$
$$\sim(\exists x)(Ax \cdot \sim Bx) \quad :: \quad (\forall x)(Ax \supset Bx)$$
$$\sim(\forall x)(Ax \supset \sim Bx) \quad :: \quad (\exists x)(Ax \cdot Bx)$$

Examples of Derivations (Unrelativized Quantification). (These correspond to 8-12 of Exercise 11e.)

I.
1. $(\exists x)[(Ax \cdot Dxb) \cdot (\forall z)(Dxz \supset Ox)]$
2. $(Aa \cdot Dab) \cdot (\forall z)(Daz \supset Oz)$ 1   EQE
3. $Aa \cdot Dab$ 2   Simp
4. Dab 3   Simp
5. $(\forall z)(Daz \supset Oz)$ 2   Simp
6. $Dab \supset Ob$ 5   UQE
7. Ob 4,6   MP

II.
1. $(\forall x)[(Bx \cdot (\exists y)(Gy \cdot Lxy)) \supset (\forall y)(Gy \supset Lyx)]$
2. $(\exists x)(Gx \cdot Lax)$
3. Ba
4. $Gc \cdot Lac$ 2   EQE
5. $(\exists y)(Gy \cdot Lay)$ 4   EQI
6. $Ba \cdot (\exists y)(Gy \cdot Lay)$ 3,5   Conj
7. $(Ba \cdot (\exists y)(Gy \cdot Lay)) \supset (\forall y)(Gy \supset Lya)$ 1   UQE
8. $(\forall y)(Gy \supset Lya)$ 6,7   MP

> 9. Gd AP
> 10. $Gd \supset Lda$ 8   UQE
> 11. Lda 9,10   MP
> 12. $Ba \cdot Lda$ 3,11   Conj
> 13. $(\exists x)(Bx \cdot Ldx)$ 12   EQI

14. $Gd \supset (\exists x)(Bx \cdot Ldx)$ 9–13   CP
15. $(\forall y)(Gy \supset (\exists x)(Bx \cdot Lyx))$ 9–14   UQI

III.
1. $(\forall x)(Fx \supset (\forall y)(Gy \supset \sim Rxy))$
2. $(\forall x)(\forall y)((Hx \cdot Hy) \supset Rxy)$
3. $(\forall x)((Fx \lor Gx) \supset Hx)$
> 4. $(\exists x)(Fx \cdot Gx)$ AP
> 5. $Fa \cdot Ga$ 4   EQE
> 6. Fa 5   Simp
> 7. Ga 5   Simp
> 8. $Fa \supset (\forall y)(Gy \supset \sim Ray)$ 1   UQE
> 9. $(\forall y)(Gy \supset \sim Ray)$ 6,8   MP
> 10. $Ga \supset \sim Raa$ 9   UQE

11.	$\sim Raa$	7,10	MP
12.	$(Fa \lor Ga) \supset Ha$	3	UQE
13.	$Fa \lor Ga$	6	Add
14.	Ha	12,13	MP
15.	$(\forall y)((Ha \cdot Hy) \supset Ray)$	2	UQE
16.	$(Ha \cdot Ha) \supset Raa$	15	UQE
17.	$Ha \cdot Ha$	14	Red
18.	Raa	16,17	MP
19.	$Raa \cdot \sim Raa$	11,18	Conj
20.	$\sim(\exists x)(Fx \cdot Gx)$	4-19	IP

IV.
1.	$(\forall x)(Fx \supset (\forall y)(Gy \supset \sim Rxy))$		
2.	$(\forall x)(Hx \supset (\exists y)(Gy \cdot Rxy))$		
3.	$(\exists x)(Hx \cdot Rxa) \supset \sim(\exists y)(Gy \cdot Ray)$		
4.	Hb		
5.	$(\exists x)(Hx \cdot Fx)$		AP
6.	$Hb \cdot Fb$	5	EQE
7.	Hb	6	Simp
8.	Fb	6	Simp
9.	$Hb \supset (\exists y)(Gy \cdot Rby)$	2	UQE
10.	$(\exists y)(Gy \cdot Rby)$	7,9	MP
11.	$Fb \supset (\forall y)(Gy \supset \sim Rby)$	1	UQE
12.	$(\forall y)(Gy \supset \sim Rby)$	8,11	MP
13.	$Gc \cdot Rbc$	10	EQE
14.	Gc	13	Simp
15.	$Gc \supset \sim Rbc$	12	UQE
16.	$\sim Rbc$	14,15	MP
17.	Rbc	13	Simp
18.	$Rbc \cdot \sim Rbc$	16,17	Conj
19.	$\sim(\exists x)(Hx \cdot Fx)$	5–18	IP
20.	$(\exists x)(Hx \cdot Rxa)$		AP
21.	$\sim(\exists y)(Gy \cdot Ray)$	3,20	MP
22.	$Ha \supset (\exists y)(Gy \cdot Ray)$	2	UQE
23.	$(\exists y)(Gy \cdot Ray)$	4,22	MP
24.	$(\exists y)(Gy \cdot Ray) \cdot \sim(\exists y)(Gy \cdot Ray)$	21,23	Conj
25.	$\sim(\exists x)(Hx \cdot Rxa)$	20–24	IP
26.	$\sim(\exists x)(Hx \cdot Fx) \cdot \sim(\exists x)(Hx \cdot Rxa)$	19,25	Conj

V.
1.	$(\forall x)(\forall y)((Fx \cdot Rxy) \supset Ryx)$		
2.	$(\forall x)(Fx \supset (\exists y)(Gy \cdot Rxy))$		
3.	$\sim(\exists x)(Gx \cdot Rxx)$		
4.	$(\exists x)(Fx \cdot Rxx)$		
5.	$Fa \cdot Raa$	4	EQE
6.	Fa	5	Simp
7.	Raa	5	Simp
8.	$Fa \supset (\exists y)(Gy \cdot Ray)$	2	UQE
9.	$(\exists y)(Gy \cdot Ray)$	6,8	MP
10.	$Gb \cdot Rab$	9	EQE

11. $(\forall y)((Fa \cdot Ray) \supset Rya)$	1	UQE
12. $(Fa \cdot Rab) \supset Rba$	11	UQE
13. Rab	10	Simp
14. $Fa \cdot Rab$	6,13	Conj
15. Rba	12,14	MP
16. $(Fa \cdot Fa) \cdot Raa$	5	Red
17. $(\exists y)((Fa \cdot Fy) \cdot Ray)$	16	EQI
18. $(\exists x)(\exists y)((Fx \cdot Fy) \cdot Rxy)$	17	EQI
19. Gb	10	Simp
20. $(x)\sim(Gx \cdot Rxx)$	3	QN
21. $(x) (\sim Gx \lor \sim Rxx)$	20	DeM
22. $(x)(Gx \supset \sim Rxx)$	21	CE
23. $Gb \supset \sim Rbb$	22	UQE
24. $\sim Rbb$	19,23	MP
25. $Raa \cdot \sim Rbb$	7,24	Conj
26. $(Raa \cdot \sim Rbb) \cdot Rab$	13,25	Conj
27. $(\exists y)((Raa \cdot \sim Ryy) \cdot Ray)$	26	EQI
28. $(\exists x)(\exists y)((Rxx \cdot \sim Ryy) \cdot Rxy)$	27	EQI
29. $(\exists x)(\exists y)((Fx \cdot Fy) \cdot Rxy) \cdot$ $(\exists x)(\exists y)((Rxx \cdot \sim Ryy) \cdot Rxy)$	18,28	Conj

EXERCISE 13c

Show that these are valid.

1. $(\forall x)(Ax \supset Bx)$
$(\forall x)(Bx \supset Cx)$
$\sim Ca$
$\therefore \quad \sim Aa$

2. $(\exists x)(Dx \cdot Fx)$
$(\forall x)[Fx \supset (Gx \lor Hx)]$
$(\forall x)(\sim Hx \lor Cx)$
$(\forall x)(Dx \supset \sim Cx)$
$\therefore \quad (\exists x)(Gx \cdot Fx)$

3. Rab
$(\exists x)Rxb \supset (\forall x)Rxb$
$\therefore \quad Rbb$

4. $(\exists x)Rxb$
$(\forall x)(Rxb \supset Fx)$
$\sim Fb$
$\therefore \quad (\exists x)Fx \cdot (\exists y)\sim Fy$

5. $(\forall x)(Ax \supset Bx)$
$(\exists x)(Ax \cdot Cx)$
$\therefore \quad (\forall x)(Cx \supset Dx) \supset (\exists x)(Bx \cdot Dx)$

6. $(\forall x)(Fx \supset Gx)$
$(\forall x)(Hx \supset \sim Gx)$
$\therefore \quad (\forall x)(Jx \supset Hx) \supset (\forall x)(Jx \supset \sim Fx)$

7. $(\forall x)((\exists y)Rxy \supset Rxa)$
$(\forall x)(Hx \supset Rxb)$
$\therefore \quad (\forall x)(Hx \supset Rxa)$

EXERCISE 13d

Show that these are valid.

1. $(\forall x)(Fx \supset (\forall y)Rxy)$
Fa
$\sim Rbc$
∴ $(\exists x)(\sim Fx \cdot (\exists y)Ryx)$

2. $(\exists x)(Fx \cdot Gx)$
$(\forall x)(Gx \supset (Hx \vee \sim Fx))$
$(\forall x)[(Fx \cdot Hx) \supset (\exists y)Rxy]$
∴ $(\exists x)(\exists y)Rxy$

3. $(\forall x)((\forall y)\sim Rxy \supset Ax)$
$(\exists x)Ax \supset (\forall y)(Ay \supset By)$
$\sim Bc$
∴ $(\exists y)Rcy$

4. $(\forall x)(\forall y)[(Fx \cdot Gy) \supset \sim Rxy]$
$(\forall x)(\exists y)(Gy \cdot Rxy)$
$(\exists x)(Hx \cdot Rxa) \supset \sim (\exists y)Ray$
∴ $\sim (\exists y)Fy \cdot$
   $\sim (\exists x)(Hx \cdot Rxa)$

5. $(\forall x)((\exists y)Lyx \supset Hx)$
Lab
$(\exists x)Hx \supset (\forall x)(Hx \supset Gx)$
$\sim (\forall x)Gx$
∴ $\sim (\forall x)(\exists y)Lyx$

6. $(\forall x)(\forall y)(Rxy \supset Ryx)$
Rab
$(\forall x)((\exists y)Rxy \supset Rxx)$
$(\exists x)\sim (\exists y)Rxy$
∴ $(Rbb \cdot (\exists y)\sim Rby) \cdot (\forall x)(Rbx \supset Rxx)$

7. $\sim (\forall x)[Ax \supset (Bx \cdot Rxa)]$
$(\forall x)(Rax \supset Rxa)$
$\sim (\exists x)(Ax \cdot \sim Bx)$
∴ $(\exists x)(Ax \cdot \sim Rax)$

8. $(\forall x)[Gx \supset (\forall y)(Fy \supset Lyx)]$
$(\forall x)(Fx \supset \sim (\forall z)Lxz)$
∴ $(\exists x)Gx \supset (\forall x)[Fx \supset ((\exists y)Lxy \cdot (\exists z)\sim Lxz)]$

14
ENGLISH ARGUMENTS

ENTHYMEMES

In representing ordinary arguments, we face a difficulty. In most cases, not everything needed for showing the validity of an argument is stated explicitly.

1. John belongs to the American Medical Association, so he must be a doctor.
2. Everyone at the meeting saw the explosion, so Betty must have seen it.

These are reasonable conclusions to draw only if additional, unstated premises are true. In case (1), the argument makes little sense unless the speaker is assuming that only doctors belong to the AMA. In case (2), the speaker seems to be assuming that Betty was at the meeting. What is said gives a fairly clear indication of what else is needed. This fact makes it possible, and even stylistically desirable, for the speaker to leave those things unsaid.

In such cases, we must make the missing premise or premises explicit before we can apply our techniques for showing validity. (We will use an '*' to mark unstated premises.)

1. Aj
   $*(\forall x: Ax)Dx$
   $\therefore \quad Dj$
2. $(\forall x: Px \cdot Mx)Sx$
   $*Pb \cdot Mb$
   $\therefore \quad Sb$

We must construct the intended argument from what is explicitly stated and from what the speaker did not explicitly state but is assuming. Ordinarily, we try to do this in a way that makes the most sense out of the speaker's words.

When a presentation of an argument omits one or more premises or the conclusion, we call that an *enthymematic* presentation of the argument. Often we are aided in identifying an unstated premise by the fact that the premise (or premises) needed to create a valid argument is well known to the speaker and the audience.

3. Whales must have lungs, because all mammals have lungs.

4. Mary can't be John's daughter, because she is his mother.

We know that whales are mammals, and we know that no one can be both mother and daughter to the same individual.

3. $*(\forall x: Wx)Mx$
$(\forall x: Mx)Lx$
$\therefore$ $(\forall x: Wx)Lx$

4. Mmj
$*(\forall x)(\forall y: Mxy)\sim Dxy$
$\therefore$ $\sim Dmj$

Another fact that is usually known to speaker and audience is whether the subject of the argument is a person or is not.

5. Everyone in the house had a good time. Dave was in the house. So Dave must have had a good time.

$(\forall x: Px \cdot Hx)Gx$
Hd
$*Pd$
$\therefore$ Gd

The premise indicated by the asterisk, that Dave is a person, would not ordinarily need to be made explicit. Such general information about the subject of the argument is usually obvious and already known.

In many other cases, a speaker's familiarity with an audience will determine how much needs to be said.

6. This record player must not be reproducing at true speed. That recording of the junior high band sounded like it ended on an E major chord. But they play only in flat keys.

The conclusion (that the record player is not reproducing at the true speed) depends on at least three unstated assumptions.

E major is not a flat key.

The ending chord of a piece is the key the piece is in.

If a recording sounds like it is in a key other than the one played, then the record player's speed is wrong.

Not everyone knows all of these facts, so not everyone could follow the argument as it was originally stated. A good writer or speaker will gauge the audience, leaving unsaid only those facts that the audience can be expected to take for granted in the conversational context.

So we have identified two factors which, alone or together, can help us to articulate unstated premises. One is that the unstated assumption is clearly indicated by context, so that the speaker can expect us to know what is being assumed. [All of (a)–(e) fulfill this condition.] The second factor, that the unstated assumption is an evident truth, or at least something that the speaker would expect the audience to take for granted, also operates in making it appropriate for a speaker to leave a premise unstated. [Arguments (c)–(e) fulfill this second condition. Whether (f) fulfills this condition depends on the audience.]

When possible, we should seek out the most obviously true premise that would validly complete the argument. This will fulfill both of these criteria. It will complete the speaker's argument in a way that makes it possible to show that it is valid and in a way that will preserve acceptability if the explicitly stated premises are already acceptable.

One fact about our way of representing English introduces a special consideration into the matter of finding missing premises. Remember that a statement of the form '$(\forall \text{v}: A \text{v}) B \text{v}$' is true whenever the sentence $A \text{v}$ is not true of anything. So consider this argument:

All naval officers wear gold buttons. $(\forall x: Nx)Gx$
∴   Some admirals wear gold buttons. ∴ $(\exists x: Ax)Gx$

One might suspect that the following unstated premise would be sufficient to guarantee validity.

All admirals are naval officers.
$(\forall x: Ax)Nx$

But such a premise is not adequate, because the two premises together

$(\forall x: Nx)Gx$
*$(\forall x: Ax)Nx$

contain nothing to guarantee that there are any naval officers. We must have an existential premise (or a premise with an individual constant) if we are to get an existential conclusion. So we can reconstruct the argument in one of the following ways:

1. (∀x: Nx)Gx
    *(∀x: Ax)Nx
    *(∃x: Ax)Ax
    ∴ (∃x: Ax)Gx
2. (∀x: Nx)Gx
    *(∃x: Ax)Nx
    ∴ (∃x: Ax)Gx

Each of these introduces some existential sentence to guarantee that there are some admirals.

Exercise 14a

Symbolize each argument and prove that it is valid. Some are presented enthymematically, and missing premises must be supplied. (Use '*Px*' for '*x* is a person' where needed.)

1. Since everyone arrived on time, it must be that no one missed the boat. (*Ax*=*x* arrived on time, *Mx*=*x* missed the boat)

2. Fruits and vegetables are nutritious and economical. Anything that is nutritious or delicious is good to eat. So bananas and carrots are good to eat. (*Fx, Vx, Nx, Ex, Dx, Gx, Bx, Cx*)

3. Everyone here is a suspect if there has been a murder. But unless someone has lied, Frank was murdered. So if no one has lied, Al is a suspect. (*Hx*=*x* is here, *Sx*=*x* is a suspect, *Mx*=*x* was murdered, *Lx*=*x* lied, *f, a*)

4. Some dogs bite, but no dogs that bite bark. Dogs that bite are terrible pets. So some dogs that don't bark are terrible pets. (*Dx, Bx*=*x* bites, *Rx*=*x* barks, *Tx*=*x* is a terrible pet)

5. All of Carl's customers know Don. Anyone who knows Don can get a discount from Ed. Anyone who has been to Al's store knows a customer of Carl. So anyone who has been to Al's store knows someone who can get a discount from Ed. (*Kxy, Dxy*=*x* can get a discount from *y*, *Cxy*=*x* is *y*'s customer, *Sxy*=*x* has been to *y*'s store)

6. Everyone in the club is from Cornell or Syracuse, and none of the people from Cornell are here. So all of the people here must be from Syracuse. (*Ix*=is in the club, *Cx*=*x* is from Cornell, *Sx*=*x* is from Syracuse, *Hx*=*x* is here)

7. Amphibians and reptiles have lungs. Anything with lungs breathes air. So frogs must breathe air. (*Ax, Rx, Lx*=*x* has lungs, *Fx*=*x* is a frog, *Ex*=*x* breathes air)

8. All lions are mammals. So any zoo that owns a lion owns at least one mammal. (*Lx*=*x* is a lion, *Mx*=*x* is a mammal, *Zx*=*x* is a zoo, *Oxy*=*x* owns *y*)

9. Everyone who has talked to Al knows the story, so Bill and Charlie must know the story, since they talked to Al. ($Txy = x$ talked to y, $Sx = x$ knows the story, a, b, c)

10. No engine without a mileage rating can be sold. No engine gets a mileage rating without being examined for safe design. Thus only the engines that have been examined for safe design can be sold. ($Rx = x$ has a mileage rating, $Dx = x$ has been examined for safe design, $Sx = x$ can be sold)

PROPERTIES OF RELATIONS

To make it possible to show the validity of an argument, we must sometimes explicitly state certain properties of relations.

Al is taller than Bill.	*Tab*
Bill is taller than Charlie.	*Tbc*
So Al is taller than Charlie.	∴ *Tac*

There are no quantifiers or compound sentences in our representation of the argument, so there is no apparent opportunity to use our system of deductive rules to derive the conclusion. Yet the argument certainly seems valid. The conclusion follows because we all know that the relation "is taller than" (Txy) is *transitive*. This means that the following general statement is true:

$$(\forall x)(\forall y)(\forall z)[(Txy \cdot Tyz) \supset Txz]$$

We could formulate this equivalently without sentential connectives:

$$(\forall x)(\forall y{:}\ Txy)(\forall z{:}\ Tyz)Txz$$

Either way, the addition of this premise will enable us to deduce the conclusion from the premises in the argument being considered.

1. *Tab*
2. *Tbc*
3. *$(\forall x)(\forall y{:}\ Txy)(\forall z{:}\ Tyz)Txz$
4. $(\forall y{:}\ Tay)(\forall z{:}\ Tyz)Taz$ 3   UQE (unrelativized)
5. $(\forall z{:}\ Tbx)Taz$ 1,4   UQE
6. *Tac*   2,5   UQE

Not all relations are transitive. If 'Txy' meant 'x tripped y', then 'Tab' and 'Tbc' could be true with 'Tac' false. The transitivity of the "is taller than" relation is an instance of a more general fact. All *comparative relations* are transitive. Thus whether 'Txy' stands for

x is taller than y
x is shorter than y
x is more terrifying than y
x is less than y
x wears nicer shirts than y
x gets better grades than y
x relies on more premises than y
x is a poorer swimmer than y

the transitivity principle will be true.

$$(\forall x)(\forall y)(\forall z)[(Txy \cdot Tyz) \supset Txz]$$

In addition, these particular comparative relations conform to an *asymmetry* principle.

$$(\forall x)(\forall y)(Txy \supset \sim Tyx)$$

[also representable as: $(\forall x)(\forall y: Txy)\sim Tyx$].
This might also figure in some arguments.

| Al is taller than Bill. | Tab |
| Thus Bill is not taller than Al. | $\therefore \quad \sim Tba$ |

With the *asymmetry* principle added, the conclusion will be derivable.

Tab
$(\forall x)(\forall y)(Txy \supset \sim Tyx)$
$\therefore \quad \sim Tba$

Comparisons made with 'more than', 'less than', or '-er' are asymmetric, but some types of comparisons are symmetric.

x is (exactly) as tall as y
x is (exactly) as smart as y
x gets grades (exactly) as good as y's

In these cases transitivity holds, but *symmetry* (rather than asymmetry) is applicable.

$$(\forall x)(\forall y)(Sxy \supset Syx)$$

"Since Al is exactly as smart as Bill, Bill is exactly as smart as Al."

Sab

*$(\forall x)(\forall y)(Sxy \supset Syx)$

∴ *Sba*

(Some comparisons are neither symmetric nor asymmetric: "x is at least as smart as y," "x is no smarter than y." Such relations are still transitive, though.)

Here is a list of some special properties that relations can have and some relations, comparative relations and others, that have those properties.

Transitivity

$(\forall x)(\forall y)(\forall z)[(Rxy \cdot Ryz) \supset Rxz]$

> x is less than y
> x is more talented than y
> x weighs (exactly) as much as y
> x is descended from y
> x is spatially enclosed within y
> x is y's ancestor

Intransitivity

$(\forall x)(\forall y)(\forall z)[(Rxy \cdot Ryz) \supset \sim Rxz]$

> x is exactly twice as heavy as y
> x is y's father

Symmetry

$(\forall x)(\forall y)(Rxy \supset Ryx)$

> x weighs (exactly) as much as y
> x is next to y
> x is y's sibling
> x is married to y

Asymmetry

$(\forall x)(\forall y)(Rxy \supset \sim Ryx)$

> x is taller than y
> x is y's parent
> x existed before y did
> x is conquering y

Reflexivity (total)

$(\forall x)Rxx$

> x weighs exactly as much as x
>
> x is (exactly) as talented as x

Irreflexivity

$(\forall x){\sim}Rxx$

> x is taller than y
>
> x is y's ancestor
>
> x is next to y
>
> x is y's sibling
>
> x is twice as heavy as y

Of course, many relations lack all of these properties. The relations 'x loves y' and 'x has seen y on TV', for example, have none of these six characteristics. (They are non-transitive, non-symmetric, and non-reflexive.)

Other Facts That Go Unstated

Consider the following argument.

All of Al's children are married.
Betty is Al's daughter.
∴ Betty is married.

To make the conclusion derivable, we must somehow connect the properties of being a child of someone and being a daughter of someone. Here are two ways that we might do it:

1. $(\forall x: Cxa)Mx$
   Dba
   *$(\forall x)(\forall y)(Dxy \supset Cxy)$
   ∴ Mb

2. $(\forall x: Cxa)Mx$
   Dba
   *$(\forall x)(\forall y)[Dxy \equiv (Cxy \cdot Fx)]$
   ∴ Mb

In (1) we state an obviously true generalization connecting these properties. In (2) we give an "analysis" of 'Dxy' (using 'Fx' for 'x is female') that connects these properties. Either way, we can then proceed to derive the conclusion.

We know many facts about family relations that might be unstated, understood premises of arguments. These are facts that everyone knows, so they generally go unstated in any argument. We can represent some of these facts using the following symbols:

Px: *x* is a person   *Fx*: *x* is female   *Mx*: *x* is male
Cxy: *x* is a child of *y*   *Dxy*: *x* is a daughter of *y*   *Sxy*: *x* is a son of *y*
Rxy: *x* is a parent of *y*   *Axy*: *x* is a father of *y*   *Oxy*: *x* is a mother of *y*
Bxy: *x* is a brother of *y*   *Txy*: *x* is a sister of *y*   *Lxy*: *x* is a sibling of *y*
Nxy: *x* is an aunt of *y*   *Uxy*: *x* is an uncle of *y*   *Wxy*: *x* is married to *y*

$(\forall x\colon Px)[(Fx \lor Mx) \cdot \sim(Fx \cdot Mx)]$
$(\forall x\colon Px)(\forall y\colon Py)(Cxy \equiv Ryx)$
$(\forall x\colon Px)(\exists y\colon Py)(Ryx \cdot Fx)$ $(\forall x\colon Px)(\exists y\colon Py)(Ryx \cdot Mx)$
$(\forall x\colon Px)(\forall y\colon Py)(Dxy \equiv (Cxy \cdot Fx))$ $(\forall x\colon Px)(\forall y\colon Py)(Sxy \equiv (Cxy \cdot Mx))$
$(\forall x\colon Px)(\forall y\colon Py)(Oxy \equiv (Rxy \cdot Fx))$ $(\forall x\colon Px)(\forall y\colon Py)(Axy \equiv (Cxy \cdot Mx))$
$(\forall x\colon Px)(\forall y\colon Py)(Bxy \equiv (Lxy \cdot Mx))$ $(\forall x\colon Px)(\forall y\colon Py)(Txy \equiv (Lxy \cdot Fx))$
$(\forall x\colon Px)(\forall y\colon Py)\{Nxy \equiv [Fx \cdot ((\exists z\colon Lzx)Cyz \lor (\exists z\colon Uzy)Wxz)]\}$
$(\forall x\colon Px)(\forall y\colon Py)\{Uxy \equiv [Mx \cdot ((\exists z\colon Lzx)Cyz \lor (\exists z\colon Nzy)Wxz)]\}$

We know many other things as well. To formulate some of them (for example, the fact that each person has exactly one mother), we need the concept of *identity* that is introduced in the next chapter.

EXERCISE 14b

Symbolize each argument and prove that it is valid. Some are presented enthymematically, and missing premises must be supplied. (Use '*Px*' to stand for '*x* is a person' where needed.)

1. Of Bob's children, only his daughters are married. Al is Bob's son. So Al is not married. (*Cxy*=*x* is *y*'s child, *Dxy*=*x* is *y*'s daughter, *Sxy*=*x* is *y*'s son, *Mx*=*x* is married)

2. Al must be married, since all of Bob's sons are married.

3. Everyone on the basketball team is taller than Al. Anyone taller than Al can reach the shelf. No one who can reach the shelf will go hungry. Charlie is taller than Bill, and Bill is on the basketball team. So Charlie will not go hungry. (*Bx*, *Txy*, *Rx*, *Hx*)

4. Since Betty is Alice's sister, Betty must be taller than Charlene. This is so because Alice is taller than Charlene, and all of Alice's sisters are taller than Alice. (*Sxy*=*x* is a sister of *y*, *Txy*=*x* is taller than *y*)

5. Anyone who works for Smith is well paid. Jones works for Smith. So Jones must be well paid. ($Wxy=x$ works for y, $Ax=x$ is well paid, $s=$ Smith, $j=$ Jones)

6. Every junior has more credits than any sophomore. Some sophomores have more credits than Al. So Bill, who is a junior, must have more credits than Al. ($Sx=x$ is a sophomore, $Jx=x$ is a junior, has more credits than y, $Cxy=x$, $a=$ Al; $b=$ Bill)

7. Everyone shorter than Bill will be excluded from the team. Al is shorter than Bill and Charlie is even shorter than Al, so they will both be excluded. ($Sxy=x$ is shorter than y, $Ex=x$ is excluded from the team, $a=$ Al, $b=$ Bill, $c=$ Charlie)

8. Some linguists receive a higher pay than Baker and Baker receives a higher pay than some philosophers. So some linguists receive a higher pay than some philosophers. ($Lx=x$ is a linguist, $Fx=x$ is a philosopher, $Hxy=x$ receives a higher pay than y, $b=$ Baker)

15

IDENTITY, DEFINITE DESCRIPTIONS, AND FUNCTION SYMBOLS

IDENTITY

Identity is a dyadic relation. To say that Mary Anne Evans is (i.e., is identical to) George Eliot is syntactically similar to saying that Mary is as tall as George, that Mary stood next to George, or that Mary saw George. But the concept of identity has a central place in many arguments, and the special inferential properties of identity have led logicians to place it in a class by itself as a *logical* relation.

We will use the symbol for identity in a way that is different from the way we use other symbols for dyadic relations. When we represent other relational sentences, the relational symbol appears at the beginning of the sentence.

Al stood next to Betty.
Nab

Al saw Betty.
Sab

But we will write the identity symbol between the two singular terms, in the way it is ordinarily written.

Al is identical to Bill.
$a = b$

In addition, we may sometimes use '$\neq$' when writing negated identities.

$\sim a = b$ $a \neq b$

$\sim a = b \supset \sim b = a$ $a \neq b \supset b \neq a$

This makes our uses of the symbol more like its ordinary uses (such as those in mathematics).

The identity symbol is very familiar in mathematics.

$2 + 4 = 6$

$(\forall x: Nx)(\forall y: Ny)(x + y = y + x)$

$|-3| = 3$

$2a + 3a + 5ab = 5a(b + 1)$

Our introduction of identity opens the way to full representation of such claims; so after a discussion of the special logical features identity, we consider some of the other resources used in expressing mathematical statements.

Representing English

Exceptives

Identity occurs as a central concept in a large class of sentences that we will call "exceptives." In these, one or more individuals are excluded from a general statement. Words and phrases such as 'except', 'other than', 'but', and 'else' are often used.

Everyone except Carol is eligible.

$(\forall x: Px \cdot \sim x = c)Ex$

Carol is taller than everyone else.

$(\forall x: Px \cdot \sim x = c)Tcx$

In many sentences the exception is understood without being expressed explicitly. Because of this, the nonidentity clause is needed even in many sentences in which it does not occur explicitly in the English.

Carol stood next to everyone.

$(\forall x: Px \cdot \sim x = c)Ncx$

Carol is taller than everyone but Harry.

$(\forall x: Px \cdot (\sim x = h \cdot \sim x = c))Tcx$

In these sentences it would be obvious that the speaker intended to make the indicated exclusion.

Only

The word 'only' also occurs in a common type of sentence that contains the identity relation.

Only Carol loves Bill.
$(\forall x{:} \sim x = c) \sim Lxb$

[It would be equivalent to write '$(\forall x{:} Lxb)x = c$'.] In such sentences with 'only', the English is actually unclear about one point. The sentence "Only Carol loves Bill" could be taken to say, in addition to what is written above, that Carol loves Bill. If it says that, it is appropriate to add a clause.

Only Carol loves Bill.
$(\forall x{:} \sim x = c) \sim Lcb \cdot Lcb$

This becomes somewhat more problematic when negation is involved.

Carol is not the only one who loves Bill.

We might interpret this in three ways. First, it could be the denial of the first version of "Only Carol loves Bill."

$\sim(\forall x{:} \sim x = c) \sim Lxb$

This is equivalent to saying that someone other than Carol loves Bill ($(\exists x{:} \sim x = c)Lxb$). It says nothing at all about whether Carol loves Bill.
   But we could also interpret the English sentence in two other ways. It could be interpreted in such a way that it would be made true by the fact that Carol does not love Bill. ("Carol is not the only one who loves Bill, simply because even she doesn't love him.") This is the interpretation we get if we take the second version of the basic (unnegated) sentence with 'only' and deny the whole conjunction.

$\sim[(\forall x{:} \sim x = c) \sim Lxb \cdot Lcb]$

[Note that this is equivalent to '$(\exists x : \sim x = c)Lxb \lor \sim Lcb$' and is made true if Carol does not love Bill.] On the other hand, we might interpret it so that the truth of the sentence ("Carol is not the only one who loves Bill") requires that Carol love Bill. This corresponds to negating only the first conjunct.

$\sim(\forall x{:} \sim x = c) \sim Lxb \cdot Lcb$

Depending on the situation, any of these three things might be meant. It is necessary to use good sense in deciding which interpretation is most appropriate in particular circumstances.

Numerical Sentences

There are three basic types of numerical claim, and we have several ways to express them. Where n is any positive integer, we can say 'at least n' 'at most n', and 'exactly n'. For each of these, we could just introduce special numerical quantifiers, but it will also be useful to explore the relationship of these numerical quantifiers to the universal and existential quantifiers.

Noting that the existential quantifier already means *at least one*, we could introduce the other numerical quantifiers for 'at least' by simply adding numerals to the existential quantifier.

At Least

At least one dog is brown.	$(\exists x: Dx)Bx$
At least two dogs are brown.	$(\exists 2x: Dx)Bx$
etc.	

Although this is satisfactory from the standpoint of the sentences' syntax and semantics, this way of representing *at least* involves introducing an infinite set of quantifiers for which there are no rules in our derivational system. Because of this, it is worth looking at the way to express *at least* with the quantifiers we already have. For example, we could express 'at least two' in the following way:

At least two dogs are brown.
$$(\exists x: Dx)(\exists y: Dy \cdot y \neq x)(Bx \cdot By)$$

The existential is the only quantifier in this verison, so we already know how to manage such sentences within the system of derivational rules. Unfortunately, this way of doing things produces sentences of rapidly increasing length when applied for larger numbers.

At least three dogs are brown.
$$(\exists x: Dx)(\exists y: Dy \cdot y \neq x)(\exists z: Dz \cdot (z \neq x \cdot z \neq y))((Bx \cdot By) \cdot Bz)$$

At least four dogs are brown.
$$(\exists x: Dx)(\exists y: Dy \cdot y \neq x)(\exists z: Dz \cdot (z \neq x \cdot z \neq y))$$
$$(\exists x_1: Dx_1 \cdot (x_1 \neq x \cdot (x_1 \neq y \cdot x_1 \neq z)))((Bx \cdot By) \cdot (Bz \cdot Bx_1))$$

General Pattern

At least **n** **A** are **B**.
$$(\exists x_1: Ax_1)(\exists x_2: Ax_2 \cdot x_2 \neq x_1)(\exists x_3: Ax_3 \cdot x_3 \neq x_1 \cdot x_3 \neq x_2) \ldots$$
$$(\exists x_n: Ax_n \cdot x_n \neq x_1 \cdot x_n \neq x_2 \cdot \cdots \cdot x_n \neq x_{n-1})(Bx_1 \cdot Bx_2 \cdot Bx_3 \cdot \cdots \cdot Bx_n)$$

(Some parentheses are omitted to make the pattern clearer.)

For the quantifier 'at most', we will use the quantifier symbol '≤' together with the appropriate numeral.

At Most

At most one dog is brown.	$(\leq 1x: Dx)Bx$
At most two dogs are brown.	$(\leq 2x: Dx)Bx$

This concept can also be expressed without the introduction of new quantifiers.

At most one dog is brown.
$(\forall x: Dx \cdot Bx)\ (\forall y: Dy \cdot By)x = y$

At most two dogs are brown.
$(\forall x: Dx \cdot Bx)\ (\forall y: Dy \cdot By)\ (\forall z: Dz \cdot Bz)(x = y \lor (x = z \lor y = z))$

General Pattern

At most n **A** are **B**.
$(\forall x_1: Ax_1 \cdot Bx_1)\ (\forall x_2: Ax_2 \cdot Bx_2) \cdots (\forall x_n: Ax_n \cdot Bx_n)\ (\forall y: Ay \cdot By)$
$(x_1 = x_2 \lor x_1 = x_3 \lor \cdots \lor x_1 = x_n \lor x_1 = y \lor x_2 = x_3 \lor \cdots \lor x_2 = x_n$
$\lor x_2 = y \lor \cdots \lor x_{n-1} = x_n \lor x_{n-1} = y \lor x_n = y)$

(This omits some parentheses.) The length of these sentences also increases rapidly with higher numbers. [An equivalent representation for "At most n **A** are **B**" could be based on the fact that this could be restated as '$\sim$(At least $n + 1$ **A** are **B**)', that is, '$\sim(\exists(n + 1)x: Ax)Bx$'. This can then be expanded according to the pattern given for *at least* $n + 1$.]

For the quantifier 'exactly', there is a variation on the existential quantifier that is often used. We can write an exclamation point after an existential quantifier to indicate that it means 'exactly n' instead of 'at least n'.

Exactly

Exactly one dog is brown. $(\exists!x: Dx)Bx$
Exactly two dogs are brown. $(\exists 2!x: Dx)Bx$

We could also express this concept without the new symbols simply by conjoining what we have already, because 'exactly n' can be expressed 'at least n and at most n'. There is also an equivalent sentence that is somewhat simpler.

Exactly one dog is brown.
$(\exists x: Dx)Bx \cdot (\forall x: Dx \cdot Bx)(\forall y: Dy \cdot By)x = y$. (At least one and at most one.)
Simpler: $(\exists x: Dx \cdot Bx)(\forall y: Dy \cdot By)x = y$

Exactly two dogs are brown.
$(\exists x: Dx)(\exists y: Dy \cdot x \neq y)(Bx \cdot By) \cdot$
$(\forall x: Dx \cdot Bx)(\forall y: Dy \cdot By)(\forall z: Dz \cdot Bz)(x = y \lor (x = z \lor y = z))$.
Simpler: $(\exists x: Dx \cdot Bx)(\exists y: (Dy \cdot By) \cdot x \neq y)(\forall z: Dz \cdot Bz)(x = z \lor y = z)$

General Pattern

Exactly *n* **A** are **B**.

$(\exists x_1: Ax_1 \cdot Bx_1)(\exists x_2: (Ax_2 \cdot Bx_2) \cdot x_2 \neq x_1)) \cdots$

$(\exists x_n: (Ax_n \cdot Bx_n) \cdot x_n \neq x_1 \cdot \cdots \cdot x_n \neq x_{n-1})(\forall y: Ay \cdot By)$

$(x_1 = y \lor x_2 = y \lor \cdots \lor x_n = y)$

EXERCISE 15a

Use the standard quantifiers '$\forall$' and '$\exists$', but no others, in representing the following sentences.

1. Alice respects Betty, but she does not respect anyone else.
2. Alice respects herself, but she does not respect anyone else.
3. Alice respects only herself.
4. Rhode Island is the only state smaller than Delaware.
5. At least two states are smaller than Connecticut.
6. Rhode Island is smaller than every other state.
7. Every author quotes at least one other author.
8. No author quotes every other author.
9. No two people are exactly the same height. (Use $Hxy = x$ is the same height as y)
10. Al quoted at most one other author.
11. Bill quoted only one author other than himself.
12. No author quoted more than two other authors.
13. Every senator other than Adams owns at least two homes.
14. No senator owns more than two homes.
15. Some senators own only one home.
16. There are exactly two senators who own more than two homes.

DEFINITE DESCRIPTIONS

One of the words most used in English is 'the'. Noun phrases made with 'the' such as "the person who ate my sandwich," "the woman who discovered radium," or "the country that occupies an entire continent," are called *definite descriptions*.

In many cases an occurrence of 'the' is merely a way of continuing a reference first made in an indefinite way.

Mary saw a man with blond hair. The man ran away.

In such cases we would indicate sameness of reference by reusing the same variable.

$(\exists x: Mx \cdot Bx)(Smx \cdot Rx)$

A single quantifier phrase governs both of the English sentences. The noun phrase with 'the' has what is called an *anaphoric* occurrence, picking up on a reference made by a previous phrase.

But in other cases the word 'the' is used to make its own reference to some single individual.

The person who ran away from this crime will suffer.

John is the person who shot Mary.

In these cases, the word 'the' is used with some predicative expression to make a noun phrase. The noun phrase refers to an individual who is, at least within the context of the conversation, the only individual to whom the predicative expression applies. This noun phrase is another type of quantifier phrase, made with the quantifier word 'the', and to represent such quantifier phrases we will introduce a new quantifier symbol, '$\imath$'.

$(\imath x\colon Px \cdot Rx)Sx$

$(\imath x\colon Px \cdot Sxm)j = x$

To adapt this quantifier to our system of derivational rules, we must do one of two things. We can either add some new rules governing this quantifier, or we can find a way to express it using the logical symbols already incorporated in the system of derivational rules. Either way is open to us, because a sentence with a definite description is equivalent to a sentence without definite descriptions. So we could eliminate the explicit use of definite descriptions.

The person who ran away will suffer.

$(\imath x\colon Px \cdot Rx)Sx$

$(\exists x\colon (Px \cdot Rx) \cdot (\forall y\colon Py \cdot Ry)y = x)Sx$

John is the person who shot Mary.

$(\imath x\colon Px \cdot Sxm)j = x$

$(\exists x\colon (Px \cdot Sxm) \cdot (\forall y\colon Py \cdot Sym)y = x)j = x$

General Pattern

The A is B.

$(\imath x\colon Ax)Bx$

$(\exists x\colon Ax \cdot (\forall y\colon Ay)y = x)Bx$

In this way we could rewrite our sentences using only the familiar quantifiers. (In the examples that follow we will provide this alternative symbolization along with the symbolization that uses the definite description symbol.) It is also worth noting some other equivalent ways of representing "The A is B."

$(\exists! x\colon Ax)x = x \cdot (\forall x\colon Ax)Bx$

$(\exists x\colon Ax)(\forall y\colon Ay)y = x \cdot (\forall x\colon Ax)Bx$

$(\exists x: Ax)(\forall y: Ay)y = x \cdot (\exists x: Ax)Bx$

$(\exists x: Bx)[Ax \cdot (\forall y: Ay)y = x]$

(Later in this chapter, derivational rules directly involving the '$\imath$' symbol will be considered.)

Like other quantifier phrases, definite descriptions can occur in all positions for noun phrases in a sentence.

John shot the man who loved Betty.

$(\imath x: Mx \cdot Lxb)Sjx$

$(\exists x: (Mx \cdot Lxb) \cdot (\forall y: My \cdot Lyb)y = x)Sjx$

Even when the definite description is not the subject of the sentence, it still is put at the beginning (just as other quantifier phrases are). This allows the quantifier to bind multiple variables after the quantifier phrase. It also allows the quantifier to be used with other quantifiers.

Carol loved the boy who drove her home and wrote to her, but she didn't write to him.

$(\imath x: Bx \cdot (Dxc \cdot Wxc))(Lcx \cdot \sim Wcx)$

$(\exists x: (Bx \cdot (Dxc \cdot Wxc)) \cdot (\forall y: By \cdot (Dyc \cdot Wyc))y = x)(Lcx \cdot \sim Wcx)$

The boy who loved Betty loved someone else too.

$(\imath x: Bx \cdot Lxb)(\exists y: Py \cdot y \neq b)Lxy$

$(\exists x: (Bx \cdot Lxb) \cdot (\forall z: Bz \cdot Lzb)z = x)(\exists y: Py \cdot y \neq b)Lxy$

Betty loved the boy who kissed her, but he loved someone else.

$(\imath x: Bx \cdot Kxb)(Lbx \cdot (\exists y: Py \cdot y \neq b)Lxy)$

$(\exists x: (Bx \cdot Kxb) \cdot (\forall z: Bz \cdot Kzb)z = x)(Lbx \cdot (\exists y: Py \cdot y \neq b)Lxy)$

The phrase 'the only' is an alternative way of expressing definite descriptions:

The only boy Betty kissed loved her.

$(\imath x: Bx \cdot Kbx)Lxb$

$(\exists x: (Bx \cdot Kbx) \cdot (\forall y: By \cdot Kby)y = x)Lxb$

Both this phrase and the single word 'the' can be used with a plural, in which case the sentence should be represented using a universal quantifier, as follows:

The only boys Betty loves are athletes.

The boys Betty loves are athletes.

$(\forall x: Bx \cdot Lbx)Ax$

In some cases the context may make it clear that it is also appropriate to add an existential clause (as with many universals):

$(\forall x: Bx \cdot Lbx)Ax \cdot (\exists x: Bx)Lbx$

Superlatives

When we have a comparative relation with '-er' or with 'more than', we can also express a superlative statement.

Comparative: Al is taller than Bill.   *Tab*
Superlative: Al is the tallest person. $(\forall x: Px \cdot x \neq a)Tax \cdot Pa$

The way that the superlative was just represented in effect says, "Al is taller than every other person." A superlative looks like a definite description, and it could be equivalently written as a definite description.

Al is the tallest person. $(\imath x: Px \cdot (\forall y: Py \cdot y \neq x)Txy)a = x$

(Al is the person who is taller than any other person.)

But the logically equivalent representation '$(\forall x: Px \cdot x \neq a)Tax \cdot Pa$' is somewhat simpler, and it does not use the special symbol '$\imath$'.

More complex superlatives follow the same pattern:

Belinda is the oldest student Carol knows.

$(\forall x: (Sx \cdot Kcx) \cdot x \neq b)Obx \cdot (Sb \cdot Kcb)$

Rather than having a simple property like being a person ('Px') to set the reference class, we have a property expressed by a more complex open sentence, '$Sx \cdot Kcx$'. But the pattern is not altered from the previous superlative example.

Possessives

Although possessives do not use the word 'the' in English, they can be thought of as definite descriptions.

Al's hat is brown. $(\imath x: Hx \cdot Oax)Bx$
(The hat that Al owns is
brown.) $(\exists x: (Hx \cdot Oax) \cdot (\forall y: Hy \cdot Oay)y = x)Bx$

Mary lost her hat. $(\imath x: Hx \cdot Omx)Lmx$
                                        $(\exists x: (Hx \cdot Omx) \cdot (\forall y: Hy \cdot Omy)y = x)Lmx$

Mary's sister is a dentist. $(\imath x: Sxm)Dx$
                                        $(\exists x: Sxm \cdot (\forall y: Sym)y = x)Dx$

Alice's uncle painted his car. $(\imath x: Uxa)(\imath y: Cy \cdot Oxy)Pxy$
$(\exists x: Uxa \cdot (\forall z: Uza)z = x)(\exists y: (Cy \cdot Oxy) \cdot (\forall x_1: Cx_1 \cdot Oxx_1)x_1 = y)Pxy$

But when there is a plurality of individuals possessed, we must use a universal quantifier rather than a definite description.

Bill loves his sisters. $(\forall x: Sxb)Lbx$

Bill's sisters love his car. $(\forall x: Sxb)(\imath y: Cy \cdot Oby)Lxy$

$(\forall x: Sxb)(\exists y: (Cy \cdot Oby) \cdot (\forall z: Cz \cdot Obz)z = y)Lxy$

EXERCISE 15b

Symbolize each sentence. If you use any quantifier other than the basic universal ('$\forall$') and existential ('$\exists$'), write an additional symbolization that does not use any quantifier other than the two basic ones.

1. The woman Al loves is a dentist.
2. The dentist Al loves is a woman, but Al loves more than one woman.
3. Al doesn't love his dentist. ($Dxy = x$ is y's dentist)
4. Only the woman who loves Bill eats with him.
5. If Carol is the woman who eats with Bill, then she loves him.
6. The tallest dentist is a woman. ($Dx = x$ is a dentist)
7. Carol loves the tallest dentist she knows.
8. Bill is the only dentist Carol knows.
9. Al and Ellen are the only dentists who eat with Bill.
10. Bill is the only dentist taller than Carol.
11. The person who loves the tallest dentist is an actor.
12. The person who loves the tallest dentist also loves someone else.
13. Bill's father is the dentist Carol loves.
14. Bill's father is not the tallest dentist.
15. Bill's father eats with everyone except Bill.
16. Dentists are the only women Bill loves.

FUNCTION SYMBOLS

Many mathematical expressions could be seen as employing definite descriptions and the concept of identity.

$2 + 3 = 5$

The sum of 2 and 3 is 5.

By making some very simple additions to our language, we can express this in a direct way using the symbol for definite descriptions. Add numerals to our stock of individual constants, and use commas where necessary to separate them. Then, using the three-place relation $Sxyz$ (x and y sum up to z) together with the definite description symbol, we can write

$$(\imath x\colon S2,3,x)x = 5$$

(This indicates that there is just one sum of 2 and 3, unlike the even simpler expression, '$S2,3,5$', which does not carry any logical guarantee of uniqueness.) Similarly, using the dyadic predicate 'Axy', 'x has an absolute value of y':

$$|3| = 3$$
The absolute value of 3 is 3.
$$(\imath x\colon A3,x)x = 3$$

(The expression $A3,3$ would carry no logical guarantee of uniqueness.)

But in mathematics, the definite description symbol is not usually explicitly used. Instead, we use *function symbols*, a device that makes an even stronger statement than is made by sentences with definite descriptions.

The mathematical symbols for addition and absolute value ('$+$' and '$|\ |$') are among the mathematicians' function symbols. Each fits together with an appropriate number of individual terms (two for addition and one for absolute value) to make a new individual term ('$2+3$' and '$|3|$'). To incorporate function symbols into our formal system, we will reserve the lowercase letters 'f', 'g', and 'h', with subscripts for additional function symbols 'f_1', 'f_2', etc., when needed. A function symbol followed by an appropriate number of individual terms in parentheses will create a new individual term. Thus if 'f' were to stand for the absolute value function and 'g' for the addition function, '$f(3)$' would be a singular term (referring to the absolute value of 3, i.e., 3) and '$g(2,3)$' would be a singular term (referring to 5).

Function symbols are used in creating a new kind of individual term. So when they are added, we need to restate our principles for creating sentences, acknowledging these new terms.

0. 0. Individual variables and individual constants are individual terms.

1. If f is an n-place function symbol and $t_1 \cdots t_n$ are n individual terms, then $f(t_1 \cdots t_n)$ is an individual term.

2. If B is an n-place predicate, and $t_1 \cdots t_n$ are n individual terms, then $Bt_1 \cdots t_n$ is a sentence.

3. Each sentence letter is a sentence.

1. 0. If p is a sentence, then $\sim p$ is also a sentence.

1. If p and q are both sentences, these are sentences:

$p \cdot q$

$p \vee q$

$p \supset q$

$p \equiv q$

$(\forall \text{\textcircled{v}}: p)q$

$(\exists \text{\textcircled{v}}: p)q$

2. Nothing else is a sentence.

This allows us to construct sentences like the following (inserting commas where useful to make for easier reading):

$Df(a)$	Al's father is a doctor.
$g(2,3) = 5$	$2 + 3 = 5$
$Lg(2,3),6$	$2 + 3 < 6$
$Lg(2,2),g(2,3)$	$2 + 2 < 2 + 3$
$(\forall x: Nx \cdot Ox)Og(x,2)$	For any odd number x, $x + 2$ is odd.

Function symbols apply to singular terms to create singular terms, so we can also have expressions like the following:

$f(f(a))$	Al's father's father
$f(g(a))$	Al's mother's father

Or, using 'f' for *absolute value* and 'g' for *addition* and 'h' for *the negative of* [i.e., $h(3)$ is -3, and $h(h(3))$ is 3], and using 'Ox' for 'x is odd', we can write sentences like these:

$f(g(3,h(4))) = 1$	$\|3 + (-4)\| = 1$
$g(f(h(3)), h(h(4))) = 7$	$\|-3\| + -(-4) = 7$
$Og(3, h(6))$	$3 + -6$ is odd.
$f(g(3, h(6))) = 3$	$\|3 + -6\| = 3$
$(\forall x: Nx \cdot Of(g(x, 2)))Ox$	For any number x such that $\|x + 2\|$ is odd, x is odd.

Each n-place function symbol can be associated with an $(n + 1) -$ place relation. For example, if 'g' stands for the function that picks out the sum of two numbers [so $g(2,3) = 5$], it corresponds to the summation relation $(S2,3,5)$. But a relation must have a special feature if it is to be associated with a function symbol. For an n-place function symbol to be appropriate, the corresponding relation must have this feature: No matter what individuals are picked for the first n places, those choices must guarantee that there is exactly one correct choice for place $n + 1$. Compare the relations "a has b as a (biological) father" (Fab) and "a has b as a sister" (Sab). If we are talking only about people, then each individual has exactly one father, so we could introduce a function symbol 'f' to create a new singular term '$f(a)$' ('a's father'). But we could not introduce a function symbol for 'a's sister', because an individual can have more than one sister or none at all. If a has two sisters, b and c, there is no definite reference for 'a's sister', so no function symbol may be used for 'sister of'.

If we introduce a function symbol for 'father of', then we have three ways to write "*a* has *b* for a father":

Fab

($\imath x$: *Fax*)*x* = *b*

f(*a*) = *b*

But these are importantly different. Nothing in the first version guarantees that *b* is *a*'s only father. (We know independently that no individual has more than one father, but nothing in the logical representation shows this fact.) The second version uses the definite description to make the guarantee that *b* is the unique father of *a*. The third version, using a function symbol, says that *b* is the unique father of *a*, but it goes even farther, because the use of the function symbol actually requires that *every* individual has exactly one father.

   Keeping the difference between function symbols and definite descriptions in mind, we can say that there are two slightly different ways to represent many sentences.

Al's father is a doctor.	($\imath x$: *Fax*)*Dx*	*D*(*f*(*a*))
2 + 3 is odd.	($\imath x$: *S2, 3, x*)*Ox*	*O*(*g*(2, 3))
If 3 is odd, then 2 + 3 is odd.	*O3* ⊃ ($\imath x$: *S2, 3, x*)*Ox*	*O3* ⊃ *O*(*g*(2, 3))
Everyone likes Al's father.	(∀*x*: *Px*)($\imath y$: *Fay*)*Lxy*	(∀*x*: *Px*)*Lxf*(*a*)

EXERCISE 15c

Use function symbols in representing the following claims. For 1–5, assume that we are talking only about people. Then we can use the following function symbols:

f(*x*) = *x*'s father   *g*(*x*) = *x*'s mother

   1. Anna's father is a librarian.
   2. Bill's mother knows Anna's father.
   3. Anna's father's mother works with Bill's mother.
   4. Carol's father is Bill's mother's father.
   5. Carol's mother loves Anna's mother's father, but he loves only Carol.

For 6–10, assume that we are talking only about numbers. Then we can use the following function symbols:

f(*x*) = |*x*| *g*(*x, y*) = *x* + *y*   *h*(*x*) = − *x*   *g*₁ (*x, y*) = *x* × *y*

   6. For any *x*, *x* + − *x* = 0.
   7. For any *x*, |*x* + 2*x*| = 3 × |*x*|.

8. For any x, $x + |x| = 0$ or $2x$.

9. For any x and y, $2(x+y) + 3x = 5x + 2y$.

10. For any x, y and z, $z \times 3(x+y) = 3zx + 3zy$.

DERIVATIONAL RULES FOR IDENTITY

There are several special logical features of identity. For example, all of the following are valid:

Transitivity	*Symmetry*	*Leibniz's Inference*
$a = b$	$a = b$	Ac
$b = c$	$\therefore \quad b = a$	$c = b$
$\therefore \quad a = c$		$\therefore \quad Ab$

In addition, the following are logical truths:

Self-identity (Reflexivity)

$(\forall x) x = x$

$\sim(\exists x)\sim x = x$

(Note that these logical truths are fully general, so it is particularly appropriate to use the unrelativized notation.)

In developing the system of derivational rules so that these inferences are included, we can take just two of these as basic: from Leibniz's inference and self-identity the others are derivable. So we can introduce these two derivational rules:

Identity Introduction (= I)
(Self-identity; Reflexivity)

$\therefore \quad \textcircled{c} = \textcircled{c}$

Identity Exploitation (= E)
(Leibniz's Inference)

$A\textcircled{c}_1$

$\textcircled{c}_1 = \textcircled{c}_2$

$\therefore \quad A\textcircled{c}_2$

The first of these is a rule of "inference" that does not require any premises. We can simply write something of the form '$\textcircled{c} = \textcircled{c}$' whenever we wish to do so. The second rule of inference is based on Leibniz's Law:

$(\forall x)(\forall y)((x = y \cdot Ax) \supset Ay)$

Letting 'Ax' stand for any open sentence with 'x' free, this says, in effect, that if $x = y$, then whatever is true of x is also true of y.

With these two rules, the other key inferences involving identity are also warranted.

Transitivity

1. $a = b$ Premise
2. $b = c$ Premise
3. $a = c$ $1,2 = E$

Here the conclusion was derived by substituting 'c' for the 'b' in the first premise. The identity in the second premise makes this possible ($= E$). We can derive the conclusion from the premise in the symmetry inference in the following way:

Symmetry

1. $a = b$ Premise
2. $a = a$ $= I$
3. $b = a$ $1,2 = E$

The identity in the first premise authorizes the substitution of 'b' for 'a' wherever it occurs. So we can substitute 'b' for the first occurrence of 'a' in '$a = a$'. The self-identity principles are of course just generalizations of the $= I$ rule. Thus we can prove them very simply be employing the rule within a universal subderivation:

1. $a = a$ $= I$
2. $(\forall x)x = x$ 1   UQI (unrelativized)
3. $\sim(\exists x)\sim x = x$ 2   QN

The two self-identity principles are established in lines 2 and 3. Similarly, we could establish Leibniz's Law $[(\forall x)(\forall y)((x = y \cdot Ax) \supset Ay)]$ in the following way:

$a = b \cdot Aa$ AP
$a = b$ Simp
Aa Simp
Ab $2,3 = E$
$(a = b \cdot Aa) \supset Ab$ CP
$(\forall y)((a = y) \supset Ay)$ UQI (unrelativized)
$(\forall x)(\forall y)((x = y \cdot Ax) \supset Ay)$ UQI (unrelativized)

There is also a principle of nonidentity equivalent to Leibniz's Law:

$(\forall x)(\forall y)((Ax \cdot \sim Ay) \supset x \neq y)$

It is easily derived using our rule $= E$.

$Ac \cdot \sim Ad$	AP
Ac	Simp
$\sim Ad$	Simp
$c = d$	AP
Ad	= E
$\sim Ad$	= E
$Ad \cdot \sim Ad$	Conj
$\sim c = d$	IP
$(Ac \cdot \sim Ad) \supset \sim c = d$	CP
$(\forall y)((Ac \cdot \sim Ay) \supset \sim c = y)$	UQI
$(\forall x)(\forall y)((Ax \cdot \sim Ay) \supset \sim x = y)$	UQI

EXERCISE 15d

Derive the conclusion.

1. $(\forall x: Ax)(\forall y: x \neq y)Rxy$
$Ab \cdot \sim Ac$
$\therefore \quad Rbc$

2. $(\exists x: Fx \cdot (\forall y: Fy)y = x)Gx$
$Fa \cdot (\forall x: Gx)Rax$
$\therefore \quad (\forall x: Fx)Rxx$

3. $(\exists x: Ax)(\exists y: Ay)y \neq x$
$(\exists x: Ax \cdot Bx)(\forall y: Ay \cdot By)y = x$
$\therefore \quad (\exists x: Ax)\sim Bx$

4. $(\exists x: Cx \cdot (\forall y: Cy)y = x)Dx$
$Ca \cdot Aa$
$Cb \cdot Bb$
$(\forall x: Dx)Rxx$
$\therefore \quad Rab$

5. $(\exists x: Ax)(\exists y: Ay \cdot y \neq x)Rxy$
$(\forall x: Ax)(\forall y: Rxy \lor Ryx)Bx$
$(\forall x: Bx)(\forall y: \sim Cy \cdot Syx)y = x$
$(\forall x: Ax)(\forall y: Ay)Sxy$
$\therefore \quad (\exists x: Cx)(\exists y: Cy)y \neq x$

6. $(\exists x: Bx)[(\forall y: By)Rxy \cdot (\forall z: (\exists y: By)Rzy)z = x]$
$(\forall x: Bx)(\forall y: By)(Rxy \equiv Cy)$
$(\forall x: Bx)(\forall y: By)(Rxy \equiv Ryx)$
$\therefore \quad (\exists x: Cx)(\forall y: Cy \cdot By)y = x$

7. $(\exists x: Ax)(\exists y: Ay \cdot y \neq x)(\forall z: Az)(z = x \lor z = y)$
$(Ab \cdot Ac) \cdot b \neq c$
$Bb \cdot Bc$
$\therefore \quad (\forall x: Ax)Bx$

DERIVATIONAL RULES FOR FUNCTION SYMBOLS

When we freely allow the use of function symbols in sentences, there is no need to add any new inference rules to govern them. Use of a function symbol carries with it much that is already provable. Suppose that we have the following premise:

$Af(b)$

(for example, "Bill's father is an actor"). Then the following claims follow:

$(\forall x)(\exists y)y = f(x)$ (Existence. "Everything has a father.")
$(\forall x)(\forall y:\ y = f(x))(\forall z:\ z = f(x))z = y$ (Uniqueness. "Each thing has at most
                                                   one father.")

Each is easily proved with rules we already have.

Existence

$f(a) = f(a)$	$= I$
$(\exists y)y = f(a)$	EQI
$(\forall x)(\exists y)y = f(x)$	UQI

Uniqueness

$f(b) = a$	
$f(b) = c$	
$a = c$	$= E$
$(\forall z:\ f(b) = z)a = z$	UQI
$(\forall y:\ f(b) = y)(\forall z:\ f(b) = z)y = z$	UQI
$(\forall x)(\forall y:\ f(x) = y)(\forall z:\ f(x) = z)y = z$	UQI

So the rules developed earlier will carry through, enabling us to prove the existence and uniqueness claims associated with the use of function symbols.

EXERCISE 15e

Derive each conclusion to show validity of each of the following arguments.

1. $Af(b)$
    $(\forall x:\ Ax)Af(x)$
    $\therefore\ \ Af(f(b))$

2. $(\forall x:\ Ax)(\exists y:\ Ay)x = f(y)$
    $(\forall x:\ Ax)Bf(x)$
    $\therefore\ \ (\forall x:\ Ax)Bx$

3. $(\forall x:\ Ax)x = f(g(x))$
    $\therefore\ \ (\forall x:\ (\exists y:\ Ay)x = g(y))(\exists z:\ Az)z = f(x)$

4. $(\forall x:\ Ax)Rxf(x)$
    $(\forall x:\ Ax)Af(x)$
    $\therefore\ \ (\forall x:\ Ax)Rf(x)f(f(x))$

5. $(\forall x\colon Ax)Bf(x)$
 $(\forall x\colon Bx)Ax$
 $\therefore$ $(\forall x\colon Ax)Af(f(x))$

6. $(\forall x\colon Ax)Bf(x)$
 $(\exists y\colon Ay)(\exists x\colon x = f(y))Ax$
 $\therefore$ $(\forall x\colon Ax)Cx \supset (\exists y\colon By)Cy$

7. $(\forall x\colon Ax)Bx$
 $(\forall x\colon x = f(x))\sim Cx$
 $(\exists x\colon Ax)x = f(x)$
 $\therefore$ $(\exists x\colon Bf(x))\sim Cf(x)$

DERIVATIONAL RULES FOR DEFINITE DESCRIPTIONS

Sentences with definite descriptions can be represented with or without the special symbol '$\imath$'.

The bassoonist is a mathematician.

$(\imath x\colon Bx)Mx$
$(\exists x\colon Bx \cdot (\forall y\colon By)y = x)Mx$

To use the first representation in derivations, we must supplement our system of derivational rules. The most evident way to do this is to introduce rules very much like those for the existential quantifier, but with an extra step for the uniqueness clause ['$(\forall y\colon By)y = x$' in the example]. Thus we would have the following rules for exploiting and for introducing the '$\imath$' symbol in sentences:

$\imath$E

$(\imath \textcircled{v}_1\colon A\textcircled{v}_2)B\textcircled{v}_1$
$\therefore$ $A\textcircled{c}$
$\therefore$ $(\forall \textcircled{v}_2\colon A\textcircled{v}_2)\textcircled{v}_2 = \textcircled{c}$
$\therefore$ $B\textcircled{c}$

where $\textcircled{c}$ is a *new* individual constant.

$\imath$I

$A\textcircled{c}$
$(\forall \textcircled{v}_1\colon A\textcircled{v}_1)\textcircled{v}_1 = \textcircled{c}$
$B\textcircled{c}$
$\therefore$ $(\imath \textcircled{v}_2\colon A\textcircled{v}_2)B\textcircled{v}_2$

As with EQE, from a sentence of the form $(\imath \textcircled{v}\colon A\textcircled{v})B\textcircled{v}$ we can derive more than one thing, introducing a new individual constant to stand in for the individual asserted to exist. As with EQE, we derive $A\textcircled{c}$ and $B\textcircled{c}$, but now we also know that there is only one individual x such that Ax, so we can also derive that $((\forall \textcircled{v}_2\colon A\textcircled{v}_2)\textcircled{v}_2 = \textcircled{c})$. The rule for introducing a definite description is analogous to that for EQI, except that a uniqueness clause must be present before the use of the definite description is justified.

EXERCISE 15f

Symbolize each, then derive the conclusion.

1. Jupiter is the largest planet. Earth is a planet other than Jupiter. So some planet is larger than Earth.

2. The doctor who treated Ellen treats only musicians. Therefore, Ellen must be a musician.

3. The oldest man in town loves Ellen, and everyone who loves Ellen is a musician. Thus the oldest man in town must be a musician.

4. Albert is the only musician in town. Smith is the only doctor. Some doctor in town is also a musician. So Albert is Smith.

5. The author of the shortest book is a mathematician. So some mathematician wrote a book that is shorter than any other book.

6. There are two musicians in town, but only one of them is a woodwind player. Only woodwind players use reeds. Thus there is at least one musician in town who does not use reeds.

7. Only Bill plays bassoon. Only bassoonists will perform. Thus only Bill will perform.

8. Any dog can bark louder than any smaller one. So the largest dog can bark louder than any other dog.

16

QUANTIFIER SEMANTICS

There has been something missing in our study of quantificational logic. When we studied sentential logic, truth-tables defining the logical symbols' meanings stood as a final judge on the question of how a compound sentence's truth-value depends on the truth-values of its simpler parts.

Al is friendly · Al is very careful

The truth-value of such a sentence depends on the truth-value of its simpler parts in the way defined by the table for the connective symbol.

p	q	$p \cdot q$	F	C	$F \cdot C$
T	T	T	T	T	T
T	F	F	T	F	F
F	T	F	F	T	F
F	F	F	F	F	F

Because we had defining tables for the symbols of sentence logic, we knew how to compute, systematically, the truth-values of complex compound sentences from the truth-values of the simple constituents. Truth-tables are the basis of a systematic truth-functional semantics.

But we have had no similar systematic account of the meaning of the quantifier symbols. Instead of employing systematic semantics, we have developed an understanding of the elements of quantificational logic by learning how to "translate" sentences with quantifier symbols into ordinary English (and vice versa).

Here we will develop a more systematic semantics for quantificational logic. But before we take on this project it will be useful to do two things. First we will consider quantifier words other than those represented by '∀' and '∃'. (We can then develop a more general semantics encompassing a wider range of quantificational concepts.) We will also want to look at another way of presenting the semantics of sentential logic, because truth-tables cannot serve as a model for the semantics of quantificational logic.

OTHER QUANTIFIERS

We have studied the quantifiers '∃' and '∀'. Those can be used to represent a wide range of English sentences, but there are also many other quantifier words.

Most men have hair.
Many men wear beards.
Few men shave their heads.
Fewer than seven men wear hairpieces.
No men have curls.

The noun phrases 'Most men', 'Many men', 'Few men', 'Fewer than seven men', and 'no men' are also quantifier phrases. Except for 'no men', these cannot be completely represented by '∃' or by '∀' or by any combination of those two quantifiers.

Note why 'no men' is an exception. We can represent "No men have beards" by

$(\forall x: Mx) \sim Bx$

$\sim(\exists x: Mx)Bx$

Although these are semantically successful, they do involve a change in structure from the simple *noun phrase* and *verb phrase* structure of the original English sentence. In the case of the quantifiers 'most', 'many', and 'few', there is no way to represent them adequately. The quantifier 'fewer than seven' could only be represented (in a fairly complicated way) if we introduced identity as a logical predicate. (This was done in Chapter 15.)

Although the quantifiers 'most', 'many', and 'few' are not as important as '∀' and '∃' for deductive logic, there are some clear deductive relations. For example, 'few men' seems equivalent to 'not many men' and 'many' seems, correspondingly, to be the negation of 'few'. 'All men are bald' entails 'most men are bald', and 'a few men are bald' seems to entail that 'some men are bald'. So it would be nice if we could easily incorporate these quantifiers. [There are several recent studies of these relationships and of the general semantics for quantifiers. For example, Philip Peterson's "On the logic of *few*, *many*, and *most*," *Notre Dame Journal of Formal Logic* 20 (1979) 155–179; John Barwise and Robin Cooper's "Generalized quantifiers and natural language," *Linguistics and Philosophy* 4 (1980) 159–219; and Mark Brown's "Generalized quantifiers and the square of opposition," *Notre Dame Journal of Formal Logic* 25 (1984) 303–322. Our semantics will follow Brown's.]

Syntactically, it is a simple matter to add quantifiers to represent these concepts. We merely need new symbols in our system.

μ	most
λ	many
σ	few
<7	fewer than seven
ν	no (none of)

(μx: Mx)Hx	Most men have hair.
(λx: Mx)Bx	Many men wear beards.
(σx: Mx)Sx	Few men shave their heads.
($<7x$: Mx)Tx	Fewer than seven men wear hairpieces.
(νx: Mx)Cx	No men have curls.

In representing 'All A are B' and 'Some A are B', we had two options. We could use relativized quantifiers

$$(\forall x: Ax)Bx$$
$$(\exists x: Ax)Bx$$

or use unrelativized quantification

$$(\forall x)(Ax \supset Bx)$$
$$(\exists x)(Ax \cdot Bx)$$

But with many other English quantifiers, there is no way to represent them using unrelativized quantification. Consider "Most men have hair," (μx: Mx)Hx. There is no way to paraphrase that as an unrelativized quantifier governing a compound sentence.

$$(\mu x)(Mx \ ? \ Hx)$$

There is no connective that will work in place of the question mark. With "Some men have hair," we can paraphrase that as "Some things are men *and* have hair," $(\exists x)(Mx \cdot Hx)$. But there is no way to paraphrase a sentence about most men into a sentence about most things. No connective will give the correct result.

Most things are men *and* have hair.
Most things are men *or* have hair.
Most things are such that if they are men, then they have hair.

The first two of these are clearly inadequate. The last, employing a conditional, may sound more promising. But if that conditional is really truth-functional (as it must be in unrelativized universals), it will not give the right result. It will be true just because most things are not men. The compound predicate '*Mx* ⊃ *Hx*' is true of most things just because '∼*Mx*' and thus '∼*Mx* ∨ *Hx*' (which is equivalent to '*Mx* ⊃ *Hx*') are true of most things. The sentence "Most things are such that if they are men then they fly" would also be true

$$(\mu x)(Mx \supset Fx)$$
$$(\mu x)(\sim Mx \vee Fx)$$

because most things are not men. We will develop a semantics that encompasses all of these quantifier words.

SYSTEMATIC SEMANTICS

In Chapter 3 we could summarize the systematic semantics of truth-functional logic with truth-tables.

p	∼*p*
T	F
F	T

p	*q*	*p · q*	*p ∨ q*	*p ⊃ q*	*p ≡ q*
T	T	T	T	T	T
T	F	F	T	F	F
F	T	F	T	T	F
F	F	F	F	T	T

This told us how the truth-value of each compound sentence depended on the truth-value of its simpler parts.

With predicate logic we have gone into the internal structure of sentences. We must say how the truth-value of complex sentences depends on the interpretation of the names, quantifier phrases, and predicates within the sentence as well as the truth-values of simpler sentences. This is most easily done if we introduce the concept of a *model* for a predicate language.

With truth-functional logic, each row of a truth-table corresponds to a *model* for the sentences being considered. Each row has one assignment of truth-values to the basic constituents, and that assignment corresponds to one way that things might have been. Consider this sentence:

Al is tall but Bill isn't
$$A \cdot \sim B$$

One way that things might be is this: *A* could be *true* and *B* could be *true*.

A	*B*	∼*B*	*A · ∼B*
T	T	F	F

In such a case, the compound sentence being considered will be false. We say that given this *model* for the truth-functional language built on basic sentences *A* and *B*, the sentence '*A* · ~ *B*' is false. The defining truth-tables for the conectives give the information that applies to all models. In English, we can say: Given any model *M*,

0. *M* must assign one truth-value to each basic sentence letter.

1. *M* assigns true to a sentence of the form '~*p*' if and only if *M* assigns false to *p*.

2. If *p* and *q* are sentences, then

  (a) *M* assigns true to '*p* · *q*' if and only if *M* assigns true to *p* and *M* assigns true to *q*.

  (b) *M* assigns true to '*p* ∨ *q*' if and only if *M* assigns true to at least one of the sentences (either to *p* or to *q*).

  (c) *M* assigns true to '*p* ⊃ *q*' if and only if *M* assigns false to *p* or *M* assigns true to *q*.

  (d) *M* assigns true to '*p* ≡ *q*' if and only if *M* assigns the same truth-value to the sentences *p* and *q*.

3. *M* assigns false to a sentence if and only if it does not assign true.

For truth-functional logic, this way of presenting the information has no advantage over truth-tables. But for predicate logic nothing like truth-tables will work in a general way to indicate how the truth-value of complex sentences depends on the interpretation of the basic elements of the sentence. We must instead give the conditions in English, as we just did for truth-functional logic.

So we need to consider the things that '*Px*' and '*Mx*' are true of in explaining how the truth-value of '(∀*x*: *Px*)*Mx*' depends on the interpretation of its parts. We will use a new term, *extension*, in describing the semantic contribution of predicates. The *extension* of a predicate is the set of things it is true *of*. For example, we have usually interpreted '*Px*' as standing for '*x* is a person.' This means that we took its *extension* to be the set of all people. (Appendix A lists the set-theoretic concepts that will be needed in developing the semantics for predicate logic.)

Combining the idea of the *extension* of a predicate with the idea of a *model* for a predicate language, we would say that a monadic predicate '*P*' has an extension in a model *M*. We have used '*P*' to stand for 'is a person', and we have most often considered the actual world (the way things actually are) as our model. In that model, the extension of '*P*' is the set of all people. But logical relations are independent of this, and we could restrict our model to things in New York State, for example, and the extension of '*P*' could be the set of people in New York State. Or we could consider models that interpret '*P*' as the set of cities in Europe, the set of all spoons in Connecticut, or any other set of things that exist in the model. (The logical connectives, though, should be the same no matter what the model is.) The truth-value of '(∀*x*: *Px*)*Mx*' in a model depends on that model's interpretation of '*Px*' and '*Mx*'. These monadic predicates do not have truth-values in the model. A predicate is not true or false in itself; it is true *of* some things and false *of* other things. For example, '*x* is a person' is true of me and you, but not true of San Francisco or Lassie.

If we let '*P*' stand for the set of all things that '*Px*' is true of (the *extension* of '*P*') and we let '*M*' stand for the set of all things that '*Mx*' is true of (the *extension* of '*M*'), we can say this

'($\forall x$: *Px*)*Mx*' is true if and only if $P \cap M = P$.

$P \cap M$ is the *intersection* of P and M, that is, the set containing each thing that belongs to P and also belongs to M. (If '*Px*' means '*x* is a person' and '*Mx*' means '*x* is mortal', then $P \cap M$ is the set of people who are mortal.) The sentence that says that all people are mortal (($\forall x$: *Px*)*Mx*) can be seen as saying that the set containing all people that are mortal ($P \cap M$) is the same as the set containing all people. In fact, we could say this more generally:

If Aⓥ and Bⓥ are sentences in which ⓥ is the only free variable, then a sentence of the form '($\forall$ⓥ: Aⓥ)Bⓥ' is true in model M if and only if $A_M \cap B_M = A_M$ (where 'A_M' refers to the extension of Aⓥ in the model M and 'B_M' refers to the extension of Bⓥ in M).

This gives us one account of universally quantified sentences. But we can do better, we can give an account that applies to quantified sentences in general and that also give us a semantical interpretation for the quantifier phrase '($\forall x$: *Px*)', indicating its role in the sentence.

Consider a quantifier word such as 'most'.

Most lemons are yellow.
(μx: *Lx*)*Yx*

We have viewed quantified sentences as being composed of a predicative expression, '*Yx*' in this case, with a quantifier phrase, '(μx: *Lx*)', prefixed to it. The quantifier phrase itself is composed of a quantifier ('μ') and a predicative expression ('*Lx*') linked by a variable (and punctuation).

Suppose that we let '$\mu(L)$' stand for a set containing sets as members. In particular, '$\mu(L)$' would be the set containing every set S of which this is true: S contains most of the individuals of which '*Lx*' is true. So suppose that in a given model M there are only five lemons, a, b, c, d, and e, so that $L_M = \{a, b, c, d, e\}$. The set '$\mu(L_M)$' is the following set:

$$\mu(L_M) = \begin{cases} \{a, b, c\} & \{a, d, e\} & \{a, b, c, d\} \\ \{a, b, d\} & \{b, c, d\} & \{a, b, c, e\} \\ \{a, b, e\} & \{b, c, e\} & \{a, b, d, e\} \\ \{a, c, d\} & \{b, d, e\} & \{a, c, d, e\} \\ \{a, c, e\} & \{c, d, e\} & \{b, c, d, e\} \\ & & \{a, b, c, d, e\} \end{cases}$$

This set has 16 sets in it. Each of those sets qualifies as 'Most lemons' because each has most of the lemons (three or more) in it. Then the sentence 'Most lemons are yellow' can be seen to say that the set of lemons that are yellow ($L_M \cap Y_M$) is one of the sets that qualifies as 'Most lemons'. Suppose that in some particular model, a, b, d, and e are yellow. Since the set $\{a, b, d, e\}$ qualifies as most lemons, it is a member of $\mu(L_M)$. So '$(\mu x: Lx)Yx$' is true in this model.

'$(\mu x: Lx)Yx$' is true in a model M if and only if $L_M \cap Y_M \in \mu(L_M)$.

For sentences in general involving 'μ':

($\mu ⓥ: A ⓥ)B \; ⓥ$ is true in M if and only if $A_M \cap B_M \in \mu(A_M)$.

An account of this general form will work for every quantifier word, not just 'μ' ('most'). The set containing every set that qualifies as *all* of the lemons is this:

$$\forall(L_M) = \{\{a, b, c, d, e\}\} = \{L_M\}$$

It is a set with only one member, the set containing every lemon.

($\forall ⓥ: A ⓥ)B ⓥ$ is true in M if and only if $A_M \cap B_M \in \forall(A_M)$.

The sentence 'All lemons are yellow' is false in the example model, because $L_M \cap Y_M = \{a, b, d, e\}$ in that model, so $L_M \cap Y_M$ is not a member of the set $\forall(L_M)$ (i.e., it is not a member of the set $\{\{a, b, c, d, e\}\}$). This corresponds to what we said earlier about the universal sentence, because $A_M \cap B_M \in \forall(A_M)$ if and only if $A_M \cap B_M = A_M$ [since $\forall (A_M) = \{A_M\}$].

Note how this works for '$\exists$'. The set $\exists(A)$ will be the set which has as members every nonempty subset of A. Thus in our example:

$$\exists(L_M) = \left\{ \begin{array}{lll} \{a\} & \{b, c\} & \{b, c, d\} \\ \{b\} & \{c, d\} & \{b, c, e\} \\ \{c\} & \{c, e\} & \{b, d, e\} \\ \{d\} & \{d, e\} & \{c, d, e\} \\ \{e\} & \{a, b, c\} & \{a, b, c, d\} \\ \{a, b\} & \{a, b, d\} & \{a, b, c, e\} \\ \{a, c\} & \{a, b, e\} & \{a, b, d, e\} \\ \{a, d\} & \{a, c, d\} & \{a, c, d, e\} \\ \{a, e\} & \{a, c, e\} & \{b, c, d, e\} \\ \{b, c\} & \{a, d, e\} & \{a, b, c, d, e\} \\ \{b, d\} & & \end{array} \right\}$$

And the sentence 'Some lemons are yellow' is true.

'$(\exists x: Lx)Yx$' is true in M if and only if $L_M \cap Y_M \in \exists(L_M)$.

$L_M \cap Y_M = \{a, b, d, e\}$, and $\{a, b, d, e\}$ is a member of $\exists(L_M)$, so the quantified sentence is true.

We can state this in a general way for all quantifiers:

If $A\textcircled{v}$ and $B\textcircled{v}$ are sentences in which $\textcircled{v}$ is the only free variable, and if Q is a quantifier, then

'$(Q\textcircled{v}: A\textcircled{v})B\textcircled{v}$' is true if and only if $A_M \cap B_M \in Q(A_M)$.

To determine a truth-value for particular sentences, we must know what each quantifier symbol means, which is to say that we must know how to determine what set $Q(A_M)$ is. Here are some examples specifying the meanings of quantifiers.

$\forall(A_M) = \{A_M\}$

$\exists(A_M) = \rho(A_M) - \{\varnothing\}$ (i.e., the set of every set that is a subset of A_M, excluding only the empty set)}

$\mu(A_M) = \{S: S \text{ is most of the } A_M\text{'s}\}$

$\lambda(A_M) = \{S: S \text{ is many of the } A_M\text{'s}\}$

$\sigma\{A_M\} = \{S: S \text{ is few of the } A_M\text{'s}\}\}$

$<7 (A_M) = \{S: S \subseteq A_M \text{ and } S \text{ has fewer than seven members}\}$

$\nu(A_M) = \{\varnothing\}$

These quantifier symbols correspond to 'every', 'at least one', 'most', 'many', 'few', 'fewer than seven', and 'no'.

SYSTEMATIC SEMANTICS FOR PREDICATE LOGIC

Now we can give the systematic semantics for predicate logic. (The necessary set-theoretic concepts are listed in Appendix A.) Each model M is associated with a universe of objects, U_M, and M assigns truth-values to sentences based on its assignments of objects and sets of objects to individual terms and predicates.

We need to use a special idea here (in addition to many concepts and notations standard to set theory). If v is some variable and u is some member of U_M, M_{vu} will be the model that is just like M except that M_{vu} will assign the object u to v (i.e., $v_{M_{vu}} = u$ and M_{vu} is otherwise like M; if $v_M = u$, then $M_{vu} = M$). This use of alternative models allows us to consider all of the possible ways of assigning objects to a variable so as to make a sentence like 'Fx' or '$Fx \cdot \sim Gx$' true. The set of all such assignments is the *extension* of the predicate or open sentence.

0. For each individual term α (a constant or a variable), $\alpha_M \in U_M$.
For each monadic predicate P, $P_M \subseteq U_M$.
For each n-adic predicate P, $P_M \subseteq (U_M)^n$.

For each sentence letter p, M assigns T to p or M assigns F to p.

If P is a monadic predicate and α is some individual term, then M assigns T to $P\alpha$ if and only if $\alpha_M \in P_M$.

If P is an n-adic predicate ($n > 1$) and $\alpha_1, \cdots, \alpha_n$ are individual terms, then M assigns T to $P\alpha_1 \cdots \alpha_n$ if and only if $<\alpha_{1M}, \ldots . \alpha_{nM}> \in P_M$

If A is some sentence, then Av_M is the set of members of U_M such that $u \in Av_M$ if and only if M_{vu} assigns T to A (i.e., $Av_M = \{u: u \in U_M$ and M_{vu} assigns T to $A\}$; Av_M is the extension of Av).

If Q is a quantifier and A is a sentence, then $Q_M (Av_M) \subseteq p(Av_M)$.

1. For any sentence A, $\sim A$ is assigned T by M if and only if A is assigned F.
2. For any sentences A and B,
   $A \cdot B$ is assigned T by M if and only if A is assigned T and B is assigned T.
   $A \supset B$ is assigned T by M if and only if A is assigned F or B is assigned T.
   $A \vee B$ is assigned T by M if and only if at least one of the sentences, A or B, is assigned T.
   $A \equiv B$ is assigned T by M if and only if A and B are assigned the same truth-value.
3. If Q is a quantifier, A and B are sentences, and v is some variable, then $(Qv: A)B$ is assigned T by M if and only if $Av_M \cap Bv_M \in Q_M(Av_M)$.
4. M assigns F to a sentence if and only if M does not assign T.

A model must interpret each of the quantifiers. E.g., we have been assuming these interpretations for three of the quantifiers we have discussed:

$$\forall_M(S) = \{S\}$$
$$\exists_M(S) = p(S) - \{\emptyset\}$$
$$\mu_M(S) = \{A: A \subseteq S \text{ and } A \text{ contains most members of } S\}$$

Example

Suppose that our language contains the usual truth-functional connectives; the three quantifiers '$\forall$', '$\exists$', and 'μ' (interpreted in the way just indicated); and the individual constants and predicates indicated below.

Constants: 'a', 'b', 'c'
Predicates: Monadic: 'F', 'G'
    Dyadic: 'R'

Now consider a model M for that language that has the following features:

U_M = { Al, Bill, Dave}
a_M = Al, b_M = Bill. c_M = Dave.   ·
F_M = { Al, Bill}
G_M = { Al, Bill, Dave}
R_M = { <Al, Al>, <Al, Bill>, <Bill, Al> }

Consider how truth-values are determined in the model.

'Fa' is true according to M, because $a_M \in F_M$ (i.e., Al is an F).

'$(\forall x: Fx)Gx$' is true according to M, because it is true that $(Fx)x_M \cap (Gx)x_M \in \forall_M((Fx)x_M)$, (i.e., $(Fx)x_M = F_M = \{$ Al, Bill$\}$; $(Gx)x_M = G_M = \{$ Al, Bill, Dave$\}$; $(Fx)x_M \cap (Gx)x_M = \{$ Al, Bill$\}$; and $\{$ Al, Bill$\} \in \{\{$ Al, Bill$\}\}$).

'$(\mu x: Gx)Rxa$' is true according to M, because $(Gx)x_M \cap (Rxa)x_M \in \mu M((Gx)x_M)$, (i.e., $\{$ Al, Bill$\} \in \{\{$ Al, Bill$\}$, $\{$ Al, Dave$\}$, $\{$ Bill, Dave$\}\}$).

When a sentence has one quantifier within the scope of another, the assignments made to the variables play a role. For the sake of specificity, let's say that our model M makes the same assignment, Al, to each of the variables:

x_M = Al, y_M = Al, z_M = Al, x_{1M} = Al, etc. for all variables.

Now we can evaluate sentences with multiple quantifiers, like '$(\forall x: Fx)(\exists y: Gy)Rxy$'. Since this is a universally quantified sentence, we begin by evaluating it accordingly:

'$(\forall x: Fx)(\exists y: Gy)Rxy$' is true if and only if $(Fx)x_M \cap ((\exists y : Gy)Rxy)x_M \in \forall_M((Fx)x_M)$.

The set $(Fx)x_M$ is the same set as F_M, because it is the set of all assignments to x such that Fx is true. But that is just the individuals in F_M (i.e., Al and Bill). The new idea is the evaluation of '$((\exists y: Gy)Rxy)x_M$'. This is the set of individuals u such that Mxu makes $(\exists y: Gy)Rxy$ true. (Mxu) is the model that is just like M except that it assigns u to 'x'.) In our example there are three such models to consider, because there are three members of U_M. $MxAl = M$, and the other two are MxBill and MxDave. So we evaluate '$(\exists y: Gy)Rxy$' relative to each of these models.

'$(\exists y: Gy)Rxy$' is true in MxAl, because MxAl $= M$ and $(Gy)y_M \cap (Rxy)y_M \in \exists_M(G_M)$. (This is because $(Rxy)y_M = \{$ Al, Bill$\}$, and $\{$ Al, Bill$\}$ is a member of $\exists_M(G_M)$ [i.e., $p(G_M) - \{\emptyset\}$]. So, Al $\in [(\exists y: Gy)Rxy]x_M$).

'$(\exists y\colon Gy)Rxy$' is true in $M x$Bill, because $(Gy)y_{MxBill}$ ∩ $(Rxy)y_{MxBill}$ ∈ $\exists_{MxBill}$ (G_{MxBill}). (This is because $(Rxy)y_{MxBill}$ = { Al}, and { Al} is a member of $\exists_{MxBill}$ (G_{MxBill}) (i.e., $p(G_M)$ − {∅}). So, Bill ∈ $((\exists y\colon Gy)Rxy)x_M$.)

'$(\exists y\colon Gy)Rxy$' is false in $M x$Dave, because $(Gy)y_{MxDave}$ ∩ $(Rxy)y_{MxDave}$ ∉ $\exists_{MxDave}$ (G_{MxDave}). [This is because $(Rxy)y_{MxDave}$ =∅, and ∅ is not a member of $\exists_{MxDave}$ (G_{MxDave}) (i.e., $p(G_M)$ − {∅}). So, Dave ∉ $((\exists y\colon Gy) Rxy)x_M$].

Testing these three models gives us the result that $((\exists y\colon Gy)Rxy)x_M$ = { Al, Bill}. Our original conditions for truth in M are

'$(\forall x\colon Fx)(\exists y\colon Gy)Rxy$' is true if and only if $(Fx)x_M$ ∩ $((\exists y\colon Gy)Rxy)x_M$ ∈ $\forall_M((Fx)x_M)$.

This now is seen to amount to

'$(\forall x\colon Fx)(\exists y\colon Gy)Rxy$' is true if and only if F_M ∩ { Al, Bill} ∈ $\forall_M(F_M)$.

But that means that '$(\forall x\colon Fx)(\exists y\colon Gy)Rxy$' is true, because F_M = { Al, Bill} and so $\forall M(F_M)$ = {{ Al, Bill}} .

Exercise 16a

For each sentence, say whether it is true or false in the model M described in the example just given.

1. Fc
2. $\sim Gb$
3. $Fa \cdot Gc$
4. $(\forall x\colon Fx)Gx$
5. $(\exists x\colon Gx) \sim Fx$
6. $(\forall x\colon Gx \cdot \sim Fx)Gx$
7. $(\forall x\colon Gx)Rax$
8. $(\forall x\colon Fx)Rxx$
9. $(\forall x\colon Gx)(\forall y\colon Rxy)Rxy$
10. $(\exists x\colon Fx)(\exists y\colon Gy)Rxy$
11. $(\exists x\colon Fx)(\exists y\colon Gy)\sim Rxy$
12. $(\forall x\colon Fx \cdot (\exists y\colon Gy)Rxy)Rxx$

APPENDIXES

A
SET-THEORETIC
CONCEPTS

Set, { *a, b, c* }

Specified by enumeration
 {Reno, Las Vegas}
Specified by a characteristic of members
 {*u*: *u* is a city in Nevada}
 The set of cities in Nevada

Membership, *x* ∈ *A*

Reno ∈ {*u*: *u* is a city in Nevada}

Subset, *A* ⊆ *B*

Every member of *A* is a member of *B*
 {Reno, Las Vegas} ⊆ {*u*: *u* is a city in Nevada}

Intersection, *A* ∩ *B*

The set consisting of the overlap of *A* and *B* (i.e., the objects that are members of *A* and also members of *B*)
 {*a, b, c*} ∩ {*b, c, d*} = {*b, c*}

Empty Set, ∅

The set that has no members
 ∅ is a subset of every set
 {*a, c, e*} ∩ {*b, d*} = ∅

Exclusion, *A* − *B*

The set containing all members of *A* except those in *B*

$\{a, b, c, d\} - \{b, d\} = \{a, c\}$

$\{a, b, c\} - \{a, c, d\} = \{b\}$

$\{b, c\} - \{a, b, c\} = \varnothing$

Ordered Pair, <*a, b* >

<Reno, Las Vegas > ≠ <Las Vegas, Reno>

Ordered *n*-tuple, <a_1, a_2, ..., a_n>

5-tuple

<Las Vegas, Reno, Boston, Reno, Detroit>

Power Set, $p(S)$

The set of all subsets of *S*

$p\{a, b, c\} = \{\varnothing, \{a\}, \{b\}, \{c\}, \{a, b\}, \{a, c\}, \{b, c\}, \{a, b, c\}\}$

Cartesian Product, S^n

The set of all *n*-tuples of members of *S*

$\{a, b, c\}^2 =$

$\{<a, a>, <a, b>, <a, c>, <b, b>, <b, c>,$
$<b, a>, <c, c>, <c, b>, <c, a>\}$

$\{a, b\}^3 =$

$\{<a, a, a>, <a, a, b>, <a, b, a>, <b, a, a>, <a, b, b>,$
$<b, a, b>, <b, b, a>, <b, b, b>\}$

B

ANSWERS
TO SELECTED EXERCISES

CHAPTER 1

Exercise 1a

2. No argument.

4. Argument. Conclusion: *Hyenas are canines.*

6. No argument.

8. No argument. (This is a conditional sentence. Note that someone who says this does not assert that Bob is opposed to killing animals or that Bob shouldn't eat meat.)

10. No argument.

Exercise 1b

2. Argument. (Conclusion: *Every doctor has attended school.*) Valid. Not sound. (Some people get degrees without attending school.)

4. Argument. (Conclusion: *Some surgeons haven't studied medicine.*) Valid. Not sound. (At least one premise is false. I'm not sure which.)

6. No argument.

8. No argument.

CHAPTER 2

Exercise 2a

2. Not a conjunction.

4. Not a conjunction if it means that they are married to each other.

6. Bob likes Fords · Bob works for GM.

8. Not a conjunction.

10. Bob owns a Ford · Bob owns a Chevrolet.

12. Al is a dentist · Al makes very little money.

14. Al is a dentist · Al makes very little money.

Exercise 2b

2. F	**4.** F
6. T	**8.** T
10. T	**12.** F
14. F	

Exercise 2c

2. Either Al or Bill speaks Italian.

4. Al and Bill don't both speak Italian.

6. Al speaks Italian, but he's studying in France this year.

8. Bill speaks French and Al doesn't, yet Al is studying in France this year.

10. Bill is studying in Italy this year even though he doesn't speak Italian.

12. Al speaks French and is studying in France this year, and Bill is studying in Italy even though he doesn't speak Italian.

Exercise 2d

2. $B \vee C$	**4.** $\sim D \vee B$
6. $\sim(B \vee C)$	**8.** $\sim\sim(B \vee A)$
10. $B \cdot (E \vee F)$	**12.** $\sim(D \vee F) \cdot E$
14. $E \vee (F \vee D)$	

Exercise 2e

2. T	**4.** F
6. T	**8.** F

Exercise 2f

2. T	**4.** F
6. F	**8.** T
10. T	**12.** F
14. T	

Exercise 2g

$\sim A \vee (B \cdot C)$ (2) $p \vee q$

$\sim(A \vee (B \cdot C))$ (1) $\sim p$

$(\sim\sim A \lor B)\cdot A$	(3) $p\cdot q$; (6) $(p\lor q)\cdot r$;
	(8) $(\sim p\lor q)\cdot r$
$\sim(A\lor B)\cdot\sim C$	(3) $p\cdot q$; (4) $\sim p\cdot q$
$\sim A\cdot((C\cdot D)\lor\sim E)$	(3) $p\cdot q$; (4) $\sim p\cdot q$; (5) $p\cdot(q\lor r)$

Exercise 2h

$p\lor q$	1, 2, 3, 5, 8, 12, 13, 15, 16, 18
$\sim p\lor q$	2, 5, 16
$p\lor(q\cdot r)$	8, 12
$p\cdot q$	10, 11, 14, 19

CHAPTER 3

Exercise 3a

2. Valid   **4.** Valid

6. Invalid   **8.** Invalid

10. Valid   **12.** Invalid

Exercise 3b

1.

		S_1		S_3		S_2
p	q	$p\lor q$	$\sim q$	$p\cdot\sim q$	$p\cdot q$	$\sim(p\cdot q)$
T	T	T	F	F	T	F
T	F	T	T	T	F	T
F	T	T	F	F	F	T
F	F	F	T	F	F	T

Consistent (row 2)

2.

					S_1	S_2	S_3
p	q	r	$\sim q$	$\sim r$	$p\lor q$	$\sim q\lor r$	$p\lor\sim r$
T	T	T	F	F	T	T	T
T	T	F	F	T	T	F	T
T	F	T	T	F	T	T	T
T	F	F	T	T	T	T	T
F	T	T	F	F	T	T	F
F	T	F	F	T	T	F	T
F	F	T	T	F	F	T	F
F	F	F	T	T	F	T	T

Consistent   (rows 1, 3, 4)

3.

				S_1		S_2	S_2
p	q		$\sim q$	$p \vee q$	$p \cdot q$	$\sim(p \cdot q)$	$p \cdot \sim q$
T	T		F	T	T	F	F
T	F		T	$\underline{T}$	F	$\underline{T}$	$\underline{T}$
F	T		F	T	F	T	F
F	F		T	F	F	T	F

Consistent   (row 2)

4.

				S_1			S_2
p	q	r	$q \cdot r$	$p \vee (q \cdot r)$	$\sim q$	$\sim p$	$\sim q \cdot \sim p$
T	T	T	T	T	F	F	$\underline{F}$
T	T	F	F	T	F	F	$\underline{F}$
T	F	T	F	T	T	F	$\underline{F}$
T	F	F	F	T	T	F	$\underline{F}$
F	T	T	T	T	F	T	$\underline{F}$
F	T	F	F	F	F	T	$\underline{F}$
F	F	T	F	$\underline{F}$	T	T	T
F	F	F	F	$\underline{F}$	T	T	T

Inconsistent

5.

				S_3		S_2	S_2
p	q	r	$\sim q$	$p \cdot r$	$\sim(p \cdot r)$	$p \vee q$	$(p \vee q) \cdot r$
T	T	T	$\underline{F}$	T	F	T	T
T	T	F	$\underline{F}$	F	T	T	F
T	F	T	T	T	$\underline{F}$	T	T
T	F	F	T	F	T	T	$\underline{F}$
F	T	T	$\underline{F}$	F	T	T	T
F	T	F	$\underline{F}$	F	T	T	F
F	F	T	T	F	T	F	$\underline{F}$
F	F	F	T	F	T	F	$\underline{F}$

Inconsistent

6.

				S_1		S_2	S_3
p	q	r	$p \vee q$	$\sim q$	$\sim q \vee r$	$p \vee r$	$\sim(p \vee r)$
T	T	T	T	F	T	T	$\underline{F}$
T	T	F	T	F	F	T	$\underline{F}$
T	F	T	T	T	T	T	$\underline{F}$
T	F	F	T	T	T	T	$\underline{F}$
F	T	T	T	F	T	T	$\underline{F}$
F	T	F	T	F	$\underline{F}$	F	T
F	F	T	F	T	T	T	$\underline{F}$
F	F	F	$\underline{F}$	T	T	F	T

Inconsistent

Exercise 3c

5.

p	q	r		$q \vee r$	$p \vee (q \vee r)$	$p \vee q$	$(p \vee q) \vee r$
T	T	T		T	T	T	T
T	T	F		T	T	T	T
T	F	T		T	T	T	T
T	F	F		F	T	T	T
F	T	T		T	T	T	T
F	T	F		T	T	T	T
F	F	T		T	T	F	T
F	F	F		F	F	F	F
					*		*

Columns match; equivalent

7.

p	q		$\sim p$	$\sim p \cdot q$	$p \cdot q$	$\sim (p \cdot q)$
T	T		F	F	T	F
T	F		F	<u>F</u>	F	<u>T</u>
F	T		T	T	F	T
F	F		T	<u>F</u>	F	<u>T</u>
				*		*

Columns do not match; not equivalent

10.

p	q		$p \vee q$	$\sim\sim(p \vee q)$	$\sim\sim p$	$\sim\sim q$	$\sim\sim p \cdot \sim\sim q$
T	T		T	T	T	T	T
T	F		T	<u>T</u>	T	F	<u>F</u>
F	T		T	<u>T</u>	F	T	<u>F</u>
F	F		F	F	F	F	F
				*			*

Columns do not match; not equivalent

Exercise 3d

2.

p	q		$\sim p$	$p \cdot q$	$(p \cdot q) \vee \sim p$
T	T		F	T	T
T	F		F	F	F
F	T		T	F	T
F	F		T	F	T

Contingent

4.

p	q		$p \vee q$	$p \cdot q$	$\sim (p \cdot q)$	$(p \vee q) \cdot \sim (p \cdot q)$
T	T		T	T	F	F
T	F		T	F	T	T
F	T		T	F	T	T
F	F		F	F	T	F

Contingent

6.

p	$p \lor p$	$\sim p$	$(p \lor p) \cdot \sim p$
T	T	F	F
F	F	T	F

Contradictory

8. $S = \sim(p \cdot q) \lor ((r \lor p) \cdot (r \lor q))$

p	q	r	$p \cdot q$	$\sim(p \cdot q)$	$r \lor p$	$r \lor q$	$(r \lor p) \cdot (r \lor q)$	S
T	T	T	T	F	T	T	T	T
T	T	F	T	F	T	T	T	T
T	F	T	F	T	T	T	T	T
T	F	F	F	T	T	F	F	T
F	T	T	F	T	T	T	T	T
F	T	F	F	T	F	T	F	T
F	F	T	F	T	T	T	T	T
F	F	F	F	T	F	F	F	T

Tautologous

10.

p	q	$\sim p$	$q \lor \sim p$	$p \lor (q \lor \sim p)$
T	T	F	T	T
T	F	F	F	T
F	T	T	T	T
F	F	T	T	T

Tautologous

Exercise 3e

Write truth-tables to verify these answers.

1. ‘$\sim(q \cdot \sim q)$’ is a tautology. So the argument is *valid*.
2. The premises are inconsistent. So the argument is *valid*.
3. Invalid
4. Invalid
5. Invalid

CHAPTER 4

Exercise 4a

2. $\checkmark\ p \lor q$
    $\checkmark\ \sim q \cdot r$
    $\checkmark\ \sim r \lor s$

4. $\checkmark\ p \cdot (q \lor r)$
    $\sim q$
    $\checkmark\ p \lor r$

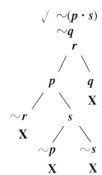

Inconsistent

√ *q* ∨ *r*
p
  / \
q   *r*
X / \
  p *r*

Consistent

6. Consistent

8. Inconsistent

Exercise 4b

See Exercise 3a.

Exercise 4c

2. Not equivalent

6. Equivalent

10. Not equivalent

4. Not equivalent

8. Equivalent

12. Not equivalent

Exercise 4d

2. Contingent

6. Contradictory

10. Contingent

14. Tautologous

18. Tautologous

4. Contradictory

8. Contingent

12. Contradictory

16. Tautologous

CHAPTER 5

Exercise 5a

2. $\sim R \supset H$

4. $O \cdot R$

6. $S \supset ((Z \cdot O) \cdot \sim L)$

8. $(\sim B \lor F) \supset E$
   Equivalent: $(\sim B \supset E) \cdot (F \supset E)$

10. $L \cdot T$

12. $H \cdot \sim F$

14. $\sim(L \cdot T) \cdot (S \supset G)$

Exercise 5b

1. $\sim(I \cdot T) \supset \sim D$
2. $\sim(D \cdot \sim(I \cdot B))$
   Equivalent: $\sim(I \cdot B) \supset \sim D$
3. $\sim(I \lor T) \supset (\sim D \supset B)$
4. $(T \cdot \sim I) \lor ((T \cdot I) \cdot D)$
5. $B \supset \sim(I \lor T)$
6. $D \supset (\sim(I \cdot T) \supset \sim B)$
7. $\sim I \supset \sim B$
8. $\sim D \supset (\sim T \supset \sim B)$
9. $B \equiv (T \cdot D)$
10. $\sim(T \lor I) \supset \sim(B \cdot \sim D)$

Exercise 5c

2. C P_2 P_1

p	q	r	$q \lor r$	$p \supset (q \lor r)$
T	T	T	T	T
T	T	F	T	T
T	F	T	T	T
T	F	F	F	F
F	**T**	T	T	**T**
F	**T**	F	T	**T**
F	F	T	T	T
F	F	F	F	T

Invalid (rows 5, 6)

4. P C

p	q	r	$q \supset r$	$p \supset (q \supset r)$	$p \supset q$	$(p \supset q) \supset r$
T	T	T	T	T	T	T
T	T	F	F	F	T	F
T	F	T	T	T	F	T
T	F	F	T	T	F	T
F	T	T	T	T	T	T
F	T	F	F	**T**	T	**F**
F	F	T	T	T	T	T
F	F	F	T	**T**	T	**F**

Invalid (rows 6, 8)

6.

							P_1	P_2	P_3
									C
p	q	r		$\sim p$	$\sim q$	$\sim r$	$p \vee q$	$\sim q \vee r$	$\sim p \vee \sim r$
T	T	T		F	F	F	T	T	F
T	T	F		F	F	T	T	F	T
T	F	T		F	T	F	T	T	F
T	F	F		F	T	T	T	T	T
F	T	T		T	F	F	T	T	T
F	T	F		T	F	T	T	F	T
F	F	T		T	T	F	F	T	T
F	F	F		T	T	T	F	T	T

Invalid (row 4)

8.

				P_1	P_2	P_3	C
p	q	r	s	$p \supset q$	$s \supset r$	$q \vee r$	$p \vee s$
T	T	T	T	T	T	T	T
T	T	T	F	T	T	T	T
T	T	F	T	T	F	T	T
T	T	F	F	T	T	T	T
T	F	T	T	F	T	T	T
T	F	T	F	F	T	T	T
T	F	F	T	F	F	F	T
T	F	F	F	F	T	F	T
F	T	T	T	T	T	T	T
F	T	T	F	T	T	T	F
F	T	F	T	T	F	T	T
F	T	F	F	T	T	T	F
F	F	T	T	T	T	T	T
F	F	T	F	T	T	T	F
F	F	F	T	T	F	F	T
F	F	F	F	T	T	F	F

Invalid (rows 10, 12, 14)

10.

				P		C
p	q	r	$q \vee r$	$p \cdot (q \vee r)$	$p \cdot q$	$(p \cdot q) \vee r$
T	T	T	T	T	T	T
T	T	F	T	T	T	T
T	F	T	T	T	F	T
T	F	F	F	F	F	F
F	T	T	T	F	F	T
F	T	F	T	F	F	F
F	F	T	T	F	F	T
F	F	F	F	F	F	F

Valid

12.

				P		C
p	q	r	$q \cdot r$	$p \supset (q \cdot r)$	$p \supset q$	$(p \supset q) \cdot r$
T	T	T	T	T	T	T
T	T	F	F	F	T	F
T	F	T	F	F	F	F
T	F	F	F	F	F	F
F	T	T	T	T	T	T
F	T	F	F	$\underline{T}$	T	$\underline{F}$
F	F	T	F	T	T	T
F	F	F	F	$\underline{T}$	T	$\underline{F}$

Invalid (rows 6, 8)

14.

$$P_1 = p \vee (q \equiv {\sim}r)$$
$$P_2 = {\sim}(q \supset p) \cdot (r \supset p)$$

		P_1				P_2	C
${\sim}r$	$q \equiv {\sim}r$	P_1	$q \supset p$	${\sim}(q \supset p)$	$r \supset p$	P_2	$r \vee p$
F	T	T	T	F	T	F	T
T	T	T	T	F	T	F	T
F	T	T	T	F	T	F	T
T	T	T	T	F	T	F	T
F	F	F	F	T	F	F	T
T	T	$\underline{T}$	F	T	T	$\underline{T}$	$\underline{F}$
F	T	T	T	F	F	F	T
T	F	F	T	F	T	F	F

Invalid (row 6)

Exercise 5d

2.

		S_1		S_2
p	q	$p \supset q$	${\sim}q$	$p \supset {\sim}q$
T	T	T	F	F
T	F	F	T	T
F	T	$\underline{T}$	F	$\underline{T}$
F	F	$\underline{T}$	T	$\underline{T}$

Consistent (rows 3,4)

4.

p	q	r	S_1 $p \supset q$	$\sim q$	S_2 $\sim q \cdot r$	$\sim r$	S_3 $p \supset \sim r$
T	T	T	T	F	F	F	F
T	T	F	T	F	F	T	T
T	F	T	F	T	T	F	F
T	F	F	F	T	F	T	T
F	T	T	T	F	F	F	T
F	T	F	T	F	F	T	T
F	F	T	<u>T</u>	T	<u>T</u>	F	<u>T</u>
F	F	F	T	T	F	T	T

Consistent (row 7)

6.

p	q	r	S_1 $p \equiv q$	S_2 $q \equiv r$	$\sim r$	S_3 $p \vee \sim r$
T	T	T	<u>T</u>	<u>T</u>	F	<u>T</u>
T	T	F	T	F	T	T
T	F	T	F	F	F	T
T	F	F	F	T	T	T
F	T	T	F	T	F	F
F	T	F	F	F	T	T
F	F	T	T	F	F	F
F	F	F	<u>T</u>	<u>T</u>	T	<u>T</u>

Consistent (rows 1, 8)

Exercise 5e

2.

p	q	r	S_1 $q \cdot r$	$p \supset (q \cdot r)$	S_2 $q \supset r$	$p \supset (q \supset r)$
T	T	T	T	T	T	T
T	T	F	F	F	F	F
T	F	T	F	<u>F</u>	T	<u>T</u>
T	F	F	F	<u>F</u>	T	<u>T</u>
F	T	T	T	T	T	T
F	T	F	F	T	F	T
F	F	T	F	T	T	T
F	F	F	F	T	T	T

Not equivalent (rows 3, 4)

4.

		S_1		S_2	
p	q	$\sim q$	$p \supset \sim q$	$\sim p$	$q \supset \sim p$
T	T	F	F	F	F
T	F	T	T	F	T
F	T	F	T	T	T
F	F	T	T	T	T

Equivalent (columns match)

6.

				S_1		S_2
p	q	r	$p \vee q$	$(p \vee q) \supset r$	$q \supset r$	$p \vee (q \supset r)$
T	T	T	T	T	T	T
T	T	F	T	**F**	F	**T**
T	F	T	T	T	T	T
T	F	F	T	**F**	T	**T**
F	T	T	T	T	T	T
F	T	F	T	F	F	F
F	F	T	F	T	T	T
F	F	F	F	T	T	T

Not equivalent (rows 2, 4)

8.

		S_1		S_2
p	q	$p \supset q$	$p \vee q$	$\sim(p \vee q)$
T	T	**T**	T	**F**
T	F	F	T	F
F	T	**T**	T	**F**
F	F	T	F	T

Not equivalent (rows 1, 3)

10.

			S_1		S_2
p	q	$p \supset q$	$\sim(p \supset q)$	$\sim p$	$\sim p \supset q$
T	T	T	**F**	F	**T**
T	F	F	T	F	T
F	T	T	**F**	T	**T**
F	F	T	F	T	F

Not equivalent (rows 1, 3)

12.

		S_1	S_2
p	q	$p \equiv q$	$q \equiv p$
T	T	T	T
T	F	F	F
F	T	F	F
F	F	T	T

Equivalent

14.

p	q	r		$q \equiv r$	S_1 $p \equiv (q \equiv r)$	$p \equiv q$	S_2 $(p \equiv q) \equiv r$
T	T	T		T	T	T	T
T	T	F		F	F	T	F
T	F	T		F	F	F	F
T	F	F		T	T	F	T
F	T	T		T	F	F	F
F	T	F		F	T	F	T
F	F	T		F	T	T	T
F	F	F		T	F	T	F

Equivalent

Exercise 5f

2.

p	q		$p \cdot q$	$(p \cdot q) \supset p$
T	T		T	T
T	F		F	T
F	T		F	T
F	F		F	T

Tautology

4.

p		$\sim p$	$p \supset \sim p$
T		F	F
F		T	T

Contingent

6.

p	q		$p \cdot q$	$q \cdot p$	$(p \cdot q) \supset (q \cdot p)$
T	T		T	T	T
T	F		F	F	T
F	T		F	F	T
F	F		F	F	T

Tautology

8.

p	q		$p \supset q$	$p \supset (p \supset q)$
T	T		T	T
T	F		F	F
F	T		T	T
F	F		T	T

Contingent

10. $p \cdot q$	$\sim p$	$\sim q$	$\sim p \vee \sim q$	$\sim(\sim p \vee \sim q)$	$(p \cdot q) \supset \sim(\sim p \vee \sim q)$
T	F	F	F	T	T
F	F	T	T	F	T
F	T	F	T	F	T
F	T	T	T	F	T

Tautology

Exercise 5g

2. $(L \cdot R) \supset \sim F$
$\sim L$
$\therefore \;\; F$
Invalid

4. $L \supset (M \supset I)$
$I \supset E$
L
$\therefore \;\; M \supset E$
Valid

6. $D \supset T$
D
$\therefore \;\; T$
Valid

8. $I \supset E$
$T \supset Y$
$(Y \cdot E) \supset \sim R$
$\therefore \;\; R \supset (\sim I \vee \sim T)$
Valid

Exercise 5h

2. $L \supset (C \cdot E)$
$E \supset (C \supset D)$
$L \cdot \sim D$
Inconsistent

4. $S \supset P$
$\sim S$
C
P
Consistent

6. $\sim B \supset \sim A$
$\sim A \supset \sim P$
B
$\sim A$
Consistent

8. $\sim G \supset S$
G
S
Consistent

CHAPTER 6

Exercise 6a

2. **1.** $\sim A$
  2. $A \vee B$
  3. $B \supset C$
  4. B 1,2   DS
  5. C 3,4   MP

4. **1.** $A \supset (B \lor C)$
    2. $A \cdot \sim B$
    3. A 2   Simp
    4. $B \lor C$ 1,3   MP
    5. $\sim B$ 2   Simp
    6. C 4,5   DS

6. **1.** $A \lor (B \cdot C)$
    2. $\sim A \cdot (B \supset D)$
    3. $\sim A$ 2   Simp
    4. $B \cdot C$ 1,3   DS
    5. $B \supset D$ 2   Simp
    6. B 4   Simp
    7. D 5,6   MP

8. **1.** $A \cdot (B \supset \sim C)$
    2. $B \cdot (C \lor D)$
    3. $D \supset E$
    4. $B \supset \sim C$ 1   Simp
    5. B 2   Simp
    6. $\sim C$ 4,5   MP
    7. $C \lor D$ 2   Simp
    8. D 6,7   DS
    9. E 3,8   MP

10. **1.** $D \lor (E \lor F)$
    2. $(E \lor F) \supset (A \supset B)$
    3. $\sim D \cdot \sim F$
    4. $E \supset A$
    5. $\sim D$ 3   Simp
    6. $E \lor F$ 1,5   DS
    7. $A \supset B$ 2,6   MP
    8. $\sim F$ 3   Simp
    9. E 6,8   DS
    10. A 4,9   MP
    11. B 7,10   MP

Exercise 6b

2. **1.** $A \lor \sim B$
    2. $\sim A \cdot D$
    3. $C \supset B$
    4. D 2   Simp
    5. $\sim A$ 2   Simp
    6. $\sim B$ 1,5   DS
    7. $\sim C$ 3,6   MT
    8. $D \cdot \sim C$ 4,7   Conj

4. **1.** $H \supset G$
    2. $\sim F$
    3. $F \lor (K \cdot \sim G)$

	4.	$K \cdot {\sim}G$	2,3	DS
	5.	K	4	Simp
	6.	${\sim}G$	4	Simp
	7.	${\sim}H$	1,6	MT
	8.	$K \cdot {\sim}H$	5,7	Conj
6.	1.	$A \supset (B \cdot {\sim}C)$		
	2.	$(D \supset C) \cdot A$		
	3.	${\sim}D \supset E$		
	4.	A	2	Simp
	5.	$B \cdot {\sim}C$	1,4	MP
	6.	B	5	Simp
	7.	$D \supset C$	2	Simp
	8.	${\sim}C$	5	Simp
	9.	${\sim}D$	7,8	MT
	10.	E	3,9	MP
	11.	$B \cdot E$	6,10	Conj
8.	1.	$(A \cdot D) \supset (C \supset E)$		
	2.	$D \supset A$		
	3.	$E \supset F$		
	4.	D		
	5.	A	2,4	MP
	6.	$A \cdot D$	4,5	Conj
	7.	$C \supset E$	1,6	MP
	8.	$C \supset F$	3,7	HS
10.	1.	$A \supset (B \vee C)$		
	2.	$D \vee {\sim}(B \vee C)$		
	3.	${\sim}A \supset (E \cdot F)$		
	4.	$E \supset {\sim}H$		
	5.	${\sim}D \cdot G$		
	6.	G	5	Simp
	7.	${\sim}D$	5	Simp
	8.	${\sim}(B \vee C)$	2,7	DS
	9.	${\sim}A$	1,8	MT
	10.	$E \cdot F$	3,9	MP
	11.	F	10	Simp
	12.	$F \cdot G$	6,11	Conj
	13.	E	10	Simp
	14.	${\sim}H$	4,13	MP
	15.	$(F \cdot G) \cdot {\sim}H$	12,14	Conj

Exercise 6c

2. **Add**
4. **DS**

Exercise 6d

2.	4.	$A \supset (C \vee E)$	1,2	HS
	5.	$D \vee F$	3,4	MP

4. $E \vee B$ 1,2,3   CD
   F 4,5   MP

Exercise 6e

2. 4. $B \vee A$ 3   Add
    5. E 1,4   MP
    6. $A \cdot C$ 2,5   MP

4. 4. $C \vee D$ 1,3   MP
    5. $\sim C$ 2,3   MP
    6. D 4,5   DS

6. 5. $B \vee A$ 2   Add
    6. $B \vee C$ 4,5   MP
    7. $\sim D \vee E$ 1,3,6   CD

Exercise 6f

2. 1. $A \supset B$
    2. $C \supset D$
    3. $E \supset (A \vee C)$
    4. E
    5. $A \vee C$ 3,4   MP
    6. $B \vee D$ 1,2,5   CD

4. 1. $(A \supset B) \supset (C \vee D)$
    2. $A \supset C$
    3. $D \supset C$
    4. $C \supset B$
    5. $A \supset B$ 2,4   HS
    6. $C \vee D$ 1,5   MP
    7. $B \vee C$ 3,4,6   CD

6. 1. $(A \vee B) \supset C$
    2. $(C \vee D) \supset E$
    3. A
    4. $A \vee B$ 3   Add
    5. C 1,4   MP
    6. $C \vee D$ 5   Add
    7. E 2,6   MP

8. 1. $(B \vee \sim A) \supset (C \vee D)$
    2. $A \supset E$
    3. $C \supset F$
    4. $D \supset G$
    5. $\sim E$
    6. $\sim A$ 2,5   MT
    7. $B \vee \sim A$ 6   Add
    8. $C \vee D$ 1,7   MP
    9. $F \vee G$ 3,4,8   CD

10. 1. $A \supset (B \cdot C)$
    2. $C \supset E$

3.	$(B \cdot C) \supset F$		
4.	$C \cdot \sim F$		
5.	$\sim F$	4	Simp
6.	$\sim(B \cdot C)$	3,5	MT
7.	$\sim A$	1,6	MT
8.	C	4	Simp
9.	E	2,8	MP
10.	$E \cdot \sim A$	7,9	Conj

12.

1.	$\sim A \supset [C \cdot \sim(D \vee F)]$		
2.	$G \supset (D \vee F)$		
3.	$B \cdot \sim A$		
4.	B	3	Simp
5.	$\sim A$	3	Simp
6.	$C \cdot \sim(D \vee F)$	1,5	Simp
7.	C	6	Simp
8.	$\sim(D \vee F)$	6	Simp
9.	$\sim G$	2,8	MT
10.	$B \cdot C$	4,7	Conj
11.	$(B \cdot C) \cdot \sim G$	9,10	Conj

14.

1.	$(A \cdot D) \supset E$		
2.	$(C \vee B) \supset \sim E$		
3.	$F \supset (A \cdot D)$		
4.	C		
5.	$C \vee B$	4	Add
6.	$\sim E$	2,5	MP
7.	$\sim(A \cdot D)$	1,6	MT
8.	$\sim F$	3,7	MT

CHAPTER 7

Exercise 7a

2.

1.	$(A \vee B) \vee C$		
2.	$C \vee (A \vee B)$	1	Comm
3.	$(C \vee A) \vee B$	2	Assoc

4.

1.	$B \supset (C \cdot \sim A)$		
2.	$D \supset \sim C$		
3.	D		
4.	$\sim C$	2,3	MP
5.	$\sim C \vee \sim\sim A$	4	Add
6.	$\sim(C \cdot \sim A)$	5	DeM
7.	$\sim B$	1,6	MT

6.

1.	$\sim(A \vee B)$		
2.	$C \supset (B \cdot D)$		
3.	$\sim A \cdot \sim B$	1	DeM
4.	$\sim B$	3	Simp
5.	$\sim B \vee \sim D$	4	Add

	6.	$\sim(B \cdot D)$	5	DeM
	7.	$\sim C$	2,6	MT
	8.	$\sim A$	3	Simp
	9.	$\sim A \cdot \sim C$	7,8	Conj
	10.	$\sim(A \lor C)$	9	DeM
8.	1.	$\sim(A \cdot (B \cdot C))$		
	2.	C		
	3.	$D \supset (A \cdot B)$		
	4.	$\sim((A \cdot B) \cdot C)$	1	Assoc
	5.	$\sim(A \cdot B) \lor \sim C$	4	DeM
	6.	$\sim\sim C$	2	DN
	7.	$\sim(A \cdot B)$	5,6	DS
	8.	$\sim D$	3,7	MT
10.	1.	$(D \cdot E) \supset (A \lor C)$		
	2.	$B \supset \sim A$		
	3.	$(B \cdot \sim A) \supset \sim C$		
	4.	$B \cdot D$		
	5.	B	4	Simp
	6.	$\sim A$	2,5	MP
	7.	$B \cdot \sim A$	5,6	Conj
	8.	$\sim C$	3,7	MP
	9.	$\sim A \cdot \sim C$	6,8	Conj
	10.	$\sim(A \lor C)$	9	DeM
	11.	$\sim(D \cdot E)$	1,10	MT
	12.	$\sim D \lor \sim E$	11	DeM
	13.	D	4	Simp
	14.	$\sim\sim D$	13	DN
	15.	$\sim E$	12,14	DS
12.	1.	$\sim(D \lor \sim A)$		
	2.	$\sim(B \cdot \sim C)$		
	3.	$A \supset (C \supset (D \cdot E))$		
	4.	$\sim D \cdot \sim\sim A$	1	DeM
	5.	$\sim D \cdot A$	4	DN
	6.	A	5	Simp
	7.	$C \supset (D \cdot E)$	3,6	MP
	8.	$\sim D$	5	Simp
	9.	$\sim D \lor \sim E$	8	Add
	10.	$\sim(D \cdot E)$	9	DeM
	11.	$\sim C$	7,10	MT
	12.	$\sim B \lor \sim\sim C$	2	DeM
	13.	$\sim B \lor C$	12	DN
	14.	$\sim B$	11,13	DS
14.	1.	$\sim(A \cdot \sim B)$		
	2.	$A \lor D$		
	3.	$\sim(C \cdot D)$		
	4.	C		
	5.	$\sim A \lor \sim\sim B$	1	DeM

6.	$\sim A \lor B$	5 DN
7.	$\sim C \lor \sim D$	3 DeM
8.	$\sim\sim\sim C$	4 DN
9.	$\sim D$	7,8 DS
10.	A	2,9 DS
11.	$\sim\sim A$	10 DN
12.	B	6,11 DS

Exercise 7b

2.	**1.**	$\sim A \supset A$	
	2.	$\sim\sim A \lor A$	1 CE
	3.	$A \lor A$	2 DN
	4.	A	3 Red
4.	**1.**	$A \supset (B \cdot D)$	
	2.	$C \supset D$	
	3.	$A \lor C$	
	4.	$\sim A \lor (B \cdot D)$	1 CE
	5.	$(\sim A \lor B) \cdot (\sim A \lor D)$	4 Dist
	6.	$\sim A \lor D$	5 Simp
	7.	$A \supset D$	6 CE
	8.	$D \lor D$	2,3,7 CD
	9.	D	8 Red
6.	**1.**	$A \supset B$	
	2.	$\sim A \lor B$	1 CE
	3.	$(\sim A \lor B) \lor C$	3 Add
	4.	$\sim A \lor (B \lor C)$	3 Assoc
	5.	$A \supset (B \lor C)$	4 CE
8.	**1.**	$\sim A \supset B$	
	2.	$\sim\sim A \lor B$	1 CE
	3.	$A \lor B$	2 DN
	4.	$(A \lor B) \lor C$	3 Add
	5.	$A \lor (B \lor C)$	4 Assoc
	6.	$A \lor (C \lor B)$	5 Comm
	7.	$(A \lor C) \lor B$	6 Assoc
10.	**1.**	$\sim[B \lor \sim(A \supset (B \cdot C))]$	
	2.	$\sim A \supset D$	
	3.	$\sim B \cdot \sim\sim(A \supset (B \cdot C))$	1 DeM
	4.	$\sim\sim(A \supset (B \cdot C))$	3 Simp
	5.	$A \supset (B \cdot C)$	4 DN
	6.	$\sim B$	3 Simp
	7.	$\sim B \lor \sim C$	6 Add
	8.	$\sim(B \cdot C)$	7 DeM
	9.	$\sim A$	5,8 MT
	10.	D	2,9 MP
	11.	$D \cdot \sim A$	9,10 Conj
12.	**1.**	$\sim A \lor (B \cdot C)$	
	2.	$C \supset (B \cdot D)$	

3.	$A \vee C$		
4.	$C \vee A$	3	Comm
5.	$\sim\sim C \vee A$	4	DN
6.	$\sim C \supset A$	5	CE
7.	$A \supset (B \cdot C)$	1	CE
8.	$\sim C \supset (B \cdot C)$	6,7	HS
9.	$\sim\sim C \vee (B \cdot C)$	8	CE
10.	$C \vee (B \cdot C)$	9	DN
11.	$(C \vee B) \cdot (C \vee C)$	10	Dist
12.	$C \vee C$	11	Simp
13.	C	12	Red
14.	$B \cdot D$	2,13	MP

14.
1.	$\sim A \vee B$		
2.	$D \vee A$		
3.	$D \supset C$		
4.	$A \supset B$	1	CE
5.	$C \vee B$	2,3,4	CD
6.	$\sim\sim C \vee B$	5	DN
7.	$\sim C \supset B$	6	CE

Exercise 7c

2. $\sim(A \cdot B)$
$\sim A \vee \sim B$
DeMorgan's Theorem

4. $A \cdot (B \vee C)$
$(A \cdot B) \vee (A \cdot C)$
Distribution

6. $(A \cdot B) \cdot C$
$A \cdot (B \cdot C)$
Associativity

Exercise 7d

2.
1.	$(A \cdot B) \supset (C \vee D)$		
2.	$(E \cdot B) \supset A$		
3.	$\sim(A \cdot B) \vee (C \vee D)$	1	CE
4.	$(\sim A \vee \sim B) \vee (C \vee D)$	3	DeM
5.	$\sim A \vee (\sim B \vee (C \vee D))$	4	Assoc
6.	$A \supset (\sim B \vee (C \vee D))$	5	CE
7.	$(E \cdot B) \supset (\sim B \vee (C \vee D))$	1,6	HS
8.	$(E \cdot B) \supset (B \supset (C \vee D))$	7	CE
9.	$[(E \cdot B) \cdot B] \supset (C \vee D)$	8	Exp
10.	$[E \cdot (B \cdot B)] \supset (C \vee D)$	9	Assoc
11.	$(E \cdot B) \supset (C \vee D)$	10	Red

4.
1.	$(A \cdot B) \supset (\sim D \supset \sim C)$		
2.	$F \supset A$		
3.	$A \supset (B \supset (\sim D \supset \sim C))$	1	Exp

4. $F \supset (B \supset (\sim D \supset \sim C))$	2,3	HS
5. $F \supset (B \supset (C \supset D))$	4	Contra
6. $F \supset ((B \cdot C) \supset D)$	5	Exp
7. $F \supset ((C \cdot B) \supset D)$	6	Comm
8. $F \supset (C \supset (B \supset D))$	7	Exp
9. $(F \cdot C) \supset (B \supset D)$	8	Exp
10. $(F \cdot C) \supset (\sim B \vee D)$	9	CE
11. $(F \cdot C) \supset (D \vee \sim B)$	10	Comm

6.
1. $A \supset (B \equiv C)$		
2. $B \cdot \sim C$		
3. $\sim A \supset D$		
4. $\sim\sim(B \cdot \sim C)$	2	DN
5. $\sim(\sim B \vee \sim\sim C)$	4	DeM
6. $\sim(\sim B \vee C)$	5	DN
7. $\sim(B \supset C)$	6	CE
8. $\sim(B \supset C) \vee \sim(C \supset B)$	7	Add
9. $\sim((B \supset C) \cdot (C \supset B))$	8	DeM
10. $\sim(B \equiv C)$	9	Bic
11. $\sim A$	1,10	MT
12. D	3,11	MP

CHAPTER 8

Exercise 8a

2.
1. $(A \supset C) \cdot (B \supset C)$		
2. $A \supset C$	1	Simp
3. $B \supset C$	1	Simp
4. $A \vee B$		AP
5. $C \vee C$	2,3,4	CD
6. C	5	Red
7. $(A \vee B) \supset C$	4–6	CP

4.
1. $A \vee (B \cdot C)$		
2. $C \supset \sim A$		
3. C		AP
4. $\sim A$	2,3	MP
5. $B \cdot C$	1,4	DS
6. B	5	Simp
7. $C \supset B$	3–6	CP

6.
1. $\sim(B \cdot \sim D)$		
2. $\sim A \supset B$		
3. $C \supset (A \supset D)$		
4. C		AP
5. $A \supset D$	3,4	MP
6. $\sim B \vee \sim\sim D$	1	DeM
7. $\sim B \vee D$	6	DN

8.	$B \supset D$	7	CE
9.	$\sim\sim A \vee B$	2	CE
10.	$A \vee B$	9	DN
11.	$D \vee D$	5,8,10	CD
12.	D	11	Red
13.	$C \supset D$	4–12	CP

8.
1.	$A \supset [B \vee (C \cdot D)]$		
2.	$E \supset \sim C$		
3.	$B \supset (E \cdot C)$		
4.	A		AP
5.	$B \vee (C \cdot D)$	1,4	MP
6.	$\sim E \vee \sim C$	2	CE
7.	$\sim(E \cdot C)$	6	DeM
8.	$\sim B$	3,7	MT
9.	$C \cdot D$	5,8	DS
10.	D	9	Simp
11.	$A \supset D$	4–10	CP

Exercise 8b

2.
1.	$\sim A \supset (B \vee C)$		
2.	$C \vee D$		
3.	$\sim B \vee \sim D$		
4.	$\sim(A \vee C)$		AP
5.	$\sim A \cdot \sim C$	4	DeM
6.	$\sim A$	5	Simp
7.	$B \vee C$	1,6	MP
8.	$\sim C$	5	Simp
9.	B	7,8	DS
10.	$\sim\sim B$	9	DN
11.	$\sim D$	3,10	DS
12.	C	2,11	DS
13.	$C \cdot \sim C$	8,12	Conj
14.	$A \vee C$	4–13	IP

4.
1.	$A \supset (D \cdot E)$		
2.	$C \vee E$		
3.	$C \supset (A \cdot \sim D)$		
4.	C		AP
5.	$A \cdot \sim D$	3,4	MP
6.	A	5	Simp
7.	$D \cdot E$	1,6	MP
8.	D	7	Simp
9.	$\sim D$	5	Simp
10.	$D \cdot \sim D$	8,9	Conj
11.	$\sim C$	4–10	IP
12.	E	2,11	DS
13.	$E \cdot \sim C$	11,12	Conj

6. **1.** $(\sim A \lor B) \supset C$
     2. $A \lor \sim D$
     3. $C \supset D$
     4. $\sim A$ AP
     5. $\sim D$ 2,4 DS
     6. $\sim C$ 3,5 MT
     7. $\sim A \lor B$ 4 Add
     8. C 1,7 MP
     9. $C \cdot \sim C$ 6,8 Conj
    10. A 4–9 IP

8. **1.** $\sim A \supset (B \supset C)$
     2. $A \lor B$
     3. $B \supset \sim C$
     4. $A \supset D$
     5. $\sim A$ AP
     6. B 2,5 DS
     7. $\sim C$ 3,6 MP
     8. $B \supset C$ 1,5 MP
     9. C 6,8 MP
    10. $C \cdot \sim C$ 7,9 Conj
    11. A 5–10 IP
    12. D 4,11 MP
    13. $A \cdot D$ 11,12 Conj

Exercise 8c

2. **1.** $A \supset \sim(C \cdot D)$
     2. $B \supset (C \lor D)$
     3. $A \cdot B$
     4. A 3 Simp
     5. B 3 Simp
     6. $C \lor D$ 2,5 MP
     7. $\sim(C \cdot D)$ 1,4 MP
     8. C AP
     9. $\sim C \lor \sim D$ 7 DeM
    10. $\sim\sim C$ 8 DN
    11. $\sim D$ 9,10 DS
    12. $C \supset \sim D$ 8,11 CP
    13. $\sim D$ AP
    14. C 6,13 DS
    15. $\sim D \supset C$ 13–14 CP
    16. $(C \supset \sim D) \cdot (\sim D \supset C)$ 12,15 Conj
    17. $C \equiv \sim D$ 16 Bic

4. **1.** $(A \cdot B) \supset C$
     2. $\sim(A \supset C)$ AP
     3. $\sim(\sim A \lor C)$ 2 CE
     4. $\sim\sim A \cdot \sim C$ 3 DeM

	5.	$\sim C$	4	Simp
	6.	$\sim(A \cdot B)$	1,5	MT
	7.	$\sim A \vee \sim B$	6	DeM
	8.	$\sim\sim A$	4	Simp
	9.	$\sim B$	7,8	DS
	10.	$\sim B \vee C$	9	Add
	11.	$B \supset C$	10	CE
	12.	$\sim(A \supset C) \supset (B \supset C)$	2–11	CP
	13.	$\sim\sim(A \supset C) \vee (B \supset C)$	12	CE
	14.	$(A \supset C) \vee (B \supset C)$	13	DN
6.	1.	$A \vee (B \supset C)$		
	2.	$A \supset (B \cdot D)$		
	3.	$B \supset (C \vee \sim D)$		
	4.	B		AP
	5.	$C \vee \sim D$	3,4	MP
	6.	$\sim C$		AP
	7.	$\sim D$	5,6	DS
	8.	$\sim B \vee \sim D$	7	Add
	9.	$\sim(B \cdot D)$	8	DeM
	10.	$\sim A$	2,9	MT
	11.	$B \supset C$	1,10	DS
	12.	C	4,11	MP
	13.	$C \cdot \sim C$	6,12	Conj
	14.	C	6–13	IP
	15.	$B \supset C$	4–14	CP
8.	1.	$(A \cdot B) \supset (C \cdot D)$		
	2.	$B \supset (A \vee C)$		
	3.	$(E \vee F) \supset \sim(B \cdot C)$		
	4.	$C \supset (D \vee E)$		
	5.	B		AP
	6.	$A \vee C$	2,5	MP
	7.	$\sim C$		AP
	8.	A	6,7	DS
	9.	$A \cdot B$	5,8	Conj
	10.	$C \cdot D$	1,9	MP
	11.	C	10	Simp
	12.	$C \cdot \sim C$	7,11	Conj
	13.	C	7–12	IP
	14.	$D \vee E$	4,13	MP
	15.	$B \cdot C$	5,13	Conj
	16.	$\sim\sim(B \cdot C)$	15	DN
	17.	$\sim(E \vee F)$	3,16	MT
	18.	$\sim E \cdot \sim F$	17	DeM
	19.	$\sim E$	18	Simp
	20.	D	14,19	DS
	21.	$D \cdot \sim E$	19,20	Conj
	22.	$C \cdot (D \cdot \sim E)$	13,21	Conj
	23.	$B \supset [C \cdot (D \cdot \sim E)]$	5–22	CP

Exercise 8d

2. 1. $C \supset (T \lor F)$
    2. $(\sim C \lor F) \supset E$
    3. $\sim E$ AP
    4. $\sim(\sim C \lor F)$ MT
    5. $\sim\sim C \cdot \sim F$ DeM
    6. $\sim\sim C$ Simp
    7. C DN
    8. $T \lor F$ MP
    9. $\sim F$ Simp
    10. T DS
    11. $\sim E \supset T$ CP
    12. $\sim\sim E \lor T$ CE
    13. $E \lor T$ DN

4. 1. $F \supset \sim S$
    2. $\sim S \supset (\sim(C \lor H \supset T)$
    3. $\sim\sim M \supset \sim T$
    4. $\sim C \cdot \sim H$
    5. F AP
    6. $\sim S$ MP
    7. $\sim(C \lor H) \supset T$ MP
    8. $\sim(C \lor H)$ DeM
    9. T MP
    10. $\sim\sim T$ DN
    11. $\sim\sim\sim M$ MT
    12. $\sim M$ DN
    13. $F \supset \sim M$ CP

Exercise 8e

1. 1. $\sim(I \lor N) \supset \sim R$
    2. $\sim N$
    3. $R \cdot \sim I$ AP
    4. $\sim I$ Simp
    5. $\sim I \cdot \sim N$ Conj
    6. $\sim(I \lor N)$ DeM
    7. $\sim R$ MP
    8. R Simp
    9. $R \cdot \sim R$ Conj
    10. $\sim(R \cdot \sim I)$ IP

4. 1. $C \supset (M \cdot L)$
    2. $L \supset ((M \supset D)$
    3. C AP
    4. $M \cdot L$ MP
    5. L Simp
    6. $M \supset D$ MP
    7. M Simp

| 8. | D | | MP |
| 9. | $C \supset D$ | | |

Exercise 8f

2.
1.	$L \supset (M \supset I)$		
2.	$I \supset E$		
3.	L		
4.	$M \supset I$		MP
5.	$M \supset E$		HS

4.
1.	$\sim E \supset \sim R$		
2.	$\sim F \supset \sim E$		
3.	$\sim F$		
4.	$\sim E$		MP
5.	$\sim R$		MP

Exercise 8g

2.
1.	$N \supset (\sim H \supset \sim E)$		
2.	$\sim H$		
3.	N		AP
4.	$\sim H \supset \sim E$		MP
5.	$\sim E$		MP
6.	$N \supset \sim E$		CP

4.
1.	$C \supset (O \vee M)$		
2.	$(O \supset R) \cdot (R \supset L)$		
3.	$M \supset \sim K$		
4.	C		AP
5.	$O \vee M$		MP
6.	$O \supset R$		Simp
7.	$R \supset L$		Simp
8.	$O \supset L$		HS
9.	$L \vee \sim K$		CD
10.	$\sim K \vee L$		Comm
11.	$C \supset (\sim K \vee L)$		CP

Exercise 8h

2.
1.	$A \equiv B$		
2.	$C \equiv D$		
3.	$\sim B \vee \sim D$		
4.	A		AP
5.	B	1,4	BI
6.	$\sim D$	3,5	DS+
7.	$\sim C$	2,6	BI
8.	$A \supset \sim C$	4–7	CP
9.	$\sim A \vee \sim C$	8	CE

4.
| 1. | $(A \cdot B) \supset C$ | | |
| 2. | $\sim B \supset C$ | | |

    3. $(C \cdot A) \equiv E$

    4. A AP

    5. $A \supset (B \supset C)$ 1   Exp

    6. $B \supset C$ 4,5 MP

    7. C 2,6 Cnvrg

    8. $C \cdot A$ 4,7 Conj

    9. E 3,8 BI

    10. $A \supset E$ 4–9 CP

6.   **1.** $[(A \cdot B) \vee C] \vee D$

    2. $\sim D \vee E$

    3. $\sim A$

    4. $[(A \cdot B) \vee C] \vee E$ 1,2 CC

    5. $(A \cdot B) \vee (C \vee E)$ 4 Assoc

    6. $\sim(A \cdot B)$ 3 Poll

    7. $C \vee E$ 5,6 DS

Exercise 8i

2(b).1. $p \vee q$

    2. p

    3. $q \vee p$

    4. $p \supset (q \vee p)$

    5. q

    6. $q \vee p$

    7. $q \supset (q \vee p)$

    8. $(q \vee p) \vee (q \vee p)$

    9. $q \vee p$

The other half of the equivalence 2(b) is established in the same way.

4.   **1.** $\sim p \vee q$

    2. $\sim p$ AP

    3. p AP

    4. $\sim q$ AP

    5. $p \cdot \sim p$ Conj

    6. q IP

    7. $p \supset q$ CP

    8. $\sim p \supset (p \supset q)$ CP

    9. q AP

    10. p AP

    11. $q \vee q$ Red

    12. q Red

    13. $p \supset q$ CP

    14. $q \supset (p \supset q)$ CP

    15. $(p \supset q) \vee (p \supset q)$ CD

    16. $p \supset q$ Red

    1. $p \supset q$

    2. $\sim(\sim p \vee q)$ AP

    3. $\sim p$ AP

4.	$\sim p \lor q$	Add
5.	$(\sim p \lor q) \cdot \sim(\sim p \lor q)$	Conj
6.	p	IP
7.	q	MP
8.	$\sim p \lor q$	Add
9.	$(\sim p \lor q) \cdot \sim(\sim p \lor q)$	Conj
10.	$\sim p \lor q$	IP

6.

$p \supset (q \supset r)$ $(p \cdot q) \supset r$

$p \cdot q$ p
p q
q $p \cdot q$
$q \supset r$ r
r $q \supset r$
$(p \cdot q) \supset r$ $p \supset (q \supset r)$

8(a).

$p \cdot (q \lor r)$ $(p \cdot q) \lor (p \cdot r)$

p $p \cdot q$
$q \lor r$ p
q q
$p \cdot q$ $q \lor r$
$q \supset (p \cdot q)$ $p \cdot (q \lor r)$
r $(p \cdot q) \supset (p \cdot (q \cdot r))$
$p \cdot r$ $p \cdot r$
$r \supset (p \cdot r)$ p
$(p \cdot q) \lor (p \cdot r)$ r
                      $q \lor r$
                      $p \cdot (q \lor r)$
                      $(p \cdot r) \supset (p \cdot (q \lor r))$
                      $(p \cdot (q \lor r)) \lor (p \cdot (q \lor r))$
                      $p \cdot (q \lor r)$

CHAPTER 9

Exercise 9a

2. p: **F**   **4.** p: **F**   or p: **F**   **6.** p: **F**
     q: **T** q: **T** q: either q: **T**
                r: **F** r: **F** s: **T**
                s: either s: **T**

Exercise 9b

2. $p \lor q$ p: **T**   **4.** $\sim q \supset \sim p$ p: **F**
     p q: **T** $\therefore \; q \supset p$ q: **T**
     $\therefore \;\; \sim q$

6. $(p \lor q) \supset r$ p: **F**   **8.** $\sim q \supset \sim p$ p: **F**
     $\sim p \cdot \sim q$ q: **F** $\therefore \;\; q \supset p$ q: **T**
     $\therefore \;\;\; \sim r$ r: **T**

10. $(p \lor q) \supset (\sim s \supset r)$ p: **F**
  $\sim(p \lor q) \cdot s$ q: **F**
  $\therefore$ $\sim r$ r: **T**
          s: **T**

Exercise 9c

2. p: **T**
  q: **F**
  r: **T**
  Invalid

4.   **1.** $(p \lor q) \supset (r \cdot s)$
   2. $\sim r$
   3. $\sim r \lor \sim s$ 2   Add
   4. $\sim(r \cdot s)$ 3   DeM
   5. $\sim(p \lor q)$ 1,4   MT
   6. $\sim p \cdot \sim q$ 5   DeM
   7. $\sim p$ 6   Simp

6.   **1.** $(p \cdot r) \lor s$
   2. $\sim r \cdot (q \supset \sim s)$
   3. $\sim r$ 2   Simp
   4. $q \supset \sim s$ 2   Simp
   5. $\sim p \lor \sim r$ 3   Add
   6. $\sim(p \cdot r)$ 5   DeM
   7. s 1,6   DS
   8. $\sim\sim s$ 7   DN
   9. $\sim q$ 4,8   MT

8. p: **T**
  q: **T**
  r: **T**
  s: **F**
  Invalid

Exercise 9d

2. $\sim p \supset \sim q$ p: **T**
    p q: **F**
    $\therefore$ q
    Invalid

4.   **1.** $\sim(T \cdot S) \supset \sim W$
   2. $\sim T$
   3. $\sim T \lor \sim S$ 2   Add
   4. $\sim(T \cdot S)$ 3   DeM
   5. $\sim W$ 1,4   MP

6. $p \supset \sim(q \cdot r)$ p: **F**
  $q \cdot \sim r$ q: **T**
  $\therefore$ p r: **F**
  Invalid

Exercise 9e

2. **1.** $A \cdot \sim B$
  2. $A \supset C$
  3. $C \supset (B \lor \sim A)$
  4. A 1   Simp
  5. C 2,4   MP
  6. $B \lor \sim A$ 3,5   MP
  7. $\sim B$ 1   Simp
  8. $\sim A$ 6,7   DS
  9. $A \cdot \sim A$ 4,8   Conj

4. **1.** $A \lor B$
  2. $A \supset C$
  3. $(A \cdot C) \supset B$
  4. $B \supset (A \cdot \sim C)$
  5. $\sim A \lor C$ 2   CE
  6. $\sim A \lor \sim\sim C$ 5   DN
  7. $\sim(A \cdot \sim C)$ 6   DeM
  8. $\sim B$ 4,7   MT
  9. A 1,8   DS
  10. C 2,9   MP
  11. $A \cdot C$ 9,10   Conj
  12. B 3,11   MP
  13. $B \cdot \sim B$ 8,12   Conj

6. **1.** $A \lor (C \cdot B)$
  2. $\sim B$
  3. $A \supset (B \cdot \sim D)$
  4. $\sim C \lor \sim B$ 2   Add
  5. $\sim(C \cdot B)$ 4   DeM
  6. A 1,5   DS
  7. $B \cdot \sim D$ 3,6   MP
  8. B 7   Simp
  9. $B \cdot \sim B$ 2,8   Conj

8. **1.** $(A \lor C) \supset (B \supset D)$
  2. $E \supset (A \cdot B)$
  3. $F \supset (B \cdot C)$
  4. $(E \cdot \sim D) \lor (F \cdot \sim D)$
  5. $(\sim D \cdot E) \lor (\sim D \cdot F)$ 4   Comm
  6. $\sim D \cdot (E \lor F)$ 5   Dist
  7. $E \lor F$ 6   Simp
  8. $(A \cdot B) \lor (B \cdot C)$ 2,3,7   CD
  9. $(B \cdot A) \lor (B \cdot C)$ 8   Comm
  10. $B \cdot (A \lor C)$ 9   Dist
  11. $A \lor C$ 10   Simp
  12. $B \supset D$ 1,11   MP
  13. B 10   Simp
  14. D 12,13   Simp

15.	$\sim D$	6	Simp
16.	$D \cdot \sim D$	14,15	Conj

Exercise 9f

2. **1.** L
　　2. $L \supset (W \cdot A)$
　　3. $\sim W$
　　4. $\sim A$
　　5. $W \cdot A$　　　　　　　　　　　　MP
　　6. W　　　　　　　　　　　　　　Simp
　　7. $W \cdot \sim W$　　　　　　　　　　Conj

4. **1.** $\sim H \supset \sim S$
　　2. $A \supset B$
　　3. $B \supset E$
　　4. $\sim S \supset E$
　　5. $\sim J \supset \sim H$
　　6. $\sim A \supset \sim J$
　　7. $\sim E$
　　8. $\sim\sim S$　　　　　　　　　　　　MT
　　9. $\sim\sim H$　　　　　　　　　　　　MT
　　10. $\sim\sim J$　　　　　　　　　　　MT
　　11. $\sim\sim A$　　　　　　　　　　　MT
　　12. A　　　　　　　　　　　　　　DN
　　13. B　　　　　　　　　　　　　　MP
　　14. E　　　　　　　　　　　　　　MP
　　15. $E \cdot \sim E$　　　　　　　　　　Conj

Exercise 9g

2. p: **F**　　**4.** p: **F**　　**6.** p:　　　**F**
　　q: **T**　　　　q: **T**　　　　q:　　　**T**
　　r: **F**　　　　　　　　　　　　r: either
　　　　　　　　　　　　　　　　　s:　　　**F**

Exercise 9h

2. p: **F**
　　q: **F**
　　s: **T**

4. **1.** $p \equiv (q \cdot s)$
　　2. $(s \cdot t) \supset r$
　　3. $(p \cdot t) \cdot \sim r$
　　4. $p \cdot t$
　　5. p　　　　　　　　　　　　　　Simp
　　6. t　　　　　　　　　　　　　　Simp
　　7. $\sim r$　　　　　　　　　　　　　Simp
　　8. $(p \supset (q \cdot s)) \cdot ((q \cdot s) \supset p)$　　Bic

9.	$p \supset (q \cdot s)$		Simp
10.	$q \cdot s$		MP
11.	s		Simp
12.	$s \cdot t$		Conj
13.	r		MP
14.	$r \cdot \sim r$		Conj

Exercise 9i

2. 1. $(p \lor q) \supset r$

    2. p AP

      3. $p \lor q$ Add

      4. r MP

    5. $p \supset r$ CP

    6. q AP

      7. $p \lor q$ Add

      8. r MP

    9. $q \supset r$ CP

    10. $(p \supset r) \cdot (q \supset r)$ Conj

    1. $(p \supset r) \cdot (q \supset r)$

    2. $p \supset r$ Simp

    3. $q \supset r$ Simp

    4. $p \lor q$ AP

    5. $r \lor r$ CD

    6. r Red

    7. $(p \lor q) \supset r$ CP

4. 1. $\sim(p \equiv q)$

    2. $\sim[(p \supset q) \cdot (q \supset p)]$ Bic

    3. $\sim(p \supset q) \lor \sim(q \supset p)$ DeM

    4. $\sim(p \supset q)$ AP

    5. $\sim(\sim p \lor q)$ CE

    6. $\sim\sim p \cdot \sim q$ DeM

    7. $p \cdot \sim q$ DN

    8. p AP

    9. $\sim q$ 7   Simp

    10. $p \supset \sim q$ 8–9   CP

    11. $\sim q$ AP

    12. p 7   Simp

    13. $\sim q \supset p$ 11,12   CP

    14. $(p \supset \sim q) \cdot (\sim q \supset p)$ Conj

    15. $p \equiv \sim q$ Bic

    16. $\sim(p \supset q) \supset (p \equiv \sim q)$ CP

    17. $\sim(q \supset p)$ AP

    18. $\sim(\sim q \lor p)$ 17   CE

    19. $\sim\sim q \cdot \sim p$ 18   DeM

    20. $q \cdot \sim p$ 19   DN

    21. q AP

22.	$\sim p$	20	Simp
23.	$q \supset \sim p$	21–22	CP
24.	$\sim\sim p \supset \sim q$	23	Contra
25.	$p \supset \sim q$	24	DN
26.	$\sim p$		AP
27.	q	20	Simp
28.	$\sim p \supset q$	26–27	CP
29.	$\sim q \supset \sim\sim p$	28	Contra
30.	$\sim q \supset p$	29	DN
31.	$(p \supset \sim q) \cdot (\sim q \supset p)$	25,30	Conj
32.	$p \equiv \sim q$	31	Bic
33.	$\sim(q \supset p) \supset (p \equiv \sim q)$	17–32	CP
34.	$(p \equiv \sim q) \vee (p \equiv \sim q)$	3,16,33	CD
35.	$p \equiv \sim q$	34	Red

1.	$p \equiv \sim q$	
2.	$(p \supset \sim q) \cdot (\sim q \supset p)$	Bic
3.	$p \supset \sim q$	Simp
4.	$\sim q \supset p$	Simp
5.	$p \equiv q$	AP
6.	$(p \supset q) \cdot (q \supset p)$	Bic
7.	$p \supset q$	Simp
8.	$q \supset p$	Simp
9.	p	AP
10.	q	MP
11.	$\sim q$	MP
12.	$q \cdot \sim q$	Conj
13.	$\sim p$	IP
14.	$\sim q$	MT
15.	$\sim\sim q$	MT
16.	$\sim q \cdot \sim\sim q$	Conj
17.	$\sim(p \equiv q)$	IP

6.	**1.**	$p \equiv q$	Bic
	2.	$(p \supset q) \cdot (q \supset p)$	Comm
	3.	$(q \supset p) \cdot (p \supset q)$	Bic
	4.	$q \equiv p$	

8.	**1.**	$(p \vee q) \cdot \sim(s \vee r)$	DeM
	2.	$(p \vee q) \cdot (\sim s \cdot \sim r)$	Comm
	3.	$(p \vee q) \cdot (\sim r \cdot \sim s)$	Assoc
	4.	$[(p \vee q) \cdot \sim r] \cdot \sim s$	Comm
	5.	$[\sim r \cdot (p \vee q)] \cdot s$	Dist

6. $[(\sim r \cdot p) \vee (\sim r \cdot q)] \cdot \sim s$ Comm

7. $[(p \cdot \sim r) \vee (q \cdot \sim r)] \cdot \sim s$

Exercise 9j

2. p: F   **4.** p: F   **6.** p: F   or p: T   **8.** p: F
    q: either q: either q: T q: F q: F
    r: F r: F r: F r: F r: F

Exercise 9k

2. Equivalent (like Exercise 9i, Problem 4)
3. p: T
     q: T
     r: F

4. **1.** $(p \supset q) \vee r$ CE

     2. $(\sim p \vee q) \vee r$ Assoc

     3. $\sim p \vee (q \vee r)$ CE

     4. $p \supset (q \vee r)$

6. Equivalent
     $p \vee \sim(q \vee r)$ DeM

     $p \vee (\sim q \cdot \sim r)$ Dist

     $(p \vee \sim q) \cdot (p \vee \sim r)$ Comm

     $(\sim q \vee p) \cdot (\sim r \vee p)$ CE

     $(q \supset p) \cdot (r \supset p)$

8. Equivalent
     1. $p \supset (p \vee r)$
     2. $\sim(q \vee \sim q)$ AP
     3. $\sim q \cdot \sim\sim q$ DeM
     4. $q \vee \sim q$ IP
     1. $q \vee \sim q$
     2. p AP
     3. $p \vee r$ Add
     4. $p \supset (p \vee r)$ CP

Exercise 9l

2. $p \cdot \sim(p \vee q)$ AP
     p Simp
     $\sim(p \vee q)$ Simp

$\sim p \cdot \sim q$　　　　　　　　　　　　　　　　　　DeM
$\sim p$　　　　　　　　　　　　　　　　　　　　Simp
$p \cdot \sim p$　　　　　　　　　　　　　　　　　　Conj
$\sim (p \cdot \sim (p \lor q))$　　　　　　　　　　　　IP

4.　　$p \cdot (\sim p \lor q)$　　　　　　　　　　　　AP
　　　　p　　　　　　　　　　　　　　　　　Simp
　　　　$\sim p \lor q$　　　　　　　　　　　　　　Simp
　　　　$\sim\sim p$　　　　　　　　　　　　　　　DN
　　　　q　　　　　　　　　　　　　　　　　DS
　　　　$q \supset r$　　　　　　　　　　　　　　　AP
　　　　r　　　　　　　　　　　　　　　　　MP
　　　　p　　　　　　　　　　　　　　　　　AP
　　　　$q \cdot r$　　　　　　　　　　　　　　　Conj
　　　　$p \supset (q \cdot r)$　　　　　　　　　　　　CP
　　　$(q \supset r) \supset (p \supset (q \cdot r))$　　　　　　CP
　　$(p \cdot (\sim p \lor q)) \supset [(q \supset r) \supset (p \supset (q \cdot r))]$　CP

6.　**1.** $p \equiv q$　　　　　　　　　　　　　　AP
　　2. $(p \supset q) \cdot (q \supset p)$　　　　　　　2　Bic
　　3. $p \supset q$　　　　　　　　　　　　3　Simp
　　4. $q \supset p$　　　　　　　　　　　　3　Simp
　　5. r　　　　　　　　　　　　　　　AP
　　6. $r \supset r$　　　　　　　　　　　　5–5　CP
　　7. $p \lor r$　　　　　　　　　　　　AP
　　8. $q \lor r$　　　　　　　　　　　3,6,7　CD
　　9. $(p \lor r) \supset (q \lor r)$　　　　　　7,8　CP
　10. $q \lor r$　　　　　　　　　　　　AP
　11. $p \lor r$　　　　　　　　　　4,6,10　CD
　12. $(q \lor r) \supset (p \lor r)$　　　　　10–11　CP
　13. $[(p \lor r) \supset (q \lor r)] \cdot [(q \lor r) \supset (p \lor r)]$　9,12　Conj
　14. $(p \lor r) \equiv (q \lor r)$　　　　　　13　Bic
　15. $(p \equiv q) \supset [(p \lor r) \equiv (q \lor r)]$　　1–14　CP

8.　　p　　　　　　　　　　　　　　　　AP
　　　$q \cdot p$　　　　　　　　　　　　　　AP
　　　q　　　　　　　　　　　　　　　　Simp
　　　$(q \cdot p) \supset q$　　　　　　　　　　CP
　　　q　　　　　　　　　　　　　　　　AP
　　　$q \cdot p$　　　　　　　　　　　　　Conj
　　　$q \supset (q \cdot p)$　　　　　　　　　　CP
　　　$((q \cdot p) \supset q) \cdot (q \supset (q \cdot p))$　　　Conj
　　　$(q \cdot p) \equiv q$　　　　　　　　　　Bic
　　$p \supset [(q \cdot p) \equiv q]$　　　　　　　CP

10.　**1.** $p \equiv q$　　　　　　　　　　　　AP
　　2. $(p \supset q) \cdot (q \supset p)$　　　　　　1　Bic
　　3. $p \supset q$　　　　　　　　　　　　2　Simp
　　4. $q \supset p$　　　　　　　　　　　　2　Simp
　　5. $\sim (p \cdot q)$　　　　　　　　　　　AP
　　6. $\sim p \lor \sim q$　　　　　　　　　　5　DeM

7.	$p \supset \sim q$	6	CE
8.	$\sim q \supset \sim p$	3	Contra
9.	$p \supset \sim p$	7,8	HS
10.	$\sim p \lor \sim p$	9	CE
11.	$\sim p$	10	Red
12.	$\sim q$	4,11	MT
13.	$\sim p \cdot \sim q$	11,12	Conj
14.	$\sim(p \cdot q) \supset (\sim p \cdot \sim q)$		CP
15.	$\sim\sim(p \cdot q) \lor (\sim p \cdot \sim q)$		CE
16.	$(p \cdot q) \lor (\sim p \cdot \sim q)$		DN
17.	$(p \equiv q) \supset ((p \cdot q) \lor (\sim p \cdot \sim q))$	1–16	CP
18.	$(p \cdot q) \lor (\sim p \cdot \sim q))$		AP
19.	p		AP
20.	$\sim\sim p$		DN
21.	$\sim\sim p \lor \sim\sim q$		Add
22.	$\sim(\sim p \cdot \sim q)$		DeM
23.	$p \cdot q$	18,22	DS
24.	q		Simp
25.	$p \supset q$		CP
26.	q		AP
27.	$\sim\sim q$		DN
28.	$\sim\sim p \lor \sim\sim q$		Add
29.	$\sim(\sim p \cdot \sim q)$		DeM
30.	$p \cdot q$	18,29	DS
31.	p		Simp
32.	$q \supset p$		CP
33.	$(p \supset q) \cdot (q \supset p)$		Conj
34.	$p \equiv q$		Bic
35.	$((p \cdot q) \lor (\sim p \cdot \sim q)) \supset (p \equiv q))$		CP
36.	$(p \equiv q) \equiv ((p \cdot q) \lor (\sim p \cdot \sim q))$	17,35	Conj, Bic

12.	$\sim(r \supset p)$	AP
	$\sim(\sim r \lor p)$	CE
	$\sim\sim r \cdot \sim p$	DeM
	$\sim\sim r$	Simp
	r	DN
	$\sim p$	Simp
	$\sim p \lor q$	Add
	$p \supset q$	CE
	$\sim q \lor r$	Add
	$q \supset r$	CE
	$(p \supset q) \cdot (q \supset r)$	Conj
	$\sim(r \supset p) \supset ((p \supset q) \cdot (q \supset r))$	CP
	$\sim\sim(r \supset p) \lor ((p \supset q \cdot (q \supset r))$	CE
	$(r \supset p) \lor ((p \supset q) \cdot (q \supset r))$	DN
	$((p \supset q) \cdot (q \supset r)) \lor (r \supset p)$	Comm
14.	$p \cdot \sim p$	AP
	$\sim q$	AP

$(p \lor p) \cdot \sim p$	1	Red
$p \cdot \sim p$	3	Red
q		IP
$(p \cdot \sim p) \supset q$		CP

Exercise 9m

2.
1.	$(p \supset (q \cdot r)) \cdot \sim (r \lor \sim p)$		
2.	$p \supset (q \cdot r)$		Simp
3.	$\sim (r \lor \sim p)$		Simp
4.	$\sim r \cdot \sim \sim p$		DeM
5.	$\sim r$		Simp
6.	$\sim \sim p$		Simp
7.	p		DN
8.	$q \cdot r$		MP
9.	r		Simp
10.	$r \cdot \sim r$		Conj

4.
1.	$((p \equiv \sim q) \equiv \sim p) \equiv \sim q$		
2.	$[((p \equiv \sim q) \equiv \sim p) \supset \sim q] \cdot$ $[\sim q \supset ((p \equiv \sim q) \equiv \sim p)]$	1	Bic
3.	$((p \equiv \sim q) \equiv \sim p) \supset \sim q$	2	Simp
4.	$\sim q \supset ((p \equiv \sim q) \equiv \sim p)$	2	Simp
5.	$\sim q$		AP
6.	$(p \equiv \sim q) \equiv \sim p$	4,5	MP
7.	$(p \equiv \sim q) \supset \sim p$	6	Bic, Simp
8.	$\sim p \supset (p \equiv \sim q)$	6	Bic, Simp
9.	$\sim p$		AP
10.	$p \equiv \sim q$	8,9	MP
11.	$(p \supset \sim q) \cdot (\sim q \supset p)$	10	Bic
12.	$\sim q \supset p$	11	Simp
13.	p	5,12	MP
14.	$p \cdot \sim p$	9,14	Conj
15.	p	9–14	IP
16.	$\sim (p \equiv \sim q)$	7,15	MT,DN
17.	$q \lor p$	15	Add
18.	$\sim \sim q \lor p$	17	DN
19.	$\sim q \supset p$	18	CE
20.	$\sim p \lor \sim q$	5	Add
21.	$p \supset \sim q$	20	CE
22.	$(p \supset \sim q) \cdot (\sim q \supset p)$	19,21	Conj
23.	$p \equiv \sim q$	22	Bic
24.	$(p \equiv \sim q) \cdot \sim (p \equiv \sim q)$	16,23	Conj
25.	q	5–24	IP
26.	$\sim ((p \equiv \sim q) \equiv \sim p)$	3,25	MT,DN
27.	$\sim p$		AP
28.	$\sim p \lor \sim q$	27	Add
29.	$p \supset \sim q$	28	CE
30.	$q \lor p$	25	Add

31.	$\sim\sim q \lor p$	30	DN
32.	$\sim q \supset p$	31	CE
33.	$(p \supset \sim q) \cdot (\sim q \supset p)$	27,32	Conj
34.	$p \equiv \sim q$	33	Bic
35.	$\sim p \supset (p \equiv \sim q)$	27–34	CP
36.	$p \equiv \sim q$		AP
37.	$(p \supset \sim q) \cdot (\sim q \supset p)$	36	Bic
38.	$p \supset \sim q$	37	Simp
39.	$\sim p$	25,38	DN,MT
40.	$(p \equiv \sim q) \supset \sim p$	36–39	CP
41.	$[(p \equiv \sim q) \supset \sim p] \cdot [\sim p \supset (p \equiv \sim q)]$	35,40	Conj
42.	$(p \equiv \sim q) \equiv \sim p$	41	Bic
43.	$[(p \equiv \sim q) \equiv \sim p] \cdot \sim[(p \equiv \sim q) \equiv \sim p]$	26,42	Conj

Exercise 9n

	Making it true	Making it false
2.	p: T	p: F
		q: F
4.	p: T or p: F	p: T
	q: T	q: F
6.	p: F or p: F or r: T	p: T
	q: F r: F	q: either
		r: F

Exercise 9o

2.
$$p \cdot q$$
$$p$$
$$p \lor q$$
$$\overline{(p \cdot q) \supset (p \lor q)}$$
Tautologous

4.	p: F	p: F	*Contingent*
	q: T	q: F	
	Makes it false	Makes it true	

6.
	1.	$(\sim p \cdot \sim q) \equiv (p \lor q)$	
	2.	$[(\sim p \cdot \sim q) \supset (p \lor q)] \cdot [(p \lor q) \supset (\sim p \cdot \sim q)]$	Bic
	3.	$(\sim p \cdot \sim q) \supset (p \lor q)$	Simp
	4.	$(p \lor q) \supset (\sim p \cdot \sim q)$	Simp
	5.	$p \lor q$	AP
	6.	$\sim p \cdot \sim q$	MP
	7.	$\sim p$	Simp
	8.	$\sim q$	Simp
	9.	q	DS
	10.	$q \cdot \sim q$	Conj
	11.	$\sim(p \lor q)$	IP
	12.	$\sim p \cdot \sim q$	DeM

13. $p \lor q$ MP
14. $(p \lor q) \cdot \sim(p \lor q)$ Conj
Contradictory

CHAPTER 10

Exercise 10a

1. Pa
2. $\sim Pc$
3. $Pa \cdot Pg$
4. $\sim(Pg \lor Pc)$
5. Tga
6. $Tga \cdot Tba$
7. $Sge \lor Sae$
8. $Sge \cdot \sim Sae$
9. $Sge \supset \sim(Sae \lor Sle)$
10. $Pg \cdot (Tcg \cdot Scg)$

Exercise 10c

1. $(\forall x{:}\ Cx)Ex$
2. $\sim(\forall x{:}\ Cx)Ex$
3. $(\forall x{:}\ Cx)Ex \cdot \sim Ch$
4. $Hh \cdot (\forall x{:}\ Hx)\sim Cx$
5. $(\forall x{:}\ Hx)Ex \cdot (\forall x{:}\ Hx)Bx$
   or
   $(\forall x{:}\ Hx)(Ex \cdot Bx)$
6. $(\forall x{:}\ Hx)Ix \cdot \sim(\forall x{:}\ Hx)Gx$
7. $(\forall x{:}\ Hx \cdot Ex)Gx$
8. $(\forall x{:}\ Hx)[Ex \lor Gx]$
9. $(\forall x{:}\ Px)Kxb$
10. $(\forall x{:}\ Px)Lxb \lor \sim(\forall x{:}\ Px)Kxb$
11. $(\forall x{:}\ Px)Kbx \cdot \sim(\forall x{:}\ Px)Lbx$
12. $(\forall x{:}\ Px)\sim Lbx$
13. $(\forall x{:}\ Px \cdot Gx)Lbx$
14. $(\forall x{:}\ Px \cdot Kxb)Lxb$
15. $(\forall x{:}\ Hx \cdot Gx)[Lxb \lor \sim Kxb]$

Exercise 10e

1. $(\exists x{:}\ Tx)Sx$
2. $(\exists x{:}\ Tx)\sim Sx$

3. $(\exists x\colon Tx)[Sx \cdot Cx]$
4. $(\exists x\colon Tx \cdot Sx)Cx$
5. $(\exists x\colon Tx \cdot {\sim}Sx)Cx$
6. $(\exists x\colon Tx \cdot Sx)Cx \cdot {\sim}(\forall x\colon Tx \cdot Sx)Cx$
7. $(Ta \cdot {\sim}Ca) \cdot Sa$
8. $(\exists x\colon Tx \cdot Kxa) \sim Sx$
9. $(\exists x\colon Tx \cdot Cx)Kax$
10. ${\sim}(\forall x\colon Tx \cdot Kax)Sx \cdot (\exists x\colon Tx \cdot Kax)Sx$

Exercise 10g

1. Aj
2. $(\forall x\colon Mx)Ax$
3. $(\forall x\colon Px \cdot Ax)Sxj$
4. $(\exists x\colon Px) \sim Ax$
5. $(\forall x\colon Px) \sim Ax$
6. $(\forall x\colon {\sim}Mx) \sim Ax$
   or
   $(\forall x\colon Ax)Mx$
7. $(\forall x\colon Px)Kxj$
8. ${\sim}(\forall x\colon Px)Kjx$
9. $(\exists x\colon Mx \cdot {\sim}Ax)Kjx$
10. $(\forall x\colon Px \cdot Kjx)Mx$
11. $(\forall x\colon Ex)Lxj$
12. $(\forall x\colon Ex)Sjx$
13. ${\sim}(\forall x\colon Ex)Ljx$
14. $(\forall x\colon Ex) \sim Ljx$
15. $(\forall x\colon Ex) \sim Ax$
16. $(\exists x\colon Ex \cdot {\sim}Ax)Kjx$
17. $(\exists x\colon Ex \cdot Kjx)Sxj$
18. $(\forall x\colon Px \cdot Kjx) \sim Sxj$
19. $(\forall x\colon {\sim}Mx) \sim Sxj$
20. $(\forall x\colon {\sim}(Mx \cdot Lxj)) \sim Sxj$

Exercise 10i

1. ${\sim}(\forall x\colon Px)Ljx$
2. $(\exists x\colon Px)(\forall y\colon Py)Lxy$
3. $(\forall x\colon Px) \sim (\forall y\colon Py)Lxy$
4. $(\forall x\colon Px)(\forall y\colon Py) \sim Lxy$
5. $(\forall x\colon Px \cdot Lxx)Wx$
6. $(\forall x\colon {\sim}Wx) \sim (\forall y\colon Py)Lxy$
7. $(\forall x\colon {\sim}Wx) \sim Lxx$
8. ${\sim}Ljj \cdot (\exists x\colon Px)Lxj$
9. ${\sim}Ljj \cdot (\exists x\colon Px)Lxx$
10. $(\forall x\colon Px) \sim Lxx$
11. $(\forall x\colon Px \cdot Lxx)Sxj$
12. $(\forall x\colon Px \cdot Lxx)(\forall y\colon Fy)Sxy$

13. $(\forall x: Px \cdot Lxx)(\forall y: Py \cdot \sim Lyy)Sxy$
14. $(\forall x: Fx)(\exists y: By)Rxy$
15. $(\exists x: Px)(\forall y: By)Rxy$
16. $(\forall x: \sim Fx)[\sim Wx \cdot \sim(\forall y: Iy)Rxy]$
or
$(\forall x: \sim Fx) \sim Wx \cdot (\forall x: \sim Fx) \sim(\forall y: Iy)Rxy$
17. $(\forall x: Fx)(\exists y: Py)Lxy$
18. $(\forall x: Fx)(\exists y: Iy)Rxy \cdot (\exists x: Fx)(\forall y: By) \sim Rxy$
19. $(\exists x: Px)[(\forall y: By \cdot (Rjy \lor Rby))Rxy \cdot (Sjx \cdot Sbx)]$
20. $(\exists x: Px)(\forall y: By \cdot (\exists z: Fz)Rzy)Rxy$
or
$(\exists x: Px)(\forall z: Fz)(\forall y: By \cdot Rzy)Rxy$

CHAPTER 11

Exercise 11b

2. **1.** $Ha \cdot Gb$
    2. $Ha \supset Ja$
    3. $Gb \supset Jb$
    4. Ha Simp
    5. Ja MP
    6. $(\exists x: Hx)Jx$ EQI
    7. Gb Simp
    8. Jb MP
    9. $(\exists x: Gx)Jx$ EQI
   10. $(\exists x: Hx)Jx \cdot (\exists x: Gx)Jx$ Conj

4. **1.** $(\forall x: Ax)Bx$
    2. $\sim Ba$
    3. Aa AP
    4. Ba UQE
    5. $Ba \cdot \sim Ba$ Conj
    6. $\sim Aa$ IP

6. **1.** $Tb \cdot Fb$
    2. $(\forall x: Tx)Rx$
    3. $(\forall x: Rx \cdot Fx)Mx$
    4. Tb Simp
    5. Rb UQE
    6. Fb Simp
    7. $Rb \cdot Fb$ Conj
    8. Mb UQE
    9. $(\exists x: Tx)Mx$ EQI

8. **1.** $(\forall x: Ax \cdot Bx)Cx$
    2. $(\forall x: Cx)[Dx \lor Ex]$
    3. $\sim Ea$
    4. $Aa \cdot \sim Da$ AP

	5.	Aa		Simp
	6.	$\sim Da$		Simp
	7.	Ba		AP
	8.	$Aa \cdot Ba$		Conj
	9.	Ca	1,8	UQE
	10.	$Da \vee Ea$	2,9	UQE
	11.	Ea	6,10	DS
	12.	$Ea \cdot \sim Ea$	3,11	Conj
	13.	$\sim Ba$		IP
	14.	$(Aa \cdot \sim Da) \supset \sim Ba$		CP
10.	1.	Rab		
	2.	$Pa \cdot Pb$		
	3.	$(\exists x: Px)Rxb \supset (\forall x: Px)Rxb$		
	4.	Pa		Simp
	5.	$(\exists x: Px)Rxb$		EQI
	6.	$(\forall x: Px)Rxb$		MP
	7.	Pb		Simp
	8.	Rbb		UQE
12.	1.	Rab		
	2.	$(\forall x: Rxb)Fx$		
	3.	$\sim Fb$		
	4.	Fa	1,2	UQE
	5.	$(\exists y: \sim Fy)Ray$	1,3	EQI
	6.	$(\exists x: Fx)(\exists y: \sim Fy)Rxy$	4,5	EQI
14.	1.	$(\forall x: Fx)(\forall y: Gy)Rxy$		
	2.	$Fa \cdot (Gb \cdot Gc)$		
	3.	$\sim Rbc$		
	4.	Fa		Simp
	5.	$Gb \cdot Gc$		Simp
	6.	Gb		Simp
	7.	Gc		Simp
	8.	Fb		AP
	9.	$(\forall y: Gy)Rby$	1,8	UQE
	10.	Rbc	7,9	UQE
	11.	$Rbc \cdot \sim Rbc$		Conj
	12.	$\sim Fb$		IP
	13.	$(\forall y: Gy)Ray$	1,4	UQE
	14.	Rab	6,13	UQE
	15.	$(\exists y: Fy)Ryb$	4,14	EQI
	16.	$(\exists x: \sim Fx)(\exists y: Fy)Ryx$	12,15	EQI
16.	1.	Hb		
	2.	$(\forall x: Fx)Gx$		
	3.	$(Ga \cdot Hb) \supset Rab$		
	4.	$(\forall x: Hx)Jx$		
	5.	Fa		AP
	6.	Ga	2,5	UQE
	7.	$Ga \cdot Hb$		Conj

8.	Rab	3,7	MP
9.	Jb	1,4	UQE
10.	$(\exists y: Jy)Ray$	8,9	EQI
11.	$(\exists x: Fx)(\exists y: Jy)Rxy$	5,10	EQI
12.	$Fa \supset (\exists x: Fx)(\exists y: Jy)Rxy$		CP

18.
1.	$Fa \cdot Ga$		
2.	$(\forall x: Gx)(Hx \lor {\sim}Fx)$		
3.	$(\forall x: Fx \cdot Hx)(\exists y: Gy)Rxy$		
4.	Fa		Simp
5.	Ga		Simp
6.	$Ha \lor {\sim}Fa$	2,5	UQE
7.	Ha	4,6	DS +
8.	$Fa \cdot Ha$		Conj
9.	$(\exists y: Gy)Ray$	3,8	UQE
10.	$(\exists x: Gx)(\exists y: Gy)Rxy$	5,9	EQI

Exercise 11c

2.
1.	$(\exists x: Fx)Gx$		
2.	Fc	1	EQE
3.	Gc	1	EQE
4.	$(\exists x: Gx)Fx$	2,3	EQI

4.
1.	$(\exists x: Fx)Gx \supset (Fa \cdot Ja)$		
2.	$(\exists x: Fx)Ex$		
3.	$(\forall x: Ex)[Gx \cdot Hx]$		
4.	$(\forall x: Jx)Kx$		
5.	Fb	2	EQE
6.	Eb	2	EQE
7.	$Gb \cdot Hb$	3,6	UQE
8.	Gb		Simp
9.	$(\exists x: Fx)Gx$	5,8	EQI
10.	$Fa \cdot Ja$	1,9	MP
11.	Ja		Simp
12.	Ka	4,11	UQE
13.	Fa	10	Simp
14.	$(\exists x: Fx)Kx$	12,13	EQI

6.
$Fa \cdot Ga$		
$(\forall x: Gx)[Hx \lor {\sim}Fx]$		
$(\forall x: Fx \cdot Hx)(\exists y: Ky)Rxy$		
$(\forall x: Kx)Jx)$		
Fa		
Ga		
$Ha \lor {\sim}Fa$		UQE
Ha		DS +
$Fa \cdot Ha$		Conj
$(\exists y: Ky)Ray$		UQU
Kb		EQE
Rab		EQE

	Jb		UQE	
	(∃*y*: *Jy*)*Ray*		EQI	
	(∃*x*: *Gx*)(∃*y*: *Ky*)*Rxy*		EQI	
8.	**1.**	(∃*x*: *Fx*)(∃*y*: *Gy*)*Rxy*		
	2.	(∀*x*: *Fx*)*Hx*		
	3.	(∀*x*: *Gx*)*Kx*		
	4.	*Fa*	1	EQE
	5.	(∃*y*: *Gy*)*Ray*	1	EQE
	6.	*Gb*	5	EQE
	7.	*Rab*	5	EQE
	8.	*Kb*	3,6	UQE
	9.	*Ha*	2,4	UQE
	10.	(∃*y*: *Ky*)*Ray*	7,8	EQI
	11.	(∃*x*: *Hx*)(∃*y*: *Ky*)*Rxy*	9,10	EQI
10.	**1.**	(∃*x*: *Fx* · (∃*y*: *Gy*)*Rxy*)*Rxa*		
	2.	*Ha*		
	3.	(∀*x*: (∃*y*: *Hy*)*Rxy*)*Hx*		
	4.	(∀*x*: *Hx*)(∀*y*: *Rxy*)*Ryx*		
	5.	*Fb* · (∃*y*: *Gy*)*Rby*	1	EQE
	6.	*Rba*	1	EQE
	7.	*Fb*		Simp
	8.	(∃*y*: *Gy*)*Rby*		Simpc
	9.	*Gc*	8	EQE
	10.	*Rbc*	8	EQE
	11.	(∃*y*: *Hy*)*Rby*	2,6	EQI
	12.	*Hb*	3,11	UQE
	13.	(∀*y*: *Rby*)*Ryb*	4,12	UQE
	14.	*Rcb*	10,13	UQE
	15.	(∃*y*: *Fy*)*Rcy*	7,14	EQI
	16.	(∃*x*: *Gx*)(∃*y*: *Fy*)*Rxy*	9,15	EQI
12.	**1.**	(∃*x*: *Fx*)∼*Kx*		
	2.	(∀*x*: *Gx*)(∀*y*: *Fy*)*Rxy*		
	3.	(∃*x*: *Gx*)*Kx*		
	4.	(∀*x*: *Gx* ∨ *Fx*)*Hx*		
	5.	(∀*x*: *Hx*)(∀*y*: *Hy* · *Rxy*)*Ryx*		
	6.	*Fa*	1	EQE
	7.	∼*Ka*	1	EQE
	8.	*Gb*	3	EQE
	9.	*Kb*	3	EQE
	10.	(∀*y*: *Fy*)*Rby*	2,8	UQE
	11.	*Rba*	6,10	UQE
	12.	*Gb* ∨ *Fb*	8	Add
	13.	*Hb*	4,12	UQE
	14.	*Ga* ∨ *Fa*	6	Add
	15.	*Ha*	4,14	UQE
	16.	(∀*y*: *Hy* · *Rby*)*Ryb*	5,13	UQE
	17.	*Ha* · *Rba*	11,15	Conj

18. Rab	16,17	UQE
19. $Rba \cdot Rab$	11,18	Conj
20. $(\exists y: \sim Ky)[Rby \cdot Ryb]$	7,19	EQI
21. $(\exists x: Kx)(\exists y: \sim Ky)[Rxy \cdot Ryx]$	9,20	EQI

14.
1. $(\forall x: Hx)(\forall y: Hy \cdot Rxy)[Fx \equiv \sim Fy]$		
2. $(\forall x: Hx \cdot \sim Fx)(\exists y: Hy)Rxy$		
3. $(\exists x: Fx \cdot (Gx \cdot Hx))(\exists y: Hy)Rxy$		
4. $(\forall x: Hx \cdot \sim Fx)Gx$		
5. $Fa \cdot (Ga \cdot Ha)$	3	EQE
6. $(\exists y: Hy)Ray$	3	EQE
7. Hb	6	EQE
8. Rab	6	EQE
9. Fa		Simp
10. $Ga \cdot Ha$		Simp
11. Ga		Simp
12. Ha		Simp
13. $(\forall y: Hy \cdot Ray)[Fa \equiv \sim Fy]$	1,12	UQE
14. $Hb \cdot Rab$	7,8	Conj
15. $Fa \equiv \sim Fb$	13,14	UQE
16. $(Fa \supset \sim Fb) \cdot (\sim Fb \supset Fa)$	15	Bic
17. $Fa \supset \sim Fb$		Simp
18. $\sim Fb$	9,17	MP
19. $Hb \cdot \sim Fb$		Conj
20. Gb	4,19	UQE
21. $(\exists y: Gy)Ray$	8,20	EQI
22. $(\exists x: Gx)(\exists y: Gy)Rxy$	11,21	EQI
23. $(\exists y: Hy)Rby$	2,19	UQE
24. Hc	23	EQE
25. Rbc	23	EQE
26. $(\forall y: Hy \cdot Rby)[Fb \equiv \sim Fy]$	1,7	UQE
27. $Hc \cdot Rbc$		Conj
28. $Fb \equiv \sim Fc$	26,27	UQE
29. $(Fb \supset \sim Fc) \cdot (\sim Fc \supset Fb)$		Bic
30. $\sim Fc \supset Fb$		Simp
31. Fc	18,30	MT +
32. $(\exists y: Fy)Rby$	25,31	EQI
33. $(\exists x: \sim Fx)(\exists y: Fy)Rxy$	18,32	EQI
34. $(\exists x: Gx)(\exists y: Gy)Rxy \cdot$ $(\exists x: \sim Fx)(\exists y: Fy)Rxy$	22,33	Conj

Exercise 11d

2.
1. $\sim(\exists x: Fx)(\exists y: Gy)Rxy$		
2. $(\exists x: Hx)Rxa$		
3. Ga		
4. $(\forall x: Fx)\sim(\exists y: Gy)Rxy$	1	QN
5. $(\forall x: Fx)(\forall y: Gy)\sim Rxy$	4	QN
6. Hb	2	EQE

7.	*Rba*	2	EQE
8.	*Fb*		AP
9.	(∀y: *Gy*)~*Rby*	5,8	UQE
10.	~*Rba*	3,9	UQE
11.	*Rba* · ~*Rba*		Conj
12.	~*Fb*		IP
13.	(∃x: *Hx*)~*Fx*	6,12	EQI
14.	~(∀x: *Hx*)*Fx*		QN

4.

1.	~(∃x: *Ax*)~*Bx*		
2.	(∀x: ~*Ax*)(∀y: *By*)*Lxy*		
3.	(∀x: *Bx*)~*Cx*		
4.	*Cd* · *Ae*		
5.	*Cd*		Simp
6.	*Ae*		Simp
7.	(∀x: *Ax*)*Bx*	1	QN
8.	*Be*	6,7	UQE
9.	~*Ce*	3,8	UQE
10.	*Ad*		AP
11.	*Bd*	7,10	UQE
12.	~*Cd*	3,11	UQE
13.	*Cd* · ~*Cd*		Conj
14.	~*Ad*		IP
15.	(∀y: *By*)*Ldy*	2,14	UQE
16.	*Lde*	8,15	UQE
17.	(∃x: ~*Cx*)*Ldx*	9,16	EQI

6.

1.	(∀x: *Fx*)[*Ax* ∨ *Gx*]		
2.	(∀x: *Mx*)(∀y: *Gy*)*Cyx*		
3.	~(∃x: *Mx*)*Cax*		
4.	*Mb* · *Ha*		
5.	(∀x: *Ax*)*Gx*		
6.	*Mb*		Simp
7.	*Ha*		Simp
8.	(∀x: *Mx*)~*Cax*		QN
9.	~*Cab*		UQE
10.	(∀y: *Gy*)*Cyb*		UQE
11.	*Ga*		AP
12.	*Cab*		UQE
13.	*Cab* · ~*Cab*		Conj
14.	~*Ga*		IP
15.	*Aa*		AP
16.	*Ga*		UQE
17.	*Ga* · ~*Ga*		Conj
18.	~*Aa*		IP
19.	*Fa*		AP
20.	*Aa* ∨ *Ga*		UQE
21.	*Ga*		DS
22.	*Ga* · ~*Ga*		Conj
23.	~*Fa*		IP

24.	$(\exists x: Hx)\sim Fx$	EQI
25.	$\sim(\forall x: Hx)Fx$	QN

8.

$(\forall x: Hx \cdot (\forall y: Hy)\sim Rxy)Ax$	
$(\exists x: Hx)Ax \supset (\forall y: Ay)By$	
$\sim Bc \cdot Hc$	
$\sim Bc$	Simp
Hc	Simp
$\sim(\exists y: Hy)Rcy$	AP
$(\forall y: Hy)\sim Rcy$	QN
$Hc \cdot (\forall y: Hy)\sim Rcy$	Conj
Ac	UQE
$(\exists x: Hx)Ax$	EQI
$(\forall y: Ay)By$	MP
Bc	UQE
$Bc \cdot \sim Bc$	Conj
$(\exists y: Hy)Rcy$	IP

Exercise 11e

2.

1.	$(\exists x: Hx)Fx \supset (\forall x: Hx)Gx$		
2.	$Ha \cdot \sim Ga$		AP
3.	Fa		AP
4.	Ha		Simp
5.	$(\exists x: Hx)Fx$		EQI
6.	$(\forall x: Hx)Gx$		MP
7.	Ga		UQE
8.	$\sim Ga$		Simp
9.	$Ga \cdot \sim Ga$		Conj
10.	$\sim Fa$		IP
11.	$(\forall x: Hx \cdot \sim Gx)\sim Fx$	2–10	UQI

4.

1.	$(\forall x: (\exists y: Hy)Rxy)Rxa$		
2.	$(\forall x: Gx)Rxb \cdot Gb$		
3.	$(\forall x: Gx)Hx$		AP
4.	$(\forall x: Gx)Rxb$		Simp
5.	Gb		Simp
6.	Hb		UQE
7.	Gc		AP
8.	Rcb		UQE
9.	$(\exists y: Hy)Rcy$		EQI
10.	Rca	1,9	UQE
11.	$(\forall x: Gx)Rxa$	7–10	UQI
12.	$(\forall x: Gx)Hx \supset (\forall x: Gx)Rxa$		CP

6.

$\sim(\forall x: Ax)[Bx \cdot Rxa]$	
$(\forall x: Rax)Rxa$	
$\sim(\exists x: Ax)\sim Bx$	
$(\exists x: Ax)\sim[Bx \cdot Rxa]$	QN
Ac	EQE
$\sim[Bc \cdot Rca]$	EQE
$\sim Bc \lor \sim Rca$	DeM

	$(\forall x{:}\ Ax)Bx$	QN
	Bc	UQE
	$\sim Rca$	DS +
	Rac	AP
	Rca	UQE
	$Rca \cdot \sim Rca$	Conj
	$\sim Rca$	IP
	$(\exists x{:}\ Ax)\sim Rax$	EQI
8. **1.**	$(\exists x{:}\ Ax \cdot Dxb)(\forall z{:}\ Dxz)Oz$	
2.	$Ac \cdot Dcb$	EQE
3.	$(\forall z{:}\ Dcz)Oz$	EQE
4.	Dcb	Simp
5.	Ob	UQE
10.	$(\forall x{:}\ Fx)(\forall y{:}\ Gy)\sim Rxy$	
	$(\forall x{:}\ Hx)(\forall y{:}\ Hy)Rxy$	
	$(\forall x{:}\ Fx \lor Gx)Hx$	
	Fa	AP
	$(\forall y{:}\ Gy)\sim Ray$	UQE
	$Fa \lor Ga$	Add
	Ha	UQE
	$(\forall y{:}\ Hy)Ray$	UQE
	Ga	AP
	$\sim Raa$	UQE
	Raa	UQE
	$Raa \cdot \sim Raa$	Conj
	$\sim Ga$	IP
	$(\forall x{:}\ Fx)\sim Gx$	UQI
	$\sim(\exists x{:}\ Fx)Gx$	QN
12.	$(\forall x{:}\ Fx)(\exists y{:}\ Gy)Rxy$	
	$\sim(\exists x{:}\ Gx)Rxx$	
	$(\exists x{:}\ Fx)Rxx$	
	Fa	EQE
	Raa	EQE
	$(\exists y{:}\ Fy)Ray$	EQI
	$(\exists x{:}\ Fx)(\exists y{:}\ Fy)Rxy$	EQI
	$(\exists y{:}\ Gy)Ray$	UQE
	Gb	EQE
	Rab	EQE
	$(\forall x{:}\ Gx)\sim Rxx$	QN
	$\sim Rbb$	UQE
	$(\exists y{:}\ \sim Ryy)Ray$	EQI
	$(\exists x{:}\ Rxx)(\exists y{:}\ \sim Ryy)Rxy$	EQI
	$(\exists x{:}\ Fx)(\exists y{:}\ Fy)Rxy \cdot (\exists x{:}\ Rxx)(\exists y{:}\ \sim Ryy)Rxy$	Conj
14. **1.**	$(\forall x{:}\ Fx)(\forall y{:}\ Fy \cdot Rxy)Ryx$	
2.	$Rab \cdot (Fa \cdot Fb)$	
3.	$(\forall x{:}\ (\exists y{:}\ Fy)Rxy)Rxx$	
4.	$(\exists x{:}\ Fx)\sim(\exists y{:}\ Fy)Rxy$	
5.	Rab	Simp

6. $Fa \cdot Fb$		Simp
7. Fa		Simp
8. Fb		Simp
9. $(\forall y\colon Fy \cdot Ray)Rya$	1,7	UQE
10. $Fb \cdot Rab$		Conj
11. Rba	9,10	UQE
12. $(\exists y\colon Fy)Rby$	7,11	EQI
13. Rbb	3,12	UQE
14. Fc	4	EQE
15. $\sim(\exists y\colon Fy)Rcy$	4	EQE
16. $(\forall y\colon Fy)\sim Rcy$	15	QN
17. $\sim Rcb$		UQE
18. $(\exists x\colon Fx)\sim Rxb$		EQI
19. $Fd \cdot Rbd$		AP
20. $(\forall y\colon Fy \cdot Rby)Ryb$	1,8	UQE
21. Rdb	19,20	UQE
22. $(\exists y\colon Fy)Rdy$	8,21	EQI
23. Rdd	3,22	UQE
24. $(\forall x\colon Fx \cdot Rbx)Rxx$		UQI
25. $Rbb \cdot (\exists x\colon Fx)\sim Rxb$		Conj
26. $[Rbb \cdot (\exists x\colon Fx)\sim Rxb] \cdot (\forall x\colon Fx \cdot Rbx)Rxx$		

(Lines 19–23 are bracketed together with an arrow pointing to line 19.)

16.	**1.** $(\forall x\colon Fx)Hxa$		
	2. $(\exists x\colon Gx)Hax$		
	3. $(\forall x\colon Fx \lor Gx)(\forall y\colon Hxy)(\forall z\colon Hyz)Hxz$		
	4. $Fb \cdot (\forall y\colon Fy)(\exists z\colon Gz)Hzy$		
	5. Fb		Simp
	6. Hba		UQE
	7. Gc	2	EQE
	8. Hac	2	EQE
	9. $Fb \lor Gb$		Add
	10. $(\forall y\colon Hby)(\forall z\colon Hyz)Hbz$	3,9	UQE
	11. $(\forall z\colon Haz)Hbz$	6,10	UQE
	12. Hbc	8,11	UQE
	13. $(\exists x\colon Gx)Hbx$	7,12	EQI
	14. $(\forall y\colon Fy)(\exists z\colon Gz)Hzy$		Simp
	15. $(\exists z\colon Gz)Hzb$		UQE
	16. Gm		EQE
	17. Hmb		EQE
	18. $Fm \lor Gm$		Add
	19. $(\forall y\colon Hmy)(\forall z\colon Hyz)Hmz$	3,18	UQE
	20. $(\forall z\colon Hbz)Hmz$	17,19	UQE
	21. Hmc	12,20	UQE
	22. $(\exists z\colon Gz)Hmz$		EQI
	23. $(\exists y\colon Gy)(\exists z\colon Gz)Hyz$		EQI
	24. $Hba \cdot (\exists x\colon Gx)Hbx$		Conj
	25. $[Hba \cdot (\exists x\colon Gx)Hbx] \cdot (\exists y\colon Gy)(\exists z\colon Gz)Hyz$		Conj
18.	**1.** $(\exists x\colon Fx)Rxx$		
	2. $(\forall x\colon (\exists y\colon Fy)Ryx)Gx$		
	3. $\sim(\exists x\colon Hx)Rxx$		

4. $(\forall x: Hx)\sim Rxx$		QN
5. Fc	1	EQE
6. Rcc	1	EQE
7. $(\exists y: Fy)Ryc$	5,6	EQI
8. Gc	2,7	UQE
9. $(\exists y: Fy)Gy$	5,8	EQI
10. Hc		AP
11. $\sim Rcc$	4,10	UQE
12. $Rcc \cdot \sim Rcc$		Conj
13. $\sim Hc$		IP
14. $(\exists x: Fx)\sim Hx$		EQI
15. $\sim(\forall x: Fx)Hx$		QN
16. $\sim Gb$		AP
17. $(\exists y: Fy)Ryb$		AP
18. Gb	2,17	UQE
19. $Gb \cdot \sim Gb$		Conj
20. $\sim(\exists y: Fy)Ryb$		IP
21. $(\forall y: \sim Gz)\sim(\exists y: Fy)Ryz$		UQI
22. $\sim(\forall x: Fx)Hx \cdot (\exists y: Fy) Gy$		Conj
23. $[\sim(\forall x: Fx)Hx \cdot (\exists y: Fy)Gy] \cdot$		
$(\forall z: \sim Gz) \sim(\exists y: Fy)Ryz$		Conj

Exercise 11f

2.	$(\forall x: Fx)(\forall y: Gy)Rxy$	
	$(\forall x: Hx)\sim Rxx$	
	$(\forall x: Fx)Hx$	
	$(\exists x: Fx)Gx$	
	Fb	EQE
	Gb	EQE
	Hb	UQE
	$\sim Rbb$	UQE
	$(\forall y: Gy)Rby$	UQE
	Rbb	UQE
	$Rbb \cdot \sim Rbb$	Conj
4.	$(\forall x: Fx)(\forall y: Gy)Rxy$	
	$(\exists x: Fx)(\exists y: \sim Fy)\sim Rxy$	
	$(\forall x: \sim Gx)Fx$	
	Fa	EQE
	$(\exists y: \sim Fy)\sim Ray$	EQE
	$\sim Fb$	EQE
	$\sim Rab$	EQE
	$(\forall y: Gy)Ray$	UQE
	Gb	AP
	Rab	UQE
	$Rab \cdot \sim Rab$	Conj
	$\sim Gb$	IP
	Fb	UQE
	$Fb \cdot \sim Fb$	Conj

6.   **1.** [∀x: Fx · (∀y: Hy)Rxy]~Rxx
    2. (∀x: Gx)(∀y: Gy)Rxy
    3. (∃x: Fx)Gx
    4. (∀x: Hx)Gx

5.	Fa	EQE
6.	Ga	EQE
7.	(∀y: Gy)Ray	2,6 UQE
8.	Hb	AP
9.	Gb	UQE
10.	Rab	UQE
11.	(∀y: Hy)Ray	UQI
12.	Fa · (∀y: Hy)Ray	Conj
13.	~Raa	1,12 UQE
14.	Raa	6,7 UQE
15.	Raa · ~Raa	Conj

Exercise 11g

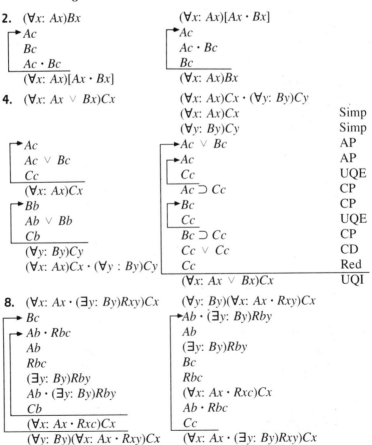

2. (∀x: Ax)Bx
    Ac
    Bc
    Ac · Bc
    (∀x: Ax)[Ax · Bx]

(∀x: Ax)[Ax · Bx]
    Ac
    Ac · Bc
    Bc
    (∀x: Ax)Bx

4. (∀x: Ax ∨ Bx)Cx

(∀x: Ax)Cx · (∀y: By)Cy
(∀x: Ax)Cx   Simp
(∀y: By)Cy   Simp

    Ac
    Ac ∨ Bc
    Cc
    (∀x: Ax)Cx
    Bb
    Ab ∨ Bb
    Cb
    (∀y: By)Cy
    (∀x: Ax)Cx · (∀y : By)Cy

Ac ∨ Bc	AP
Ac	AP
Cc	UQE
Ac ⊃ Cc	CP
Bc	CP
Cc	UQE
Bc ⊃ Cc	CP
Cc ∨ Cc	CD
Cc	Red
(∀x: Ax ∨ Bx)Cx	UQI

8. (∀x: Ax · (∃y: By)Rxy)Cx
    Bc
    Ab · Rbc
    Ab
    Rbc
    (∃y: By)Rby
    Ab · (∃y: By)Rby
    Cb
    (∀x: Ax · Rxc)Cx
    (∀y: By)(∀x: Ax · Rxy)Cx

(∀y: By)(∀x: Ax · Rxy)Cx
    Ab · (∃y: By)Rby
    Ab
    (∃y: By)Rby
    Bc
    Rbc
    (∀x: Ax · Rxc)Cx
    Ab · Rbc
    Cc
    (∀x: Ax · (∃y: By)Rxy)Cx

Exercise 11h

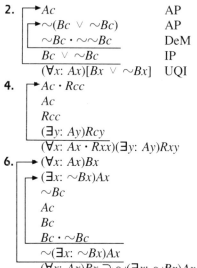

2.
```
 ┌─►Ac                        AP
 │ ┌─►~(Bc ∨ ~Bc)            AP
 │ │  ~Bc · ~~Bc             DeM
 │ └──Bc ∨ ~Bc               IP
 └────(∀x: Ax)[Bx ∨ ~Bx]     UQI
```

4.
```
 ┌─►Ac · Rcc
 │  Ac
 │  Rcc
 │  (∃y: Ay)Rcy
 └──(∀x: Ax · Rxx)(∃y: Ay)Rxy
```

6.
```
 ┌─► (∀x: Ax)Bx
 │ ┌─► (∃x: ~Bx)Ax
 │ │   ~Bc
 │ │   Ac
 │ │   Bc
 │ └── Bc · ~Bc
 │     ~(∃x: ~Bx)Ax
 └─────(∀x: Ax)Bx ⊃ ~(∃x: ~Bx)Ax
```

Exercise 11i

2. (∃x: Ax · Bx)[~Bx ∨ ~Ax]
Ac · Bc
~Bc ∨ ~Ac
~(Bc · Ac)
~(Ac · Bc)
(Ac · Bc) · ~(Ac · Bc)

4. (∃x: Ax · Bx)(∀y: By)Rxy · (∀z: Bz)~Rzz
(∃x: Ax · Bx)(∀y: By)Rxy
(∀z: Bz)~Rzz
Ac · Bc
(∀y: By)Rcy
Bc
Rcc
~Rcc
Rcc · ~Rcc

6. (∃x: Ax)(∀y: Ay)[Rxy ≡ ~Rxx]
Ac
(∀y: Ay)[Rcy ≡ ~Rcc]
Rcc ≡ ~Rcc
(Rcc ⊃ ~Rcc) · (~Rcc ⊃ Rcc)
```
 ┌─►Rcc
 │  Rcc ⊃ ~Rcc
 │  ~Rcc
 └──Rcc ⊃ ~Rcc
    ~Rcc
```

$\sim$*Rcc* ⊃ *Rcc*
Rcc
Rcc · $\sim$*Rcc*

10. $\sim$(∀*x*: *Ax*)(∃*y*: *By*)*Rxy* · (∃*y*: *By*)(∀*x*: *Ax*)*Rxy*

$\sim$(∀*x*: *Ax*)(∃*y*: *By*)*Rxy*	Simp
(∃*x*: *Ax*)$\sim$(∃*y*: *By*)*Rxy*	QN
(∃*x*: *Ax*)(∀*y*: *By*)$\sim$*Rxy*	QN
(∀*y*: *By*) $\sim$*Rxy*	EQE
Ac	EQE
(∃*y*: *By*)(∀*x*: *Ax*)*Rxy*	Simp
Ba	EQE
(∀*x*: *Ax*)*Rxa*	EQE
Rca	UQI
$\sim$*Rca*	UQI
Rca · $\sim$*Rca*	Conj

CHAPTER 12

Exercise 12a

2. Consistent; model:
   Two individuals: a, b
   Aa $\sim$*Ba*   *Ca*
   Ab   *Bb* $\sim$*Cb*

4. Inconsistent

Exercise 12b

2. Inconsistent

4. Consistent; model:
   Two individuals: b, c
   Ab   *Bb*   *Cb*   *Db*
   Ac   *Bc* $\sim$*Cc*   *Dc*

Exercise 12c

2. Invalid; model:
   Two individuals: a, b
   Aa $\sim$*Ba* $\sim$*Ca* $\sim$*Da*
   Ab   *Bb* $\sim$ *Cb* $\sim$*Db*

4. Invalid; model:
   Two individuals: a, b
   Aa $\sim$*Ba* $\sim$*Ca* $\sim$*Da*
   $\sim$*Ab* $\sim$*Bb*   *Cb*   *Db*

6. Invalid; model:

   Three individuals: a, b, c

~Aa   Ba   Ca
~Ab   Bb   ~Cb
Ac   ~Bc   Cc

Exercise 12d

2. Model:
Two individuals: a, b
Aa   Ba   ~Ca
Ab   Bb   Cb
(∀x: Ax · Bx)~Cx   false
(∃x: Ax)(Bx · ~Cx)   true

4. Model:
Two individuals: a, b
Aa   Ba
Ab   ~Bb   ~Cb
(∀x: Ax)[Bx ∨ Cx]   false
(∃x: Ax)Bx ∨ (∃x: Ax)Cx   true

6. Model:
One individual: a
Aa   ~Ba   Ca
(∀x: Ax)~[Bx ∨ Cx]   *false*
(∀x: Bx)~[Ax ∨ Cx]   *true*

Exercise 12e

2. Two models:
Model I: One individual: *a*; ~*Aa*; makes sentence true
Model II: One individual: *a*; *Aa*, *Ba*, ~*Ca*; makes sentence false

4. Two models:
Model I: One individual: *a*; ~*Aa*; makes sentence false
Model II: One individual: *a*; *Aa*, *Ba*; makes sentence true

6. Two models:
Model I: One individual: *a*; ~*Aa*; makes sentence true
Model II: One individual: *a*; *Aa*, *Ca*; makes sentence false

8. Two models:
Model I: One individual: *a*; ~*Aa*; makes sentence true
Model II: One individual: *a*; *Aa*, ~*Ba*, *Ca*; makes sentence false

CHAPTER 13

Exercise 13b

1. (∀x: Ax)[Bx · Cx]

2. $(\forall x: Ax)[(\exists y: By)Rxy]$
3. $(\forall x: Ax)Bx \supset (\exists y: Cy)Dy$
4. $(\forall x: Cx \lor \sim Cx)Ax \supset (\exists y: By)By$
5. $\sim(\forall x: Ax)Bx$
6. $(\forall x: Ax)\sim Bx$
   or
   $(\forall x: Cx \lor \sim Cx)\sim(Ax \cdot Bx)$
7. $(\exists x: Ax)\sim Cx \cdot (\exists y: By)Dy$
8. $(\forall x: (\exists y: Ay \lor \sim Ay)Rxy)[(\exists y: Ay \lor \sim Ay)Ryx]$

Exercise 13c

1. **1.** $(\forall x)(Ax \supset Bx)$
    2. $(\forall x)(Bx \supset Cx)$
    3. $\sim Ca$
    4. $Aa \supset Ba$ 1   UQE
    5. $Ba \supset Ca$ 2   UQE
    6. $\sim Ba$ 3,5 MT
    7. $\sim Aa$ 4,6 MT
2. **1.** $(\exists x)(Dx \cdot Fx)$
    2. $(\forall x)[Fx \supset (Gx \lor Hx)]$
    3. $(\forall x)(\sim Hx \lor Cx)$
    4. $(\forall x)(Dx \supset \sim Cx)$
    5. $Dc \cdot Fc$ 1   EQE
    6. Dc 5   Simp
    7. Fc 5   Simp
    8. $Fc \supset (Gc \lor Hc)$ 2   UQE
    9. $Gc \lor Hc$ 7,8 MP
    10. $Dc \supset \sim Cc$ 4   UQE
    11. $\sim Cc$ 6,10 MP
    12. $\sim Hc \lor Cc$ 3   UQE
    13. $\sim Hc$ 11,12 DS
    14. Gc 9,13 DS
    15. $Gc \cdot Fc$ 7,14 Conj
    16. $(\exists x)(Gx \cdot Fx)$ 15   EQI
3. **1.** Rab
    2. $(\exists x)Rxb \supset (\forall x)Rxb$
    3. $(\exists x)Rxb$ 1   EQI
    4. $(\forall x)Rxb$ 2,3 MP
    5. Rbb 4   UQE
4. **1.** $(\exists x)Rxb$
    2. $(\forall x)(Rxb \supset Fx)$
    3. $\sim Fb$
    4. $(\exists y)\sim Fy$ 3   EQI
    5. Rcb 1   EQE
    6. $Rcb \supset Fb$ 2   UQE

	7.	Fb	5,6 MP
	8.	$(\exists x)Fx$	7 EQI
	9.	$(\exists x)Fx \cdot (\exists y){\sim}Fy$	4,8 Conj
5.	**1.**	$(\forall x)(Ax \supset Bx)$	
	2.	$(\exists x)(Ax \cdot Cx)$	
	3.	$(\forall x)(Cx \supset Dx)$	AP
	4.	$As \cdot Cs$	2 EQE
	5.	As	4 Simp
	6.	Cs	4 Simp
	7.	$As \supset Bs$	1 UQE
	8.	Bs	5,7 MP
	9.	$Cs \supset Ds$	3 UQE
	10.	Ds	6,9 MP
	11.	$Bs \cdot Ds$	8,10 Conj
	12.	$(\exists x)(Bx \cdot Dx)$	11 EQI
	13.	$(\forall x)(Cx \supset Dx) \supset (\exists x)(Bx \cdot Dx)$	3–13 CP
6.	**1.**	$(\forall x)(Fx \supset Gx)$	
	2.	$(\forall x)(Hx \supset {\sim}Gx)$	
	3.	$(\forall x)(Jx \supset Hx)$	AP
	4.	Jc	AP
	5.	$Jc \supset Hc$	3 UQE
	6.	Hc	4,5 MP
	7.	$Hc \supset {\sim}Gc$	2 UQE
	8.	${\sim}Gc$	6,7 MP
	9.	$Fc \supset Gc$	1 UQE
	10.	${\sim}Fc$	8,9 MT
	11.	$Jc \supset {\sim}Fc$	4–10 CP
	12.	$(\forall x)(Jx \supset {\sim}Fx)$	4–11 UQI
	13.	$(\forall x)(Jx \supset Hx) \supset (\forall x)(Jx \supset {\sim}Fx)$	3–12 CP
7.	**1.**	$(\forall x)((\exists y)Rxy \supset Rxa)$	
	2.	$(\forall x)(Hx \supset Rxb)$	
	3.	Hc	AP
	4.	$Hc \supset Rcb$	2 UQE
	5.	Rcb	3,4 MP
	6.	$(\exists y)Rcy$	5 EQI
	7.	$(\exists y)Rcy \supset Rca$	1 UQE
	8.	Rca	6,7 MP
	9.	$Hc \supset Rca$	3–8 CP
	10.	$(\forall x)(Hx \supset Rxa)$	3–9 UQI

Exercise 13d

2.	**1.**	$(\exists x)(Fx \cdot Gx)$
	2.	$(\forall x)(Gx \supset (Hx \lor {\sim}Fx))$
	3.	$(\forall x)[(Fx \cdot Hx) \supset (\exists y)Rxy]$

4.	$Fa \cdot Ga$	1	EQI
5.	Fa		Simp
6.	Ga		Simp
7.	$Ga \supset (Ha \lor \sim Fa)$	2	UQE
8.	$Ha \lor \sim Fa$		MP
9.	Ha		DS +
10.	$Fa \cdot Ha$		Conj
11.	$(Fa \cdot Ha) \supset (\exists y)Ray$	3	UQE
12.	$(\exists y)Ray$		MP
13.	$(\exists x)(\exists y)Rxy$	12	EQI

4.

$(\forall x)(\forall y)[(Fx \cdot Gy) \supset \sim Rxy]$		
$(\forall x)(\exists y)(Gy \cdot Rxy)$		
$(\exists x)(Hx \cdot Rxa) \supset \sim(\exists y)Ray$		
$(\exists y)Fy$		AP
Fc		EQE
$(\exists y)(Gy \cdot Rcy)$	2	UQE
$Gb \cdot Rcb$		EQE
Gb		Simp
Rcb		Simp
$(\forall y)[(Fc \cdot Gy) \supset \sim Rcy]$	11	UQE
$(Fc \cdot Gb) \supset \sim Rcb$		UQE
$Fc \cdot Gb$		Conj
$\sim Rcb$		MP
$Rcb \cdot \sim Rcb$		Conj
$\sim(\exists y)Fy$		IP
$(\exists x)(Hx \cdot Rxa)$		AP
$\sim(\exists y)Ray$		MP
$(\exists y)(Gy \cdot Ray)$	2	UQE
$Ge \cdot Rae$		EQE
Rae		Simp
$(\exists y)Ray$		EQI
$(\exists y)Ray \cdot \sim(\exists y)Ray$		Conj
$\sim(\exists x)(Hx \cdot Rxa)$		IP

6.

$(\forall x)(\forall y)(Rxy \supset Ryx)$		
Rab		
$(\forall x)((\exists y)Ryx \supset Rxx)$		
$(\exists x)\sim(\exists y)Rxy$		
Fc		EQE
$\sim(\exists y)Rcy$		EQE
$(\forall y)\sim Rcy$		QN
$(\exists y)Ryb$	2	EQI
$(\exists y)Ryb \supset Rbb$	3	UQE
Rbb		MP
$\sim Rcb$		UQE
$(\forall y)(Rby \supset Ryb)$	1	UQE
$Rbc \supset Rcb$		UQE
$\sim Rbc$		MT

(∃y)~Rby	EQI

Rbe	AP
(∃y)Rye	EQI
(∃y)Rye ⊃ Ree	UQI
Ree	MP
Rbe ⊃ Ree	CP
(∀x)(Rbx ⊃ Rxx)	UQI
Rbb · (∃y)~Rby	Conj
[Rbb · (∃y) ~Rby] · (∀x)(Rbx ⊃ Rxx)	Conj

8. (∀x)[Gx ⊃ (∀y)(Fy ⊃ Lyx)]
(∀x)[Fx ⊃ ~(∀z)Lxz]

(∃x)Gx	AP
Ga	EQE

Fb	AP
Fb ⊃ ~(∀z)Lbz	UQE
~(∀z)Lbz	MP
(∃z)~Lbz	QN
Ga ⊃ (∀y)(Fy ⊃ Lya)	UQE
(∀y)(Fy ⊃ Lya)	MP
Fb ⊃ Lba	UQE
Lba	MP
(∃y)Lby	EQI
(∃y)Lby · (∃z)~Lbz	Conj
Fb ⊃ ((∃y)Lby · (∃z)~Lbz)	CP
(∀x)[Fx ⊃ ((∃y)Lxy · (∃z) ~Lxz)]	UQI
(∃x)Gx ⊃ (∀x)[Fx ⊃ ((∃y)Lxy · (∃z)~Lxz)]	CP

CHAPTER 14

Exercise 14a

2. (∀x: Fx ∨ Vx)(Nx · Ex)
(∀x: Nx ∨ Dx)Gx
*(∀x: Bx)Fx · (∀x: Cx)Vx
∴ (∀x: Bx ∨ Cx)Gx

4. Not enthymematic
(∃x: Dx)Bx · (∀x: Dx · Bx)~Rx
(∀x: Dx · Bx)Tx
∴ (∃x: Dx · ~Rx)Tx

6. (∀x: Px · Ix)(Cx ∨ Sx)
(∀x: Px · Cx)~Hx
*(∀x: Px · Hx)Ix
∴ (∀x: Px · Hx)Sx

8. Not enthymematic
$(\forall x: Lx)Mx$
$\therefore$ $(\forall x: Zx \cdot (\exists y: Ly)Oxy)(\exists z: Mz)Oxz$

10. Not enthymematic
$(\forall x: \exists x \cdot \sim Rx)\sim Sx$
$(\forall x: Ex \cdot Rx)Dx$
$\therefore$ $(\forall x: \exists x \cdot \sim Dx)\sim Sx$

Exercise 14b

2. $(\forall x: Sxb)Mx$
*Sab
$\therefore$ Ma

4. Sba
$Tac \cdot (\forall x: Sxa)Txa$
$*(\forall x)(\forall y: Txy)(\forall z: Tyz)Txz$
$\therefore$ Tbc

6. $(\forall x: Jx)(\forall y: Sy)Cxy$
$(\exists x: Sx)Cxa$
Jb
$*(\forall x)(\forall y: Cxy)(\forall z: Cyz)Cxz$
$\therefore$ Cba

8. $(\exists x: Lx)Hxb$
$(\exists x: Fx)Hbx$
$*(\forall x)(\forall y: Hxy)(\forall z: Hyz)Hxz$
$\therefore$ $(\exists x: Lx)(\exists y: Fy)Hxy$

CHAPTER 15

Exercise 15a

2. $Raa \cdot (\forall x: Px \cdot x \neq a)\sim Rax$

4. $(\forall x: Ex \cdot x \neq r)\sim Sxd \cdot Srd$

6. $(\forall x: Ex \cdot x \neq r)Srx$

8. $(\forall x: Ax) \sim(\forall y: Ay \cdot y \neq x)Qxy$

10. $(\forall x: (Ax \cdot x \neq a) \cdot Qax)(\forall y: (Ay \cdot y \neq a) \cdot Qay)x = y$

12. $(\forall x: Ax)\sim(\exists y: Ay \cdot y = x)(\exists z: Az \cdot z \neq x)(\exists x_1: Ax_1 \cdot x_1 \neq x)[(y \neq z \cdot y \neq x_1) \cdot z \neq x_1]$

14. $(\forall x: Sx) \sim(\exists y_1: Hy_1 \cdot Oxy_1)(\exists y_2: Hy_2 \cdot Oxy_2)(\exists y_3: Hy_3 \cdot Oxy_3)[(y_1 \neq y_2 \cdot y_1 \neq y_3) \cdot y_2 \neq y_3]$

16. $\{ \exists x: Sx \cdot (\exists y_1: Hy_1 \cdot Oxy_1)(\exists y_2: Hy_2 \cdot Oxy_2)$
$(\exists y_3: Hy_3 \cdot Oxy_3) ((y_1 \neq y_2 \cdot y_1 \neq y_3) \cdot y_2 \neq y_3)\}$
$\{ \exists x: Sx_2 \cdot (\exists y_1: Hy_1 \cdot Ox_2y_1)(\exists y_2: Hy_2 \cdot Ox_2y_2)(\exists y_3: Hy_3 \cdot Ox_2y_3)$
$((y_1 \neq y_2 \cdot y_1 \neq y_3) \cdot y_2 \neq y_3)\}$

$[x \neq x_2 \cdot$
$\{ \forall x_3 \colon Sx_3 \cdot (\exists y_1 \colon Hy_1 \cdot Ox_3y_1)(\exists y_2 \colon Hy_2 \cdot Ox_3y_2)(\exists y_3 \colon Hy_3 \cdot Ox_3y_3)$
$((y_1 \neq y_2 \cdot y_1 \neq y_3) \cdot y_2 \neq y_3)\} [x_3 = x \ \lor \ x_3 = x_2]]$

Exercise 15b

2. $(\imath x \colon Dx \cdot Lax)Wx \cdot (\exists x \colon Wx \cdot Lax)(\exists y \colon Wy \cdot Lay)x \neq y$

4. $(\forall x \colon \sim(\imath y \colon Wy \cdot Lyb)x = y)\sim Exb$

6. $(\imath x \colon Dx \cdot (\forall y \colon Dy \cdot y \neq x)Tyx)Wx$

10. $(\imath x \colon Dx \cdot Txc)b = x$

12. $(\imath y \colon Dy \cdot (\forall z \colon Dz \cdot z \neq y)Tyz)(\imath x \colon Px \cdot Lxy)$
$\quad (\exists y_2 \colon (Py_2 \cdot y_2 \neq y) Lxy_2)$

14. $(\imath x \colon Fxb)(\imath y \colon Dy \cdot (\forall z \colon Dz \cdot z \neq y)Tyz)x \neq y$

16. $(\forall x \colon \sim Dx)\sim(Wx \cdot Lbx)$

Exercise 15c

2. $Kg(b)f(a)$

4. $f(c) = f(g(b))$

6. $(\forall x \colon Nx)g(x, h(x)) = 0$

8. $(\forall x \colon Nx)[g(x, f(x)) = 0 \ \lor \ g(x, f(x)) = g_1(2, x)]$

10. $(\forall x \colon Nx)(\forall y \colon Ny)(\forall z \colon Nz)$
$\quad [g_1(z, g_1(3, g(x, y))) = g(g_1(g_1(3, z), x), g_1(g_1(3, z), y))]$

Exercise 15d

2.
1. $(\exists x \colon Fx \cdot (\forall y \colon Fy)y = x)Gx$		
2. $Fa \cdot (\forall x \colon Gx)Rax$		
3. Fa	2	Simp
4. $(\forall x \colon Gx)Rax$	2	Simp
5. $Fc \cdot (\forall y \colon Fy)y = c$	1	EQE
6. Gc	1	EQE
7. Fc	5	Simp
8. $(\forall y \colon Fy)y = c$	5	Simp
9. Fd		AP
10. $d = c$	8,9	UQE
11. $d = d$		=I
12. $c = d$	10,11	=E
13. Gd	6,12	=E
14. Rad	4,13	UQE
15. $a = c$	3,8	UQE
16. $a = d$	12,15	=E
17. Rdd	14,16	=E
18. $(\forall x \colon Fx)Rxx$		

4.
1. $(\exists x \colon Cx \cdot (\forall y \colon Cy)y = x)Dx$
2. $Ca \cdot Aa$
3. $Cb \cdot Bb$

4.	$(\forall x: Dx)Rxx$		
5.	$Cc \cdot (\forall y: Cy)y = c$	1	EQE
6.	Dc	1	EQE
7.	Rcc	4,6	UQE
8.	$(\forall y: Cy)y = c$	5	Simp
9.	Ca	2	Simp
10.	$a = c$	8,9	UQE
11.	Cb	3	Simp
12.	$b = c$	8,11	UQE
13.	$b = b$		$=$ I
14.	$c = b$	12,13	$=$ E
15.	Rcb	7,14	$=$ E
16.	$a = a$		$=$ I
17.	$c = a$	10,16	$=$ E
18.	Rab	15,17	$=$ E

6.

1.	$(\exists x: Bx)[(\forall y: By)Rxy \cdot (\forall z: (\exists y: By)Rzy)z = x]$		
2.	$(\forall x: Bx)(\forall y: By)(Rxy \equiv Cy)$		
3.	$(\forall x: Bx)(\forall y: By)(Rxy \equiv Ryx)$		
4.	Bc	1	EQE
5.	$(\forall y: By)Rcy \cdot (\forall z: (\exists y: By)Rzy)z = c$	1	EQE
6.	$(\forall y: By)Rcy$	5	Simp
7.	$(\forall z: (\exists y: By)Rzy)z = c$	5	Simp
8.	$Ca \cdot Ba$		AP
9.	Ca	8	Simp
10.	Ba	8	Simp
11.	Rca	6,10	UQE
12.	$(\forall y: By)(Rcy \equiv Ryc)$	3,4	UQE
13.	$Rca \equiv Rac$	10,12	UQE
14.	$(Rca \supset Rac) \cdot (Rac \supset Rca)$	13	Bic
15.	$Rca \supset Rac$	14	Simp
16.	Rac	11,15	MP
17.	$(\exists y: By)Ray$	4,16	EQI
18.	$a = c$	7,17	UQE
19.	$(\forall y: Cy \cdot By)y = c$	8–18	UQI
20.	$(\forall y: By)(Rcy \equiv Cy)$	2,4	UQE
21.	$Rcc \equiv Cc$	20,4	UQE
22.	Rcc	4,6	UQE
23.	$(Rcc \supset Cc) \cdot (Cc \supset Rcc)$	21	Bic
24.	$Rcc \supset Cc$	23	Simp
25.	Cc	22,24	MP
26.	$(\exists x: Cx)(\forall y: Cy \cdot By)y = x$	19,25	EQI

Exercise 15e

2.

1.	$(\forall x: Ax)(\exists y: Ay)x = f(y)$		
2.	$(\forall x: Ax)Bf(x)$		
3.	Ac		AP
4.	$(\exists y: Ay)c = f(y)$	1,3	UQE

5. Aa	4	EQE
6. $c = f(a)$	4	EQE
7. $Bf(a)$	2,5	UQE
8. $c = c$		$=$I
9. $f(a) = c$	6,8	$=$E
10. Bc	7,9	$=$E
11. $(\forall x\colon Ax)Bx$	3–10	UQI

4.

1. $(\forall x\colon Ax)Rxf(x)$		
2. $(\forall x\colon Ax)Af(x)$		
3. Ac		AP
4. $Af(c)$	2,3	UQE
5. $Rf(c)f(f(c))$	1,4	UQE
6. $(\forall x\colon Ax)Rf(x)f(f(x))$	3–5	UQI

6.

1. $(\forall x\colon Ax)Bf(x)$		
2. $(\exists y\colon Ay)(\exists x\colon x = f(y))Ax$		
3. $(\forall x\colon Ax)Cx$		AP
4. Ac	2	EQI
5. $(\exists x\colon x = f(c))Ax$	2	EQI
6. Cc	3,4	UQE
7. $Bf(c)$	1,4	UQE
8. $a = f(c)$	5	EQI
9. Aa	5	EQI
10. Ca	3,9	UQE
11. $Cf(c)$	8,10	$=$E
12. $(\exists y\colon By)Cy$	7,11	EQI
14. $(\forall x\colon Ax)Cx \supset (\exists y\colon By)Cy$	3–12	CP

Exercise 15f

2.

1. $(\imath x\colon Dx \cdot Txe)(\forall y\colon \sim My)\sim Ty$		
2. $\sim Me$		AP
3. $Dc \cdot Tce$	1	$\imath$E
4. $(\forall y\colon Dy \cdot Tye)y = c$	1	$\imath$E
5. $(\forall y\colon \sim My)\sim Tcy$	1	$\imath$E
6. $\sim Tce$	2,5	UQE
7. Tce	3	Simp
8. $Tce \cdot \sim Tce$	6,7	Conj
9. Me	2–8	IP

4.

1. $(\forall x\colon x \neq a)\sim(Mx \cdot Tx)$		
2. $(\forall x\colon x \neq s)\sim(Dx \cdot Tx)$		
3. $(\exists x\colon Dx \cdot Tx)Mx$		
4. $Dc \cdot Tc$	3	EQE
5. Mc	3	EQE
6. $a \neq s$		AP
7. $\sim(Dx \cdot Tx)$	2,6	UQE
8. $c \neq s$		AP
9. $\sim(Dc \cdot Tc)$	2,8	UQE
10. $(Dc \cdot Tc) \cdot \sim(Dc \cdot Tc)$	4,9	Conj

11.	$c = s$	8–10	IP
12.	$s = a$		AP
13.	$a \neq a$	6,12	$=$ E
14.	$a = a$		$=$ I
15.	$a = a \cdot a \neq a$	13,14	Conj
16.	$s \neq a$	12–15	IP
17.	$\sim(Ms \cdot Ts)$	1,16	UQE
18.	Tc	4	Simp
19.	$Mc \cdot Tc$	5,18	Conj
20.	$Ms \cdot Ts$	11,19	$=$ E
21.	$(Ms \cdot Ts) \cdot \sim(Ms \cdot Ts)$	19,20	Conj
22.	$a = s$	6–21	IP

6.

1.	$(\exists x: Mx \cdot Tx)(\exists y: My \cdot Tx)x \neq y \cdot$		
	$(\exists z: Mz \cdot Tz)(\forall x: (Mx \cdot Tx) \cdot Wx)x = z$		
2.	$(\forall x: \sim Wx)\sim Rx$		
3.	$(\exists x: Mx \cdot Tx)(\exists y: My \cdot Ty)x \neq y$	1	Simp
4.	$(\exists z: Mz \cdot Tz)(\forall x: (Mx \cdot Tx) \cdot Wx)x = z$	1	Simp
5.	$Ma \cdot Ta$	3	EQE
6.	$(\exists y: My \cdot Ty)a \neq y$	3	EQE
7.	$Mc \cdot Tc$	6	EQE
8.	$a \neq c$	6	EQE
9.	$Md \cdot Td$	4	EQE
10.	$(\forall x: (Mx \cdot Tx) \cdot Wx)x \neq d$	4	EQE
11.	Wa		AP
12.	$(Ma \cdot Ta) \cdot Wa$	5,11	Conj
13.	$a = d$	10,12	UQE
14.	$d \neq c$	8,13	$=$ E
15.	Wc		AP
16.	$(Mc \cdot Tc) \cdot Wc$	7,15	Conj
17.	$c = d$	10,16	UQE
18.	$d \neq d$	14,17	$=$ E
19.	$d = d$		$=$ I
20.	$d = d \cdot d \neq d$	18,19	Conj
21.	$\sim Wc$	15–20	IP
22.	$\sim Rc$	2,21	UQE
23.	$(\exists x: Mx \cdot Tx)\sim Rx$	7,22	EQE
24.	$Wa \supset (\exists x: Mx \cdot Tx)\sim Rx$	11–23	CP
25.	$\sim Wa$		AP
26.	$\sim Ra$	2,25	UQE
27.	$(\exists x: Mx \cdot Tx)\sim Rx$	3,26	EQE
28.	$\sim Wa \supset (\exists x: Mx \cdot Tx)\sim Rx$	25–27	CP
29.	$\sim(Wa \lor \sim Wa)$		AP
30.	$\sim Wa \cdot \sim\sim Wa$	29	DeM
31.	$Wa \lor \sim Wa$	29–30	IP
32.	$(\exists x: Mx \cdot Tx)\sim Rx \lor (\exists x: Mx \cdot Tx)\sim Rx$	24,28,3	1CD
33.	$(\exists x: Mx \cdot Tx)\sim Rx$	32	Red

8.

1.	$(\forall x: Dx)(\forall y: Dy \cdot Lxy)Bxy$		
2.	$Dc \cdot (\forall y: Dy \cdot y \neq c)Lcy$		AP

3.	*Dc*	2	Simp
4.	(∀*y*: *Dy* · *y*≠*c*)*Lcy*	2	Simp
→**5.**	*Da* · *a*≠*c*		AP
6.	*Lca*	4,5	UQE
7.	(∀*y*: *Dy* · *Lcy*)*Bcy*	1,3	UQE
8.	*Da*	5	Simp
9.	*Da* · *Lca*	6,8	Conj
10.	*Bca*	7,9	Conj
11.	(∀*z*: *Dz* · *z*≠*c*)*Bcz*	5–10	UQI
12.	(∀*x*: *Dx* · (∀*y*: *Dy* · *y*≠*x*)*Lxy*)		
	(∀*z*: *Dz* · *z*≠*x*)*Bxz*	2–12	UQI

CHAPTER 16

Exercise 16a

2.	F	**4.**	T
6.	T	**8.**	F
10.	T	**12.**	F

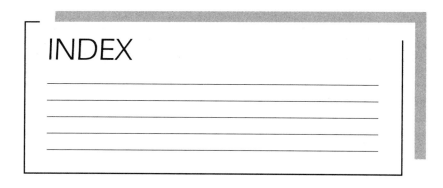

INDEX

Note: * indicates an occurrence in an explanatory chart, table, or summary list.

A

A sentence 205–206
absorption 157, 252
addition (Add) 115, 119*, 162*
anaphoric *the* 302–303
antecedent 80
any 194–195
argument 4, 15
  form 36, 39, 43
associativity (Assoc) 124, 133*, 162*
  biconditional 155
assumption
  subderivation 135–137
  ordinary argument 287–295
asymmetry
  showing validity, invalidity 47–49
  of relations 292–293
at least 199, 299–300
at most 300–301

B

biconditional 84
  additional rules for 154–155
biconditional (Bic) (rule) 132, 133*, 162*
bound variable 216–217
  accidental 218–219
Barwise, Jon vi, 317
Brown, Mark vi, vii, 317

C

cartesian product 330
cases, argument by 116, 127–128, 149, 150
Church, Alonzo 256
closed formula 217
commutativity (Comm) 123, 133*, 162*
  biconditional 155
completeness (of a system of rules) 108, 138, 233
conclusion 4, 15*
  recognizing 5–6
conditional 79–81
conditional distribution (CDist) 157
conditional exchange (CE) 128–129, 133*, 156, 162*
conditional proof (CP) 135–137, 162*
conjunction 18–20, 23–24, 42
conjunction (Conj) 112, 119*, 161*
connective
  symbol 18
  truth-functional 19
  word 17, 18, 42
consequence 15
consequent 80
consistency 7–8, 15, 50–52, 59*, 62–70, 168–170, 183*, 258–262
constructive dilemma (CD) 116, 119*, 162*
contingent 58–59, 59*, 76–77, 183, 184*, 271–272

contradiction 57–58, 59*, 76–77,
    181–182, 184*, 250
contradiction (X) (rule) 157
contradictories 55, 204–206
contradictory
    pair of sentences 55*, 204
    sentence 57–58, 59*, 76–77, 181–182,
        184*, 250
contraposition 130–131, 133*, 156, 162*
contraries 54–55, 204
convergence (cnvrg) 156
conversion (conv) 252
Cooper, Robin vi, 317
correctness (of a system of rules)
    107–108, 142–143
counterexample 10–12, 164–166, 254

D

decision procedure 255–256, 260,
    263–265
deductive 13, 15
definite description 302–306
    derivational rules 314
De Morgan, Augustus 125
De Morgan's Theorems (DeM) 125,
    133*, 156, 162*
derivation 107
derelativization (DR) 252, 277
destructive dilemma (DD) 156
disjunction 28–30, 42
disjunctive syllogism (DS) 109, 119*,
    156, 161*
distribution (Dist) 128, 133*, 156, 162*
    conditional (CDist) 157
double negation (DN) 122–123, 133*,
    162*
    avoidance of 155–156
dyadic predicate; dyadic relation
    188–189

E

E sentence 205–206
either-or 28–30
empty set 329
entail 15, 54
enthymeme 287–295

equivalence 53–54, 59*, 73–75,
    174–177, 183*, 247–248
equivalence rules 122–124, 133*, 162*,
    233, 238*
every 194–195
evil, problem of 145–146
exactly 301–302
exceptives 298
excluded middle (EM) 157
exclusion, set 330
existential quantifier exploitation (EQE)
    228, 238*
existential quantifier introduction (EQI)
    214–215, 218, 239*
extension 320

F

family 295
free variable 217
follow from 15
form
    argument 36, 39, 43
    sentence 26, 35–40, 42
    set 51
function symbol 306–309
    derivations 312–313

G

Gupta, Anil vi

H

hypothetical syllogism (HS) 113, 119*,
    161*

I

I sentence 205–206
identity 297–298
    derivational rules 310–312
identity exploitation (=E) 310
identity introduction (=I) 310
implicational rules 119, 223
imply 15

inconsistency 7–8, 15, 50–52, 59*,
    62–70, 168–170, 183*, 244–246,
    258–260
  of premises 60–61
  relationship to validity 70–71,
    170–172
indicator words 5–6, 15
indirect proof (IP) 143–144
individual constant 201
individual variable 191, 201
inductive 12–15
inequivalence 53–56, 59*, 73–75,
    174–175, 183*, 268–271
infer 15
inference rules 105–108, 110
instance
  of a form 36–40
  ©|Ⓥ 218
intersection 330
invalid (*see* valid *and* validity)
  showing 11, 46, 47–49, 59*,
    163–164, 183*, 265–268
irreflexivity 294

L

Leibniz's inference 310
Leibniz's Law 310–311
logic 3, 5
  Aristotelian vi, 204–206
logical truth 57, 59*, 76–77, 178–180,
    184*, 249
  in conclusion 60

M

McCawley, James vi
membership, set 329
model 10, 63–65, 256, 258–262,
    319–320
model path 64–69, 163–164
modus ponens (MP) 108, 119*,
    161*
modus tollens (MT) 112, 119*,
    155, 161*
monadic predicate 188
Montague, Richard vi
most 317–319, 321–322, 324

N

name, proper 189
negating a conditional (NC) 157
negation 17, 25–26, 42
neither-nor 30
non-contradiction (NOX) 157
noun phrase 189

O

O sentence 205–206
only 207, 298–299, 304
  only if 85–86
  if and only if 87–88
open formula 217

P

parentheses 31–32
Peterson, Philip vi, 317
pollution (Poll) 156
possessives 305–306
possibility 9–13
power set 330
predicate 188, 190, 200*
  compound 195
  dyadic 188–189
  monadic 188
predicative context 188, 217
premises 4, 5, 15
  inconsistent 60–61
  recognizing 5–6
prenexation (Prenex) 253

Q

quantification 189–326
  relativized v, 193–275, 297–326
    derivation 214–253, 310–314
    models 254–275
    semantics 316–326
    symbolization 193–207, 297–306
  unrelativized 276–286
    translation 277–278
    derivation 280–285

quantificational contraposition (QContra) 252
quantificational distribution (QDist) 252
quantificational modus tollens (QMT) 251
quantifier 189, 201*
  existential 199
  intermediate 317–319
  numerical 299–302, 317–318
  phrase 189, 194–195
  universal 194
  word 189
quantifier exportation (QExp) 253
quantifier negation (QN) 233, 238*
quantifier reordering (Reord) 252
quasi-name 230

R

reflexives 210
reflexivity 294
  of identity 310–311
relation 22–23, 188–189, 191
  property of 291
  comparative 291–293
relational context 189
relative clause 24, 192–193, 196
relettering (Relet) 252
reductio ad absurdum 144
redundancy (Red) 127, 162*

S

schematic letter 26, 36–40
self-identity 310
semantics 34–35, 40, 316–327
  quantifier 323–324
  truth-functional connective 84–85
sentence
  atomic 18, 42
  compound 18, 42
  form 26, 35–40, 42
set 329
  of beliefs 7–8
  of sentences 50–52
set-theoretic terminology 329–330
  cartesian product 330
  empty set 329

  exclusion 330
  intersection 321, 329
  membership 329
  ordered n-tuple 330
  power set 330
  subset 329
short dilemma (SD) 157
simplification (Simp) 108, 119*, 161*
sound 9, 15, 61
strength, inductive 12–14, 15
subderivation 137, 140–141, 236–237
subset 329
superlative 305
support 15
syllogism 109
symmetry 292–293
syntax 34, 40, 201
System S (a smaller system) 158–160

T

tautology 56–57, 59*, 76–77, 178–180, 184*
transitivity 291–293
  of identity 310–311
truth-functional 18–21
  compound 18–19, 42
  connective 19, 42
truth-table 19, 34, 42*, 46–47
  size 46–47, 62, 105
truth-value 19
truth-tree 62–78, 92–95, 255–275
  rules 67, 78*, 94–96*, 257, 259–260, 275*

U

universal syllogism (US) 253
universal quantifier 193–194
universal quantifier exploitation (UQE) 220–221, 238*
universal quantifier introduction (UQI) 235–237, 239*
unless 86–87

V

valid 8–10, 15
validity
  deciding 5, 45–46, 255–256, 260
  recognizing 3, 12, 16
  relationship to inconsistency 70–71,
    170–172
  showing 3, 9, 10–12, 16, 44–49, 59*,
    70–73, 106–108, 110, 183*
  understanding 3, 9, 12, 16

variables
  individual 191
    bound 217
    free 217
  sentence 26

W

without 90–91

SYMBOLS INDEX

∴ 8
· 18
∼ 25
∨ 28
⊃ 79
≡ 84
∷ 123
∀ 194
∃ 199
= 297
≠ 298
∃n 300
≤n 300
∃! 301

∃n! 301
ɿ 303
μ 318
λ 318
σ 318
<n 318
ν 318
∩ 321, 329
∈ 329
⊆ 329
∅ 329
− 330
ρ 330

TRUTH-FUNCTIONAL CONNECTIVES

p	$\sim p$
T	F
F	T

p	q	$p \cdot q$	$p \vee q$	$p \supset q$	$p \equiv q$
T	T	T	T	T	T
T	F	F	T	F	F
F	T	F	T	T	F
F	F	F	F	T	T

TRUTH-TREE RULES

Double Negation

$\sim\sim p$
.
.
.
p

Conditional

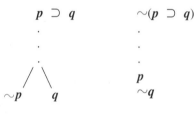

Conjunction

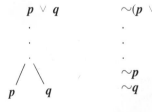

Biconditional

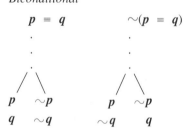

Disjunction